METHODS OF SOCIAL MOVEMENT RESEARCH

Social Movements, Protest, and Contention

Series Editor: Bert Klandermans, Free University, Amsterdam

Associate Editors: Ron R. Aminzade, University of Minnesota
David S. Meyer, University of California, Irvine
Verta A. Taylor, University of California, Santa Barbara

For more books in the series, see page 355.

METHODS OF SOCIAL MOVEMENT RESEARCH

**Bert Klandermans and
Suzanne Staggenborg, Editors**

Social Movements, Protest, and Contention
Volume 16

University of Minnesota Press
Minneapolis • London

Published by the University of Minnesota Press
111 Third Avenue South, Suite 290
Minneapolis, MN 55401-2520
http://www.upress.umn.edu

Library of Congress Cataloging-in-Publication Data

Methods of social movement research / Bert Klandermans and Suzanne
Staggenborg, editors.
   p. cm. — (Social movements, protest, and contention ; v 16)
Includes bibliographical references and index.
   ISBN 0-8166-3594-3 (HC : alk. paper)
   ISBN 0-8166-3595-1 (PB : alk. paper)
   1. Social movements. 2. Social movements—Research. 3. Social
surveys. I. Klandermans, Bert. II. Staggenborg, Suzanne. III. Series.
   HM881 .M475 2002
   303.48'4'07—dc21

2002003435

12 11 10 09 08 07 06 05 04 03 02   10 9 8 7 6 5 4 3 2 1

Contents

Preface

We decided to collaborate in editing a book on methods of social movement research because we share a belief in the importance of empirical work for the development of theoretical ideas and an enthusiasm for studying social movements. We paired up as editors because we have different strengths in quantitative and qualitative methods, but our mutual admiration for all types of theoretically informed empirical research is far stronger than our own preferences for particular methods. In our view, empirical research has been key to the substantial progress of the field in understanding social movements. However, few discussions of research methods exist; by systematically laying out the major methods used by social movement theorists, we hope to encourage even more empirical work and to provide new generations of scholars with methodological guidelines.

With these goals in mind, we solicited chapters from outstanding social movement scholars with expertise in various research methods. We aimed to make the volume as comprehensive as possible in covering the major methods used in studying social movements, from quantitative to qualitative techniques, and from micro to macro levels of analysis. The chapters lay out the strengths and weaknesses of different methods, and lead students and scholars interested in learning these methods to additional sources. Although the book will be of special interest to those working in the area of social movements, it should also be helpful to students and scholars in other areas who are interested in learning how theory can be developed through careful empirical research.

We are very grateful to the authors of the chapters in this volume for agreeing to write them and for producing outstanding discussions that strike a difficult balance between being both methodologically sophisticated and accessible to readers with a range of backgrounds. We were quite demanding editors, asking authors to go through several rounds of revision, but we think the end products are worth the effort. We were very fortunate in receiving detailed comments from Thomas Rochon, who reviewed both the proposal and the manuscript for the University of Minnesota Press. His comments were extremely useful, both to us as editors and to individual authors, and the book is stronger as a result.

We owe a special debt to Sid Tarrow, who, in addition to coauthoring the concluding chapter with us, provided us with advice from start to finish, including detailed comments on our introduction. We are also grateful to other colleagues who read and commented on various chapters, including David Knoke, John McCarthy, and Rod Nelson. Finally, we thank editor Carrie Mullen and production assistant Mike Stoffel for their assistance.

Introduction

Bert Klandermans and Suzanne Staggenborg

"Theory-bashing," as John Lofland (1993) called it, is the ritual knocking down of a simplistic theoretical model erected for the occasion before the author goes on to announce his or her own contribution. Social movement scholars, in Lofland's view, have been among those most committed to this intellectual ritual. Social psychological and breakdown theories, resource mobilization theory, and, most recently, political process theory have all enjoyed the dubious honor of serving as targets. Doubting that scientific progress is served by this habit, Lofland regretted that it had become so pervasive in the social movement literature and, although on the wane in the 1990s, was still common. Yet Steven Buechler's (2000, p. xi) recent assessment seemingly belies Lofland's forebodings: "Social movement theory and research have recently become some of the most active areas within the discipline, producing a tremendous volume of work on diverse aspects of collective action." Along with many others, we agree with this observation; social movement theory has made significant progress. Was Lofland then wrong? Was what he saw as ritualized theory-bashing in fact lively debate that has pushed the study of social movements forward? Yes and no. We propose that the "secret" of the success of social movement theory and research has, indeed, been its characteristic openness to criticism and new approaches, but only in so far as this has been accompanied by a readiness to put new ideas to empirical test. This, and the creative employment of a variety of research methods, has in our view turned the study of social movements into a real empirical science and a successful enterprise.

The success of social movement studies is evidenced by both the profusion of research and the popularity of courses on social movements. The area is no longer just a subfield of sociology but an increasingly important area in other disciplines as well. In fact, cross-fertilization of sociological research with work from political science, history, psychology, and, recently, anthropology and cultural studies is one important reason for its stunning growth. In addition to cross-discipline exchange, numerous transatlantic and cross-national collaborations in the past twenty years have contributed greatly to the area's theoretical and methodological development.

Of course, the proliferation of movement studies has not only been a matter of theoretical advances. Social movements themselves expanded in visibility and importance during the "cycle of contention" of the 1960s and early 1970s (Tarrow 1998). The migration of movements from the fringes of society to the mainstream, and the increasing centrality of movement organizations to the political process have been critical in expanding academic studies of social movements (see Jenkins and Klandermans 1995; Meyer and Tarrow 1998 for discussions of the growing importance of social movements in society). In this volume, we will mostly leave the external influences on the field aside and concentrate on the internal dynamics of the discipline, but we will return to some of these broader issues in our conclusion.

We argue that approaches such as resource mobilization theory have advanced the social movement area not only by criticizing their predecessors and proposing new theoretical ideas, but by offering concepts and research questions with clear empirical referents, enabling scholars to use a variety of methodological approaches and techniques to study social movements. Researchers studying different movements with different methods have all contributed to the collective enterprise of developing social movement theory. After some thirty years of growth, social movement research continues to thrive, but future development of the field depends on our ability to expand our theories with new concepts and questions that lend themselves to empirical research with new and existing methods.

Resource mobilization theory triggered an expansion of social movement research by changing the core question of the field from "Why are people aggrieved?" to "Why do aggrieved people protest when they do?" Criticizing previous explanations of social movements that focused on societal breakdown, the theory proposed that resources make a difference to mobilization and success. This argument provided movement scholars with a specific set of empirical concerns about the differential availability, mobilization, and allocation of resources. Collective actors and their allies and targets differ in terms of the resources they command, their preparedness to make resources available, and their ability to use their resources effectively. New research argued that sponsorship by established organizations, rather than resources from aggrieved populations, led to movement success (Jenkins and Perrow 1977). This research led to debate over the role of resources and to further expansion of theory in studies stressing indigenous rather than elite resources in movement mobilization (Morris 1984). Other analysts continued to refine the concept of resources (Freeman 1979; Gamson, Fireman, and Rytina 1982) and to test the theory's assumptions (Cress and Snow 1996). What is striking in these works is the array of methodological approaches, from quantitative analysis of event data to qualitative research to experimental design, along with a common focus on developing the theoretical insights of resource mobilization theory.

Of course, to inspire so much research, resource mobilization theory did more than focus on resources. In their seminal articles developing this approach, John McCarthy and Mayer Zald (see their collected papers, Zald and McCarthy 1987) introduced key concepts such as *social movement organization, social movement industry,* and *countermovement,* which enabled researchers to identify concrete units of analysis. They also posed provocative questions and developed specific hypotheses about the costs and benefits of participation and the professionalization of movements. In short, McCarthy and Zald and other early developers of resource mobilization theory (e.g., Oberschall 1973; Gamson 1990 [first edition 1975]) produced concepts and ideas that could be observed and measured. In doing so, they inspired a generation of social movement scholars who went out to collect evidence that could confirm or falsify their hypotheses and further develop the theory.

Political process theory in its turn criticized resource mobilization theory for neglecting the fact that social movements develop and act in political arenas that significantly influence their trajectories. It offered the field theoretical ideas and core concepts such as *political opportunities* (see Eisinger 1973; Kitschelt 1986; McAdam 1999 [first edition 1982]; Tarrow 1989). The answer of political process theory to the question of why movements arise (or fail to do so) and why movements take different trajectories is that political opportunities differ across contexts and over time. Changing opportunities help explain why movements emerge at one point in time rather than another, and differences in political opportunities help explain why movements are successful in some countries or regions and not in others. The concept pointed to the various political environments that social movement organizations face, leading social movement scholars to build variations in political opportunity structure into their explanations of the fates of movement organizations.

Political process theory also offered an innovative method: protest event analysis provided a way of measuring the effects of political opportunities in comparative designs (see Koopmans and Rucht in this volume). This approach began with Shorter and Tilly's (1974) work on strikes and developed with Tilly's attempts to map contention in France and Great Britain (see Tilly 1978, 1986, 1995). The *protest event* became the unit of analysis in an influential new approach to social movement research that used newspapers as a data source. More recently, other sources such as police files and reports of press agencies have been used. But the fundamental methodological approach has remained the same, resulting in a virtual industry of protest event data analysis in the study of social movements and other forms of contention.

Recently, both resource mobilization and political process theory have been criticized for being overly structural and for neglecting such factors as identity, culture, and emotions (Goodwin and Jasper 1999). A number of scholars are beginning to develop methodological approaches to studying cultural processes such as the exercise of creativity within movements, the development of collective identity, the influence of discourse on protest, and the interplay between culture and structure (Jasper 1997; Melucci 1989, 1996; Polletta 1997, 1998; Steinberg 1999). This "cultural turn" may herald a new direction for the field, but, as we will argue in the concluding chapter, unresolved methodological and measurement problems with regard to identity, emotion, and culture may frustrate the development of this cultural perspective into a new paradigm.

Thus, theoretical innovations that encourage empirical investigation and offer methodological tools have contributed considerably to the growth of social movement research. But equally important in our view has been the absence of methodological dogmatism in the social movement field. Students of social movements have conducted quantitative and qualitative studies, surveys and in-depth interviews, archival studies and participant observation, single-case studies and complex comparative designs, mathematical simulations and protest event analyses, ecological studies of multi-organizational fields and life-history interviews, discourse analysis and studies of narratives. In short, a full range of methods has been fruitfully applied in the study of social movements, resulting in a flourishing field that produces enough good empirical work to fill conference programs, scientific journals, edited collections, and monographs, year after year. We are not claiming that all this work is of uniformly high quality, but we do claim that over the years the field has attracted a critical mass of qualified researchers who have moved the domain ahead considerably.

Compared to thirty years ago, we know a lot more about such core questions as: Why do people participate in social movements? How are social movements structured? How do social movements develop over time? How do movements influence one another? How do political opportunities affect social movements? How do social movements influence public policies? This is not the place to elaborate on the answers to these questions, but we do want to emphasize that a variety of research methods have been instrumental in finding these answers. Survey research, in-depth interviews, mathematical modeling, network analysis, and participant observation have all helped us to understand processes of mobilization and social movement participation. Organizational analyses, participant observation, archival studies, and network analysis have informed us about movement structures and how movements influence one another. Protest event analysis, comparative studies, historical analyses, and case studies have helped to map how movements develop over time and how political opportunities influence a social movement's history.

Of course, methods are only tools for testing and building theory. Social movement research thrives because analysts continue to develop theoretical ideas and engage in spirited debate over concepts and ideas (see, for example, the exchanges between Zald [2000] and his critics in *Mobilization*, and between Goodwin and Jasper [1999] and others in *Sociological Forum*). Although such debates witness the vitality of the field, they would be futile if scholars did not go out into the field to test and develop theories with empirical data. When key concepts have been defined such that they can be turned into measurable and observable variables, we have made progress in the social movements area.

Let us be clear: we are not arguing that the expansion of social movement research is exclusively the result of quantitative hypothesis testing. A look at the table of contents of this volume shows that what we mean by empirical is not limited to a single or even a restricted set of methods. On the contrary, we mean that social movement scholars have time and again shown a readiness to confront their thinking with evidence. At times, new evidence and the contributions of other scholars have led theorists to amend even their own well-established theories (see McAdam 1999, new preface; McAdam, Tarrow, and Tilly 2001). It is precisely the rich variety of methods employed in the endeavor of developing theory with empirical evidence that has made it successful.

Expanding on an earlier effort by Diani and Eyerman (1992), this book is an attempt to take stock of current methodological advances and to make the accumulated methodological experience and know-how of movement analysts available to new generations of movement scholars. Without turning it into a cookbook with ready-made recipes, we wanted to put together a book that will help students learn to do research on social movements, and also aid established scholars interested in mastering new methods. We wanted to show them that there is a wide range of methods and techniques available, each with strengths and weaknesses that need to be assessed in choosing the methods that fit their research problems.

At the same time, we want to challenge the scholarly community of social movement researchers by pointing to ongoing theoretical and methodological problems of the field. Although we may sound self-congratulatory in our description of the state of the area, we recognize that much is lacking in our practice as researchers. This is not only a matter of the weaknesses and limitations of the methods we have at our disposal. To be sure, there is room for improvement, and each chapter in this volume discusses the shortcomings as well as strengths of different approaches and methods. However, it is also a matter of questions we have not even begun to answer, either because we lack theories that are concrete and detailed enough to allow us to go into the field, or because we do not have the appropriate methods to actually conduct research, or both. For example, emotions, culture, and identity are topics in social movement theory that we are just beginning to figure out how to study empirically (see Aminzade et al. 2001 for a promising effort to address new issues in social movement research). We are convinced that theoretical and methodological advances are linked, and we will elaborate this theme in more detail in our concluding chapter.

Ultimately, we want to encourage more theoretical integration in our field. Although social movement theorists generally avoid mindless empiricism and engage in healthy theoretical debates, several writers have expressed concern about the dispersed condition of the field and alerted us to the need for more synthesis (Lofland 1993; McAdam, Tarrow, and Tilly 1996, 1997, 2001). Developing a synthesis is a matter of theory rather than method, but it requires a body of strong empirical research. The goal of empirical research, using a range of methods, should be the creation of sound theories that can be synthesized into a comprehensive understanding of social movements. Sound theories in our view are not abstract, free-floating entities, but systems of ideas that can stand empirical tests and serve practical needs; after all, there is nothing so practical as a good theory. To develop good theory, we need to select appropriate methods, and we hope this volume will aid researchers in making methodological choices.

Choosing Methods to Study Social Movements

A researcher who sets out to study social movements is faced with a range of methodological possibilities. Although the choices are limited by the questions the research tries to answer, we would encourage students of social movements to approach their research questions from various angles and to employ multiple methods. We are not, of course, suggesting that every individual researcher needs to use the whole range of methods. Although a multi-method approach is desirable, few researchers are able to use more than a few methods in a single research project, owing to inevitable financial and logistic restrictions, time constraints, deficits of experience, and other limitations. Nevertheless, the field as a whole should maintain and nourish methodological pluralism. Different methods contribute different types of evidence and theoretical insights that add to the collective enterprise; restricting ourselves to a limited methodology would necessarily make us fall short of the theoretical synthesis needed.

What, then, are the options available, and how can a choice be made? For this volume we selected the most significant methodological approaches and techniques employed within the social movement domain. Obviously, it is beyond the limits of this volume to provide an extended treatment of all methods used by social movement scholars. However, most of the research methods and approaches employed in the area are covered here, and some methods that do not receive full treatment (e.g., focus groups and experiments) are discussed within various chapters. Some of the methods covered are strictly quantitative (survey research, protest event analysis, mathematical modeling); some are strictly qualitative (participant observation, in-depth interviewing); and some can be either quantitative or qualitative (network analysis, discourse analysis, archival and historical research, macro-organizational analysis, case studies, comparative politics). Different methods are appropriate for different topics, and each chapter in this book specifies what research questions the method discussed is best suited for. Here we provide some initial guidelines and criteria that can be used in the selection of research methods.

Level and Unit of Analysis

One important consideration is the level and unit of analysis. If the research questions posed are at the individual level of analysis, survey research and in-depth interviews are possible choices. Surveys are particularly appropriate when the researcher wants to generalize to a population, whereas in-depth interviews are more useful in developing theoretical ideas about complicated processes. The typical unit of analysis of survey research is intended or reported behavior; other possibilities are group identification, attitudes, grievances, relative deprivation, and cognition. The unit of analysis for in-depth interviews is less concrete, but the method is especially useful in assessing feelings, emotions, motives, life histories, and interpretations of complex phenomena.

Survey research of movement organizations is obviously aimed at the organizational level of analysis, which is also frequently true of case studies, participant observation, archival and historical studies, network analysis, and macro-organizational analysis. The unit of analysis of these methods varies, however. Organizational surveys may aim at the organization's tactics or effectiveness, or at organizational characteristics. Case studies, participant observation, and archival and historical studies typically take one or more movement organizations as their unit of analysis, although they may also study some larger unit, such as a community. For case studies, participant observation, and archival and historical studies, time is an important factor as well. Each of these methods is used to describe or reconstruct the evolution of a movement or organization over time.

Network analysis and macro-organizational analysis take multi-organizational fields as their level of analysis. But the unit of analysis varies: network analysis is concerned with ties between organizations, and macro-organizational analysis is concerned with the birth and death of organizations. Protest event analysis and comparative politics take societies or political systems as their level of analysis. In the case of protest event analysis, however, protest events are obviously the unit of analysis, whereas in the case of comparative politics, it is social movements or entire movement sectors that are the unit of analysis.

Discourse analysis and mathematical modeling can be located at various levels of analysis. The typical unit of analysis in the case of discourse analysis is text, which might be produced by an individual, an organization, or some other institutional actor. Analysis of text usually aims at understanding its source, so the level of analysis depends on the source. Mathematical modeling may model individual behavior, but it may also model acts of organizations, governmental institutions, or other actors.

Research Question

The types of questions that can be answered with the different methods vary as well. Individual participation can be investigated via surveys, in-depth interviewing, case studies, and participant observation. Occasionally, discourse analysis—when it concerns an analysis of a personal statement or account of why someone participates in a movement—may teach us why individuals participate as well. We may also try to model mathematically the dynamics that lead individuals to participate. Answers to the question of why movements rise or decline and have various impacts can be provided by case studies, protest event analyses, archival and historical studies, and comparative politics. Dynamics within the social movement sector or within a movement's multi-organizational field can be investigated by network analyses or organizational analyses. Allies and opponents, overlapping memberships, changing coalitions, mergers, and competition are the typical subjects of these research methods. In this context, discourse analysis may reveal interesting patterns of ideological kinship or heritage between movement organizations. Again, one may try to model these dynamics mathematically in order to understand the working of such complex systems. Finally, a comparative approach, using protest event analysis and/or archival and historical studies can be used to examine the interface of movements and societies or political systems.

Cost

A final criterion we want to mention here is cost. Obviously, research varies in the costs that are involved. Yet differences in costs are not linked to the methods used in a simple way, as every method has its high- and low-budget forms. If we compare surveys and in-depth interviews, for example, a longitudinal survey with face-to-face interviews is expensive, but so is transcription and coding of in-depth interviews (not to mention translation costs if the interviews are to be conducted in different languages). On the other hand, a printed questionnaire distributed among members of an organization or by volunteers in a neighborhood costs almost nothing, and so does an interview when all the work is done by a single researcher. Labor and expertise, rather than equipment, are the main requisites of social movement research, and their costs determine whether methods are cheap or expensive. Indeed, recent advances in software have made it feasible for a single researcher with a personal computer to analyze a wealth of data that two decades ago would have taken a research grant and a team of assistants to organize. We do not think any method is necessarily prohibitively expensive, although some are easier to employ with a low budget than others. The kind of research question one wants to answer, and the level and unit of analysis are in our view the crucial criteria in the selection of methods. The resources available may further determine whether one can employ a high- or low-budget version of the method.

How the Book Is Organized

We invited prominent social movement researchers who are experts on the particular approaches or methods to write the following chapters. We asked our authors to include the following elements in their chapters: (1) a methodological discussion of topics such as the types of research questions for which the method is appropriate, the level of analysis for which the method is most appropriate, and the strengths and the limitations of the method; (2) one or more good examples of studies employing the method (either from the authors' own research or other); and (3) some "how to" discussion that will provide practical guidance to readers interested in learning the method. This task proved to be more complicated than either the editors or the authors initially anticipated. We want the book to be useful to both students and established scholars interested in learning new methods. But as a result of our intended dual audience, most of the authors found it difficult to decide how much detail to include and exactly what level of audience to address. Each author ultimately made numerous compromises, but all produced chapters that will point readers in the right direction for learning the methods and assessing their usefulness.

We considered various ways of ordering the volume's chapters, none of them completely satisfactory. One option would have been to organize the book into sections on qualitative and quantitative methods, but some approaches, such as case studies and comparative politics, defied such a division. Another option we considered was a distinction between general approaches, such as the case study, and particular techniques, such as participant observation. But where in this division would network analysis or historical studies fit? We concluded that no ordering would be completely satisfactory, but we eventually chose an organizing principle based on the levels of analysis for which the methods are mostly appropriate. Thus, we employ a loose micro to macro progression, beginning with methods most suited to individual-level analyses and ending with those that are clearly intended to deal with macro-level questions. In the end, our failure to find a hard and fast way to divide up these methods reflects our approach: methods are not goals in themselves but means that scholars should use and combine liberally to test and build their theories.

In our concluding chapter, "Blending Methods and Building Theories in Social Movement Research," written with Sidney Tarrow, we discuss the art of doing scholarly work by linking theory and method. We identify some methodological weaknesses that we observe in the field and discuss how they might be solved with a multi-method approach. We look at examples of topics on which we have made progress with existing theory and available methods, and we identify the types of issues that still need to be addressed in the social movement area. We close by raising broader questions about the relations of social movements to other forms of contention, to social and policy outcomes, and to institutional politics. We hope these unresolved issues will be addressed by researchers armed with future methodological innovations as well as the methods detailed in this volume.

References

Aminzade, Ronald R., Jack A. Goldstone, Doug McAdam, Elizabeth Perry, William H. Sewell Jr., Sidney Tarrow, and Charles Tilly. 2001. *Silence and Voice in the Study of Contentious Politics.* Cambridge: Cambridge University Press.

Buechler, Steven M. 2000. *Social Movements in Advanced Capitalism.* New York: Oxford University Press.

Cress, Daniel M., and David A. Snow. 1996. "Mobilization at the Margins: Resources, Benefactors, and the Viability of Homeless Social Movement Organizations." *American Sociological Review* 61 (6): 1089–1109.

Diani, Mario, and Ron Eyerman, eds. 1992. *Studying Collective Action.* London: Sage.

Eisinger, Peter K. 1973. "The Conditions of Protest Behavior in American Cities." *American Political Science Review* 67: 11–28.

Freeman, Jo. 1979. "Resource Mobilization and Strategy: A Model for Analyzing Social Movement Organization Actions." In *The Dynamics of Social Movements: Resource Mobilization, Social Control, and Tactics,* edited by Mayer N. Zald and John D. McCarthy, 167–89. Cambridge, Mass.: Winthrop.

Gamson, William A. 1990. *The Strategy of Social Protest.* 2d ed. Belmont, Calif.: Wadsworth.

Gamson, William A., Bruce Fireman, and Steven Rytina. 1982. *Encounters with Unjust Authority.* Homewood, Ill.: Dorsey Press.

Goodwin, Jeff, and James M. Jasper. 1999. "Caught in a Winding, Snarling Vine: The Structural Bias of Political Process Theory." *Sociological Forum* 14 (1): 27–54.

Jasper, James. 1997. *The Art of Moral Protest: Culture, Biography, and Creativity in Social Movements.* Chicago: University of Chicago Press.

Jenkins, J. Craig, and Bert Klandermans, eds. 1995. *The Politics of Social Protest: Comparative Perspectives on States and Social Movements.* Minneapolis: University of Minnesota Press.

Jenkins, J. Craig, and Charles Perrow. 1977. "Insurgency of the Powerless: Farm Workers Movements, 1946–1972." *American Sociological Review* 42: 249–68.

Kitschelt, Herbert P. 1986. "Political Opportunity Structures and Political Protest: Anti-Nuclear Movements in Four Democracies." *British Journal of Political Science* 16 (1): 57–85.

Lofland, John. 1993. "Theory-Bashing and Answer-Improving in the Study of Social Movements." *The American Sociologist* 24 (2): 37–58.

McAdam, Doug. 1999. *Political Process and the Development of Black Insurgency.* 2d ed. Chicago: University of Chicago Press.

McAdam, Doug, Sidney Tarrow, and Charles Tilly. 1996. "To Map Contentious Politics." *Mobilization* 1 (1): 17–34.

———. 1997. "Toward an Integrated Perspective on Social Movements and Revolution." In *Comparative Politics: Rationality, Culture, and Structure,* edited by Mark I. Lichbach and Alan S. Zuckerman, 142–73. New York: Cambridge University Press.

———. 2001. *Dynamics of Contention.* Cambridge: Cambridge University Press.

Melucci, Alberto. 1989. *Nomads of the Present: Social Movements and Individual Needs in Contemporary Society.* Philadelphia: Temple University Press.

———. 1996. *Challenging Codes: Collective Action in the Information Age.* Cambridge: Cambridge University Press.

Meyer, David S., and Sidney Tarrow, eds. 1998. *The Social Movement Society.* Lanham, Md.: Rowman and Littlefield.

Morris, Aldon D. 1984. *The Origins of the Civil Rights Movement: Black Communities Organizing for Change.* New York: Free Press.

Oberschall, Anthony. 1973. *Social Conflict and Social Movements.* Englewood Cliffs, N.J.: Prentice-Hall.

Polletta, Francesca. 1997. "Culture and Its Discontents: Recent Theorizing on the Cultural Dimensions of Protest." *Sociological Inquiry* 67 (4): 431–50.

———. 1998. "'It Was Like a Fever . . .' Narrative and Identity in Social Protest." *Social Problems* 45 (2): 137–59.

Shorter, Edward, and Charles Tilly. 1974. *Strikes in France, 1830–1968.* Cambridge: Cambridge University Press.

Steinberg, Marc W. 1999. *Fighting Words: Working-Class Formation, Collective Action, and Discourse in Early Nineteenth-Century England.* Ithaca, N.Y.: Cornell University Press.

Tarrow, Sidney. 1989. *Democracy and Disorder: Protest and Politics in Italy 1965–1975.* Oxford: Oxford University Press.

———. 1998. *Power in Movement: Social Movements and Contentious Politics.* 2d ed. New York: Cambridge University Press.

Tilly, Charles. 1978. *From Mobilization to Revolution.* Reading, Mass.: Addison-Wesley.

———. 1986. *The Contentious French: Four Centuries of Popular Struggle.* Cambridge, Mass.: Harvard University Press.

———. 1995. *Popular Contention in Great Britain, 1758–1834.* Cambridge, Mass.: Harvard University Press.

Zald, Mayer N. 2000. "Ideologically Structured Action: An Enlarged Agenda for Social Movement Research." *Mobilization* 5 (1): 1–16.

Zald, Mayer N., and John D. McCarthy, eds. 1987. *Social Movements in an Organizational Society: Collected Essays.* New Brunswick, N.J.: Transaction Books.

METHODS OF SOCIAL MOVEMENT RESEARCH: FROM MICRO TO MACRO

1

Survey Research: A Case for Comparative Designs

Bert Klandermans and Jackie Smith

Survey research continues to be a frequently employed methodology in social movement research. According to Crist and McCarthy (1996), one-fifth of the studies published in the 1980s and early 1990s used surveys as one of their data sources. In this chapter, we discuss the uses and limitations of survey research for the study of social movements, including the less common but potentially rich method of the organizational survey. There are many excellent source books for researchers who want to apply survey methodology (see, for example, Babbie 1990; Fink 1995; and Robson 1993), and we refer readers to these textbooks for more guidelines about survey methodologies. We attempt to aid the researcher in considering the potentials and pitfalls of survey methods by taking into account the specific characteristics of the social movement domain.

In social movement research, survey techniques are employed both with individuals and organizations as the unit of analysis. In the prototypical *individual survey* a sample of individuals fill in a questionnaire encompassing questions about knowledge, beliefs, attitudes, behavior, demographics, and other personal characteristics. Examples are Walsh's study of people living in the Three Mile Island area following a nuclear accident (1988), Opp's studies of participants in legal and illegal protest (1988, 1989), and Klandermans's studies of participation in collective action staged by various movements (Klandermans 1984, 1993, 1997; Klandermans and Oegema 1987; Oegema and Klandermans 1994). An additional way that individual-level surveys can be used by analysts of social movements is demonstrated by the work of Rochon (1998) and Harris (1999). These scholars used pre-existing, publicly available surveys of public opinion and social behavior, which also included measures of organizational and church participation, to evaluate relationships between social movement mobilizations and broader social factors such as public opinion and social and political engagement.

In an *organizational survey*, spokespersons of social movement organizations are questioned about their organization's structure, resource acquisition and allocation, tactics, collective action, and policy. Such studies are much rarer, but a few good examples exist, including Knoke's study of voluntary associations (1989), which involved extensive interviews with 459 informants who provided information on bureaucratization, centralization, and resource use and mobilization. Colwell and Bond (1994) conducted a panel survey of peace movement organizations during the height of antinuclear mobilization and again after the movement subsided in the early 1990s. Dalton employed survey techniques in his study of environmental organizations in Western Europe (1994), and Minkoff (this volume) discusses in depth the organizational surveys of anti–drunk driving organizations by McCarthy. Extending the method further, Smith used survey methods to analyze transnational human rights organizations (Smith, Pagnucco, and Lopez 1998) and coalition affiliates of a transnational environmental and social justice organization (Smith 1999).

This chapter attempts to improve survey techniques as they are employed in social movement research, particularly by stressing the use of comparative designs. Survey research can use cross-sectional or more sophisticated longitudinal or comparative designs. Too much survey research on social movements takes the first, simpler approach. Although intellectually more demanding and more costly, survey designs that draw comparisons across movements, space, or time provide immense empirical leverage that can help advance theories of social movements. The intelligent use of such designs turns surveys into a powerful tool for the study of social movements. In the following pages we discuss a variety of techniques of data collection, sampling techniques, and research designs, with an emphasis on how they can be employed in comparative settings.

The Use of Survey Research in the Study of Social Movements

The most frequent use of surveys is for description: the description of members, of participants, of potential participants, of different types of participants (male/female, black/white, young/old, etc.), and of their opponents. Some key questions of this type of research revolve around motivations of different categories of participants. Examples of such studies include Oliver (1984) and Ennis and Schreuer (1987). Sometimes these studies are simple descriptions, and sometimes they are rooted in theories that are operational-ized in the questionnaire and tested against survey responses. One example of such research is Opp's work within the rational choice theoretical frame-work on the antinuclear power movement in Germany (1989), and on the democratization movement in former East Germany (Opp and Gern 1993). The problem with such studies is that often they lack a valid standard of comparison. To understand the dynamics of participation, one needs to compare participants with nonparticipants. In addition, one needs to know whether specific characteristics are typical for all participants or not.

Addressing this problem, McAdam (1986) emphasizes that nonpartici-pants do not necessarily provide appropriate standards for comparison. This is especially true of attitudinal comparisons. Typically, two groups are com-pared, and the involvement of the participants is attributed to any attitudi-nal differences observed between the two groups. But McAdam cautions that the attitudinal differences between participants and nonparticipants might *result from* rather than constitute an underlying motivation for ac-tivism. McAdam's and other studies show that participants' beliefs and con-sciousness are transformed in the course of their participation in a move-ment. Yet it is also likely that individuals participate in a particular social movement because they share some of the beliefs of the movement. Unless we obtain measurements that both precede and follow participation or ex-posure to movement activities, we will not be able to determine the extent to which individuals participate because of their beliefs and the extent to which their beliefs are shaped by their participation.

Moreover, comparisons of participation are problematic, since partici-pants may be more or less intensively involved in a movement and since par-ticipation itself affects later possibilities for action. Participation is therefore a process that can be conceived in four steps where each step represents a decision point where people move toward or away from participation. For instance, an individual becomes a sympathizer or not, becomes a target of a mobilization attempt or not, is motivated to participate or not, and over-comes barriers to participation or not. Comparisons must be made between people at the same point in this process. If we do not separate these compari-sons, we miss the point that at each decision point different mechanisms are at work to shape individuals' decisions. As a consequence, our comparison of participants with nonparticipants encompasses each of the four types of nonparticipation and thus is blurred. The strength of McAdam's study of participants in Freedom Summer was that he made the right comparison. It is reasonable to assume that all student applicants were motivated to partici-pate in Freedom Summer. They all completed the application forms and were accepted into the project. Yet one quarter of the applicants did not participate. McAdam used the information available on the application forms to identify characteristics of those who participated and those who withdrew. The data were longitudinal since the application procedure took place earlier in the year.

In summary, the study of movement participants requires proper comparisons so that we are able to make sense of our findings. But there is more to comparison than distinguishing participants from nonparticipants. We will argue that it is far more useful to survey several smaller samples in a comparative design than one large sample noncomparatively. For instance, fifty interviews each of two different groups of informants at three points in time will tell us considerably more about movement participation than three hundred interviews with one group at a single point in time. Similarly, a cross-sectional study that distinguishes respondents according to how they fit among the four steps of the process of movement participation will tell us more than a study that does not allow for such comparisons. It is such comparisons that help us to understand movement participation. After all, movement participation is a process, and we cannot investigate a process with a single-shot measure. Thus, much of this chapter is devoted to discussion of comparative designs.

Comparison

Comparative designs may incorporate comparisons of movements, or comparisons of events or other features of social movements across space or time (or some combination of these comparisons). Such comparisons are rare. Yet, comparative research of movement participation is important. It tells us that what holds for a participant in one movement, or at one point in time, or at one place is not necessarily true for a participant in another movement, or at a different time or place. Comparisons across different social movements are uncommon. One example is Klandermans's (1993) comparison of participants in the labor movement, the peace movement, and the women's movement. This comparison used similar measurements and concepts within a unified theoretical framework and found that a different mix of motives spurred participation in each of these movements.

Comparisons across space are the most common. Maguire's surveys of the peace movement in Italy and Great Britain (1995), and Opp and colleagues' surveys in Germany, Israel, and Peru (1995) are examples. The latter investigated participation in legal and illegal protest in these three countries. These researchers found that the traditional pattern of protest being more common on the left wing of the political spectrum, and lowest on the right held only in Germany. In the other countries rightists and extreme rightists were more active than centrists, and in some locations people from the right were as active or even more active than those on the nonextreme left. The results suggest that the association between ideology and protest behavior can vary widely according to country context. Findings like this demonstrate the crucial importance of comparison of space. Indeed, such comparative studies gave rise to the so-called social geographic approach to social movements (Miller 2000), which made comparisons of space and place its basic paradigm. Miller demonstrated how social geographic differences such as differences in class composition, educational levels, economic history, and history of activism between regions (in the Cambridge, Massachusetts, area) could explain the differences between the Freeze Campaigns in these regions.

Comparisons involving time are equally important, as levels of participation tend to vary cyclically over time. Klandermans's research on the peace movement provides a dramatic example. In June 1985, he and his colleagues interviewed samples of the population of four Dutch communities. Sixty-nine percent said that they would sign a petition against the deployment of cruise missiles in the Netherlands. The interviews were repeated again in November, when just two-thirds of those who had said that they would sign reported that they actually signed. Of the initial petition supporters remaining, two-fifths indicated that in fact they wanted to sign but failed to do so, but three-fifths said that they had never wanted to sign. Had the researchers only interviewed the sample in November after the petition drive took place, they would not have found this significant group of people who changed their positions completely (Oegema and Klandermans 1994).

Another important area of research involves studies of biographical consequences of movement participation (Marwell, Aiken, and Demerath 1987; Marwell, Demerath, and Aiken 1993; McAdam 1989; Stewart, Settles, and Winter 1998). By surveying movement participants many years after their active participation in social movements, these studies have convincingly demonstrated that movement participation has long-lasting biographical consequences.

How Is Survey Research Done?

Designs, sampling techniques, questionnaires, and statistical analyses are the building blocks of survey research. The study of social movements has some peculiarities that necessitate specific modifications of these methodological tools. Before discussing the basic "nuts and bolts" of survey research, we review varieties of comparative designs that are applicable to the study of social movements.

Comparative Designs

Designs are meant to structure the research environment so that the questions guiding the research can indeed be answered. Designs specify the comparisons that are necessary for an answer to be extracted from the data. The three main types of comparison are of movements, of space, and of time. Ideally, we should conceive of studies that combine these three comparisons, for example, a study of the changing characteristics of the participants in the women's movement and the peace movement in the Netherlands and Germany between 1975 and 1980. Such a design would help us account for the context of movement participation. Yet, to our knowledge nobody has ever tried such a design, most likely because such a design is extremely demanding: comparable questions must be asked of participants of both movements, in both countries at the two points in time. Indeed, most comparative studies keep one or two of the three dimensions constant. Klandermans and colleagues' (2001) study of farmers' protest in the Netherlands and Spain is an example of a study that kept one dimension (the movement dimension) constant. During three subsequent years, these scholars investigated farmers' responses to agricultural policies of the European Union. More common, however, are studies that keep two dimensions of comparison constant by comparing, for instance, two or more movements within the same country at a single point in time, the same movement in two or more different countries at a single point in time, or the same movement in a single country at two or more different points in time. These are the three designs that will be discussed and illustrated in the next few pages.

Comparison of Movements

The most common question in a comparison of movements concerns the similarities and differences between participants in different movements. These differences may concern demographic characteristics, motivational dynamics, identity, attitudes, and ideology. An example is Klandermans's (1993) comparison of participants in the labor, peace, and women's movements in the Netherlands. Drawing on Turner and Killian's (1987) distinction of action orientations, the study tests the hypothesis that each movement appealed to different action orientations: a power orientation in the case of the labor movement, a value orientation in the case of the peace movement, and a participation orientation in the case of the women's movement. But the study also illustrated an important challenge for this kind of comparison, namely the development of operational definitions of participation and comparable measurements of action orientations in very different movements. This is not a trivial matter. After all, the definition of participation and the measures of action orientation define the comparison.

In this study Klandermans contrasted preparedness to participate and actual participation in activities staged by the movements: industrial action for the labor movement, a demonstration for the peace movement, and participation in some women's groups in the community for the women's movement. Common categories of motivation were used to assess the action orientation of participants in these different movements. Value and power orientations were defined in terms of the collective incentives for participation, and the participation orientation was defined in terms of selective incentives. A value orientation was thus defined as an emphasis on the motivation to participate on the value of the collective goal, a power orientation as an emphasis on the expectation that the goal can be achieved, and a participation orientation as an emphasis on participation as a goal in itself. These definitions to some extent determine the outcome of the comparison.

Comparison of Space

Comparisons of space examine the same movement in different locations. A prominent example is Walsh's study of citizens and activists in Middletown, Newberry, Harrisburg, and Lancaster, four communities in the neighborhood of Three Mile Island (1988). Other examples are Miller's study of the Freeze Campaign in Cambridge, Lexington, and Waltham (2000), and Oegema and Klandermans's study of participants and nonparticipants in a petition against cruise missiles in four Dutch communities (1994). Each study demonstrates that the dynamics of participation are shaped by characteristics of the local communities in which movements are embedded. Had these authors neglected to make these comparisons (either by restricting themselves to a single community or by simply analyzing aggregated, national-level data), we would have erroneously believed that the dynamics of participation in each community were the same. Such comparisons are important because they may reveal diverging political, economic, or social psychological dynamics of movement participation. The reason behind comparison of space may be a need for careful description, or investigation into the impact of contextual variation, or to test some theory about the differences between the groups being studied.

Methodologically, two key issues are to ensure that both the sampling frames for the different populations and the questionnaires are comparable. These are issues in any comparison, but in the context of comparisons of space they require special attention. Making sampling and questionnaires comparable is easier said than done. It is crucial, for instance, to have consistently defined samples in each locale. After all, we want to be able to attribute the differences we find between two or more samples to real contextual differences rather than to sampling biases. But it may not always be easy to draw comparable samples, because one cannot always identify comparable sampling frames. A sampling frame is a list of units (i.e., individuals or organizations) that comprise the population from which the sample is to be drawn. If available lists are not identical samples from the populations being studied, these samples will not be comparable. But in different countries, regions, or locales, records are often kept according to different procedures and with varying levels of accuracy. Movement organizations in country A may have reliable membership lists, but their counterparts in country B may have less formal registration procedures. Differences in regulations may have the same effect. The bylaws of organization X may make it impossible to use its membership list for sampling, while organization Z may have no qualms about releasing its list. Comparing organizational populations across countries is immensely difficult. One can find a wealth of fairly comparable organizational registries for groups in North America and Europe but must rely on a range of sources of variable quality and consistency in order to move beyond these regions. Many more examples of sampling pitfalls can be identified, but the message is clear: in order to draw equivalent samples, one needs comparable sampling frames of the groups one wants to compare.

In addition to equivalent samples, we need comparable questionnaires. That is, questions must not only have comparable wording, but they must also have the same *meaning* for each group in a study. It is difficult enough to find wordings that have the same meaning to respondents from the same cultural background, let alone to respondents from different cultures. Pretesting questions and exploring their meaning in qualitative pilot studies with both social science colleagues and with people who make up the sample population are of crucial importance. Where possible, pretests should include interviews with at least two representatives of the sample population (and key variations within this population) where the informant can help the researcher identify wording or formatting that may pose problems of clarity or construct validity for those asked to complete the survey.

If we are conducting our research in more than one country, we must solve both problems of translation and problems of cultural differences. Problems of translation can be solved by careful procedures such as translation and back-translation to guarantee that the questions are indeed the same. But such procedures do not necessarily solve the problem of cultural differences. For example, being a member of a farmers' organization has a totally different meaning in the Netherlands (where farmers' organizations are part of neocorporatist structures dating back to the era of pillarization) than in Spain (where the main political groupings in the country have their associated farmers' organizations). But even within the same culture, the same word can have a different meaning. For example, in Klandermans's study the word *action* had a meaning among the elderly that associated much more with unruliness than it did among the younger generations in other studies. The same was true in comparisons of black and white South Africans. While the former had a long history of sometimes very militant collective action, the latter had no experience whatsoever. As a consequence, taking part in moderate action had a very different meaning for whites than for blacks. Given these realities, careful translation of questionnaires requires both language skills and appreciation of the cultural differences between and within countries.

Comparison of Time

Movement participation and mobilization are processes that evolve over time. Movements expand and contract in phases of mobilization and demobilization. These waves of expansion and contraction can be analyzed in comparisons of time. In fact, movement participation is not as spontaneous as is sometimes assumed, and it is often possible to foresee fluctuations in participation. Movement participation can be conceived of as a response to mobilization attempts. On quite a few occasions we *can* predict that a movement organization will mobilize its constituency. If we are on good terms with an organization, the organization might be willing to inform us about impending campaigns and might even take an interest in our research. Such a collaborative relationship may not even be necessary because organizations often publicize their intentions to mobilize mass action.

As long as we know beforehand that a movement organization is setting out to mobilize, we can design our research accordingly. But what if we do not know? How can we predict the courses of mobilization campaigns in order to design appropriate ways to study them? We can find at least a partial solution to our problem in the fact that movements evolve cyclically. No single movement is able to keep its constituency continuously mobilized. At the very least, movements experience seasonal cycles: even movement activists go on vacation, and every year, when the summer (in their part of the world) is over, the movements' programs and activities must be revived. Any researcher planning to investigate participation in a specific movement must first consider the kind of cycles the movement and its participants might go through. Survey research designs in particular must be sensitive to the time frames affecting potential respondents or informants. Below we review some of the ways cyclical patterns affect movements.

Seasonal Cycles

Nearly every movement experiences seasonal cycles. In the fall a movement begins new activities, creates new opportunities for participation, and re-invigorates already existing plans and programs. Consequently, it tries anew to persuade individuals to take part in the activities of the movement. Most university campuses, for instance, have fixed days at the start of the academic year during which voluntary organizations can try to recruit new participants, and academic calendars can have important effects on movements involving large numbers of students. Also, cross-national surveys involving groups or individuals in both the Northern and Southern Hemispheres must account for two summer seasons in the timing of the survey. The work of Briet, Klandermans, and Kroon (1987) provides an example of how this seasonal rhythm can be incorporated into a study of a movement, in this case, the Dutch women's movement.

Cycles Generated by Recurrent Instances of Collective Action

Some movement organizations go through institutional cycles. Labor unions have their yearly contract negotiations, which are frequently accompanied by mobilization campaigns. The gay and lesbian movement has annual parades. Election periods tend to stimulate collective action by many different groups. Other movements may have similar institutionally anchored days, periods, or events for which they try to mobilize and broaden their constituency. It is not always easy to foresee whether these events will create any excitement at all, but occasionally they do, and sometimes we can predict this outcome.

Action Mobilization Cycles

It is not unusual for a movement organization to announce in advance that it will organize a demonstration, rally, or some other kind of mass action. Because such activities require much preparation, they are typically planned well in advance. Accordingly, they provide excellent opportunities for longitudinal research. Before the event, one can ask individuals whether they are aware of the imminent event and whether they intend to participate; after the event, a researcher can go back to these same individuals and ask whether they did in fact participate. Klandermans's study of the 1983 peace demonstration in The Hague (Klandermans and Oegema 1987) is an example of how research on movement participation can take advantage of an action mobilization cycle.

Cycles Generated by Events

Sometimes observers and researchers can anticipate that political events will generate mass mobilization. Klandermans's study of the Dutch peace movement exploited the fact that the Dutch government had openly committed itself to decide on the deployment of cruise missiles before 1 November 1985. It was easy to predict that, given this commitment, the movement would try to mobilize its constituency. More recently, meetings of such institutions as the World Bank and the IMF have attracted a diverse set of movement organizations that have mobilized their constituencies to demonstrate. Knowing that such events are coming up, one can make arrangements to collect data. When organizations, rather than individuals, are to be surveyed at such events, researchers must be sensitive to the ways that such mobilizations and events affect the likelihood that knowledgeable organizational leaders will take the time to participate in a survey. One must balance the need to collect information near key moments or events with the risk of low response rates due to the fact that the most important informants are often working overtime to make such events happen. In some cases, events have to be avoided. For example, Smith's survey of international human rights organizations had to be timed so that it would not coincide with the annual United Nations Human Rights Commission meeting, which lasts for six weeks every March–April (Smith, Pagnucco, and Lopez 1998).

Growth and Decline Cycles

Movements grow and decline, a process that implies an initial increase but an eventual falling off in participation. Such cycles are inherent in the life of a movement. We have witnessed such cyclical patterns in the movements against cruise missiles all over Europe. Every time a government decided to deploy the missiles, the movement declined (Klandermans 1991; Rochon 1988). In fact, one could have predicted that whatever decision a government made would set the movement back: a decision to deploy would imply a major failure for the movement; a decision not to deploy—although a major success—would eliminate the movement's foremost grievance. In the literature both eventualities are cited as causes of movement decline. If we can anticipate such cycles, we can design our research in accordance with them.

Survey Research Designs

The first decision a researcher must make when considering a survey research design is what unit of analysis is most appropriate to the questions being asked. A first choice is whether one is principally concerned with answering questions about individuals or organizations. But once that choice is made, one must ask whether the individuals of interest are the general public, participants in movement events, leaders of movement organizations, or targets of movement efforts. On the organizational side, one might be interested in learning about local, national, or international organizations or about relationships among these. Populations of the relevant types of organization must be identified for a survey of individuals, exemplified in the previously mentioned survey of human rights organizations (Smith, Pagnucco, and Lopez 1998). A study of organizations might involve, for instance, a survey of the organizational affiliates of a loose coalition or of a more formal organization (e.g., Smith 1999).

Sampling

Once we have identified the unit of analysis for our study, we must find a way to identify those who fit in this population we are interested in, the *sampling frame*. The real problem in social movement research is the sampling frame (the list of individuals or organizations that comprise the research population). Once we find an appropriate sampling frame, sampling is a technical matter. Depending on whether our research question concerns potential participants or, alternatively, actual participants, the research population can be (some subset of) the general population or the participants in a social movement. Sometimes every citizen is a potential participant as is the case for the peace movement or the animal rights movement, but often the potential participants are some subset of the general population, such as farmers, females, gays or lesbians, the elderly, or the people living in a particular neighborhood. If the general population is the research population, one can use a telephone book, postal codes, postal addresses, or population registers as sampling frames. One can restrict sampling to a single city or even a neighborhood, provided that the city or neighborhood is reasonably representative of the general population. Far more complicated is sampling subsets of the population or movement participants. Often, reliable lists of individual members of some subgroup are either not available or not accessible to third parties for privacy reasons. As a consequence, we must work with some alternative sampling frame that is as proximate to the research population as possible. For example, in the farmers' protest study, Klandermans and colleagues (2001) approached *every* farmer in each of a set of selected farming communities. In a study of political participation of the elderly, one may approach homes for the elderly or draw samples of the population in graying neighborhoods. Neighborhoods may have a specific composition (socioeconomic, political) that might make them useful as a sampling frame. Organizations may be willing to open their networks or to sell their mailing lists. In some cases, one can make use of professional companies that deliver a sample upon request.

Sampling movement participants can be even more problematic, as many movements do not maintain reliable lists of participants. Sampling potential participants to find actual participants is not efficient. Usually, actual participants account for only a small proportion of the mobilization potential. One may easily end up approaching ten to twenty potential participants to find one active participant. Another option is to sample participants at events: the people who attend a meeting, take part in a demonstration, or sign a petition. In this case some smart thinking about sampling technique is needed. Petitions are easy: one can sample from the list of signatures, provided that names and addresses are made available. But how might one sample in mass meetings or at demonstrations? One possibility is to divide a meeting space into cells and to sample cells by approaching every person who occupies a sampled place (see Drury, Reicher, and Scott 1999 for an example of this approach to sampling during collective action). Apart from the technical problems of sampling participants at events, it is obvious that the kind of activity influences who participates. The people who attend a meeting are not necessarily the same as the people who participate in the demonstration or who sign the petition. Yet, all three groups of people are and probably see themselves as participants in the same movement.

Although ideally the researcher would like his or her principal questions to determine the research design, limitations on the availability of and access to information often demand that the researcher adapt the design to fit available data sources. As we have noted, survey designs demand at least some credible measure of the population of individuals or organizations one seeks to understand. In other words, we need to identify an unbiased and appropriate *sampling frame* from which we will choose potential informants. At times we may be able to combine what we know to be biased lists of organizations or individuals within our population with efforts to compensate for this known bias. If one is interested in surveying local, national, or international movement organizations from different countries, one might seek to compile as comprehensive a sampling frame as possible by drawing from multiple organizational directories published independently by private or government agencies (see also Minkoff, this volume).

When surveying organizational leaders, consultations with activists in the movement or with other analysts of that particular movement can yield a "snowball" sample of those individuals who are seen as leaders in a given movement. The United Nations and other international bodies compile lists of organizations registered to attend special international conferences, and these lists may also be of use for particular research questions. The lesson one can draw from this discussion is that good researchers must often find creative ways to overcome the limitations of readily available data sources. If an unbiased sampling frame simply cannot be found, a study may still be worth doing as long as the biases inherent in the sampling frame are considered in the interpretation of survey results. Obviously, generalization is possible only to the population as defined by the sampling frame that is used. Thus, the researcher should always provide a careful description of the sampling frame.

The handbooks on survey methods cited earlier provide a variety of *sampling strategies*. In addition to the considerations raised there, however, researchers of social movements may face problems that are particular to this area of research. In the first place they may choose designs that weight samples in order to expand the number of cases representing a relatively understudied group. For instance, Smith's survey of affiliates of a transnational social movement organization oversampled affiliates based in developing country regions for two reasons: (1) to overcome anticipated problems of nonresponse caused by less reliable postal systems in these regions, and (2) to ensure that a sufficient number of cases from these regions would be generated in the study to enable generalizations about that relatively underexamined subset of organizations. Stratified samples are also useful when the researcher has reason to believe that a subset of the population in question has a particularly important impact on conflict dynamics. This was the case in the peace movement survey initiated by Colwell and her colleagues (Colwell and Bond 1994), where groups with relatively large budgets, which were assumed to have a greater impact on peace movement mobilizations, were oversampled. Finally, as many movement organizations are structured in branches, we have often no choice but to draw samples of branches first and then individuals within the sampled branches. Such samples require multilevel data analysis during data processing. We will return to that matter in the section on data processing. The important methodological matter to keep in mind here is that generalizations can be made about the entire population only if results are based on probability samples of that population. Where others types of samples are employed, conclusions are limited by the sampling biases in the study's design.

Choosing the Type of Survey

Survey questionnaires can be mailed to respondents, completed in face-to-face or telephone interviews (often computer assisted), or—the newest development—transmitted via the Internet. Each of these techniques has its advantages and disadvantages, which the researcher should consider early in the research process.

Costs

Face-to-face interviews are the most expensive form of data collection, and the Internet is the cheapest option. Mailing questionnaires is cheaper than telephone interviews, but the difference between the two is much smaller than one would be inclined to believe, especially if the interviewers are inputting responses directly into a computer database.

Response Rates

Each survey method influences response rates differently: face-to-face interviews tend to have the highest response rates, and mailed questionnaires the lowest. Telephone interviews occupy a position in between, but nearer to face-to-face interviews than to mailed questionnaires. Moreover, some researchers employ incentives to encourage participation, although care must be taken to assure that incentives do not introduce new biases into the study. As the Internet is a recent development in this area, no systematic information on response rates is available yet. However, the number of individuals and organizations connected to the Internet is growing so rapidly that this route will become more and more attractive, and thus it will not be long before this information becomes available. Smith's (1999) work suggests, however, that this avenue may have its limitations. She experimented with Internet-based responses by allowing organizations that were contacted by mail the option of completing their surveys via the Internet. Only one of the more than five hundred groups in the sample chose this route (although a number of groups did request e-mail versions of the survey). This might reflect relatively low access to the Internet, although half the respondents reported having access to this technology. What is more likely is that the exercise of completing the survey involves a number of staff members or even deliberation among organizational participants, making a hard-copy questionnaire the preferred option.

Mailed questionnaires seldom generate response rates higher than 30 percent for individual surveys, and 50 percent for organizational ones. Face-to-face interviews easily reach response rates of 60 percent to 70 percent, and telephone interviews finish somewhat lower, at 50 percent to 60 percent. Indeed, telephone interviews are often the most cost-effective approach (that is, the costs per completed interview). In general, organizational surveys have also been associated with lower response rates than those of individual surveys (Tomaskovic-Devey, Leiter, and Thompson 1994: 439).

Timing

Surveys take time. Telephone and Internet surveys, however, can be organized on much shorter notice than mail and face-to-face surveys. Someone who has access to the appropriate facilities can organize a telephone or Internet survey almost overnight. The Internet is by far the speediest form of data collection. If the sample is set up in advance—as is usually the case—the questionnaire can be mailed in a few seconds, and one can have the answers returned within a few days. Telephone interviews take more time for the simple reason that reaching informants by phone and conducting interviews takes time. They also may be less appropriate for some types of organizational surveys, since it is often difficult to reach large numbers of busy organizational leaders by phone, and since some movements with small and geographically dispersed organizations that cross many time zones may not lend themselves to such designs. Smith (1999) has sought to employ telephone surveys in her work on affiliates of transnational associations and has found tremendous costs associated with difficulties in reaching targeted informants and with language and other communication difficulties. Nevertheless, assuming that telephone surveying is more localized and computer assisted, one can have the first results within a few hours after the last interview is conducted. Mail and face-to-face surveying are more complicated and labor-intensive. Sampling, mailing, and returning the questionnaires, or training the interviewers can easily take several weeks or longer, if one seeks to maximize response rates. Interviews take time but can often be computer assisted.

Substance

Not every kind of question can be asked via each approach. For example, knowledge cannot be assessed in mailed questionnaires or via the Internet, unless one does not mind if the respondent looks up the correct answer. But organizational studies often require some searching on the part of the respondent for accurate information about, for instance, the founding date of an organization. Open-ended questions fare better in face-to-face interviews, where the researcher can ask probing questions to explore themes that arise in the course of a response. In heterogeneous samples one will typically find people who are not used to verbalizing let alone to writing about their beliefs, attitudes, or behavior. Interviews leave the respondent the possibility of talking rather than writing. Mailed questionnaires and questionnaires on the Internet have the advantage that people can take their time and work on their response when it suits them. They can reread what they filled in, reconsider their answers, and correct answers if they want. All this is more difficult in interview settings, especially in telephone interviews. Telephone interviews need to be limited in length. Thirty minutes is the typical time limit for an effective survey, but if the subject is of much concern to the respondent, this time can be extended to three-quarters of an hour. Mailed questionnaires and questionnaires on the Internet can be longer. However, long questionnaires lower the response rate and may make people less serious in their responses.

Time Frame

A final, more general design question regards the time frame of the survey. Is the study designed to provide a picture of some aspect of a movement at a single point in time, or does the researcher intend to engage in a longitudinal study involving pre- and post-event surveys or surveys at various points in a movement cycle? Since multiple-time surveys enhance our analytical leverage by providing comparison points, designs that incorporate them are important. Even if one began a study assuming a one-shot survey of movement participants or organizations, an opportunity may arise to go back and resurvey the same groups or individuals. This was the case in the Colwell survey of the peace movement mentioned earlier. Thus, it is wise for a researcher to conceptualize the survey with the idea that he or she or some other researcher may repeat a survey of the same population at a later time.

There are several possible designs to move beyond one-time surveys. In an appendix on research methods, Klandermans (1997) discusses three core designs for social movement research: (1) panel studies, (2) separate sample designs, and (3) separate sample pretest-posttest designs. We will discuss only the main characteristics and refer to this appendix for details.

Panel Studies

Panel studies can be conceived of as within-subject designs and can be described as follows:

$$R\, O_1\, X_1\, O_2\, X_2\, O_3 \ldots X_n\, O_n,$$

where X stands for event; O stands for observation; subscripts 1 through n refer to the sequential order of events ($X_1 \ldots X_n$) or of observations ($O_1 \ldots O_n$); and $R_1 \ldots R_n$ stands for groups that are randomly formed.

A random sample of individuals is interviewed before and after events of interest. This design may provide us with data on fluctuations in participation and relevant beliefs. It allows us to apply sophisticated correlational analyses, such as cross-lagged correlations, and to test complicated over-time models with techniques such as LISREL. With more than two measurements in time, this design can help us make causal inferences. An example of such research is Taylor's study of the Boston school segregation conflict (1986), in which Taylor tried to investigate how leaders, events, and circumstances caused people to engage in an active fight against desegregation. Over a twenty-two-month period, Taylor surveyed a sample of residents of the Boston area five times to determine their beliefs about race relations and desegregation, and the relation of these beliefs to the anti-busing protest.

Panel studies have a number of weaknesses. First, they do not control for *history;* that is, after we have assessed a change in belief, attitude, or behavior, we still have the difficulty of attributing the change to specific events. Any event—not only the event we were interested in—that occurs in between two observations may be responsible for the observed changes. The longer the period between two observations, the greater the number and variety of events that could provide rival explanations. Second, panel studies may create *testing* problems; that is, an individual's responses to a particular question may change over time because he or she has been asked the same questions a number of times. Moreover, individuals may become irritated, bored, and frustrated when they have to fill out the same questionnaire on more than one occasion. In contrast to the effects of history, testing effects are stronger if the time interval in between two measurements shortens. A third weakness of panel studies is *subject mortality:* a study can lose its respondents for all kinds of reasons (it may be impossible to trace or contact them again, they may be unwilling or unable to cooperate again, or they may have died). The longer the study lasts, the more serious a problem mortality can become. One advantage, of course, is that we know a lot about the dropouts from the previous interviews. We can therefore estimate the degree of bias in the data.

Separate Sample Designs

As the name indicates, separate sample designs, unlike panel studies, are based on several separate samples employed to collect data over time in the following way:

$$
\begin{array}{lllll}
R_1 O_1 & X_1 & X_2 & \cdots & X_n \\
R_2 & X_1 & O_2 X_2 & \cdots & X_n \\
R_3 & X_1 & X_2 O_3 & \cdots & X_n \\
\cdots & \cdots & \cdots & \cdots & \cdots \\
R_n & X_1 & X_2 & \cdots & X_n O_n
\end{array}
$$

If the study involves a large population, samples can be drawn independently of each other at various times. Klandermans, Roefs, and Olivier (2001) employed this design in their study of social movements in South Africa. From 1994 until 2000, these authors interviewed random samples of the South African population, asking questions about grievances, relative deprivation, trust in government, participation in grassroots organizations, and protest participation.

The major advantage of this type of design is that *testing* is no longer a problem. Because respondents are interviewed only once, none of the problems related to repeated measurement arises. *Subject mortality* will not become a problem either when groups are sampled independently at the appropriate time. Equivalence of the various groups (because of sampling biases or nonresponse) is a problem that always needs attention, especially when groups are small. We are, of course, able to assess to what extent two groups are equivalent. If needed, statistical controls (analysis of covariance with the differences between groups as covariates) may help to correct for the observed nonequivalence.

Separate sample designs also have disadvantages. As in panel designs, *history* is not controlled for as an alternative explanation of the assessed changes. In fact, all comparisons of time in field research struggle with this problem.

Separate Sample Pretest-Posttest Designs

We can obtain within-subject analyses of changes by adding a posttest to the separate sample design. This addition leads to the following arrangement:

$$R_1 O_1 \quad X_1 \quad O_2 \quad X_2 \quad \quad X_3 \quad \quad \cdots \quad X_n$$

$$R_2 \quad X_1 \quad O_3 \quad X_2 \quad O_4 \quad X_3 \quad \quad \cdots \quad X_n$$

$$R_3 \quad X_1 \quad \quad X_2 \quad O_5 \quad X_3 \quad O_6 \quad \cdots \quad X_n$$

$$\cdots \quad \cdots \quad \cdots \quad \cdots \quad \cdots \quad \cdots \quad \cdots \quad \cdots \quad \cdots$$

$$R_n \quad X_1 \quad \quad X_2 \quad \quad X_3 \cdots \quad O_{2n-1} \quad \cdots \quad X_n \quad O_{2n}$$

The separate sample pretest-posttest design combines the merits of the two preceding designs. It enables us to perform all the analyses that can be done with the separate sample design, when comparing O_1, O_3, O_5, and so on. In addition, this design allows us to make within-subject analyses of changes over time (comparing O_1 with O_2, O_3 with O_4, etc.) without the problems inherent in panel studies. Subjects are never interviewed more than two times. If it is possible to interview each separate sample three times, a powerful design results, which allows for robust causal analyses as well. Moreover, this design controls for *testing* effects introduced by repeated measurements. If O_2 does not differ from O_3, testing cannot be a rival explanation of differences between O_1 and O_2. *Mortality,* too, is controlled for: the comparison of O_1 with O_2 may be flawed because of mortality; that of O_1 with O_3 is not. Thus, if the O_1-O_2 comparison confirms the O_1-O_3 comparison, mortality can be ruled out as an alternative explanation. The one problem that remains unresolved is *history.* Klandermans (1984) applied this design in his study of a mobilization campaign of a Dutch labor union.

Response Rates and Nonresponse Bias

The reliability and validity of survey findings depend on high survey response rates, which reduce the possibility that the sample of respondents is systematically different from the population the study investigates. Nonrandom differences between survey respondents and nonrespondents, or *nonresponse bias,* are often difficult to avoid. For instance, one would expect that people who are less interested in the goals of a movement or who are overworked leaders of small and resource-poor organizations would not take the time to complete a survey. Because a biased pool of respondents limit one's ability to generalize from survey results, the researcher must take every possible step both to limit nonresponse bias and, if possible, to understand its dimensions.

Nonresponse threatens the reliability and validity of our findings more than sample size. Therefore, researchers' efforts should emphasize achieving high response rates rather than large samples. Indeed, it is better to draw a smaller sample and aim at as high a response rate as possible than to draw a larger sample to compensate for a low response rate. Scholars using survey methodologies have developed a variety of strategies for maximizing response rates (for a detailed discussion, see Spaeth and O'Rourke 1994). McCarthy and his collaborators (McCarthy, Shields, and Hall, 1997; McCarthy and Wolfson 1996) mailed an abbreviated version of the questionnaire to nonresponders, including only questions researchers deemed most central to their principal analyses. With this method, data on key variables were collected from an additional 22 percent of the nonrespondents in a survey of groups working to combat drunk driving. McCarthy and his collaborators have also used, with considerable success, follow-up telephone calls to organizations, reminding them to return their survey. Smith's (1999) work on organizational surveys employed these multiple types of efforts to encourage nonrespondents to complete the surveys, and each contact effort generated some added level of response. When designing a study, researchers should define an appropriate targeted response rate and time frame within which surveys will be collected. Probably no more than a 50 percent response rate can be expected for organizational surveys. The design should include multiple and varied follow-up communications to nonrespondents until that target response rate is reached and/or the time frame has expired.

In some cases, particularly in organizational studies, researchers may have access to data on the population of interest *prior* to beginning a survey. For instance, organizational directories provide details about a group's goals, location, founding date, and membership (see Minkoff, this volume). Lists of individuals or organizations provide details about where a target informant is located. Such information can be used to compare respondents with the entire sample (or population) of individuals or organizations to identify potential nonresponse biases (for an example of such a study, see Smith 1997). While these tests are limited to the few variables for which data are available, the researcher can at a minimum determine whether the pool of respondents overrepresents particular geographic areas, types of organizations, economic groups, or other categories. This knowledge can improve the validity of one's conclusions from an imperfect sample by allowing a more accurate interpretation of survey results.

Questionnaire Design

The typical survey questionnaire in the social movement domain encompasses a mixture of questions regarding knowledge, opinions, and attitudes about the movement and its goals; reported participation in movement activities in the past and intended participation in the future; perceived costs and benefits of participation; ideology and identity; affective components such as commitment to the movement; and demographic characteristics such as gender, age, profession, income and education, position in social networks, and political affiliation. Organizational surveys might ask about an organization's goals, structure and procedures, strategies and activities, involvement with members or volunteers, and resources.

Questionnaire design must be sensitive to informants' situations and sentiments. Of crucial importance is the appearance of the survey instrument, which should have an appealing and clear layout. The researcher must also pay close attention to whether the questions address controversial issues appropriately, whether they reflect comparable levels of specificity, and whether they are ordered in such a way as to avoid undue influence on a respondent's answers. Survey respondents may be reluctant to answer questions on matters such as involvement in illegal activities, personal income, or political views. To ensure that respondents complete such questions, the design must seek to reduce any suspicions the informant might have by, for instance, selecting wording and placement of questions that increase the likelihood that informants will provide honest answers. Pretesting of the questionnaire can help identify sensitive questions. Also, the researcher can take steps to cultivate the trust of respondents by, for instance, guaranteeing informant confidentiality, securing endorsements of the study by respected movement leaders or organizations, and providing certain incentives, such as promising to make the survey results available to respondents.

On the matter of question specificity, Ajzen and Fishbein (1977) stressed the need to pay close attention to the level of specificity in each survey question. *General* attitudinal questions are unlikely to correlate strongly with *specific* behavioral questions, but they do correlate with composite behavioral measures, such as a list of possible activities people could participate in, or the general question whether people are prepared to participate in any kind of collective action organized by a movement. If one wants to understand why people participate in a specific movement activity, it is best to assess the attitude toward that specific activity rather than a general attitude toward collective action or the movement's goals in general.

Surveys in the movement domain usually encompass attitudinal *and* behavioral questions (intentions or reported behavior), creating possibilities for problems with *order effects*. Asking a list of attitudinal questions may prime the informant to answer subsequent behavioral questions in particular ways. Someone who has expressed supportive attitudes toward the movement's goals and actions may have difficulties saying that he or she will not participate in movement activities. On the other hand, someone who has indicated repeatedly that he or she will participate in movement activities may find it necessary to justify this expressed intention if attitudinal questions follow behavioral ones. Either scenario produces artificially high correlations between attitudes and behavior. The common preventive measure in such circumstances is to vary the order in which questions are presented to the interviewee and/or to include multiple questions that ask for the same information. If the answers to the two sets of questions do not vary depending on the order in the questionnaire, order effects can be ruled out as an alternative explanation.

Standardization is crucial to effective questionnaire design. If only we could agree on identical or at least comparable measures for key concepts, we would make comparisons much easier. Indeed, one could then compare results of studies of different places and movements even where these studies were conducted by different researchers. Standardized questions measuring core concepts in the study of social movements should seek to replicate others' work or at least to consider possibilities for future replication. Communication among researchers is necessary to encourage such standardization, and a first step could be the inclusion of exact versions of questionnaires in appendixes to publications (see Knoke and Wood 1981; Opp 1989; and Walsh 1988 for examples).

Data Analysis

Survey research on social movements uses all of the common statistical techniques. We refer the reader to the relevant handbooks for the technical details. In line with our emphasis on comparison, we suggest that it is important to disaggregate the impact of movement, time, and space on the individuals' behavior. Moreover, as most of our variables are correlated among themselves, it is necessary to conduct multivariate analyses and not to stick with zero-order relations and univariate analyses.

Of special importance is the issue of multilevel analysis. If we sample participants from different branches, or citizens in different communities, we may need to conduct multilevel analysis to separate the effects of variation between branches/communities and variation between individuals within the same branch or community. Indeed, organizational surveys reveal important variations caused by differences in organizational structure, size, scope, or location, and these kinds of differences should be considered in any research design. Such statistical designs are especially useful in the case of stratified sampling. For instance, one may expect the sample of individuals within a branch or community to be more homogeneous than a random sample of citizens. Multilevel analysis is designed to separate the two sources of variance. The following example from Klandermans's (1994) peace movement study illustrates the point.

Between November 1985 (when the Dutch government decided to deploy cruise missiles) and June 1987, a quarter of the peace activists left their peace group. Interestingly, two-thirds of those who had left the group by 1987 had already considered leaving before the summer of 1985, as compared to only one-third of those who were still involved in 1987. This finding suggests that it was the less committed and less active members who left first after the government decision. To the researchers' surprise, they did not find any difference in the hours per month spent in 1985 in activities for the peace movement between those who left and those who stayed. However, comparisons of the group averages yielded telling differences. Those who left typically spent less time on movement activities than *their group's average*. Indeed, it was the less active members who withdrew from the movement, but they were less active relative to their local group rather than to the overall sample.

Conclusions: Limitations and Advantages of Survey Research

Surveys are certainly not appropriate tools for addressing all research questions in social movements, and there are important limitations to survey research. Research that takes the individual as its unit of analysis necessarily restricts itself to the explanation of individual opinions, attitudes, and behaviors. It can help us to understand why individuals participate in social movements once they have emerged but is not able to tell us much about the emergence of social movements. It may tell us how many citizens are dissatisfied with some governmental policy and why, and it may tell us how many of those who are dissatisfied are prepared to take part in protest, had there been some, but it can tell us little about the organizations and actors that stage movement events. Social movements require both people who are motivated to participate in collective action and actors that supply opportunities to protest. Appropriately designed surveys can tell us how ideology, capacity, and opportunities are brought together. Surveys with good comparative designs—especially comparisons of time—may be able to tell us how and why demand for protest developed. The supply side of protest, however, is a different matter that cannot be assessed at the individual level with the individual as the unit of analysis. Surveys of movement organizations may tell us some part of the story, but we need information about dynamics at the macro level as well. In short, surveys can help us answer some questions if they are designed and implemented carefully, but the answers they provide are often constrained by the practical limitations to obtaining preferred sampling frames and implementing effective surveys. When analyzed along with other sources of evidence about broader contexts, however, surveys can provide rich insights into movement dynamics.

A second limitation is the costs. Properly designed surveys are generally quite time-consuming, and they can be expensive. As most survey costs cover telephone, mail, and personnel to interview and enter the data in the computer, anything that can cut down on those items reduces costs. Of course, some surveys of committed members of movement organizations can be conducted without many costs if the questionnaires can be distributed and collected through organizational networks. But one cannot always count on such organizational networks, and one's research questions may demand a different set of subjects from this readily reached group.   .

A third limitation concerns the logistics of surveying. Organizing a survey cannot be done overnight. Designing and printing questionnaires, making questionnaires ready for computer-assisted interviewing or for use on the Internet, drawing samples, organizing a mailing, and hiring interviewers are time-consuming matters. To be sure, much time can be saved if one has the appropriate facilities in place, and standardized measures speed question-naire design considerably. But not everything can be standardized, and not everybody has professional facilities available. As a method of data collection, surveys are generally more complicated than other, more qualitative forms of data collection, such as participant observation or in-depth interviews. And surveys are less effective in documenting what may be crucial details about social movement action. The best way a researcher can overcome these limitations to survey methods is to devote ample time and attention to pretesting survey instruments and consulting with other experts before conducting a survey.

A fourth limitation relates to the survey questionnaire as a device to acquire information. We are dependent on what informants are prepared to tell us. The answers to our questions can be socially desirable answers or rationalizations. There is no guarantee that people are telling us the truth. Although sometimes informants may provide false or made-up responses, attempts by survey researchers to assess this potential problem have revealed no indications that it takes place on a large scale. Occasionally, one is in the position to compare reported behavior with actual behavior: as a rule the differences are small. Similarly, checks for social desirability seldom reveal major problems. And surveys completed by different organizational leaders or staff revealed similar responses (Smith, Pagnucco, and Lopez 1998; Weed 1987). Even when efforts are taken to overcome this limitation, we may nevertheless assume that answers to questions on sensitive matters will be subject to significant nonresponse and will likely be biased in some ways.

Surveys in the social movement domain share the limitations of surveys in any domain. Basically, these limitations are related to the use of quantitative methods. The measures used in surveys are generally abstract and superficial. Feelings and emotions, people's uncertainties, doubts, and fears, all the inconsistencies and the complexities of social interactions and belief systems are matters that are not easily tapped with survey questionnaires. In-depth interviews, focus group discussions, and similar qualitative techniques may be more useful in that regard, perhaps in combination with surveys.

If used in proper ways, survey research is a powerful tool for the study of social movements. It is especially valuable if employed in comparative designs. Rather than conducting large-scale, one-time surveys, researchers might put their time and resources to more productive use by comparing smaller samples drawn from different movements or places or at different points in time. After all, social movement participation is to a large extent context dependent. Comparative designs do justice to context dependency because variability in context is built into the design. Moreover, the sophisticated statistical techniques of today enable us to separate different sources of variance to unravel complex patterns of causal, moderating, and intervening variables. Researcher resourcefulness and creativity in identifying population samples and attentive efforts to minimize nonresponse bias, in part by selecting smaller samples, can contribute much toward improving survey evidence about social movements. The appropriate use of individual and organizational survey designs can enhance important aspects of our understandings of social movement dynamics.

References

Ajzen, I., and A. Fishbein. 1977. "Attitude-Behavior Relations: A Theoretical Analysis and Review of Empirical Research." *Psychological Bulletin* 84: 888–918.

Babbie, Earl. 1990. *Survey Research Methods.* 2d ed. Belmont, Calif.: Wadsworth.

Briet, Martien, Bert Klandermans, and Frederike Kroon. 1987. "How Women Become Involved in the Women's Movement." In *The Women's Movements of Western Europe and the United States: Changing Theoretical Perspectives,* edited by Carol Mueller and Mary Katzenstein, 44–67. Philadelphia: Temple University Press.

Colwell, Mary Anna Culleton, and Doug Bond. 1994. "American Peace Movement Organizations: The 1988 and 1992 Surveys." Working Paper No. 21. San Francisco: Institute for Nonprofit Organization Management, University of San Francisco.

Crist, John T., and John McCarthy. 1996. "'If I Had a Hammer': The Changing Methodological Repertoires of Social Movement Research" *Mobilization* 1: 87–102.

Dalton, Russell J. 1994. *The Green Rainbow: Environmental Groups in Western Europe.* New Haven, Conn.: Yale University Press.

Drury, John, Steve Reicher, and Clifford Scott. 1999. "Shifting Boundaries of Collective Identity: Intergroup Context and Social Category Change in an Anti-Roads Protest." Unpublished paper, University of Sussex, Sussex.

Ennis, James G., and Richard Schreuer. 1987. "Mobilizing Weak Support for Social Movements: The Role of Grievance, Efficacy and Cost." *Social Forces* 66: 390–409.

Fink, Arlene. 1995. *The Survey Kit.* Thousand Oaks, Calif.: Sage.

Harris, Frederick C. 1999. *Something Within: Religion in African-American Political Activism.* New York: Oxford University Press.

Klandermans, Bert. 1984. "Mobilization and Participation in a Social Movement: Social Psychological Expansions of Resource Mobilization Theory." *American Sociological Review* 49: 583–600.

————, ed. 1991. *Peace Movements in Western Europe and the United States,* International Social Movement Research, vol. 3. Greenwich, Conn.: JAI Press.

————. 1993. "A Theoretical Framework for Comparisons of Social Movement Participation." *Sociological Forum* 8: 383–402.

————. 1994. "Transient Identities: Changes in Collective Identity in the Dutch Peace Movement." In *New Social Movements: From Ideology to Identity,* edited by Hank Johnston, Joseph Gusfield, and Enrique Laraña, 168–85. Philadelphia: Temple University Press.

————. 1997. *The Social Psychology of Protest.* Oxford: Blackwell.

Klandermans, Bert, and Dirk Oegema. 1987. "Potentials, Networks, Motivations and Barriers: Steps towards Participation in Social Movements." *American Sociological Review* 52: 519–32.

Klandermans, Bert, Marlene Roefs, and Johan Olivier. 2001. *The State of the People: Citizens, Civil Society, and Governance.* Pretoria, South Africa: HSRC.

Klandermans, Bert, Jose-Manuel Sabucedo, Marga de Weerd, and Mauro Rodriguez. 2001. "Framing Contention: Dutch and Spanish Farmers Confront the EU." In *Contentious Europeans: Protest and Politics in an Emerging Polity,* edited by Doug Imig and Sidney Tarrow. Lanham, Md.: Rowman and Littlefield.

Knoke, David. 1989. "Resource Acquisition and Allocation in U.S. National Associations. In *Organizing for Change: Social Movement Organizations in Europe and the United States,* edited by Bert Klandermans, 129–154. Greenwich, Conn.: JAI Press.

Knoke, David, and James R. Wood. 1981. *Organization for Action, Commitment in Voluntary Associations.* New Brunswick, N.J.: Rutgers University Press.

Maguire, Diarmuid. 1995. "Opposition Movements and Opposition Parties: Equal Partners or Dependent Relations in the Struggle for Power and Reform?" In *The Politics of Social Protest: Comparative Perspectives on States and Social Movements,* edited by J. Craig Jenkins and Bert Klandermans, 199–229. Minneapolis: University of Minnesota Press.

Marwell, Gerald, Michael Aiken, and N. J. Demerath III. 1987. "The Persistence of Political Attitudes among 1960s Civil Rights Activists." *Public Opinion Quarterly* 51: 359–75.

Marwell, Gerald, N. J. Demerath III, and Michael T. Aiken. 1993. "1960s Civil Rights Workers Turn Forty: A Generational Unit at Midlife." In *Research in Political Sociology,* edited by Ph.C. Wasburn, 175–95. Greenwich, Conn.: JAI Press.

McAdam, Doug. 1986. "Recruitment to High-Risk Activism: The Case of Freedom Summer." *American Journal of Sociology* 92: 64–90.

————. 1989. "The Biographical Consequences of Activism." *American Sociological Review* 54: 744–60.

McCarthy, John D., Joseph Shields, and Melvin Hall. 1997. "The American Catholic Bishops and the Empowerment of the Poor through Community Development." In *Social Justice Philanthropy*, edited by John H. Stanfield, 97–120, Research in Social Policy, vol. 5. Greenwich, Conn.: JAI Press.

McCarthy, John D., and Mark Wolfson. 1996. "National Federating Structure and Local Resource Mobilization: The Case of the Early Drunk Driving Movement." *American Sociological Review* 61: 1070–88.

Miller, Byron. 2000. *Geography and Social Movements: Comparing Antinuclear Activism in the Boston Area*. Minneapolis: University of Minnesota Press.

Oegema, Dirk, and Bert Klandermans. 1994. "Non-conversion and Erosion: The Unwanted Effects of Action Mobilization." *American Sociological Review* 59: 703–22.

Oliver, Pamela E. 1984. "If You Don't Do It, Nobody Else Will: Active and Token Contributors to Local Collective Action." *American Sociological Review* 49: 601–10.

Opp, Karl-Dieter. 1988. "Community Integration and Incentives for Political Protest." In *From Structure to Action: Comparing Social Movement Participation across Cultures,* edited by Bert Klandermans, Hanspeter Kriesi, and Sidney Tarrow, 83–103. Greenwich, Conn.: JAI Press.

———. 1989. *The Rationality of Political Protest*. Boulder, Colo.: Westview.

Opp, Karl-Dieter, Steven E. Finkel, Edward N. Muller, Gadi Wolfsfeld, Henry Dietz, and Jerrold Green. 1995. "Left-Right Ideology and Collective Political Action: A Comparative Analysis of Germany, Israel and Peru." In *The Politics of Social Protest: Comparative Perspectives on States and Social Movements*, edited by J. Craig Jenkins and Bert Klandermans, 63–96. Minneapolis: University of Minnesota Press.

Opp, Karl-Dieter, and Christiane Gern. 1993. "Dissident Groups, Personal Networks, and the East German Revolution of 1989." *American Sociological Review* 58: 659–80.

Robson, Collin. 1993. *Real World Research. A Resource for Social Scientists and Practitioner-Researchers*. Oxford: Blackwell.

Rochon, Thomas R. 1988. *Mobilizing for Peace: The Antinuclear Movements in Western Europe*. Princeton, N.J.: Princeton University Press.

———. 1998. *Culture Moves: Ideas, Activism, and Changing Values*. Princeton, N.J.: Princeton University Press.

Smith, Jackie. 1997. "Nonresponse Bias in Organizational Surveys: Evidence from a Survey of Groups and Organizations Working for Peace." *Nonprofit and Voluntary Sector Quarterly* 26 (3): 359–68.

———. 1999. "Global Actions: Report on a Survey of EarthAction Partner Organizations." Department of Sociology, SUNY-Stony Brook, Stony Brook, N.Y.

Smith, Jackie, Ron Pagnucco, and George Lopez. 1998. "Globalizing Human Rights: Report on a Survey of Transnational Human Rights NGOs." *Human Rights Quarterly* 20: 379–412.

Spaeth, Joe L., and Diane P. O'Rourke. 1994. "Designing and Implementing the National Organization Study." *American Behavioral Scientist* 37: 872–90.

Stewart, J. Abigail, Isis H. Settles, and Nicholas Winter. 1998. "Women and the Social Movements of the 60s: Activists, Engaged Observers and Nonpartici-pants." *Political Psychology* 19: 63–94.

Taylor, D. Garth. 1986. *Public Opinion and Collective Action.* Chicago: University of Chicago Press.

Tomaskovic-Devey, Donald, Jeffrey Leiter, and Shealy Thompson. 1994. "Organi-zational Survey Nonresponse." *Administrative Science Quarterly* 39: 439–57.

Turner, Ralph H., and Lewis M. Killian. *Collective Behavior.* 3d. ed. Englewood Cliffs, N.J.: Prentice Hall.

Walsh, Edward J. 1988. *Democracy in the Shadows: Citizen Mobilization in the Wake of the Accident at Three Mile Island.* Westport, Conn.: Greenwood Press.

Weed, Frank J. 1987. "Grass Roots Activism and the Drunk Driving Issue: A Survey of MADD Chapters." *Law and Policy* 9: 259–78.

2

Formal Models in Studying Collective Action and Social Movements

Pamela E. Oliver and Daniel J. Myers

Our purpose in this chapter is to explain the value of mathematical modeling of social movement phenomena. We have the daunting task of speaking to two different audiences: those comfortable with mathematics who want to develop mathematical models relevant to social movements, and those uncomfortable with mathematics who want to learn helpful things about movements from the mathematics-based work of others. We will try to speak to both audiences, and we ask the forbearance of each toward those sections aimed at the other.

To those who feel that mathematics is an alien and even dehumanizing tool, we suggest that mathematical language can be understood in cultural terms, as a mode of communication that uses particular symbols and patterns to convey meaning. Like any unfamiliar culture, the modes of expression seem alien at first, but when you know the language and its meanings, you can recognize its beauty and discover that some ideas can be expressed more clearly in that language than in any other. Mathematics is a language that permits thoughts and new ideas that simply cannot be expressed in other ways. If you do not speak the language of mathematics, it is like reading poetry in translation: you get some of the ideas but never the full power and beauty of the original.

To expand this point further, consider an example from statistics (not formal models), but one familiar to most sociologists: a table of multivariate regression coefficients. Such a table summarizes information that would otherwise require several pages to explain and does so in a format that is easier to understand and evaluate than a verbal description ever could be.

You do need to learn the cultural practice or language of a regression table to understand it, but if you know the language, it is a very efficient and clear mode of communication. Knowing the language of a regression table is essential for a sociologist, and so is knowing enough mathematical notation to read basic algebraic equations, even if you do not want to do mathematical sociology yourself.

why models

The translation metaphor also has meaning for those who do "speak" mathematics. There is value in carefully translating mathematics into words, so that those who do not readily grasp equations can appreciate the ideas they convey. And just as some have been inspired to learn Italian or Arabic to appreciate Dante or the Koran, some sociologists have been inspired to learn more mathematics from the interest sparked by verbal translations of mathematical sociology.

In this spirit, we welcome all of you to a discussion of mathematical models in the study of collective behavior and social movements. We approach this enterprise with an assumption that the full understanding of any social phenomenon requires many different approaches and methodologies, and that our task is to explain the value of mathematical models as one of them. Analogies to poetry notwithstanding, we still have the language problem. All but the very simplest mathematical formulations cannot be explained without equations, and a full exposition of any complex model can require twenty pages or more. Just as the chapters about survey research or participant observation cannot let you actually experience the research method, we are reduced to writing about mathematical methods while only demonstrating them on a cursory level.

The Problem of Collective Action

Let's begin where math models in social movements began, with the problem of collective action. Although *collective action* might refer to anything people do together, most social scientists have defined it as an action that provides a shared good, deriving their view from Mancur Olson's *The Logic of Collective Action* (1965). Olson woke up social science by claiming that "rational, self-interested individuals will not act to achieve their common or group interests" (1965: 2). Prior to Olson, sociologists assumed a natural tendency led people to act on shared interests. But economists had long argued that coercive taxation is necessary because rational individuals would not voluntarily contribute to public goods such as armies, public schools, or sewage systems, which could not be withheld from those who did not pay. Olson argued that all group interests were subject to the same dilemma because when benefits cannot be withheld from noncontributors, rational individuals are motivated to free ride on the contributions of others. Olson influenced early resource mobilization theory by focusing attention on the problem of getting people to participate in collective action.

Olson accompanied his verbal arguments with equations. By the 1970s, however, many had argued that Olson's equations were too limited for use in further theorizing and began to develop other ways of expressing the problem. In the process, they stopped asking if collective action is rational and began identifying conditions where collective action was more or less likely (see Hardin 1982 and Oliver 1993 for reviews).

One line connected Olson's problem to the Prisoners' Dilemma (PD). The original "story" of the PD game is that two criminals are caught for committing a burglary together and interrogated separately. If neither confesses (both cooperate), each will get a two-year sentence. If both confess (both defect), each will get a six-year sentence. If one confesses (defects) while the other does not, the defector gets immunity while the cooperator gets ten years. The PD game reflects Olson's problem because both players are tempted to "free ride" on the cooperation of the other given that each always benefits from defecting. Hardin (1971) argued that collective action was a prisoners' dilemma between "self" and "the group," and the PD tradition continues to be a major framework for analysis. Others (e.g., Chong 1991; Cortazar 1997; Hamburger 1979; Heckathorn 1996; Runge 1984), however, argued that collective action can also be an "assurance game" in which all benefit if all cooperate but are hurt if someone defects. Game theory provides a rich history of considering the strategies derived from various payoff structures, rules about repeating the game, and how players communicate. But while this tradition is useful for analyzing strategic interaction in two-actor systems and certain small group situations, it is too cumbersome and intractable for modeling action in large heterogeneous groups.

The approach that has proved more flexible in the long run begins with decision theory equations. Decision equations are based on the idea that people will do things that bring them net benefits. Theorists have developed various ways of expressing an individual's benefits as a function of his or her own actions and the actions of others in the group. To translate this kind of idea into mathematics, we will identify five important elements. First, there is the outcome of the model, which we will call G_i, which is the net gain to any individual i. The second element is the costs of contributions to the collective good. We will allow individual contributions of different sizes and call a contribution size r, and call C_i the cost to the individual of making a contribution of size r. In addition, we will represent the contributions of all others as R. The third element, P, is the amount of the collective good that is provided (to everyone) based on the total contribution ($R + r$ if i contributes, and R if i does not contribute). Of course, levels of provision have different value to each individual, so we will call v_i the value of P to an individual. Finally, we allow for selective incentives, I, which is the value of any private incentives given to contributors. Following Oliver (1980), then, these elements are combined into a general model:

$$G_i(r) = v_i[P(R + r) - P(R)] + I - C_i(r),$$

in which the net gain to i is a function of the value v_i accruing from their contribution level r plus selective incentives, minus the costs incurred.

We then need a rule for how behavior is affected by the net payoff $G_i(r)$. A "determinate" decision rule common in economics says that a person will choose the action with the highest payoff, regardless of whether contributing versus not changes the payoff by 1 unit or 100 units. Psychologists predict behavior more probabilistically. If the payoff difference between contributing and not is 51 versus 49, they would predict that actors would contribute 51 percent of the time and not contribute 49 percent of the time, while if the payoff from contributing is 95 and of not contributing is 5, actors would contribute 95 percent of the time and withhold only 5 percent. By contrast, a determinate model would predict contributing 100 percent of the time in both cases because it is the option with the highest payoff. Determinate decision rules are easier to represent and manipulate in equations, while probabilistic decision rules usually fit empirical data better.

Using the simpler determinate decision model, we can predict cooperation if the net payoff is greater than zero, that is, $G_i(r) > 0$. We can use elementary algebra to show that $G > 0$ if $[P(R + r) - P(R)] > (C_i(r) - I)/v_i$. The term $[P(R + r) - P(R)]$ is a production function, which gives the difference in the payoff P produced by a contribution r. If r makes no difference in P (as Olson argued), this term will be zero, and no level of contribution is ever rational unless $0 > (C_i(r) - I)/v_i$ which is true only if the selective incentive is greater than the cost ($I > C_i(r)$). This is exactly the situation Olson had in mind; the collective good (P) makes no difference in the outcome, *only* the relation between the cost and the incentive matters. However, if $P(R + r) > P(R)$, then collective action might be rational without incentives, depending on the cost.

There are several important aspects of this example that recur in models of collective action, and mathematical models more generally. First, the example lays out a clear way of talking about the problem and identifying what factors are to be considered. Second, standard mathematical rules, in this case algebra, allow us to derive new relations from the given information.

Third, while the new derivations were completely present in the original equation, they may not have been obvious until we performed the manipulation. Finally, and most importantly, we cannot "solve" this equation to determine if collective action is rational. The most important factor is whether r makes a difference in P, and nothing in the equation tells us whether or not that is so. We will have to make some additional assumptions about the nature of that relationship to get an answer. Theorists have had spirited arguments about which assumptions are reasonable and the conditions under which different assumptions are reasonable, but there is no mathematical proof that can resolve the matter. These untested assumptions are called the "scope conditions" of a theory, and we will say more about them below.

Determinate individual decision models are also used as parts of more complex models of interdependent decisions involving many heterogeneous individuals. Modeling multiple actors requires developing additional rules for how their actions affect each other. Oliver, Marwell, and Teixeira (1985) assumed that people make decisions sequentially, and showed that heterogeneous groups behave differently from single individuals or homogeneous groups, depending on the shape of the production function P. They emphasized the "critical mass," the subset of actors with high interest in the collective good who play special roles in collective action. In some cases, the production function is *decelerating* so that the difference $P(R + r) - P(R)$ gets smaller as the total number of prior contributions increases: in this case, the critical mass provides the good while everyone else free rides. In other cases, the production function is *accelerating* so that the difference $P(R + r) - P(R)$ gets larger as the total number of prior contributions increases: in this case, the critical mass overcomes start-up costs and creates conditions that motivate the rest to participate. Oliver and Marwell (1988) also argued that the relationship between a group's size and the rationality of collective action varies depending on the production function, critiquing Olson's (1965) claims that large groups cannot provide collective goods.

Many scholars have taken up the problem of collective action, and we can mention only a few examples here. Macy (1990, 1991a, 1991b, 1993, 1997) has focused on changing the core decision rule from determinate to a probabilistic model of adaptive learning. Macy assumes that the baseline is not a no-cost zero point but an aversive situation that motivates actors to try other options. Collective action happens when several actors probabilistically try cooperation at the same time and produce better outcomes. Heckathorn (1988, 1990, 1993, 1996) has developed models in which actors can coerce each other into cooperating. A wide variety of outcomes can occur depending on the configuration of payoffs and incentive systems. In two interesting results, he shows that "hypocritical cooperation" (making others cooperate while you privately defect) can generate collective action, and that some situations create an "altruist's dilemma" in which those who do what is good for others cause worse overall outcomes compared to people who behave selfishly. Kim and Bearman (1997) assume that interests can change, rather than remain fixed. People will change their interests and expect others to change as well when they encounter cooperators who have higher interests and defectors with lower interests.

Although collective action theory is often called "rational action" theory, theorists have developed models that modify the assumption of self-interested egoism. One example is Gould (1993), who assumes that individuals are motivated by fairness norms. He assumes that people neither like being exploited nor wish to be viewed as exploiters, so they adjust their contributions to match others. These fairness rules lead to cascades of adjustment until a steady-state equilibrium is reached in which everyone's fairness norm is satisfied. Although his model is too complex to explain completely here, the first step gives the core notion of the approach. In the model, one person starts contributing independently of others, and everyone else begins trying to "match" their contribution to everyone else's average contribution. As the contribution levels move away from zero, they are governed by this equation:

$$c_i(t) = \lambda \frac{\sum_{j}^{N} c_j(t-1)}{N-1}, \ i \neq j$$

This equation says that i's contribution at time t equals the average of everyone else's contributions at time $t-1$ multiplied by λ, a parameter that ranges between 0 and 1, where 1 means individuals match the average perfectly, and 0 means individuals contribute zero no matter what others do. Using this model, Gould examines the effects of network density and the position within the network of initial contributors by assuming that the fairness equation above considers only those people to whom an actor has network ties.

Notice that we cannot directly test the model to see if Gould's "fairness maximizer" assumption is better than the "self-interested egoist" assumption. Instead, different theorists make different assumptions about the core principal by which people make decisions, and then derive the consequences of those assumptions. Most sociologists would agree that different people operate under different principles, and that the same people operate under different principles in different settings. Thus, theories with different core assumptions should not be evaluated as "right" or "wrong," but as more or less applicable to different situations.

Generating and Analyzing Mathematical Models

In the balance of this chapter, we discuss some of the fundamental principles in generating and analyzing a formal mathematical model. We outline the steps to model building and discuss some of the issues involved in each. In the process, we summarize some published works that illustrate the issues and give some brief examples from our own ongoing work in modeling the diffusion of protest and collective violence. Readers who are more interested in reading and evaluating models than in writing them should find our discussion serves as a solid pointer to issues to consider in evaluating others' models.

1. Acquire knowledge about the process you want to model. Before developing a model of a social process, it is critical to know as much as possible about the process. You should be familiar with relevant empirical patterns and previous theorizing (verbal or formal) related to the process. For example, a growing body of published data shows counts of protest or collective violence events over time. We note several empirical generalizations about these data plots: (1) they tend to be wavelike, that is, they go up and then come down; (2) they tend to be fairly peaked or "spiky," rising and falling much more rapidly than most continuous mathematical functions; and (3) they exhibit smaller waves within larger waves. Another example is that repression sometimes suppresses protest, and other times spurs more protest. Most scholars believe that the effect of repression on protest is curvilinear: moderate repression spurs protest, while severe repression destroys it, and zero repression makes it look unimportant. Elegant mathematical models may be published in technical journals, but they will not have an impact on sociology unless they are well linked to broader theoretical and empirical issues. Knowing the literature will also help you avoid "reinventing the wheel," and produce a real advance by building on the work of others.

Finally, we want to emphasize the importance of looking to other disciplines and past work for mathematical forms that may be useful. For example, Macy (1990) adapted a standard learning theory model for his analysis of collective action, while Chong (1991) adapted an economics model of supply and demand. Oliver and Myers (2000) suggest that the interdependent diffusion of collective action and regime responses might adapt biological models of the coevolution of species. Having some familiar terrain in your models will make it easier to understand their behavior and make them more stable. As much as possible, build models using standard mathematical forms with well-known properties.

2. Clearly specify the kind of problem you wish to solve. Supposing that you want to explain the rise and fall of protest over time. Conceptually, there are two general approaches. The first takes one or more well-defined empirical instances for which there are data and attempts to create a mathematical model that fits the data well. Such models are widely used in engineering and physical sciences to represent specific physical systems, such as manufacturing production processes or predator-prey relationships. Once the model is constructed, it can be used to determine how the outcomes of the system would change if some elements in the system were altered. Demographers use this approach to construct models of populations, showing how they change in response to a particular influence, such as an increase in contraceptive use or an increase in AIDS infection. Once a model of one particular instance has been created, it can be modified to represent other similar processes. Empirical models, therefore, can be aggregated to develop more abstract theory. In our work modeling protest cycles, we have found that the best type of mathematic model for representing the basic "look" of empirical protest cycles starts with a set of actors who are assumed to emit protest with some relatively low probability. This simple stochastic or probabilistic model generates some of the waves and spikes seen in empirical data (and also is a plausible representation of the underlying process producing protest events).

The second kind of model seeks to represent a single abstracted process and is more squarely a theory development enterprise. Rather than representing any empirical case, the model represents a unitary process involved in a wide variety of empirical instances. Examples of unitary processes are rational choice, adaptive learning, and strategic interaction. Instead of being tied to data, the mathematical model itself is taken as a given because it is a plausible representation of the process of interest, and analysis focuses on following the model through to its logical conclusions to predict outcomes. Tests of predictions are generally left to subsequent researchers, who may compare the predictions of competing theories. In our work, we have developed a formal model that assumes that protest cycles are the net result of two diffusion processes in which ideas spread through a population, the first idea being the encouragement to protest, and the second being the repression of protest; this model fits the data better than prior simpler models.

In general, models should either represent a unitary process (or the interaction of a few well-studied unitary processes) or should be closely tied to empirical data. Complex models that attempt to represent the interactions among many processes without empirical ties have too many degrees of freedom and are usually impossible to analyze or validate in any systematic way.

3. Select the basic modeling strategy. There are many different approaches to constructing mathematical models, and different kinds of mathematical representations will be more or less effective in capturing the process of interest. First, there are the number of equations involved in representing the system. Some processes can be modeled with a single equation that can be manipulated by standard mathematical operations and transformed to produce predictions about the outcomes of the process. In some cases, a series of equations representing subprocesses can be resolved into a single equation that predicts outcomes. On the other end of the spectrum are models in which there is a separate equation governing the behavior of each individual, and these equations interact with each other to produce the outcomes of the system. Single equation, or "analytic," models are much more prestigious in the aesthetics of mathematics and are advantageous because they allow standard mathematical operations, such as integration, taking derivatives, solving for equilibria or optima, finding asymptotes, solving for thresholds, and so forth. It is much harder (if not impossible) to obtain straightforward "analytic" solutions to multi-equation systems, forcing the analyst to find numeric solutions or generate outcomes via simulation. A single equation can sometimes summarize the behavior of a homogeneous group in which everyone is identical, but multiple equations are generally necessary to represent the interdependent actions of a heterogeneous group. As we work on the problem of modeling protest waves, for example, we are finding that they are best represented as the accumulation of randomly determined actions by a set of different actors whose actions affect each other. Such models involve creating large arrays in which each row represents an actor, and each column represents actors' characteristics (e.g., interest, resources); models that include network ties among actors have another matrix representing the presence or absence of all possible ties. Even if determinate individual decision models are used, such multi-actor systems can be very large and complex, and are not amenable to elegant solutions. Instead, the systems are represented in computer programs that perform large numbers of calculations to yield each result. A multi-equation approach that we do not have space to discuss is "cellular automata," in which equations are written to describe how individuals react probabilistically to those near to them, and then these relations predict large-scale phenomena: for example, equations describe how water molecules react to each other, and then can be aggregated into macro phenomena such as river flows (see Gaylord and D'Andria 1998). Such models may be appropriate for the spread of ideologies or protest through populations.

Multi-equation systems have been used to model the behavior of people in temporary gatherings or crowds. McPhail's cybernetic control theory says collective action is coordinated by individuals adjusting their behavior to bring their perceptual signals in line with a reference signal; models based on this theory show how clusters, arcs, and rings form in crowds as a consequence of common orientations (McPhail 1991, 1993). Feinberg and Johnson (Feinberg and Johnson 1988, 1990a, 1990b; Johnson and Feinberg 1977, 1990) model the well-established empirical phenomenon of "milling" in a crowd, wherein people move around and talk with others near them. Processes built into these models include the influence of other people nearby, the influence of a central agent who is trying to influence the crowd, and the backing away of those who disagree with the emerging consensus. Johnson and Feinberg's insight, that consensus is a product of both influence and exit, is important for understanding the processes of action within a wide range of collectivities, and the construction and diffusion of a social movement ideology might work according to similar principles.

Another type of modeling strategy specifies the general form of a model based on assumptions about a social process, but the exact shape of the function that represents it is not determined until the model is fit to data. In such cases, there are one or more parameters in the model that are left unspecified until the function is matched to data, and the values of the parameters are selected to provide the best fit between model and data. This approach to modeling has been very popular in the diffusion literature and was used by Pitcher, Hamblin, and Miller (1978) to model collective violence diffusion. The core assumption in the model was that the expression of collective violence is controlled by imitation and inhibition processes that are informed by vicarious learning from the outcomes of prior events. For both imitation and inhibition effects, a scale parameter is introduced in the model that relates the relative impact of prior adoptions on later ones.

Although the authors could have treated their model analytically and shown how it responds to systematic variations in the parameters, they chose instead to estimate the parameters of their model by "fitting" it to empirical data. The approach has its strengths and weaknesses. One weakness is that the model cannot be tested empirically without first using the data to determine the final form of the model. With enough free-floating parameters, models can fit extremely well to nearly any empirical situation. On the other hand, if that model is well conceived, and each parameter has clear substantive meaning, the parameters can be compared to tell something about a social situation that cannot be related by models that do not depend on the empirical data. For example, if a parameter conveys the infectiousness of an event within a diffusion process, comparing the estimated parameters for

different empirical cases tells us about differences in the strength of inter-
actor influence in different contexts.

Further complexity is introduced into the modeling process when we
consider the difference between determinate models and stochastic models.
Determinate models give a definite single result for each combination of
inputs—no matter how many times predictions from the model are computed, the result will always be the same. Rational action models are generally determinate models: at each decision point, the actor is assumed to choose
the single action with the highest payoff. A stochastic model is one in which
some of the variables are probability distributions rather than single numbers. Adaptive learning models (e.g., Macy 1990) are stochastic models,
because, at a given time, each actor's behavior is not determined but instead
reflects a probability distribution. Our work on modeling protest cycles indicates that stochastic models produce simulated event time series that
most resemble empirical protest event time series. Because of the random
element involved in stochastic models, the predicted outcomes are considerably more complex—each time the model is run, a different prediction can
be produced. These kinds of models therefore produce probability distributions of predicted outcomes for each combination of inputs, and the character of these distributions becomes central to understanding the model and
assessing how well it models an empirical process.

4. Start simply and build carefully. Before developing and testing a model
with all the complexity you ultimately wish to capture, start by testing the
behavior of the simplest possible model under very simple conditions to be
sure that it is free of "glitches." If your model produces the desired pattern,
then begin to add factors or features parsimoniously—just enough to capture the process of interest. If the model has subprocesses, validate each
completely before allowing them to interact. If you do not fully understand
the behavior of simple constituent processes, the results of an elaborate
model can be extremely misleading.

Once you begin working with your full model, make certain you test it
under the full range of possible conditions. Consider the reasonable range of
every variable, and check the behavior of the model under combinations of
extremes, for example, when one variable is zero, another is very large, and
another is very small. You should also verify that the model is being calculated correctly by running tests of the model with simple "round" numbers and
checking the results by hand (or at least through independent computations
via a spreadsheet). If there are relevant empirical data or published simulation results from others' work, put those values into the model to see if it
generates the correct output.

5. *Face the problem of metric.* Variables in mathematical models are inherently tied to some scale of measurement, or metric. Failure to recognize different metrics in a model can distort the results and even make parameters completely nonsensical. Problems with metric recently made big news when a Mars landing module malfunctioned because data had been entered in the English (inches, feet, miles) system instead of the metric system. Unfortunately, there is almost no discussion of metric in social science, and many published mathematical models fail to treat metric properly. It is all too common to see published models in which parameters have been chosen arbitrarily to give "interesting" numerical results with no attention at all to what those numbers might mean.

There are two ways to handle metric correctly. The first is to explicitly specify the metric for every variable in the model. When all factors have the same metric, the metric can be ignored, as it "cancels out." More commonly, attention has to be paid to the translation between metrics. For example, models of the interactions between movements and states (either state policies or state repression) require an explicit attention to metric that is not easily resolved. Mobilization is usually measured as numbers of events, or numbers of participants (although these only incompletely capture the disruptiveness and intensity of mobilization). But in what units should repression or state policies be measured? And what specifically is the relation between a unit of repression and a unit of protest? These are not easy questions to answer, but they must be to produce a meaningful model.

The second choice is to normalize, or standardize, the model so that every term in the model is either expressed in the same metric or is metric-free. Physical scientists typically use the term *normalize,* while social scientists generally use the term *standardize* for the same general concept. Computing standard scores (subtracting the variable's mean and dividing by its standard deviation) is one example of standardization, although not commonly used in modeling. One common strategy is to express some variables as functions of others. Another is to express variables as proportions reflecting their location between meaningful maximum and minimum values. Complex normalizations usually require both strategies. Marwell and Oliver (1993: 27–28), for example, standardize their model by assuming there is a maximum or high provision level that can be set equal to 1 (so that all other provision levels are expressed as proportions of this level), and carefully define contributions, costs, and benefits in terms of these standardized provision levels.

6. *Explicitly identify the scope conditions and assumptions.* All theories, whether verbal or mathematical, positivist or constructionist, contain a variety of assumptions taken to be true without proof. Unfortunately, these

assumptions are often unacknowledged in much verbal theorizing. One advantage of formal mathematical theory is that the logic of the mathematics itself forces theorists to specify their assumptions, or at least makes them manifest the mathematics of the model. Three kinds of assumptions are important in mathematical models. The first is that the mathematical form used is an adequate representation of a process of interest. In empirical modeling, this assumption need not be taken as a given but may be based on empirical data. In theoretical modeling, the justification for form is grounded in a belief that it imitates the process of interest. For example, rational action models express in an equation a conscious thought process of weighing costs and benefits that people are believed to use in decision making. In other cases, theorists have written models in which they do not know exactly how the process works, but instead they assume the process works a particular way and determine the consequences implied by that assumption.

Writing a mathematical model therefore forces you to pin down just how you think things work. Is the relation between protest and repression linear or nonlinear? What kind of nonlinear? Does the relation interact with other factors? Exactly how? As soon as you start constructing equations or writing computer code, you are forced to become specific about how you think the process works. This is much harder than just writing a verbal theory that says one thing "affects" another. Even so, some assumptions are not always obvious, and the theorist must take care to make them explicit. For example, Oliver and Marwell's models permit "rich" people with high resources to make partial contributions, while Macy's, Heckathorn's, and Kim and Bearman's models assume that actors must contribute all their resources if they contribute anything; these embedded assumptions can make big differences in the outcomes of the models.

The second kind of assumption is called a *scope condition*. Scope conditions limit the context in which the theory is expected to operate. This principle is too often ignored in verbal theorizing. For example, consider the classic resource mobilization claim that there are always enough grievances, and the real predictor of protest is resources. Not surprisingly, empirical researchers quickly demonstrated that aggrieved people protest more than nonaggrieved people, a proposition that resource mobilization theorists would never have disputed in the first place. And, in fact, the initial statement would have more fruitfully been initially stated as "*for those issues about which there is a grievance*, the resources of the aggrieved groups determine which ones will be acted upon," where the underlined clause is a scope condition. If a scope condition is not true, the theory does not apply. Finding examples of empirical instances that do not meet the scope conditions of a theory in no way disproves it. Instead, the concern is whether there are some instances that *do* meet the assumptions, and whether the model's predictions are true when the assumptions are met.

The third important kind of assumption in mathematical theorizing is a *simplifying assumption.* In this case, the theorist knows that the process is actually more complex than the model, but some factors are purposely ignored, or relationships are represented with approximations that are known not to be strictly correct. Simplifying assumptions are made so that a model can be made tractable, that is, capable of being analyzed mathematically. All models (and all theories) require simplifying assumptions. For one, they have to ignore some factors that might influence the outcomes. While in reality everything may have some connection to everything else, it is impossible to develop any kind of theory by considering everything at once. Theorists must use boundaries and assume that the factors outside the boundary have insignificant effects. Apart from bounding the model, other simplifying assumptions are often necessary, especially in the initial stages of development. If a simplified model is shown to transcend the simplifying restrictions, then the model is said to be "robust." If, however, the results change dramatically when simplifying assumptions are relaxed, the assumptions must either become scope conditions for the model, or must be systematically varied and analyzed.

7. Analyze your model. Determine its behavior under limiting conditions. Identify the reduced forms of equations. Conduct experiments and map the response surface. Once your model is known to be working correctly, you need to analyze it. It is not enough to tweak the parameters so that you can make it behave like one example or make it generate several different "interesting" patterns. Instead you need to determine systematically how the model behaves with all the possible combinations of inputs and parameters. The key ideas for doing this are the *response surface* and *experimental design.* Although the term is rarely used by sociologists, the concept of a response surface is common in statistics and engineering, and is straightforward. You have an output or criterion variable whose behavior you are interested in, such as the amount of protest. This is just the dependent variable, or y, that sociologists are used to. If you have only one independent variable or input (x), you can plot a standard two-dimensional graph of a line showing how y changes with x. That is a two-dimensional response surface. If there are two independent variables, or inputs, you can plot the outcome, or y variable, as a function of the inputs on a three-dimensional graph, in which case the plot is a surface, rather than a line. The general concept of the response surface simply extends this idea into n-dimensional space. The goal of response surface analysis is to understand how the output variable changes as a function of multiple inputs.

What can be difficult is to recognize that we are often interested in treating parameters as variables. To take a simple example, consider the linear equation $Y = a + bX$. If a and b are given numbers (such as 3 and 5), the equation $Y = 3 + 5X$ yields a specific line relating Y and X. But in response surface analysis, we could be interested in how the relation between Y and X varies as a and b vary, so we would imagine a 4-dimensional space in which the location of the line relating X and Y moves up and down the Y axis depending on a, and the slope of the line gets steeper or flatter and tips to the right or the left depending on b.

We do not do a response surface analysis of a linear equation because we know that it is exactly the same for all possible values of a and b. However, most collective action models are nonlinear systems in which the shape or form of the function changes with different combinations of the parameters. It is common that the response surface is qualitatively different in different regions of the input space, that there are steep changes or discontinuities between regions, and that maximizing outputs involves optimizing rather than maximizing inputs. In collective action models, there are often thresholds for combinations of inputs below which the output is constant, and above which the output changes with the inputs, often discontinuously. Once you understand the idea of a response surface, it is a straightforward extension to recognize that the output does not necessarily have to be a continuous quantitative number but can be qualitatively different states. You may also be interested in multiple outputs.

If possible, begin by analyzing your model symbolically using standard mathematical approaches such as algebra and differential or integral calculus to solve for maxima and minima, thresholds, limits, equilibrium states, reduced forms, and the like. Obviously, the more mathematics you know, the more likely you are to be able to conduct these analyses, and it is always worthwhile to spend some time with appropriate texts learning or reviewing basic mathematical approaches to the class of equations you are working with. Even for complex multi-equation models, you can often find analytic solutions for some variables when others are held constant.

Experimental design is another powerful framework for analyzing complex response surfaces, and it is essential that you understand the basic principles of experimental design. In an experiment, you hold some factors constant and systematically vary others. Your research purpose or theory should tell you which elements of your model should be held entirely constant in your analysis. These constants become scope conditions for the results of your analysis.

Your analysis should involve a combination of exploration and focused comparison. First, you explore the model, looking for thresholds, limits, equilibria, and the like, guided as much as possible by your prior analysis. Be sure to examine the model under the full range of extremes, including unrealistic ones. It is easy to make false assumptions about the realistic ranges of variables, or to extrapolate falsely from too narrow a range of values. Oliver (1993) found that one of the results Heckathorn (1988) reported about group size and social control changed for very low probabilities of detection of deviance. What extremes are realistic? Try to consider the kinds of empirical situations to which they might apply and come up with some estimates. For example, Oliver developed a model involving the degree of group heterogeneity, operationalized as the standard deviation of a standardized lognormal distribution (mean = 1) of contribution levels. Initial analyses were conducted with standard deviations in the .3 to 3 range. A little research revealed that (as of 1990) the U.S. income distribution was roughly lognormal with a standard deviation of .8 of its mean, indicating that this initial range was plausible. However, some additional computation revealed that a standard deviation of 20 was well within the limits of empirical plausibility (e.g., a distribution in which the vast majority give almost nothing, and one person in 5,000 gives $300 or more, or in which the average time contribution is an hour a year, but one in 5,000 gives 6 hours a week). It turned out that the response surface of the model changed dramatically for such high standard deviations. Thus, we presented results for standard deviations of .3, 1, 3, 10, and 20 (see Marwell and Oliver 1993: 134–35).

Group size often matters in collective action models. Groups of size 2 and 3 have their own peculiar dynamics. Real social groups often involve at least thousands of members, possibly millions. Can a model with, say, 100 or even just 10 actors in it be trusted to give results that would apply to 1,000,000 actors? Different theories would give different answers. What we can say is that you should give some theoretical attention to the group size question, should not use very small groups unless you are specifically interested in small groups, and should probably run your model with at least two and preferably at least three different group sizes, so that you can get some information about whether group size affects the results. If you are running a model in which group size is a parameter (N) instead of the number of interacting individuals in a model, test group sizes of different magnitudes (e.g., 10, 100, 1,000, 10,000, 100,000) that are reasonable for the kinds of groups you are modeling.

After sufficient exploration to ensure that you understand your models, design focused comparisons to test theoretical propositions, to compare your model to other models, or to assess the possible impact of some particular change. Determine which elements should be held constant for this purpose, and which should be varied. Design a systematic data generation procedure. One approach is to select values at equal intervals from the full range for each variable. If you have two inputs that are each sampled at six levels in a fully crossed experimental design including all possible combinations, you would need to generate 6^2, or 36 "cases," while for five inputs that are each sampled at six levels, a fully crossed design would yield 6^5, or 7,776 distinct data points, so sample sizes can increase rapidly as you systematically test a model. If your model is determinate, you need to run it only once for each design cell, and if it can be calculated quickly on a computer, it may not be difficult to program a loop that generates all the input combinations and calculates and stores all the output combinations in a data base. Another possibility is to use a random number generator to select a value for each input from its range, and repeat the experiment as many times as you can afford to. The result of either procedure will be a data set of inputs and outputs that you can plot in various ways. However, whenever the relationships in your model are not linear, equally spaced intervals will not necessarily give the best information about your response surface. Your initial analysis may reveal that there are particular regions of the space that require more detailed analysis. Because we are unable to convey n-dimensional spaces on two-dimensional paper, presentation of your results usually requires generating graphical cross sections of different regions of the response space. You generate a cross section by holding all but one or two inputs constant at a particular level and generating a two- or three-dimensional graph of the output as a function of the varying inputs.

Even a complex determinate model might take too long to calculate to make it feasible to generate enough outputs to represent adequately the whole response surface. If the model is stochastic, you need multiple cases per design cell so that you can identify the probability distribution of outcomes in that cell. How many cases per cell? The answer lies in sampling theory and depends both on how variable the outcome is for a given combination of input parameters, and the degree of precision you desire for your estimate. But even if you are willing to settle for small samples per design cell (and 10 is a very small sample by any criterion), if you have a large number of design cells, the number of data points involved can quickly become enormous. And since stochastic models by their nature require much more computation than determinate models, the amount of time necessary to generate those data points could become impossibly large. It is at this point that a solid understanding of experimental design and the principles of mathematical analysis can guide you in designing a smaller, more manageable experiment that will generate useful results by helping you to focus on "interesting" regions of the response surface and generate focused comparisons between different regions. If practical constraints force you to hold many potentially variable factors of your model constant, you should either report these as scope conditions for your results, or be able to explain why these constant factors would not change the dynamics of the variables you are modeling.

Random number generators play an important role in analyzing mathematical models and simulations. Many statistical packages, mathematical programs, and spreadsheets have built-in procedures for generating random numbers from a number of distributions, and some also have built-in procedures or add-in procedures available to assist with simulation procedures. You need to give serious attention to the particular statistical distribution you use in generating a random number, depending on its role in the model. If you are generating random numbers for inputs to use in collecting data on a response surface, you would use a uniform distribution to get equal coverage of all regions of the surface as the random analogue to equally spaced intervals. But if you know that the output changes more quickly in some regions than others, a more efficient design would use a random distribution that generates more data points near the critical area, and fewer where the output changes more slowly. When you are analyzing a determinate model, the choice of distribution affects only the efficiency of data collection. But if there is a stochastic component to your model, the form of the distribution from which probabilities or other random elements are drawn can make a big difference in the outcomes, and you should not blindly use a uniform or normal distribution without considering theoretically what kind of process underlies the random element. A serious discussion of statistical distributions is beyond the scope of this chapter. (See Myers and Montgomery 1995 for an advanced treatment of issues of experimental design and response surface analysis; see Law and Kelton 2000 for an advanced treatment of principles of simulation modeling and experimental analysis.)

8. Assess the fit of your model to criterion data. If the purpose of a model is to represent an empirical instance, testing the fit of the model is obviously required. But even if the purpose is to develop theory, it is appropriate to determine if the theory seems to fit appropriate empirical instances, and there are usually at least some data relevant to elements of the model. Fit can be assessed with respect to the assumptions and the predicted outcomes of a model. The assumption that people seek to maximize their own payoffs can be assessed in bargaining experiments by asking players what factors they are considering (e.g., Michener and Myers 1998a,b). Opinion data can be used to assess whether people's interests remain relatively fixed, as Marwell and Oliver (1993) assumed, or change over time, as Kim and Bearman (1997) assumed, and so forth. Finding some cases that do not fit a theory's assumptions does not disprove it, but if no cases fit the assumptions, the usefulness of a theory is called into question.

Finding data relevant to a theoretical model can sometimes be difficult, but often some indirect evidence can be used. For example, early resource mobilization theory argued that external resources cause protest. But McAdam (1982) presented data on the civil rights movement, showing that rises in mobilization preceded rises in external funding, thus sparking a reconsideration of the role of external resources in protest. Models of protest mobilization should be compared to the basic patterns of protest data: wavelike, spiky, and having waves within waves. Theoretical modeling is often useful precisely when relevant data are not readily accessible, but models should still be subjected to basic "reality checks" against what data are available.

Even when appropriate empirical data exist, "fitting" the model is not necessarily a straightforward process. The first inclination of sociologists trained in regression approaches is to calculate a χ^2 or R^2 test. However, in some cases, these tests can be worse than useless. If the data are cumulative event counts, for example, R^2 tests are quite misleading. Consider the plots in Figure 2.1 of the density and cumulative distributions for constant, exponential growth, and diffusion models over time. The correlation between the cumulative logistic diffusion curve and a line with the same minimum and maximum yields an R^2 of .94, even though the correlation between the density functions of the *same curves* is 0. The correlation between a cumulative logistic diffusion curve and a cumulative exponential growth curve is +.78, yielding an R^2 of .6, even though the correlation between the density functions is actually negative, -.47. Pitcher, Hamblin, and Miller (1978) fit their diffusion model against 25 data series and found R^2 values generally exceeding .95. As impressive as this seems, the results are misleading because the data are cumulative event counts, and any S-shaped function will necessarily have very high correlations with the data. In short, models that produce the wrong basic shape should be readily discarded, but if the basic shape is correct, more rigorous and detailed assessments of fit are required.

9. Write about your model. The final step in any research project is communicating the results. Your goal is to contribute to sociology, not just to play with numbers and graphs. Clearly identify the process(es) you are

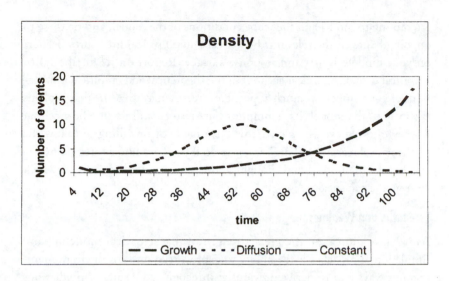

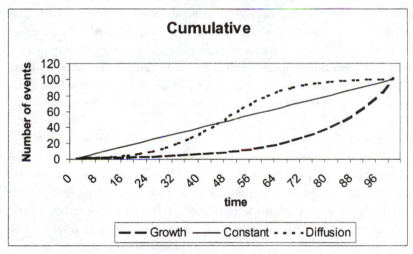

Figure 2.1. Comparing three models of protest over time: constant (the amount of action is steady across the time period), growth (the amount of action increases by a constant percentage of the prior amount), diffusion (the amount of action is a function of the product of the proportion who have already acted and those who have not acted yet). The top panel shows the density function; the bottom panel shows the cumulative amount of action over time. All three curves begin and end at the same cumulative amounts of action, but get there in different ways. The density function for the constant action model has a zero correlation with the others, while the growth and diffusion models are negatively correlated; the cumulative functions for all three are highly positively correlated.

attempting to model and the scope conditions of the model, and tie these to ongoing issues in the relevant theoretical and empirical literatures. Report on your model's limits and response surface. Report on its fit (if any) to empirical data. Give a clear account of the theoretical and empirical implications of your model. As much as possible, create a narrative line that explains the logic of the model, its assumptions, its results, and its significance that can be followed even by a reader who is unable or unwilling to follow the mathematical reasoning. This is easier to do if you have not cheated on step 1, and have actually read and thought about the broader literature to which your model can speak.

Strengths and Weaknesses

As we have indicated, the great strength of mathematical modeling and simulation approaches is the ability to express relationships in clear, unambiguous ways and to derive previously unrecognized results or predictions from them. These approaches are useful for developing abstract theory that may be applied across many instances, and are appropriately compared to abstract verbal theory approaches, rather than to empirical research. Any theoretical representation is necessarily an abstraction that by its nature lacks content about particular historical events, ideologies, or personalities. The relationship between theory and empirical data is always a dialectic between the general and the particular. There are often proposed relationships from verbal theory that cannot be readily or clearly stated in mathematical terms, but this most commonly points to ambiguity in the verbal theory, or to the modeler's lack of knowledge of mathematical forms to represent particular kinds of relationships. Mathematical models in sociology are generally much simpler than complex empirical relationships, but so is any verbal theory. Physical and biological scientists building on a more substantial base of well-confirmed simple relationships have, in fact, been able to build complex representations of complex empirical systems. Obviously, mathematical approaches need to be used in combination with other methods that provide either quantitative or qualitative information about empirical patterns and relationships. Modeling should be viewed as an important complement to empirical research, not a substitute for it. However, the researcher doing modeling will often draw on or inspire other scholars' empirical research, rather than combining modeling and empirical research in the same article or book. Knowledge accumulates when scholars build on each other's work, rather than expecting that any one research project can provide the one perfect definitive answer.

Conclusion

Both mathematical sociologists and postmodernists have been accused of trying to write in ways that others cannot understand, and are often assumed by others to have nothing useful to say if it cannot be said in "plain English." We are not competent to comment on postmodernist writing, but we are prepared to say that people "speak mathematics" not as an arcane jargon to shut out others, but because it is an elegant and effective mode for communicating certain kinds of ideas. We do not believe that formal mathematical models are the only way to do sociology. Rather, we believe that sociologists are bound in a Durkheimian organic solidarity based on a division of labor in which different kinds of theory and methods each play an important role. In this respect, formal models do a particular kind of work. Most importantly, the process of writing a formal model forces you to pin down exactly what you mean, to operationalize relationships, and to specify mechanisms. Turning thoughts into equations reveals ambiguities and contradictions very quickly. In addition, a good model can permit a "what if" analysis, allowing you to explore possibilities that do not actually exist. If you can adequately represent the mechanisms in "what is," you can explore what would happen if some elements of the system change.

We have mostly written as if the audience is made up of potential modelers, and we hope some of you will be motivated to try modeling. But we know that most readers are more interested in evaluating others' models than in writing their own, so we end by summarizing the principles to use in evaluating a formal model.

First, what is the model about? What empirical phenomena does it attempt to represent? What examples do the authors give? Do they cite literature, or give other bases for suggesting that their image of the empirical phenomenon is correct? Or if it is a purely theoretical article, what is the core process in the model? Is this a kind of "normative" theory, in which the point is not to model actual behavior but to provide a baseline by showing what the results would be if certain assumptions were true?

Second, what are the scope conditions and simplifying assumptions? These should be spelled out. Some of the scope conditions will be implicit in the way the equations are written and may be difficult to find if you cannot read the equations. Remember, however, that you should not be focusing on whether you can think of any exceptions to the scope conditions—there will always be cases that do not fit the scope of a theory. Rather you should consider whether there are cases that *do* fit the scope conditions. Also look for the author's discussions of how the model changes if some of the simplifying assumptions are relaxed: is the model robust?

Third, how is the model analyzed? It is helpful to the non-mathematical reader to have a narrative that explains how the model works, but the analysis should be more than just storytelling, more than writing equations that can do the same thing as you can do verbally. There should be some analysis that shows how the model changes as the parameters of the model change. There should be a presentation of controlled comparisons within the model, and if it is compared to other similar models, there should be controlled comparisons with the other theories.

Finally, consider the empirical credibility of the model. It is usually not possible to publish an extended model and an extended data analysis in the same article. But any presentation of relevant data is a plus, and there should at least be some discussion of the kinds of examples the model should apply to. Look at the outcomes the model produces. Do they seem to fit what you know about the empirical data? Do they seem to illuminate the mechanisms involved? Again, do not reject a model because you know of some counterexample or, worse, because you do not like the implications of the results. And do not accept it just because you can think of one example that seems to fit, or you do like the implications. But it is appropriate to bring to bear what knowledge you do have about the phenomenon in evaluating the model.

As one element of a diverse repertoire of methodologies designed to illuminate different aspects of collective action and social movements, mathematical models can make important contributions. We invite you to explore the works we have listed in the bibliography and to undertake some modeling of your own.

Appendix: Tools and Resources

Many people who write formal models also write their own computer programs to analyze them, using whatever computer language they happen to know. It is possible to do a great deal of analysis using a spreadsheet. There are also more specialized computer programs particularly suited for working with mathematical models or simulations. We list some we have found to give you an idea of what is available. Prices are as of the date we searched; editions and prices are continually evolving. Academic prices for proven members of educational institutions are substantially lower than commercial prices.

Mathematics Programs

Mathematica by Wolfram, Inc., and Maple by Waterloo Maple, Inc., are complex and powerful programs that do symbolic mathematics as well as numerical computations; they can also create impressive 3-D graphical images. You can do formal analysis of models with these packages as well as design simulations. There are ongoing debates between users of each program about which is better, and they differ in their syntax and underlying programming logic. Both are relatively difficult to learn to use. Mathematica has a richer library of add-ons and third-party software products and books, and supports a wide variety of modeling and simulation activities. Maple is generally less expensive. Academic editions are available for under $1,000, and student editions are considerably less expensive.

For more information on Mathematica, contact Wolfram, Inc., at http://www.wolfram.com. The corporate headquarters for Wolfram Research, Inc., is located at 100 Trade Center Drive, Champaign, IL 61820-7237. For sales and order inquiries in the United States and Canada, call 800-WOLFRAM (965-3726) or 800-441-MATH (6284). The fax number is 217-398-0747. Sales inquiries may also be sent by e-mail to info@wolfram.com.

In Europe, contact Wolfram Research Europe Ltd., 10 Blenheim Office Park, Lower Road, Long Hanborough, Oxfordshire OX8 8LN, United Kingdom. The telephone number for this office is 44-(0)1993-883400, and the fax number is 44-(0)1993-883800. Sales inquiries may be sent to info@wolfram.co.uk.

In Asia, contact Wolfram Research Asia Ltd., Oak Ochanomizu Building 5F, 3-8 Ogawa-machi Kanda, Chiyoda-ku, Tokyo 101-0052, Japan. The telephone number for this office is 81-(0)3-3518-2880, and the fax number is 81-(0)3-3518-2877. Sales inquiries may be sent to info@wolfram.co.jp.

For more information on Maple, contact Waterloo Maple, Inc., 57 Erb Street West, Waterloo, Ontario, Canada N2L 6C2. This office may be reached by telephone at 519-747-2373, and by fax at 519-747-5284. Sales inquiries in North America may call 800-267-6583. Information on Maple is available through e-mail at info@maplesoft.com, and on the Internet at http://www.maplesoft.com.

Graphical Simulation Programs

Graphical simulation programs make it easy to construct certain kinds of models with icons and links between icons. Most of these are specialized products oriented to engineers designing manufacturing or business processes, computer networks, and the like. We have found two packages that are suitable for the more general needs of academic social scientists. As compared with programming languages, these programs are much easier to use: it is possible to produce a basic model and get results quickly. This ease of use makes it possible to focus on thinking about the design of the model instead of figuring out how to write a program and deal with error messages. However, the graphical programs are less flexible and powerful. Whether the limitations are a problem depends on your particular model.

Stella, from High Performance Systems, Inc., is a general-purpose simulation package with a graphical interface that is especially well suited for representing feedback processes that occur over time, for example, predator-prey relations. You represent the model as stocks and flows, and you can specify the exact equation representing a relationship. Unlike most graphical packages, Stella produces an equations page to complement the graphical representation. It has special features for setting up computer- or Web-based interfaces for educational presentations. The user interface is easy to use, although it can be cumbersome for large batch-oriented data generation, but it can link to spreadsheets for large input-output tasks. There are stochastic functions. The more expensive research edition can handle arrays. The documentation emphasizes the principles of model building. There is a less expensive basic edition, and a research edition that has much higher capacity and extra features. Student prices start under $100, educator prices are $300 to $550, depending on the version. A free demo is available for download. (Note: The same firm produces iThink, which is exactly the same program marketed to business applications.)

For more information on Stella, contact High Performance Systems, Inc., 45 Lyme Road, Suite 300, Hanover, NH 03755-1221. The telephone numbers for this office are 800-332-1202 and 603-643-9636. Information is available on the Internet at http://www.hps-inc.com.

Extend, from Imagine That, Inc., is a general-purpose simulation package with pedagogic materials. Everything is an icon, even adding and subtracting, and the icons are highly specialized, not really equation or functionally oriented. Icons generate C-like code, which apparently can be edited, although that feature was not available in the demo we examined. Models can generate processes that can be animated with icons you choose. You can do sensitivity analyses, and interface with other programs. Academic licenses begin at $350; prices for a limited edition for students or evaluation purposes begin at $60. You can download a free demonstration version.

For more information, contact Imagine That, Inc., 6830 Via Del Oro, Suite 230, San Jose, CA 95119. This office may be reached by telephone at 408-365-0305, by fax at 408-629-1251, or through e-mail at extend@

imaginethatinc.com. The Web site for Imagine That, Inc., is found at http://www.imaginethatinc.com.

Simulation Languages

Simulation languages are powerful programming languages with special constructs to make it easier to write and test simulations. They are generally easier to learn to program than general programming languages (or Mathematica or Maple) but require more learning than graphical packages. The firms offering simulation languages also market graphical packages.

Wolverine Software sells GPSS/H, a version of the long-standing GPSS simulation language, and SLX, which is a powerful multilayered simulation product. A student version of SLX is available free, and a student version of GPSS/H is available for $40; these are limited versions that can be used for evaluation purposes. The student version of GPSS/H includes a textbook and examples. Academic versions of SLX and GPSS/H are about $750 to $1,000.

For more information, contact Wolverine Software Corporation, 2111 Eisenhower Avenue, Suite 404, Alexandria, VA 22314-4679. Telephone numbers for this office are 800-456-5671 and 703-535-6760; the fax number is 703-535-6763. The company may be reached through e-mail at mail@wolverinesoftware.com. Information is also available at its Web site, http://www.wolverinesoftware.com/products.htm.

Simscript 11.5 and Simprocess are products of CACI, Inc. Simscript is a free-form, English-like, general-purpose programming language with simulation constructs and built-in features for experimental design and response surface analysis. Its core simulation constructs are entities and activities. It is built on a C++ compiler, available for mainframe and PC, and has a menu-oriented user interface. It has graphical user interfaces and animation capabilities, self-documenting code, and built-in constructs for discrete-event and combined discrete/continuous process–oriented simulations. CACI also has a graphical-interface product called Simprocess, which is available in a student version that can be downloaded as a demo. Its orientation is entities (e.g., customer calls) going through activities; it is well designed for cost accounting and simulating business processes but appears too specialized for more general sociological modeling. Pricing information is not available without talking to a representative.

For more information, go to the CACI corporate Web site at www.caci.com. Information about Simscript and Simprocess is available at http://www.caciasl.com. E-mail inquiries should be directed to simscript@caciasl.com; for telephone inquiries, call 619-542-5228.

Other Useful Resources

The Web page on social simulation at http://www.soc.surrey.ac.uk/research/ simsoc/simsoc.html includes many links to other social simulation sites. It is well organized and offers a good set of links.

The *Journal of Artificial Societies and Social Simulation* (JASSS) is the premier journal in the field of social simulation and the best source for a diversity of social simulations, as well as discussions about simulation principles (http://www.soc.surrey.ac.uk/research/simsoc/cress.html).

The *Journal of Mathematical Sociology* publishes a wide variety of mathematical models in sociology, including many relevant to collective action, and is the best single source for exploring the diversity of mathematical modeling in sociology. The editor of the journal is Patrick Doreian, and inquiries should be directed to the journal at the Department of Sociology, University of Pittsburgh, Pittsburgh, PA 15260. The telephone number for the office is 412-648-7537, and the fax number is 412-648-2799. E-mail inquiries should be sent to pdjms+@pitt.edu. Subscriptions are held by most libraries. The journal's publisher is the Gordon and Breach Publishing Group.

References

Axelrod, Robert M. 1984. *The Evolution of Cooperation.* New York: Basic Books.

Chong, Dennis. 1991. *Collective Action and the Civil Rights Movement.* Chicago: University of Chicago Press. A supply-demand model; careful mathematical analysis; weaknesses are inadequate treatment of metric and poor fit to empirical patterns.

Coleman, James Samuel. 1964. *Introduction to Mathematical Sociology.* New York: Free Press of Glencoe. A widely read classic.

Cornes, Richard, and Todd Sandler. 1996. *The Theory of Externalities, Public Goods, and Club Goods.* 2d ed. Cambridge: Cambridge University Press.

Cortazar, Rene. 1997. "Non-Redundant Groups, the Assurance Game and the Origins of Collective Action." *Public Choice* 92: 41–53.

Davis, Morton D. 1983. *Game Theory: A Nontechnical Introduction.* New York: Basic Books.

Fararo, Thomas J. 1978. *Mathematical Sociology: An Introduction to Fundamentals.* Huntington, N.Y.: R. E. Krieger. A useful classic.

Feinberg, William E., and Norris R. Johnson. 1988. "'Outside Agitators' and Crowds: Results from a Computer Simulation Model." *Social Forces* 67: 398–423.

————. 1990a. "Elementary Social Structure and the Resolution of Ambiguity: Some Results from a Computer Simulation Model." *Sociological Focus* 23: 315–31.

————. 1990b. "Radical Leaders, Moderate Followers: Effects of Alternative Strategies on Achieving Consensus for Action in Simulated Crowds." *Journal of Mathematical Sociology* 15: 91–115.

Gaylord, Richard J., and Louis J. D'Andria. 1998. *Simulating Society: A Mathematica Toolkit for Modeling Socioeconomic Behavior.* New York: Springer. Cellular automata models.

Gilbert, G. Nigel, and Klaus G. Troitzsch. 1999. *Simulation for the Social Scientist.* Buckingham; Philadelphia, Pa.: Open University Press. A general discussion with programs in a programming language called lisp.

Gould, Roger V. 1993. "Collective Action and Network Structure." *American Sociological Review* 58: 182–96.

Hamburger, Henry. 1979. *Games as Models of Social Phenomena.* San Francisco: W. H. Freeman and Co.

Hardin, Russel. 1971. "Collective Action as an Agreeable N-prisoner's Dilemma." *Behavioral Science* 16: 472–81.

————. 1982. *Collective Action.* Baltimore: Johns Hopkins University Press.

Heckathorn, Douglas D. 1988. "Collective Sanctions and the Creation of Prisoners-Dilemma Norms." *American Journal of Sociology* 94: 535–62.

————. 1990. "Collective Sanctions and Compliance Norms: A Formal Theory of Group-Mediated Social-Control." *American Sociological Review* 55: 366–84.

————. 1993. "Collective Action and Group Heterogeneity: Voluntary Provision versus Selective Incentives." *American Sociological Review* 58: 329–50.

————. 1996. "The Dynamics and Dilemmas of Collective Action." *American Sociological Review* 61: 250–77.

Johnson, Norris R., and William E. Feinberg. 1977. "A Computer Simulation of the Emergence of Consensus in Crowds." *American Sociological Review* 42: 505–21.

————. 1990. "Ambiguity and Crowds: Results from a Computer Simulation Model." *Research in Social Movements, Conflicts and Change* 12: 35–66.

Jones, Anthony J. 1979. *Game Theory: Mathematical Models of Conflict.* New York: Halsted Press.

Kim, HyoJoung, and Peter S. Bearman. 1997. "The Structure and Dynamics of Movement Participation." *American Sociological Review* 62: 70–93.

Lave, Charles A., and James G. March. 1975. *An Introduction to Models in the Social Science.* New York: Harper & Row. Widely read and very useful.

Law, Averill M., and W. David Kelton. 2000. *Simulation Modeling and Analysis.* 3d ed. Boston: McGraw-Hill. A standard simulation text widely used by professionals; the focus is experimental design and using simulation to understand an empirical problem, not programming.

Macy, Michael W. 1990. "Learning-Theory and the Logic of Critical Mass." *American Sociological Review* 55: 809–26.

———. 1991a. "Chains of Cooperation: Threshold Effects in Collective Action." *American Sociological Review* 56: 730–47.

———. 1991b. "Learning to Cooperate: Stochastic and Tacit Collusion in Social-Exchange." *American Journal of Sociology* 97: 808–43.

———. 1993. "Backward-Looking Social-Control." *American Sociological Review* 58: 819–36.

———. 1997. "Identity, Interest and Emergent Rationality: An Evolutionary Synthesis." *Rationality and Society* 9: 427–48.

Marquette, Jesse F. 1981. "A Logistic Diffusion Model of Political Mobilization." *Political Behavior* 3: 7–30.

Marwell, Gerald, and Pamela E. Oliver. 1993. *The Critical Mass in Collective Action: A Micro-Social Theory.* New York: Cambridge University Press.

McAdam, Doug. 1982. *Political Process and the Development of Black Insurgency, 1930–1970.* Chicago: University of Chicago Press.

McPhail, Clark. 1991. *The Myth of the Madding Crowd.* New York: Walter DeGruyter.

———. 1993. "From Clusters to Arcs and Rings: Elementary Forms of Sociation in Temporary Gatherings." In *The Community of the Streets,* edited by S. E. Cahill and L. H. Lofland. Greenwich, Conn.: JAI Press.

McPhail, Clark, W. T. Powers, and C. W. Tucker. 1992. "Simulating Individual and Collective Action in Temporary Gatherings." *Social Science Computer Review* 10: 1–28.

Michener, H. Andrew, and Daniel J. Myers. 1998a. "Probabilistic Coalition Structure Theories: An Empirical Comparison in 4-Person Superadditive Sidepayment Games." *Journal of Conflict Resolution* 42 (6): 830–60.

———. 1998b. "A Test of Probabilistic Coalition Structure Theories in 3-Person Sidepayment Games." *Theory and Decision* 45 (1): 37–82.

Myers, Raymond H., and Douglas C. Montgomery. 1995. *Response Surface Methodology.* New York: Wiley. A standard text in its third edition that integrates experimental design and problems of optimization.

Oliver, Pamela E. 1980. "Rewards and Punishments as Selective Incentives for Collective Action: Theoretical Investigations." *American Journal of Sociology* 85: 1356–75.

———. 1993. "Formal Models of Collective Action." *Annual Review of Sociology* 19: 271–300.

Oliver, Pamela E., Gerald Marwell, and Ruy A. Teixeira. 1985. "A Theory of the Critical Mass: Interdependence, Group Heterogeneity, and the Production of Collective Action." *American Journal of Sociology* 9: 522–56.

Oliver, Pamela E., and Gerald Marwell. 1988. "A Theory of the Critical Mass:

The Paradox of Group-Size in Collective Action." *American Sociological Review* 53: 1–8.

Oliver, Pamela E., and Daniel J. Myers. 2000. "Diffusion Models of Cycles of Protest as a Theory of Social Movements." American Sociological Association's Collective Behavior and Social Movements Section Working Paper Series, no. 2.

Olson, Mancur. 1965. *The Logic of Collective Action.* Cambridge: Harvard University Press.

Owen, Guillermo. 1995. *Game Theory.* San Diego: Academic Press.

Pitcher, Brian L., Robert L. Hamblin, and Jerry L. L. Miller. 1978. "The Diffusion of Collective Violence." *American Sociological Review* 43: 23–35.

Rapoport, Anatol. 1970. *N-Person Game Theory: Concepts and Applications.* Ann Arbor: University of Michigan.

Runge, C. Ford. 1984. "Institutions and the Free Rider: The Assurance Problem in Collective Action." *Journal of Politics* 46: 154–81.

Sandler, Todd. 1992. *Collective Action: Theory and Applications.* Ann Arbor: University of Michigan Press.

3

Verification and Proof in Frame and Discourse Analysis

Hank Johnston

Over the past two decades ideational and cultural approaches to social movements have spawned small movements of their own within the field. Frame analysis has become a popular trend. It entered the scene in the early 1980s and since then has given rise to research identifying over a hundred different movement-specific, collective-action frames. Another popular trend is discourse analysis. In the early 1980s it became fashionable in the fields of history, literary criticism, and cultural studies and has been applied to questions related to social movements under several rubrics: rhetorical analysis, narrative analysis or narrativity, dialogic analysis, story-grammar analysis, content analysis, and semantic text analysis. The multiplicity of these labels suggests that the subfield of discourse analysis is far from theoretically coherent. It embraces differing perspectives and methodologies that mix and match linguistic and interpretative methods, cultural criticism, and varying degrees of methodological rigor. The same can be said about the framing literature. Benford's "insiders critique" (1997) notes that sometimes the concept of frame is applied too generally, reflecting both scholarly enthusiasm for the role of ideas in collective action and differing perspectives on their influence. The goal of this chapter is to take stock of the trends in both approaches, review the methods that they most commonly use, and make some methodological suggestions that might nudge forward our understanding of cultural processes in social movements.

Frame and discourse analyses pose two sets of challenges to the social movement researcher in the areas of data collection, analysis, and final presentation of results. First, there is a set of challenges that relates to definitions and conceptualizations. Ideational concepts are inherently imprecise, and distinctions between frames, ideologies, and discourses are frequently blurred. Discourse and frames are related and sometimes overlap. Cultural discourses can include frames, and some discourses can be characterized as the broadest kinds of frames. Ideologies often do the same things frames do and are sometimes called frames, as in a "feminist frame" or "Marxist frame" (see Oliver and Johnston 2000). It is common to find discourse analysis using the language of framing and vice versa (see Ellingson 1995: 101). There is a Chinese saying that to call things by their right name is the beginning of knowledge. With that in mind, this chapter begins with brief review of what we mean by frames and discourse, so that these concepts may be used clearly and consistently in research designs.

A second set of challenges relates to verification and proof. Both frame and discourse analyses confront the difficult tasks of describing and presenting evidence for concepts that reside in the black box of mental life. Gaining access to mental life has always been a challenge to social science, but with the use of questionnaires or focus groups, or by inferring from common texts or observed behavior, it is possible to represent mental constructs within the constraints of the chosen method. Yet, in my reading of the social movement literature, theoretical arguments for frames and discourse, often based on the selective use of cases, are much stronger and more numerous than empirical investigations that demonstrate the influence of frames or discourse on social movement success, maintenance, decline, and consequences. In this chapter, I will review several strategies of frame and discourse analysis with the goal of linking concepts with empirical observation in a clear and convincing way, strategies that can help in making systematic comparisons between cultural and ideational influences. If frame and discourse analyses are to have long-lasting influence in the field, research must be designed to convincingly demonstrate to a wide audience of social scientists that collective action frames and social movement discourses influence start-ups, trajectories, successes, failures, and consequences of social movements and protest.

What Is a Frame?

In 1954 Gregory Bateson introduced the concept of a frame as a mental construct that defines "what is going on" in interactive situations ([1954] 1972). He showed that participants always apply interpretative frameworks in order to ascertain how others' actions and words are to be understood. Frame concepts were introduced to sociological theory by Erving Goffman in *Frame Analysis* (1972), and later in *Forms of Talk* (1981). In these books,

Goffman examined layers of framing in interaction and focused his analysis on the conversational conventions that mark the application of and changes in interpretative frames. His approach to frames stressed that the close analysis of naturally occurring speech is the best way to study framing activities.

Frames are interpretative schemata "that enable participants to locate, perceive, and label occurrences" (Snow et al. 1986: 464), "selectively punctuating and encoding objects, situations, events, experiences, and sequences of actions within one's present or past environment" (Snow and Benford 1992: 137). In other words, in one's scope of experience, frames indicate what to look at and what is important, and thereby indicate what is going on. A frame may also indicate, by directing attention away from other things, what is not important. Applied to social movement research, this definition implies several fundamental elements of a frame.

First, a frame has content. Schank and Abelson (1977) demonstrate this by showing how frames orient our expectations based on past experience, such as ordering food in a restaurant. "John went into the restaurant. He ordered a hamburger and a coke. He asked the waitress for the check and left" (quoted in Tannen 1993). Schank and Abelson point out that it does not strike us as unusual that we can refer to "the" waitress and "the" check, "just as if those objects had been previously mentioned," even though they were not. The reason these words sound correct is that a "restaurant frame" (or "script," the term they use) implicitly introduces them as part of the total restaurant schema in which waitresses and checks plus numerous other items, such as menus, tables, table settings, booths, counters, and so on, are *mentally* present. Collective action frames similarly include numerous items, such as "the" protesters, "the" police, "the" grievances, "the" protest songs, and "the" movement, that are organized in memory and accessed as experiences arise.

Second, a frame is a cognitive structure, or schema, to use Snow and colleagues' term. This means that its contents can be thought of as hierarchically organized. Gerhards and Rucht's (1992: 76) visual portrayal of a master frame for a German anti-IMF campaign is one way to present the relationships between various components in a frame schema. Figure 3.1 is a slightly modified representation of their schema. It shows that, in addition to the general description of the anti-IMF frame (summarized in the box at the top), there are subordinate elements that occur at three sublevels. These represent the detailed contents of the frame. These points of information, or nodes in the frame structure, were drawn from close analysis of anti-IMF flyers calling for protest mobilization.

Third, like other ideational factors that shape human behavior, frames

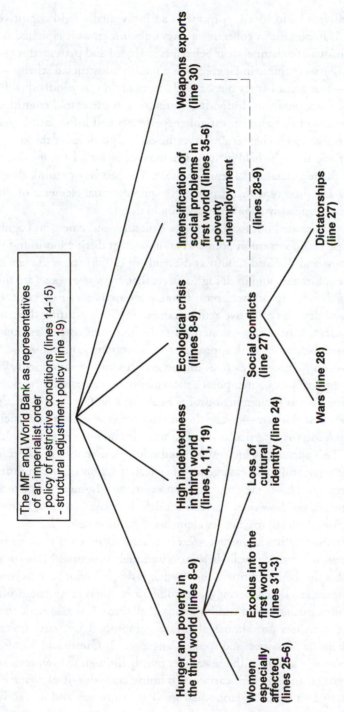

Figure 3.1. *Master frame of the Anti-IMF campaign. Adapted from Gerhards and Rucht 1992. Copyright University of Chicago Press; reprinted by permission of the University of Chicago Press.*

The IMF and World Bank as representatives
of an imperialist order
- policy of restrictive conditions (lines 14-15)
- structural adjustment policy (line 19)

Hunger and poverty in
the third world (lines 8-9)

High indebtedness
in third world
(lines 4, 11, 19)

Ecological crisis
(lines 8-9)

Intensification of
social problems in
first world (lines 35-6)
-poverty
-unemployment

Weapons exports
(line 30)

Women
especially
affected
(lines 25-6)

Exodus into the
first world
(lines 31-3)

Loss of
cultural
identity (line 24)

Social conflicts
(line 27)

(lines 28-9)

Wars (line 28)

Dictatorships
(line 27)

are *both* individual and social. A frame is an individually held cognitive schema but is important in collective action only insofar as it is shared by enough individuals to channel their behaviors in shared and patterned ways. The anti-IMF master frame in Figure 3.1 is a socially constructed schema—a *social* fact—that actually may not be "held mentally" by any individual in that specific representation. Individual variations in the actual cognitive structure are assumed, based on variable experiences and information (see also Klandermans 1997, chapter 2). Nevertheless, for purposes of the analysis, these variations can be held in abeyance in favor of a model that evinces a good fit with the general social representation. The best way to think about Figure 3.1 is as a prototype that captures the quintessential elements of the frame and simultaneously allows for variation in details.

Fourth, frames are both fixed cognitive structures and emergent cognitive processes. This observation points to an important distinction in frame research. Snow and Benford (2000) and Steinberg (1998) stress the emergent qualities of frames, and in doing so assert that *framing processes* are the proper research focus. In contrast, most framing research uses surveys or textual analysis to describe collective action frames, implicitly treating them as fixed structures captured in a moment of time, and then correlates them with movement behaviors. Both approaches are important, however. A focus on the verb—on *framing*—describes important activities in movement development, especially as contemporary movements concentrate on marketing themselves via frame alignment processes. A focus on the noun—on *the frame's content and structure*—reveals the interpretative repertoire of participants and/or leaders at a particular point in time during the movement's development. This approach requires the methodological artifice of freezing the ongoing negotiation and emergence of collective action frames in order to take soundings. This is the only way to measure how frames change over time, how much, and how these variations might be related to other factors in mobilization. Both approaches are elements of framing research.

Fifth, frames are based on text. *Text* is a fashionable term that, in its broadest sense, refers to symbolic behaviors and their structure. Most commonly, it takes the form of written documents; verbal behavior such as conversations, speeches, slogans, songs; and sometimes visual representations, such as pictures, cartoons; and combinations of all three. It is axiomatic that (1) framing activities are almost always accomplished by participants through the media of written and spoken language, (2) frames and framing activities become available to the researcher mostly through written texts or spoken language, and (3) verification of framing activities or of a frame's content is based on evidence embodied in what people say and do. To be convincing, the frame analysis must not journey too far from the original texts on which it is based, and must maintain a continual evidential dialogue with them. All too often a frame is "discovered" through participant interviews, movement documents, speeches, songs, and slogans. The analysis then moves on and rarely looks back to what the frame means in its full detail to those who use it. Verification and proof of frame analysis require clear references to the texts on which frames or framing processes are based.

What Is Discourse?

Discourse, like frames, is based on text. A discourse refers to the sum total of the "manifestos, records of debates at meetings, actions of political demonstrators, newspaper articles, slogans, speeches, posters, satirical prints, statutes of associations, pamphlets, and so on" of a time, a place, and a people (Sewell 1980: 8–9). For the social movement researcher, common data sources are organizational documents and newspaper articles, but they can also include the spoken words of social movement participants, leaders, opponents, and bystanders, which are audio-recorded and transcribed. A related term is the *discursive field* of a social movement, described as the "symbolic space or structure" of what is being talked about, often "defined by some fundamental opposition of binary concepts" (Wuthnow 1989: 13). It draws on the conflicts, struggles, and political cleavages of the broader social and cultural environment, and articulates these elements such that the transformative power of the ideas is challenging yet familiar.

The contentious aspect of discourse is often represented by the use of its plural form, *discourses.* To recognize more than one discourse emphasizes that what is being discussed and acted on is never unanimous but often challenged and negated by opposing groups. Like the emphasis on framing *processes* mentioned earlier, there is a genre of discourse analysis that stresses the emergent and socially constructed nature of textual production. In this view, variously called the discursive/rhetorical approach (Billig 1992), the rhetorical turn (Simon 1990), or dialogic theory (Steinberg 1998, 1999), all meaning is context-specific, multifaceted, ever evolving, dialectical, and conflict-rived. It focuses on what is actually said or written—the performative aspects of discourse—rather than on the knowledge embodied in mental structures that textual production presumes. Research in this vein is typically descriptive of how discourse changes or how it is related to broader discursive fields, rather than causal.

In the 1960s, discourse analysis was a new area of inquiry in the field of linguistics. It grew in response to Chomsky's transformational grammar, which focused on the sentence as the unit of analysis. A group of linguists emphasized that it was necessary go beyond isolated sentences and consider nearby text in order to grasp full meaning and thereby understand how meaning is produced. The argument was that broader speech episodes in which themes and ideas were fully developed and brought to closure contained information that was critical to full interpretation. Since then, the basic principle that the holistic text is the proper unit of analysis has been embraced by historians, literary theorists, and social and political scientists of the "discursive turn" (or "narrative turn"; see, for example, Somers 1992) and extended to include contextual factors residing in the social conditions of textual production. This brand of "macro" discourse analysis (as opposed to the micro focus of linguistic discourse analysis [Johnston 1995]) concentrates on the global meaning of texts and on their interpretation and "deconstruction" according to social factors such as status, politics, and economic interests.

Applied to social movements, there are different levels of discourse. The broadest are world-historical discourses (or *mentalités*) of the Reformation, Enlightenment, Islamism, and so on, and then the more circumscribed discursive fields of specific movements such as gay rights, liberation theology, and ecology. To describe these discourses, the analyst must choose texts that are representative, such as documents that are widely recognized as seminal or definitive of a movement—the Port Huron statement, for example, as a text for the U.S. student movement, or Luther's Invocavit sermon of 1522 for the Reformation (see Wuthnow 1989).

A second level is organizational discourse. When a movement is structured according to different social movement organizations (SMOs), their textual production forms part of the polyphonous voice of a movement's discourse. The producers of organizational discourse are the activists, committees, and functionaries at various levels of the SMO. It is common that the discourse produced by intellectuals and movement leaders is taken as representative of organizational discourse. Rochon (1998) points out that this level is often reflective of discursive elements that resonate among the larger populace, akin to processes of frame alignment and frame bridging. Demonstrating this nesting phenomenon, that subordinate levels draw on and reflect the essential elements of broader discourses, is a common research goal in discourse studies.

The third level refers to the individual production of text and speech by participants and activists. This focus is in line with traditional linguistic discourse analysis. It seeks to explain what is said by expanding the analysis to broader textual units, such as the speech episode for spoken language and the complete text for written language. Both are defined by the development and resolution of themes and by their own internal structures. Linguistic theory offers several rules of thumb that direct the analyst's attention to channels and sources of meaning that are often ignored or overlooked (see Figure 3.3 at the end of this chapter for a summary). The relevant point for our purposes is that there is a relationship between the individual level of discourse and the more general levels because texts are usually produced by individuals. Key texts are partly shaped by the writer's biographical context, the roles he or she occupies within the organization, and individual goals that may vary from organizational goals. Accurate interpretation of organizational or world-historical texts may require micro-data about the writer/speaker.

Qualitative Approaches

Frame and discourse analyses commonly utilize qualitative methods of data reduction and presentation. Qualitative data reduction orders a wide variety of written or spoken textual materials by categories that represent more general factors. The coding of texts by these categories is based on the judgment of the researcher. Presentation of findings relies on texts that are presumed to be representative of a given category, and without numerical measures of the categories' contents. Because textual data come contextually embedded and are often gathered in ways that offer insights into their interpretation that are lost in survey techniques, qualitative analysis offers higher validity of the findings but less reliability. Coding categories are generated either from theoretical interests or from an initial round of analysis. It is typical that textual materials are analyzed in a two-step process, first, to refine theoretical categories and generate new ones, often by review of an exploratory sample of texts, and second, to apply newly refined codes to the broad body of text.

Qualitative Discourse Analysis

Most qualitative discourse analysis intensively analyzes textual materials with the goal of laying bare the relationships between movement discourse and the discursive field of the broader culture. A convincing case for this kind of "discursive embeddedness" may be made by moving between a movement's textual materials and those of the broader culture, but this is a research strategy that only secondarily and implicitly can take up the central "why questions" of the field, such as why a movement succeeds, why a movement fails, or why a movement has a particular trajectory. Qualitative discourse analysis is characterized by an intensive focus on movement-related texts to identify patterns, linkages, and structures of ideas. This usually precludes systematic examination of patterns over time and how they may vary according to other influences, a practical constraint of the method rather than intrinsic to its logic. We will see later how quantitative methods of discourse analysis might better answer these kinds of questions with longitudinal comparisons. In contrast, it is typical that qualitative discourse analysis, by virtue of its intensive focus, explores or describes relationships related to the "how questions." How is it that a movement expresses its grievances a certain way? How does a movement come to mix ideologies and frames? How does a movement use broader cultural symbols? Two recent studies are good examples of what qualitative analysis can do in this vein: Jessie Daniels's monograph *White Lies* (1997) and Marc Steinberg's *Fighting Words* (1999).

Daniels's study demonstrates parallels between the discourse of white racist SMOs and the larger culture; in other words, it lays bare the racism of the broader culture by showing that the extremism of small racist groups is not that extreme. In this sense, it is not strictly a study of social movement development. She examines white supremacist discourse by employing "ethnographic content analysis" of white supremacist newsletters and publications produced between 1977 and 1991. These publications were part of the collection of Klanwatch, a division of the Southern Poverty Law Center in Montgomery, Alabama. The unit of analysis is the article, editorial, or cartoon within the publications. In reviewing these materials, Daniels notes "the themes which emerged while foregrounding . . . theoretical questions about the intersections of race, class, gender and sexuality."

> In stage one of the process I noted words, images, and recurring themes in the publications. This preliminary reading and the early "field" notes were useful to me as I moved on to stage two. Stage two was much longer and included most of the analysis. This stage included choosing a unit of analysis [the article], developing categories and a system for noting them; textual, visual, compositional analysis, and finally, explanation. (141)

Steinberg's study, like Daniels's, looks closely at language, symbols, and images. His research has three goals, which are mostly descriptive rather than explanatory: (1) to show how discourse was shaped by changing economic and political contexts; (2) to show how two groups, Spitalfield silk weavers and Lancaster cotton weavers in the early nineteenth century, developed discursive repertoires based on material interests; and (3) to demonstrate the reciprocity between discourse and protest actions. He shows how what was written—and presumably talked about in 1830—influenced protest action, which in turn influenced what was talked about again. Discourse and text become an element in the progress of events, not simply vehicles of information. This is a theoretical orientation drawing on the work of Mikhail Bakhtin, which stresses the recursive and processual nature of discourse. Thus, while Steinberg's research relies heavily on the historian's craft, and he takes issue with narrativist critiques of E. P. Thompson's work on class formation, what he does with his archival materials is strongly influenced by a particular theoretical perspective within the "linguistic turn" of cultural analysis.

Both studies also reflect the "linguistic turn" in their methodologies. For example, Steinberg intensively examines a key text representing a campaign for a Wages Protection Bill (114–17). He closely analyzes a petition supporting the bill, which he chose in part because it was widely distributed (it gathered 20,000 signatures). Intensive textual analysis must always balance its insights with the looming question of whether the text is representative enough to generalize about its patterns. The choice of widely distributed and/or milestone documents, such as Steinberg's petition, can increase confidence in generalizability. For Daniels, the claim of generalizability is based on a large sample size for discourse analysis, 369 issues of white supremacist newsletters, and she discusses straightforwardly her sampling decisions and problems with representativeness. Her analysis of textual materials is even more intensive than Steinberg's. She broadens textual analysis by considering other sources of meaning, especially the arrangement of written material and visual components—for example, racist cartoons—which she labels "compositional analysis." Daniels argues that the arrangement of text relative to other symbolic elements can be an input to meaning and provide clues for interpretation. Compositional analysis could also include the positioning of articles (front page versus inner pages), their clustering, and their distribution by article type.

Together these two studies show the close relation between discourse analysis as a method and discourse as a theoretical construct. Both are descriptive studies that utilize textual analysis to show relationships between what is talked about and written about in movements and broad cultural templates. Steinberg demonstrates how hegemonic discourses of early capitalists shaped how workers came to terms with the injustices they faced, and thus influenced their collective action. Daniels's task is to demonstrate parallels in extremist discourse and dominant discourses. Certainly, the practical constraints of intensive textual analysis by a researcher or a researcher's team limit qualitative discourse analysis to certain kinds of issues, such as relations between movement cultures and broader cultures. The penetrating gaze this strategy offers is particularly well suited to laying bare the deep structures of ideas and their relations within a movement, and to mapping the ideological processes in movement formation. It is useful for suggesting with whom movements might form coalitions (those that share discursive repertoires), what movements might be successful (those that draw on resonating templates), and what ideologies might mobilize (those that successfully engage the hegemonic discourse). Qualitative strategies are best employed in exploring these relations in specific movements, but in so far as they are labor intensive, they will tend to constrain research to case studies, and to a focus on the "hows" of ideation in movement development rather than the "whys" of general mobilizing processes.

Qualitative Frame Analysis

Qualitative approaches to textual data, like those described above, are also commonly used in frame analysis. Framing studies typically rely on convenience samples of movement documents and/or transcribed ethnographic interviews with movement activists as the database. Johnston and Aarelaid-Tart (2000) used transcriptions of seventy-two biographical interviews with activists and intellectuals to identify two master frames in the national resistance in Estonia. Mooney and Hunt (1996) reviewed secondary sources for information about twenty-one contemporary and historical agrarian mobilizations and conducted interviews with current movement leaders to specify three master frames. Capek (1993) relied on twenty in-depth interviews plus movement documents to posit an environmental justice frame. However, despite a shared qualitative orientation to texts, there seem to be two key differences between frame and discourse studies. First, because they embrace different theoretical concepts, different research questions are asked. Framing studies mostly describe collective action frames and their role in movement development. Discourse studies treat cultural processes and their effect on what gets talked about. Second, as one might expect, framing studies offer less reference to the actual texts on which the frames are based, while discourse studies tend to analyze texts more closely.

The framing literature in linguistics and cognitive studies often portrays a frame as a hierarchical cognitive structure or decision-making algorithm that moves from general to increasingly specific behaviors. Frame analysis in social movement studies, however, rarely reproduces frame structures that contain levels of cognitive orientations and behaviors. One exception, as mentioned earlier (see Figure 3.1), is Gerhards and Rucht's depiction of frame structures for the anti-IMF and anti-Reagan campaigns in Germany (1992: 76–79). These were based on two widely distributed leaflets, which were reproduced in an appendix to their article. There are several advantages in their strategy. First, because the actual texts are presented, the analysts' interpretations can be easily evaluated. Second, a schematic diagram makes clear the relation among the various framing concepts. These too can be compared with the actual texts. Third, the analysis is based on a plausible assumption that the flyers are representative of the master frames. These flyers were signed and supported by all groups supporting the campaigns and therefore were taken as valid indicators of those elements of the master frames that were shared.

Gerhards and Rucht's approach to empirical verification of frame concepts is similar to the strategy described in my own work (Johnston 1995), which describes a formalized method of presenting the different levels within a frame schema. A simple tactic that clarifies the textual basis of frame analysis is to list the lines of the text on which the categories at various levels are based. I have taken the liberty to demonstrate this with Gerhards and Rucht's figure. The line numbers in Figure 3.1 were inserted by me and were not included in the original article. For example, the second-level element, "high third-world indebtedness," in Figure 3.1 refers to line numbers 4, 11, and 19 of the original text (presented in an appendix), where the reader can verify the interpretation.

Similarly, when frame analysis is based on a sample of several texts rather than just one or two, the presentation strategy in Figure 3.2 helps verification. Like Figure 3.1, this figure presents the hierarchical structure of a frame that contains its various elements and their relationships to each other. The higher levels represent more general categories, and the lower levels are subcategories of the frame based on review of interview texts. Rather than the lines of text, the number of respondents holding the frame who mention the subcategory is provided as a measure of generality and distribution of each subcategory. Figure 3.2 represents the structure of a collective-action master frame of the radical branch of the Estonian national opposition to the Soviets (Johnston and Aarelaid-Tart 2000). Thirty-four respondents gave evidence of this frame in their interviews ($N = 72$ in the study; the remaining 38 described a master frame that oriented actors toward accommodation with the communists). Figure 3.2 is for illustrative purposes and was not part of the published research.

Other researchers have also seen the need for systematic exposition of frame content. In a study of media framing and grassroots organizing Charlotte Ryan (1991) uses qualitative methods to distill the essence of both media and movement frames. Her analysis systematically lists key frame elements in charts, each of which present four general themes: (1) the key issue in the frame; (2) responsibility/solution proposed in the frame, or its diagnosis and prognosis; (3) the symbols used, especially visual images, metaphors, historical examples, stereotypes, and catch phrases; and (4) the supporting arguments, especially in terms of historical roots of the grievance,

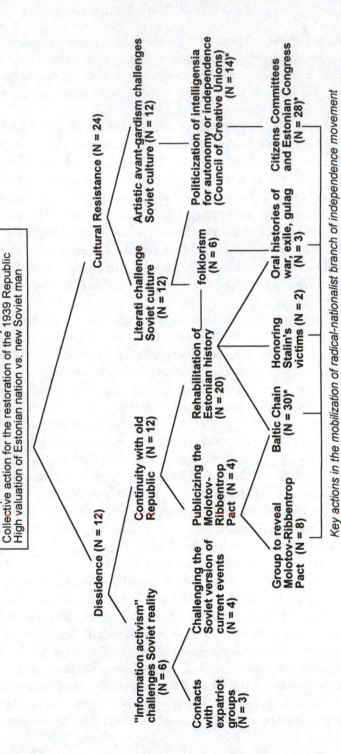

Figure 3.2. *Pure-nationality master frame for the Estonian National Opposition (N = 34). The asterisk indicates popular actions that drew upon both dissidents and cultural resisters.*

consequences of the frame's success, and appeals and links to broader cultural values. Ryan's approach has been applied by Fuks (1998) in his analysis of environmental conflict in Rio de Janeiro.

Qualitative frame analysis lends itself to certain theoretical questions, such as strategic framing by SMOs, consciousness raising (which is a reframing activity), building collective identity (which has been analyzed as a framing activity by Hunt, Benford, and Snow 1994, and Bernstein 1997), and fostering collective solidarity through strong mobilizing frames. These are processes that are best revealed by the in-depth focus and high validity that qualitative analysis offers. Yet as Benford (1997) points out, the majority of qualitative frame analyses focus on movement-specific frames. This is partly due to the lack of systematic methods to describe frames across different movements, partly due to a lack of standardized measures for key framing concepts, such as diagnostic, prognostic, and motivational framing, and partly due to the practical constraints that—as in qualitative discourse analysis—an intensive focus on movement texts imposes. Comparing the variable strength of these factors across movements could help move forward our understanding of generic framing processes.

Quantitative Methods

Quantitative studies of collective action frames and movement discourse are designed to produce numerical measures of frequency and intensity of relevant categories. One genre of quantitative methods uses responses to sample surveys to produce numerical data. Another approach uses content analysis, often with the aid of computer programs, to translate written text into quantitative outputs. A third approach is story-grammar analysis, which also frequently employs computer analysis but with a different analytical logic. All three have advantages but are also subject to methodological constraints in translating text into numerical data.

Sample Surveys

The survey method is well suited for testing the content of collective action frames or discourse and verifying and refining previous research that has identified frames or discursive strategies. It is not well suited, however, for first ventures into plotting the meaning structures of frames or exploratory research in discourse. These goals require an inductive logic that moves from the specific (textual materials) to the general (e.g., frame categories and subcategories). This contrasts with the logic of survey analysis that tends to work deductively, from general theoretical understandings or interests to specific questionnaire items. Also, measuring the intensity or distribution of ideational elements among a population, a task that survey questionnaires are eminently able to accomplish, has traditionally not been a goal of frame and discourse analyses. Another limitation of survey data is the risk that statistical operations may recast the operational definition of a frame from its originally powerful usage as an interpretative schema to other higher-level generalizations about shared orientations (such as goals, values, beliefs, and ideologies) of movement membership or SMOs.

One example of frame-oriented survey analysis is Marullo, Pagnucco, and Smith's (1996) study of SMO decline and frame changes in the U.S. peace movement. Their study was based on a stratified sample ($N = 411$) of grassroots peace organizations, whose staff or leadership filled out the questionnaires. Nineteen items about the organization's goals, strategies, and values were included on the questionnaire to gather information about collective action frames. Six higher-level factors were identified by factor analysis of responses to these questions, which the authors defined as organizational frames. These were then grouped according to three even more general factors—presumably master frames of the peace movement—identified as a "great powers framework," a "world order framework," and a "nonviolence framework," and traced over time.

This is an innovative method of identifying master frames, but one that functions under several constraints. First, a large sample size is necessary for factor analysis of responses. Second, the questionnaire items on which the factor analysis is based must be comprehensive enough to embrace the permutations of frame content and structure. In the peace movement study, it is appropriate to ask whether the original nineteen questionnaire items adequately reflected and/or investigated the variety of information in frame structures since they were derived from general-interest questions about organizational values, goals, and strategies and not from what was already known about peace movement activists' cognitive orientations. Third, the logic behind identifying higher-level factors as frames must be specified in the analysis. This requires a systematic presentation of the original questionnaire items, the range of responses, the logic behind how they combine, and the logic behind combining the original six factors into three master frames. If this can be done satisfactorily, factor analysis can be a useful method to identify the general focus of collective action frames, but not the details of a frame's content.

Survey analysis creates questions whose responses provide ways to test hypotheses and gain insights into social movement culture, for example, the intensity or distribution of frames or discourses. It makes sense that a researcher might compose questions that measure whether a social movement participant carries a particular frame—identified by previous research—or explore the different meanings of frames or discursive strategies in order to plot their distribution among SMOs. But these are not research questions that are widely asked in frame and discursive approaches, although they are good ones and well suited to the method. To date, the application of survey research to frame analysis has been somewhat limited.

Content Analysis

The term *content analysis* has been used for over a half-century (e.g., Shils 1948) to describe researchers' meticulous steps to reduce raw textual data to categorical units, and to assign numerical measures of occurrence and intensity. Shapiro and Markoff (1998: 20) observe that many methodologies claim the term *content analysis,* including intuitive interpretation of texts that have nothing to do with enumeration, but for our purposes, we will adopt the following definition: Content analysis is the methodical conversion of textual materials to numerical frequency and/or intensity of meaningful categories that are standardized and statistically manipulable. The assignment to categories is based on clearly stated operational techniques such that they can be repeated by other researchers without significant variation.

It is best to draw a clear distinction between content analysis and discourse analysis. The latter emerged from linguistic understandings of naturally occurring speech in which *the context* of speech or textual production is emphasized as a vehicle of meaning and understanding. Content analysis, on the other hand, tends to focus only on words, or at best word combinations. Most content analysis today is accomplished by text-analysis computer programs that are able to number crunch key-word or word-combination occurrences and provide opportunities for the ongoing refinement of exactly what gets counted. For example, Carroll and Ratner's (1996) examination of master frames in several Vancouver SMOs used Ethnograph, a textual analysis program (Seidel, Kjolseth, and Seymour 1988) to produce numerical outputs of transcribed interviews. Based on thousands of lines of interview text, their analysis identified three master frames: a political-economy frame, a liberal frame, and an identity frame. In this approach, the distribution of words and the interpretation of how they cluster are substitutes for the "sensitive reading" of texts that typify qualitative methods.

The logic behind this brand of content analysis is that counting words provides a *measure of meaning* that is for the most part sufficient, especially when there are huge amounts of text to be analyzed. If there are errors due to changing or unclear meanings of words, these are overshadowed by the predominance of standardized usage of the words. Whether these assumptions are acceptable is a decision that a researcher must make, but accepting these assumptions is different from assuming that tabulating word occurrences provides a valid representation of what a text is about. The context of the "speech situation" or the context of textual production is often where additional and often critical inputs to meaning are located, and frequently this kind of information can completely turn around the meaning of a word. While it is true that textual analysis programs have provisions for feedback and refinement of word occurrences in order to capture semantic variations, including homonyms (words that carry several meanings must be recognized, such as "text" as in written text versus "text" as in textbook), in some cases the programs will still miss a great deal of contextual information. Correct interpretation often requires reference to broader textual context, cultural and biographical understandings, and, in spoken text, tonal variations. These are data that do not enter into content analysis.

In sum, the variability, complexity, and recursiveness of human language have to date made valid and reliable computer analysis difficult, but this field is rapidly progressing. Recent published reviews of state-of-the-art programs are Popping (1997) and Palmquist, Carley, and Dale (1997). In a personal communication, Tom Rochon described a program developed by Educational Testing Service that analyzes the logic of written essays with 95 percent accuracy to human evaluation. Computer evaluation is based on structural similarities in hundreds of essays scanned into readable text and on their evaluations done by trained reviewers. The coded evaluations serve as the basis for analyzing the structure of new essays. Essays are not spoken discourse, and they are written in standardized settings that control for varying definitions of the situation—a long way from the spoken and written discourse of social movements. Nevertheless, that a computer program can analyze the logical structure of a whole text suggests how rapidly technology is changing and that more powerful and reliable computer applications certainly lie in the future. Even so, as with the analysis of these essays, it is likely that computer text processing will remain highly dependent on human input at different points in the analysis.

Story-Grammar Analysis

One way to reduce the errors characteristic of simple word counts is to structure analysis so that humans and machines specialize in what they do best. The complexities of human linguistic processing remain the sole province of coders who translate text into basic *story grammars,* or "semantic structures" that represent the essence of what is said. Computers do the data crunching. This division of labor represents a basic change from the traditional coding task of reducing complex textual data to higher-level theoretically relevant codes, as in coding protest events from newspaper reports. Instead, coders are charged with applying their natural abilities as competent, culturally aware speaker-hearers—with all the tacit linguistic resources that this implies, especially regarding interpreting context and nuance—to "translate" the texts into machine-readable codes. These codes hypothetically represent all the possibilities of "what gets said" in the collection of texts being reviewed, rather than higher-level, theoretically relevant, analytical categories—the typical end point of coding procedures. The reasoning behind the story-grammar strategy is that coders use natural language skills to understand what is being said, not to analyze it and categorize it. They then recast the meanings they extract into simple symbol sequences that the computer can read and manipulate. The data-crunching abilities of computers enable large quantities of text to be analyzed, often detecting patterns or covariates that, for practical reasons, qualitative analysis would not be able to identify.

Shapiro and Markoff (1998) recently completed a long-term project that utilizes this approach. They sampled and coded the *cahiers de doléances* of the French Revolution, a set of documents produced by more than forty thousand of France's local and regional bodies (parishes, towns, guilds, etc.) called to assemble at the Estates-General in 1789. The *cahiers de doléances* (books of grievances) might be said to represent the regional bodies' negotiating positions to be haggled over with the king's representatives. Clearly this set of documents has a great deal to say about the causes of the French Revolution, the groups that supported it, and regional variation. Shapiro and Markoff's research, however, is not about frames or discursive fields of the Revolution. Rather the authors use their machine-readable translations of grievances to track variations according to social, political, and economic factors. Quantification of the text allows for statistical manipulation of the demands posed by different groups by these variables.

Shapiro and Markoff charged their coders with identifying the units of grievances or demands in the text. Each unit can be parsed (analyzed by grammatical units, as indicated by < >) in terms of a <subject>, "ordinarily a social institution or a social problem," and an <action> that is demanded (79). A third element is the <object> toward which actions might be directed. Finally, there are certain standardized <qualifications> that coders may use to make their "translations" more precisely capture the meaning of the text. The subject-verb-object sequence is the fundamental grammar for declarative sentences. The assumption is that all texts can be reduced to these codes provided that they are guided by a higher-level understanding of the texts at the outset, and adaptable and expandable as the coding progresses.

Briefly the translation proceeds as follows. If one of the grievances stated in the text is about taxes, "all taxes are within the broadest category of government, so their codes always begin with a 'G.' To indicate that they are taxes [as opposed to military expenditures] the code then has the symbol 'TA.' If we are dealing with an indirect tax, G, TA is followed by 'IN,' and if that indirect tax is the salt tax, it is symbolized 'GA' (for *gabelle*)" (Shapiro and Markoff 1998: 85). It is expected that these coding rules are further refined and elaborated as the data analysis proceeds. The semantic texture and syntactic complexity of the original documents preordain that there will be some coder errors, but the authors are content to live with these because (1) simplification of the coding task should mean (the authors assume) that errors will be relatively few, (2) the benefits of computer-based analysis are great, and (3) the large sample size compensates for the few errors (for a fuller description of how codes can be changed and expanded, see Shapiro and Markoff 1988: 84–96). Rather than describing Shapiro and Markoff's methodology in more detail, I direct the interested reader to their book (see also Franzosi 1999 and Roberts 1997b, similar treatments of this approach, which they label "semantic text analysis").

Although not to date applied in research in frame and discourse analyses, story-grammar analysis or semantic-text analysis holds potential for more empirical rigor. We can begin by noting that an <action> in response to a grievance is a basic function of framing and ideologies, namely making a prognosis of action (Snow and Benford 1992). These could plausibly be <street protests>, <legislative strategies>, <nonviolent site occupation>, <petitions>, and so on. It makes sense that other framing functions such as diagnosis (the direction of attention to the causes of the problem), motivation, triggering, or keynoting (indicating injustice) can be isolated by parsing text and translating them into machine-readable codes. Based on what we already know about collective action frames, written or spoken texts can be reduced to a finite number of basic grammars—what frames do, who does them, to whom, and how—and these can be specified so that the coder of movement documents would be able to identify a frame element and translate it into a code for quantitative processing. They can then be assembled in the form of a schema that portrays the deep structure of the text similar to Figures 3.1 and 3.2.

This observation derives from an assumption in Shapiro and Markoff's method that there are a limited number of actions within any culturally specific textual form, such as social movement recruitment literature or flyers for protest marches. Franzosi (1998) builds on this insight by applying a story-grammar approach to quantify different kinds of interaction among actors in situations of contention. He uses the term *story grammars* to describe the skeletal structures of syntax that are composed of the parsed elements of a textual episode and arranged hierarchically from general to specific elements. These elements vary in length but are identified by breaking down the episode into its grammatical forms and functions. Again, <subject>, <action>, and <object> pertain to the various actors in a contentious situation and to what they do. Then there are <modifiers> for each that specify more information for the subject, action, and objects of action. For example, an action might be a <street protest>, and its <modifier> would indicate the type of actor, <SMO>; its size, <large>; and/or organization, <organized march> or <disorderly> or <nonviolent>. For the action, the modifier might indicate <time>, <action type>, <outcome>, <instrument>. The assumption is that most textual material can be reduced to the essential story-grammar elements. "Information in a story grammar is organized according to a relational format, with subjects related to their actions, actors and actions related to their modifiers, and subjects and objects (both social actors) related to one another via their actions" (Franzosi 1999: 133).

With proper theoretical and empirical fine tuning, it is easy to imagine a dictionary of codes based on what is known about a movement, its opponents, its political context, resources, and so on (and flexible enough to embrace more categories) that could be applied to publications or activist-interview texts to translate what they say and do into machine-readable codes. Applied to research on framing activities, if a large sample of activist interviews, or movement documents, or newspaper articles was employed, the story grammar of collective action frames could be depicted with numerical assignments at each node denoting how widely they were reported. Because codes are hierarchically descriptive, going from general to specific (government action → police presence → use of tear gas), unitization of various nodes in a frame structure can be easily accomplished. With the help of computer processing, the same kind of structure represented by Figures 3.1 and 3.2 could be produced.

This method holds promise for some of the elements most difficult to verify in framing theory. For example, frame bridging can be analyzed by taking large samples of texts from different SMO publications. Frame structures can then be constructed based on coding categories (or nodes in the structure), and frame bridging empirically demonstrated by statistically correlating the nodes in different frame structures for different SMOs. The strength of linkages among nodes within different story grammars can be statistically evaluated, and measures of strength obtained. Also, whether the bridging was in terms of actions or objects can be measured, and the level at which the linkages occur demonstrated. Similar analyses can be applied to frame amplification: different frame structures can be represented at different points in the movement's trajectory to demonstrate the growing importance of what had been minor nodes in the frame structure, or the addition of new elements.

A master frame is a powerful concept in the framing perspective but is studied by "sensitive readings" of texts rather than standardized procedures to measure frame characteristics and effects. Among different social movements, clustering behaviors could be matched with counts of elements at the higher levels in the frame structure, where hypothetically the master frame would be operating. Movement-level differences would be demonstrated at the lower levels. A story-grammar approach ensures that master frames are empirically based because they are constructed directly from their textual representation rather than measured by survey questions, a strategy that runs the risk of taking the frame as a given rather than demonstrating its structure.

Quasi Experiments, Group Research, and Focus Groups

One of the early studies to elaborate framing concepts was Gamson, Fireman, and Rytina's examination of group rebellion (1982). They designed a quasi-experimental approach that used videotaped interaction occurring in groups of eleven people to study the emergence of injustice frames and to track other framing processes. Ten years later, as the framing perspective gained momentum, Gamson (1992) directed another study that used "conversational groups" to examine how people used media messages to develop collective action frames. Both studies were based on interactional data from group settings. These were *not exactly* focus groups, strictly defined, but they were very close. Neither study was about a particular social movement, or SMO, but rather explored more general social psychological elements and cultural processes of frame construction.

In the first case, the premise of group formation was to explore community values in what was ostensibly represented to the subjects as a market-research focus-group study. This provided "cover" for the real research goal of studying framing. Participants did not know each other, and a facilitator and an assistant choreographed the interaction so that it seemed that they were deceitfully manipulating the "focus group" to produce information to serve their ends in a court case. In other words, the slow revelation that the group was being lied to and manipulated introduced the dependent variable of this quasi experiment, the perception of injustice. Group interaction was examined in terms of the social construction of an injustice frame that guided rebellion against the "market researchers." I call it a quasi experiment because all variables were not controlled, and the goal was not to measure the variable effects of injustice but rather to trace framing processes more generally.

In the second case, the participants were friends and acquaintances who were recruited snowball-fashion from initial contacts in working-class communities. It is unusual for focus group participants to know each other, but Gamson chose this strategy based on the assumption that friendly discussion groups would be less artificial and closer to naturally occurring settings in which political themes are the fodder of social conversation. In other ways, however, these groups were closer to traditional focus groups in that the interaction was guided by a facilitator following a scripted list of open-ended questions, and discussions were used to probe participants' often unvoiced ideas. Conversations focused on political themes that were part of current public discourse and discussed in the mass media. The interaction was recorded on audiotape, transcribed, and analyzed by a coding scheme based on various frames that existed in public discourse (see Gamson 1992: 189–257, for detailed methodological appendixes). Taken together, these studies point the student of frames and discourse in two related directions regarding social movement research.

First, convening focus groups is an ideal strategy to explore social construction processes. Given the recent emphasis on frame construction, identity construction, and the emergent and recursive nature of discourse, it is surprising that social movement researchers have not used focus groups more frequently. Twenty years ago, European approaches developed by Alain Touraine and Alberto Melucci proposed convening small groups as the best way of gaining insight into these processes, but their methods are not used widely today. Touraine labeled his method "sociological intervention" (1981). Briefly, he gathered social movement participants into discussion groups with the goals of observing the "struggles" that typify social movements and providing feedback of the researcher's analysis as an element of the movement's "self-analysis." Melucci and his colleagues elaborated Touraine's method as a contractual relationship between researchers and actors in several of the studies in *Altri Codici* (1984). Melucci's theoretical positions on social movement collective identity construction are inexorably linked with his methodological preference for small-group discussions (see also Melucci 1989, 1992).

It is perhaps understandable that Touraine's and Melucci's proactive view of the researcher-movement relationship has not gained wide acceptance in North America, but it is puzzling that discussions among social movement participants and activists as a data gathering strategy are not used more often. Focus groups can provide insights into numerous concepts that have great currency in social movement studies: diagnostic processes, action frames, frame bridging, goal expansion and contraction, collective identity construction, cultural outcomes, suddenly imposed grievances, quotidian resistance, to name a few. Focus groups are also ways of examining less logical and less reasoned elements of attitudes and beliefs (Morgan 1998: 59) and hold potential for exploring the relations among emotions and mobilization, another area of research that has gained more attention recently (Goodwin, Jasper, and Polleta 2000).

Second, focus groups are ideally suited for gathering insights into thought processes that would be otherwise difficult to gauge. In-depth interviews can do this but may be limited by respondents' one-on-one concerns about self-presentation, and by the interviewer's skills in encouraging personal revelation. Focus groups have the advantage of creating temporary speech situations in which members share the understanding that active participation is expected and that verbalizing vague and incomplete thoughts is encouraged. For this reason, focus groups are well suited for probing tacit preferences and prejudices and revealing the workings of deep-seated thought processes. Focus groups are commonly used by businesses to gather information for product design, advertisement testing, and marketing, and are also widely applied in political campaigns (for mostly the same reasons!). There is a large literature, which the student can consult for planning the practical elements and structuring the questions (Barbour and Kitzinger 1999; Greenbaum 1997; Krueger 1994; Morgan 1998). Discussions centering on ideas that interest the researcher can be recorded and analyzed. It has been observed that videotaping and audiotaping (to a lesser degree) often inhibit discussion, but it is my experience that with proper facilitation to "frame the discussion" at the outset, and after a short period of settling in, participants eventually ignore the presence of recording technology. The point at which the shift occurs is often evident in a change to a more relaxed speech style.

There are drawbacks to focus groups. It is possible that the participants may not have considered the themes that the researcher is interested in before the group session. This can produce discussions that are dominated by the relatively more informed members, in which pressures to conform are strong (Morgan 1998: 50). Gamson (1992: 21) notes that uninformed participants can adopt a conversational style of "cynical chic" whereby the importance of the issue is discounted, thereby thwarting the goals of the group. It is widely recognized that focus groups are better for gathering insights about subgroups and population segments than broad populations. Despite extensive efforts, Gamson found it difficult to form focus groups that were highly representative of the population because there was a strong element of self-selection (1992: 190).

In sum, focus groups are an underutilized method to generate discussion that closely approximates naturally occurring speech. When the groups are made up of social movement participants, they hold the potential for insights into their motivations, aspirations, and fears that may not have been previously considered and would not be available from other methods. Focus groups are a means of text production rather than analysis, and both the qualitative and quantitative methods discussed in the previous sections hypothetically apply. In business and political applications, verbal transcripts are usually coded based on qualitative, informed interpretation. I have not seen an application of syntactical parsing and story-grammar analysis applied to focus group texts as a means of quantification, although in my judgment it holds potential. Just how much attention should be paid to contextual detail and nuance to make accurate interpretations is both a practical and theoretical decision. Gamson (1992) began by using a detailed method of transcription to capture nuance and speech acts but found that the costs outweighed the benefits, and eventually stopped. It is important that the analyst consider how much meaning is contained in these details, because once the coding is done, they are usually irretrievable. Figure 3.3 contains five elements of verbal exchange derived from linguistic discourse theory that should be considered when using focus group discussions to produce texts. Note that points 2, 3, and 4 can apply to written texts and documents as well.

Summary and Conclusions

The study of discourse and frames in the last two decades of the twentieth century has been characterized by a body of research that has brought culture and language back into social movement analysis. This chapter has presented several strategies for refining and strengthening the analysis of collective action frames and social movement discourse. The goal has been to move forward the standardization of research designs in cultural processes with the ultimate goals of making their findings accessible to scholars working from within other perspectives and to better synchronize the findings of culturalists with other perspectives. Drawing on the previous discussion, several key observations, caveats, and recommendations can be identified with this goal in mind.

1. Discourse and frame analysis are prone to blurred and overlapping definitions. It is crucial that the concepts be clearly defined and used consistently from the initial study design to the final write-up.

1. Shared understandings of the speech situation comprise the context of textual production. A speech situation is a bounded episode of verbal interaction for which there are shared understandings of appropriate speech behaviors. Knowing how a speech situation is defined is a key datum for interpreting text. Social movement cultures embrace various speech situations that, if ignored, may lead to misunderstanding of interview or focus-group transcripts. Also, definitions of speech situations often change during discussions, and are often marked by changes in intonation, pitch, facial expressions, and body language.

2. The text is a holistic construction. Most verbal exchanges, including focus groups and interviews, are comprised of several episodes of connected discourse with different subjects, objects, story lines, themes, and goals. Accurate interpretation may require going outside the segments being analyzed for additional information. Each part of the text should be analyzed in terms of the whole. Information needed for interpretation of textual units is often found in sections that are quite distant from the unit of speech under consideration.

3. Verbal texts are produced from role perspectives. Speech in focus groups or interviews may vary according to changes in the role perspectives from which interlocutors speak. People talk differently if they are acting as an expert, a friend, or a father. Accurate textual analysis requires knowledge of the speaker/writer's role repertoire, which is sometimes available elsewhere in the text, or can be gathered from organizational sources and from preliminary questionnaires. When textual materials do not evince internal consistency, the answer may lie in alternation in role perspectives from which the speaker is talking.

4. Speech is shaped by interactional goals. Beyond just passing information, people often have goals that they seek to accomplish in their speech. In interviews or focus-group discussions, misapprehension of pragmatic intent raises the possibility of invalid interpretations. Pragmatic intent is often revealed by looking at the overall structure of the text, especially toward the end when the goals of interaction often become more transparent. If pronouncements do not correlate with statements in other parts of the discussion, inconsistencies (and outright lies) can nevertheless be taken as data if one can reconstruct the pragmatic intent behind them.

5. In face-to-face interaction, nonverbal channels of information can change meanings significantly. Gumperz (1982) has shown that nonverbal information often marks changes in role status, speech situation, and discursive style. Nonverbal channels are especially relevant in emotional communication. Interviews and focus groups are complex speech situations in which this kind of information may be crucial for valid interpretations. Specifying nonverbal data is labor intensive. They are often lost when spoken texts are transcribed for coding. A parsimonious strategy is to retrieve them case by case from audio- or videotapes when there is difficulty in making sense of a section, or if an analyst, employing his or her own cultural sensitivity, suspects something is being communicated beyond the words alone.

Figure 3.3. Guidelines for intensive analysis of verbal texts.

2. Frames and discourse become available to the researcher through texts, either documents or transcriptions of speech. To make sense to the broader community of scholars who may be less persuaded about the utility of cultural analysis, concepts should be linked with empirical observation in a clear and convincing way. Frame and discourse analyses must not journey too far from the original texts on which they are based, and should maintain a continual dialogue with them. Adhering to the five guidelines in Figure 3.3 can significantly bolster confidence in interpretation of texts.

3. The criteria for selection of texts, either written or spoken, should be specified for the reader. Part of these criteria include an understanding of how the texts are produced, either by the movement or by movement participants, and how these texts are related to the movement development and participation. Full disclosure of sampling procedures at all levels imparts greater confidence about the accuracy and generality of the findings.

4. The use of systematic methods of presentation, such as schematic representations, standardizes frame analysis, increases confidence in interpretations, and makes comparisons easier. The analysis of frames and discourse should at least help specify for the reader the usually tacit processes of data reduction by specific reference to key texts and/or the proportion (relative to the total N) of the texts containing the items.

5. Methodological operations translating textual material to numerical data often run the risk of mutating the operational definition of a frame from its originally powerful usage as an interpretative schema to other higher-level generalizations about ideation (such as goals, values, beliefs, and ideologies) of movement membership or SMOs.

6. In quantitative analysis of texts, incorrect or biased coding is probably the greatest source of error. Once coded and enumerated, the basis of the coding decision is lost to the analyst. Keeping the coding processes as simple as possible is a useful strategy to reduce coding errors. Using panels of judges to review samples of coding decisions is another way to reduce coder error.

7. Computer analysis of textual material is currently limited by the complexity and recursiveness of naturally occurring speech, and for the foreseeable future will require a lot of human input, as in Shapiro and Markoff's approach. Yet this is an area that is rapidly progressing, and the student is advised to research the up-to-date programs that are available before deciding on a text-analysis protocol.

8. Schematic representation of frames can be enhanced if textual materials

are converted to elementary story grammars specifying framing functions and their actions, subjects, objects, and appropriate modifiers. This enables the researcher to make a quantitative case for frame structure and its elements. This is also an alternative way of providing evidence for framing functions such as bridging, amplification, and master frame effects. Linkages between nodes in different frame structures can be statistically tested, thereby increasing confidence in the strength of these relationships. In the past, analyses of these linkages typically have relied on subjective and interpretative arguments.

9. Focus groups with social movement activists are underutilized as a research method. They are ideally suited for producing texts about framing processes such as bridging, amplification, resonance, emotional reactions, and elements of social construction such as identity, strategy, and motivation.

Taken together, frame and discourse analysis represent part of the cultural turn in the social sciences. As we have seen, they are perspectives that embrace a number of different methodologies, and that, by their definition of what is important and what is not, highlight a particular kind of evidence and logic of argumentation. Applied to social movements, they ask different kinds of questions and demand different kinds of data than structuralist and rationalist approaches. It would be regrettable if the perspective becomes so focused and involuted that the kinds of questions that interest the rest of the field—what I have called the why questions of social movement research—are not addressed. This chapter represents a broad review of how some scholars, including myself, have approached the challenge to prevent this from happening.

References

Barbour, Rosaline S., and Jenny Kitzinger. 1999. *Developing Focus Group Research.* Newbury Park, Calif.: Sage.

Bateson, Gregory. 1972 [1954]. *Steps to an Ecology of Mind.* New York: Ballantine.

Benford, Robert. 1997. "An Insider's Critique of the Social Movement Framing Perspective." *Sociological Inquiry* 67: 409–30.

Bernstein, Mary. 1997. "Celebration and Suppression: The Strategic Uses of Identity by the Lesbian and Gay Movement." *American Journal of Sociology* 103: 531–65.

Billig, Michael. 1992. *Talking of the Royal Family.* London: Routledge.

Capek, Stella. 1993. "The 'Environmental Justice' Frame: A Conceptual Discussion and an Application." *Social Problems* 40 (1): 5–24.

Carroll, William K., and R. S. Ratner, 1996. "Master Framing and Cross-Movement

Networking in Contemporary Social Movements." *Sociological Quarterly* 37: 601–25.

Daniels, Jessie. 1997. *White Lies.* New York: Routledge.

Ellingson, Stephen. 1995. "Understanding the Dialectic of Discourse and Collective Action: Public Debate and Rioting in Antebellum Cincinnati." *American Journal of Sociology* 101: 100–144.

Franzosi, Roberto. 1998. "Narrative Analysis—Why (and How) Sociologists Should Be Interested in Narrative." In *The Annual Review of Sociology,* edited by John Hagan, 517–54. Palo Alto, Calif.: Annual Reviews.

———. 1999. "The Return of the Actor: Interaction Networks among Social Actors during Periods of High Mobilization in Italy, 1919–1922." *Mobilization* 4: 131–49.

———. 2000. *From Words to Numbers: Narrative as Data.* Cambridge: Cambridge University Press.

Fuks, Mario. 1998. "Arenas of Public Action and Debate: Environmental Conflicts and the Emergence of the Environment as a Social Problem in Rio De Janeiro." Paper presented at the XIV World Congress of Sociology, July 26–August 1, Montreal, Quebec, Canada.

Gamson, William A. 1992. *Talking Politics.* New York: Cambridge.

Gamson, William A., Bruce Fireman, and Steven Rytina. 1982. *Encounters with Unjust Authority.* Homewood, Ill.: Dorsey.

Gerhards, Jurgen, and Dieter Rucht. 1992. "Mesomobilization: Organizing and Framing in Two Protest Campaigns in West Germany." *American Journal of Sociology* 98: 555–95.

Goffman, Erving. 1972. *Frame Analysis.* New York: Harper and Row.

———. 1981. *Forms of Talk.* Philadelphia: University of Pennsylvania Press.

Goodwin, Jeffery, James Jasper, and Francesca Polleta. 2000. "Return of the Repressed." *Mobilization* 5: 65–71.

Greenbaum, Thomas L. 1997. *The Handbook for Focus Group Research.* Newbury Park, Calif.: Sage.

Gumperz, John J. 1982. *Discourse Strategies.* Cambridge: Cambridge University Press.

Hunt, Scott, Robert Benford, and David Snow. 1994. "Identity Fields: Framing Processes and the Social Construction of Movement Identities." In *New Social Movements,* edited by Enrique Laraña, Hank Johnston, and Joseph Gusfield, 185–208. Philadelphia: Temple University Press.

Johnston, Hank. 1995. "A Methodology for Frame Analysis: From Discourse to Cognitive Schemata." In *Social Movements and Culture,* edited by Hank Johnston and Bert Klandermans, 217–46. Minneapolis: University of Minnesota Press.

———. 1991. *Tales of Nationalism.* New Brunswick, N.J.: Rutgers University Press.

Johnston, Hank, and Aili Aarelaid-Tart. 2000. "Generations, Microcohorts and Long-Term Mobilization: The Estonian National Movement 1940–1991." *Sociological Perspectives* 43 (4): 671–98.

Klandermans, Bert. 1997. *The Social Psychology of Protest.* Oxford: Blackwell.

Krueger, Richard A. 1994. *Focus Groups.* Thousand·Oaks, Calif.: Sage.

Marullo, Sam, Ron Pagnucco, and Jackie Smith. 1996. "Frame Changes and Social Movement Contraction: U.S. Peace Movement Framing of the Cold War." *Sociological Inquiry* 66: 1–28.

Melucci, Alberto. 1984. *Altri Codici. Aree di movimento nella metropoli.* Bologna: Mulino.

———. 1989. *Nomads of the Present: Social Movements and Individual Needs in Contemporary Society.* Philadelphia: Temple University Press.

———. 1992. "Frontier Land: Collective Action between Actors and Systems." In *Studying Collective Action,* edited by Mario Diani and Ron Eyerman, 238–58. Newbury Park, Calif.: Sage.

Mooney, Patrick H., and Scott A. Hunt. 1996. "A Repertoire of Interpretations: Master Frames and Ideological Continuity in U.S. Agrarian Mobilization." *Sociological Quarterly* 37: 177–97.

Morgan, David L. 1998. *The Focus Group Guidebook.* Thousand Oaks, Calif.: Sage.

Oliver, Pamela A., and Hank Johnston. 2000. "What a Good Idea!: Frames and Ideology in Social Movement Research." *Mobilization* 5: 50–65.

Palmquist, Michael, Kathleen M. Carley, and Thomas A. Dale. 1997. "Applications of Computer-Aided Text Analysis: Analyzing Literary and Non-Literary Texts." In *Text Analysis for the Social Sciences: Methods for Drawing Statistical Inferences from Texts and Transcripts,* edited by Carl Roberts, 171–89. Hillsdale, N.J.: Lawrence Erlbaum Associates.

Popping, Roel. 1997. "Computer Programs for the Analysis of Texts and Transcripts." In *Text Analysis for the Social Sciences: Methods for Drawing Statistical Inferences from Texts and Transcripts,* edited by Carl Roberts, 209–21. Hillsdale, N.J.: Lawrence Earlbaum Associates.

Roberts, Carl, ed. 1997a. *Text Analysis for the Social Sciences: Methods for Drawing Statistical Inferences from Texts and Transcripts.* Hillsdale, N.J.: Lawrence Earlbaum Associates.

———. 1997b. "Semantic Text Analysis: On the Structure of Linguistic Ambiguity in Ordinary Discourse." In *Text Analysis for the Social Sciences: Methods for Drawing Statistical Inferences from Texts and Transcripts,* edited by Carl Roberts, 55–77. Hillsdale, N.J.: Lawrence Earlbaum Associates.

Rochon, Thomas R. 1998. *Culture Moves.* Princeton, N.J.: Princeton University Press.

Ryan, Charlotte. 1991. *Prime Time Activism.* Boston: South End Press.

Schank, Roger C., and Robert P. Abelson. 1977. *Scripts, Plans, Goals and Under-standing.* Hillsdale, N.J.: Lawrence Erlbaum Associates.

Seidel, John V., Rolf Kjolseth, and Elaine Seymour. 1988. *The Ethnograph. A User's Guide.* Corvallis, Oreg.: Qualis Research Associates.

Sewell, William. 1980. *Work and Revolution in France.* Cambridge: Cambridge University Press.

Shapiro, Gilbert, and John Markoff. 1998. *Revolutionary Demands: A Content Analysis of the Cahiers de Doléances of 1789.* Stanford, Calif.: Stanford University Press.

Shils, Edward. 1948. *The Present State of American Sociology.* Glencoe, Ill.: The Free Press.

Simon, Herbert W. 1990. *The Rhetorical Turn: Invention and Persuasion in the Conduct of Inquiry.* Chicago: University of Chicago Press.

Snow, David A., and Robert D. Benford. 1988. "Ideology, Frame Resonance, and Participant Mobilization." In *From Structure to Action: Comparing Social Movement Participation across Cultures,* edited by Bert Klandermans, Hanspeter Kriesi, and Sidney Tarrow, 197–218. Greenwich, Conn.: JAI Press.

———. 1992. "Master Frames and Cycles of Protest." In *Frontiers in Social Movement Theory,* edited by Aldon Morris and Carol McClurg Mueller, 133–55. New Haven, Conn.: Yale University Press.

———. 2000. "Mobilization Forum: Comment on Oliver and Johnston." *Mobilization* 5: 55–60.

Snow, David A., E. Burke Rochford Jr., Steven K. Worden, and Robert D. Benford. 1986. "Frame Alignment Processes, Micromobilization and Movement Participation." *American Sociological Review* 51 (4): 546–81.

Somers, Margaret. 1992. "Narrativity, Narrative Identity and Social Action: Rethinking English Working-Class Formation." *Social Science History* 16: 591–630.

Steinberg, Marc. 1998. "Tilting the Frame: Considerations of Collective Action Framing from a Discursive Turn." *Theory and Society* 27: 845–72.

———. 1999. *Fighting Words.* Ithaca, N.Y.: Cornell University Press.

Tannen, Deborah. 1993. "What's in a Frame?" In *Framing in Discourse,* edited by Deborah Tannen, 14–56. New York: Oxford University Press.

Touraine, Alain. 1981. *The Voice and the Eye.* Cambridge: Cambridge University Press.

Wuthnow, Robert. 1989. *Communities of Discourse: Ideology and Social Structure in the Reformation, the Enlightenment, and European Socialism.* Cambridge, Mass.: Harvard University Press.

4

Semi-Structured Interviewing in Social Movement Research

Kathleen M. Blee and Verta Taylor

"You used my words." That comment, uttered by a woman Verta Taylor interviewed for her research on a women's self-help movement after hearing Taylor lecture on the topic several years later, illustrates that interviews are one of the primary ways researchers actively involve their respondents in the construction of data about their lives. An interview is, quite simply, a guided conversation. But unlike most other conversations, the purpose of an interview is to elicit specific kinds of information (Denzin 1989; Lofland and Lofland 1995; Berg 1998). Interviews have always been central to social movement research as a means of generating data about the motives of people who participate in protest and the activities of social movement networks and organizations.

Interviews can be structured or semi-structured. In a *structured interview,* the interviewer uses a preestablished schedule of questions, typically referred to as a *questionnaire,* with a limited set of response categories, and asks each respondent the same set of questions in order to ensure comparability of the data. Structured interviews are generally used in survey research and opinion polling. In contrast to the rigidity of this type of interview, in a *semi-structured interview* the interviewer relies on an *interview guide* that includes a consistent set of questions or topics, but the interviewer is allowed more flexibility to digress and to probe based on interactions during the interview. Semi-structured interviews are particularly useful for understanding social movement mobilization from the perspective of movement actors or audiences. They provide greater breadth and depth of information, the opportunity to discover the respondent's experience and interpretation of reality, and access to people's ideas, thoughts, and memories in their own words rather than in the words of the researcher, but at the cost of a reduced ability to make systematic comparisons between interview responses.

In the field of social movements, semi-structured interviewing is a common methodological tool, especially useful in studies where the goals are exploration, discovery, and interpretation of complex social events and processes and when combined with participant observation and/or documentary methods (Morris 1984; Fantasia 1988; McAdam 1988; Staggenborg 1991; Whittier 1995; Robnett 1996; Ray 1999). But the semi-structured interview can also be used as a streamlined means of obtaining the rich, detailed data typically generated through field research without committing the investigator to prolonged involvement in the lives and activities of social movements (Blee 2001), or as a way of investigating research questions or propositions derived from social movement theory (Tarrow 1977; Rochon 1988; Meyer 1990; Dalton 1995; della Porta 1995).

We begin this chapter by exploring the usefulness of semi-structured interviewing in social movement research. Next, we address how the researcher's position influences semi-structured interviewing. We then draw from our own research on a variety of social movements to illustrate the major subtypes of semi-structured interviews: oral histories, life histories, key informant interviews, and focus groups. We conclude with a discussion of strategies for analyzing qualitative interview data and a consideration of ethical issues.

Why Use Semi-Structured Interviews?

Semi-structured interviewing methods have been used to great advantage in a wide variety of social movement studies. Such interviewing strategies have been particularly useful in research on loosely organized, short-lived, or thinly documented social movements and in studies that explore issues for which it is difficult to gather data through structured questionnaires, field observation, or documentary analysis. The following are some ways that semi-structured interviewing can be valuable in social movement research.

First, through interviewing methods, scholars can gain access to the motivations and perspectives of a *broader* and *more diverse* group of social movement participants than would be represented in most documentary sources. The propaganda and internal documents of social movement organizations, as well as the personal testimonies and recollections of participants, are often produced by official leaders and those who are articulate, educated, and confident about the historic importance of their movement activities. Additionally, the writings and statements of those who are prominent, wealthy, or influential in society are more likely to be recorded and preserved over time, which disproportionately favors men over women, higher-class participants over those from lower classes, and movement leaders or spokespersons over rank-and-file participants. Interviewing is one means of counteracting the biased availability of documentary material about social movements, allowing researchers access to members of social movements whose activities and understandings would otherwise be lost or filtered through the voices of others (Thompson 1988: 125). To illustrate, Robnett's (1996) interviews with African American women who were active in the civil rights movement uncovered a distinct form of grassroots leadership, which she terms "bridge leadership," carried out by women who were prevented from occupying formal leadership positions by the exclusionary practices of the Black church. This behind-the-scenes leadership that was central to mobilizing mass participation and creating solidarity in the civil rights movement was not acknowledged by earlier studies that relied on documents and interview samples constructed from archival sources generated by mainstream civil rights organizations and leaders (McAdam 1988; Morris 1984).

Any type of interviewing can be used to gain information from a broad range of social movement participants. In semi-structured interviewing, however, it is not only information but also themes and categories of analysis that are generated from the responses of diverse movement participants. The open-ended nature of such interviewing strategies makes it possible for respondents to generate, challenge, clarify, elaborate, or recontextualize understandings of social movements based on earlier interviews, documentary sources, or observational methods. This is particularly helpful for understanding little-studied aspects of social movement dynamics and for studying social movements that are difficult to locate, generate few documents, or have unclear or changing memberships. For example, interviews with members of gay employee groups and human relations officers in Fortune 1000 companies allowed Raeburn (2000) to discover the existence of an elaborate but submerged network of gay activists that has spearheaded the adoption of domestic partner benefits and other gay-inclusive policies in a growing number of American corporations.

Second, semi-structured interviewing strategies make it possible to scrutinize the semantic *context* of statements by social movement participants and leaders. It is often valuable to understand activists' talk in the context of wider social understandings and discourses. For example, a study of the British fascist movement found that some supporters made statements of racial tolerance and eschewed open expressions of prejudice yet still participated avidly in the agenda of the National Front (Cochrane and Billig 1984).

Social movement scholars often need to assess the context of motivations, beliefs, and attitudes of social movement participants for which it can be misleading to rely on the discrete statements and categorical answers generated by structured interviews or questionnaires (Potter and Wetherell 1988).

Third, semi-structured interviewing allow scrutiny of *meaning*, both how activists regard their participation and how they understand their social world. Social movement scholars have found such attention to subjective meaning particularly useful for understanding how social movement participants make sense of and justify their actions (Taylor and Whittier 1992; Jenness and Broad 1997). Thompson's (1988: 138) observation that "what the informant believes is indeed a *fact* (that is, the *fact* that he or she believes it) just as much as what 'really' happened" underscores the importance of understanding social movements from the point of view of their participants. Through semi-structured interviewing, researchers can gain insight into the individual and collective visions, imaginings, hopes, expectations, critiques of the present, and projections of the future on which the possibility of collective action rests and through which social movements form, endure, or disband. Through interviews with women in Italian revolutionary organizations, for example, Passerini was able to describe crucial, but intangible, motivations for women's participation in revolutionary social movements such as the women's expressed "illusion of a free and adventurous life" and their sense of being "worthless, unable to exist, outside the group" (Passerini 1992: 170).

Fourth, semi-structured interviews are able to provide a *longitudinal* window on social movement activism. They can capture the rhythms of social movement growth and decline, and participant involvement and withdrawal over time. In addition to providing information on how activists become involved when social movements are strong, as, for example, women's mobilization into the U.S. feminist movement in the 1970s, semi-structured interviews can illuminate how activists are mobilized or politically sustained during periods of relative quiescence or inactivity (Taylor 1989). Moreover, such interviewing strategies permit social movement researchers to probe complexities of cause and effect that are often neglected in cross-sectional data. Using interviewing to explore activists' lives over time, for example, scholars have challenged the assumption that involvement in social movements is necessarily preceded by beliefs consistent with the movement (Blee 2001).

Fifth, semi-structured interviews allow social movement scholars access to such nuanced understandings of social movement outcomes as the construction of collective and individual *identities* (Melucci 1989; Taylor 1996;

Whittier 1995). Rather than assuming that identities are simple reflections of background characteristics, scholars have become increasingly attentive to how social movement identities are formed and how they relate to social and political activism, as in Passerini's finding that female revolutionary identities are the result rather than the precipitator of involvement in political violence (Passerini 1992; Taylor and Whittier 1992). Such analyses require researchers to probe deeply into the self-understandings of respondents, listening carefully to how social movement participants describe themselves and their movement practices and to the emotional investments participants make in activist identities. To the extent that emotions are what connect activists to one another and that emotions play an important role in channeling collective action (Taylor 1996; Goodwin, Jasper, and Polletta 2000), intensive interviews are the best method for probing deep emotional issues.

Sixth, semi-structured interviews bring *human agency* to the center of movement analysis. Qualitative interviews are a window into the everyday worlds of activists, and they generate representations that embody the subjects' voices, minimizing, at least as much as possible, the voice of the researcher (Ragin 1994). Concepts that account for human agency—elite support, organization, indigenous networks, strategy, and rationality—are central to resource mobilization and political process approaches to social movements (Morris forthcoming). To the extent that qualitative interviews seek in-depth data that record subjects' own descriptions and understandings of events, they are particularly useful for discovering why the theory being tested may not fit the data well. For example, Morris's interviews (1984) with civil rights leaders revealed the various strategies used by Black activists as early as the 1910s to construct openings in the political system that facilitated the emergence of a mass-based civil rights movement in the mid-1950s. This information led Morris to a formulation of resource mobilization theory that assigns greater weight to the causal role that indigenous institutions (specifically, the Black church and Black colleges) play in mobilizing protest. Similarly, Staggenborg's (1991) interviews with pro-choice activists advanced social movement theory by demonstrating the importance of two distinct types of mobilizing structures—professional leadership and formalized organizational structures as well as indigenous, loosely organized grassroots networks—for the continued mobilization of the pro-choice movement following the legalization of abortion in 1973.

Finally, semi-structured interviewing allows scholars to scrutinize the ways in which messages of social movements are *received* by members, targeted recruits, intended audiences, and others (Gamson 1998). Studies of media reception find that people understand, assimilate, and use messages very differently, depending on their own identities, social positions, values, relationships to the broadcaster, and other factors. This finding suggests the importance of analyzing both the messages of social movements and their reception by intended audiences and others. Various types of in-depth interviewing allow social movement scholars to assess the complex ways in which movement ideas are interpreted both cognitively and emotionally by different audiences throughout the duration of a social movement.

Positioning the Researcher

All social research involves what Thorne (1978: 73) describes as a "problematic balance, a dialectic between being an insider, a participant in the world one studies, and an outsider, observing and reporting on that world." That balance is absolutely fundamental for collecting rich data in social movement research. Successful qualitative interviewing depends on the interviewer's understanding of their own position vis-à-vis participants in the social movement under study.

Insider versus Outsider Roles

Certainly, being a *participant* can facilitate access to a movement and promote the trust and rapport necessary for collecting sound data. Feminist scholars and others have shown the benefits of the interviewer and interviewee sharing a common standpoint before the interview takes place, emphasizing especially the way the ideological compatibility of the researcher and those being studied enhances rapport, empathy, and trust (Collins 1991). It would have been very difficult for Rupp, Taylor, and Whittier to conduct their research on lesbian feminist communities in the United States had they not been involved over a long period of time in the lesbian feminist community (Taylor and Whittier 1992). In describing the benefits of their sexual identities, Taylor and Rupp (1996) emphasize that it is not that insider status gave them a privileged vantage point from which they could write a more authentic account of the community, but rather that they had knowledge of ephemeral developments that might not appear in any written sources or oral histories and were able to interview some women—particularly radical lesbian separatists—who were only willing to speak to them because they knew they were lesbians and trusted that they would generate their analysis from a lesbian feminist standpoint.

Despite the obvious advantages of an insider position, being a nonparticipant also has benefits. *Outsiders* can provide valuable perspectives on the taken-for-granted assumptions of social movement participants. They may be better able than would participants to elicit full rationales of and extensive interpretive accounts from social movement participants (Snow, Bedford, and Anderson 1986). Yet nonparticipants can also have difficulty obtaining or retaining access to certain social movements. Consider what happened to Lofland when he was researching an aspiring new religion for his book *Doomsday Cult* (1977). When a local leader decided that Lofland's sociological interests, which he had expressed from the outset, were more sincere than his religious interests and that he was never going to convert to the religion, Lofland lost access to the group.

Movement Factions

Nearly all social movements contain factions. It would not be overstating the matter to say that the researcher who does not encounter differences of opinion, cliques, and conflicts in the course of doing field research on protest groups has probably failed to obtain accurate information about the movement being studied. In the data collection stage, the trick in handling factions and conflicts is to figure out how to remain neutral, because taking sides with one group most assuredly will mean being denied access to the other group. When it comes to dealing with highly factionalized movements, being a participant makes it less likely that the researcher can remain truly an outsider to disputes. One way to handle situations where complete neutrality is not possible is for the researcher to align with a single faction or group and be open about being "on your group's side" in any conflicts (Lofland and Lofland 1995). This is the standpoint Fantasia took in his study *Cultures of Solidarity* (1988), based on the modern labor movement. Fantasia was working at a small iron foundry when a wildcat strike occurred, a situation that allowed him to develop close personal relationships and sympathies with workers involved in labor struggles but that necessitated little contact with management.

For nonparticipants, it is particularly important to avoid making alignments with factions during the early stages of fieldwork when a researcher is seeking entrée and trying to build rapport with participants. In her study of a women's self-help movement, Taylor (1996) established her first contact with Depression After Delivery, the East Coast branch of the postpartum support movement, only to discover that there was another, West Coast group, Postpartum Support International, that had arisen earlier to address postpartum illness. Fortunately, this mistake did not jeopardize Taylor's initial access to either faction. However, the ongoing competition, differences of opinion, and personal conflicts between the leaders of these two groups were a minefield that had to be negotiated at every stage of the fieldwork. To maintain access to both groups, Taylor tried to make light of the conflict by

openly discussing the tendency of all social movements to give rise to factions, conflicts, and disagreements and providing concrete examples of the
divisions that plagued other social movements. She emphasized that she was
studying both sides and would uphold strict confidentiality regarding the
nature of each side's personal views.

Strategies for Conducting Effective Interviews

All types of semi-structured interviewing require the active and visible engagement of the researcher to create an authentic dialogue with interviewees.
Researchers make use of several strategies to encourage interviewees to provide comprehensive answers that will make rich qualitative data. The first
step is to construct an interview guide that takes into consideration the central aims of the research as well as the social and demographic characteristics
of the interview sample (see Lofland and Lofland 1995 and Berg 1998 for
more specific guidelines regarding the construction of semi-structured interview schedules). Both the order of the questions and the level of language
should be adapted to the sample so as to promote rapport between the interviewer and interviewee. As a general rule, it is best to end rather than begin a
semi-structured interview with a short written list of demographic questions, since the closed-ended format of such an instrument may discourage
the open-ended discussion, reflection, and rapport that make for an effective
qualitative interview. Perhaps most importantly, it is necessary at the outset
of an interview to clearly explain the purposes of the interview, the topics in
which the researcher is interested, and the depth of responses the researcher
is seeking (Rubin and Rubin 1995).

Once the interview begins, the interviewer should not feel too constrained by the guide. Follow-up questions, probes for clarification, and additional inquiries can be added when appropriate to the flow of the interview to encourage interviewees to provide more detailed responses, to give
examples, to return to an earlier point, to convey intangible feelings and
emotions, and to present a vivid sense of themselves and their experiences.
In some situations, interviewers give respondents a great deal of latitude to
direct the interview, and interject questions only when a particular avenue of
discussion has been fully explored. Other times, especially with reticent informants, researchers play a more active role in directing the interview, presenting new issues or additional factors for a respondent to consider. Some
social movement researchers report that the problem with interviewing
activists who are highly committed to a cause is not drawing them out but
rather keeping the interviewee focused on the type of information sought
(Taylor and Rupp 1991). In every case, interviewers must be sufficiently

directive to cover the topics being researched but at the same time allow unexpected responses by interviewees to direct the study toward different and
potentially useful topics.

Semi-structured interviews typically are conducted face-to-face with
one individual, but they can also take the form of face-to-face conversations
with groups (Melucci 1988) or can even be conducted by telephone, mail,
or self-administered questionnaires. Interviews can range in length from a
brief conversation to an interview that takes place over multiple sessions
that last several hours or even days. Because social movements strategies and
beliefs are likely to shift over time, interviews with social movement leaders
sometimes take place over several sessions (Taylor 1996).

In semi-structured interviewing, interviewees are chosen in a deliberate,
but rarely random, sampling process. Individuals are selected because they
have particular experiences in social movements, such as different levels of
activism or participation in different factions of a movement, rather than because their experiences are representative of the larger population. Sampling
may proceed in stages as a researcher's increasing insight into the group or
activist network under study raises new questions and requires additional or
different types of respondents. At each stage, sampling is guided by theoretical considerations rather than solely a concern with representativeness.
Sampling choices reflect the underlying questions and theories guiding the
research and the emergent understandings garnered in the study.

Rubin and Rubin (1995) suggest that sampling for qualitative interviews
follow two principles. First, sampling should strive for *completeness*. Social
movement researchers choose respondents who are knowledgeable about the
topic under investigation, and continue to add new interviewees until the
topic is saturated, that is, the interviews are garnering the same kinds of narratives and interpretations. Second, sampling should follow the principle of
similarity and *dissimilarity*. Interviewees are chosen to see how the interpretations or accounts of similarly situated respondents compare, as well as to
ascertain how those respondents with very different characteristics or in different circumstances differ. In her study of activists from the 1960s, Klatch
(1999) used both methods, relying on snowball sampling to identify a pool
of respondents who were former activists in a prominent "new left" group
and those who had been active in a major "new right" movement organization, and then selecting additional respondents to increase the diversity of
interviewees in terms of geography, ideologies, and organizational positions.

Taylor's (1996) study of a women's self-help movement illustrates
a number of advantages of semi-structured interviewing, including how
intensive interviews can maximize description, discovery, and the active

involvement of participants in social movement research, as well as how interviewing methods can be used to create new theoretical insights. Initially Taylor hypothesized that postpartum illness was connected to the cultural and oppressive aspects of motherhood. In an effort to understand women's experiences of postpartum illness from their own point of view, Taylor initially relied on fifty-two semi-structured interviews conducted with women who self-identified as having suffered "emotional problems" in the year following the birth or adoption of a child, and a comparison group of fifty women who had given birth to or adopted a child within the previous two years. When, in the course of conducting the interviews, Taylor discovered that a national self-help movement focused on postpartum depression was emerging and was playing a role in women's self-definitions, this opened the door for her to begin thinking about the role of social movements in the construction of illness. The open-ended nature of the interviews revealed that women use the term *postpartum illness* not in a strict clinical sense, but rather to communicate a complex of distressing emotions that violate gendered emotion norms of appropriate motherhood. Further, Taylor's interviewees pointed to women's organizing around postpartum illness as a means of questioning the male-dominated medical establishment and resisting the orthodox white and middle-class view of the selfless, devoted, glowing mother by conveying the variety of women's experiences of motherhood. As Taylor's focus shifted to the self-help movement mobilized around postpartum illness, she supplemented use of the interview method with a participatory action approach that incorporated both her own participation in the activist community and empowerment of the community by encouraging their involvement in the research process (see Naples and Clark 1996). She sought the advice of self-help activists in designing the study, identifying interviewees and obtaining other data sources, and interpreting results (Taylor 1998; Taylor 2000).

In providing an explanation of the postpartum self-help movement that links it to gendered norms and practices, Taylor also developed a theoretical framework that opened the way for research on such topics as the role of emotion in constructing the collective identities deployed by social movements, in defining the grievances that motivate activism, and in the distinctive rituals and cultural codes that characterize different social movement cultures (Taylor and Whittier 1992; Robnett 1996; Blee 1998; Goodwin, Jasper, and Polletta 2000; Taylor 2000). As this study illustrates, one of the main uses of qualitative interviewing strategies is to allow the researcher to explore social movement participants' views of reality in order to revise and extend existing theory (Burawoy et al. 1991).

Types of Semi-Structured Interviews

In addition to simple respondent interviews, there are four types of semi-structured interviews that are used extensively in social movement research. These involve somewhat different interviewing strategies, although many studies use elements of several approaches. Below we discuss interviewing strategies based on oral histories, life histories, key informant interviews, and focus group interviews.

Oral History Interviewing

Oral history interviews aim to elicit a robust or "thick" description of a historical period or situation from the perspective of those who lived through that time. Researchers use oral history interviewing to understand social movements of the past (Morris 1984) or past periods of current social movements (Rupp and Taylor 1987; Staggenborg 1991). This technique is particularly valuable for social movements for which little documentary evidence has been preserved, such as those populated by the poor, those that are marginal or fleeting, and those that operate out of public view or through informal networks. Oral history interviewing also may be the best source of information on certain historical aspects of social movements—such as the role of influential allies and other shifting political opportunities in movement success, perceptions and experiences of rank-and-file members, and the internal dynamics of movement organizations—for which there are few other sources.

The goal of oral history interviewing, aptly summarized by Portelli (1997: ix), is to scrutinize "[t]he relationship between private and public histories, experiences, and narratives." Oral history interviewing thus operates as a technique of bridging, seeking to understand social contexts through stories of individual experiences and to comprehend experiences of the past through stories told in the present. McAdam's (1988) in-depth study of the 1964 Freedom Summer campaign in Mississippi used oral histories to develop important propositions pertaining to the significance of social networks for mobilization and to the short-run and long-run biographical consequences of participation in high-risk social movement activism. Oral history interviewing projects are often based on multiple interviews, seeking perspectives and accounts from those in various social groups and social positions at the time.

Blee's (1991) study of women who joined the massive Ku Klux Klan of the 1920s suggests some of the strengths and weaknesses of research based on oral history interviewing. Most histories of the Klan based on documentary sources focus entirely on men members, assuming that women were minor, incidental players, mere window dressing behind which men carried out the real politics of hatred and bigotry. Blee's oral histories of former Klanwomen, however, tell otherwise. Women played a significant role in this Klan's vicious campaigns of rumor, boycotts, and intimidation of African Americans, Catholics, Jews, and other minorities.

Moreover, Blee's work illuminates how oral narratives can help develop new theoretical perspectives on social movements. Her oral histories revealed what documentary sources concealed: that many Klanwomen held complicated attitudes about gender and support for women's rights (the rights of white, native-born, and Protestant women only, of course) with rigid adherence to nationalism, racial hierarchies, and Christian supremacy. These understandings—which raise questions about the extent to which the personal beliefs of participants match the ideologies of social movement organizations—are inaccessible except through oral interviews.

On the other hand, Blee's work shows that oral accounts can be misleading if not used with proper caution. In their oral histories, Klanwomen related experiences with "clannish" Catholics and Jews, offensive African Americans, or troublesome immigrants to explain why they joined the Klan. But these are not likely to be true accounts of personal experience, as they mirror the stories circulated in Klan propaganda (Blee 1993). Moreover, the perspectives of Klan members provide little information on macro-level factors that influence social movement mobilization or outcomes. Thus it is important for social movement researchers to compare oral history accounts from differently situated persons and to compare oral histories with documentary and other historical data (Naples 1999: 10).

Life History Interviewing

In contrast to oral history interviewing's focus on historical events and processes, life histories in social movement research are more oriented toward understanding the activist experiences of individual respondents over time, or to exploring the interaction between macro events such as protests and social movements with individual actions and identities (Connell 1995; Rubin and Rubin 1995). In life history interviewing, the informant her/himself often is the subject of study, in addition to serving as an observer and narrator of the past. Scholars using life histories pay close attention to how individuals tell stories about their past and to how their accounts of social movement participation fit with other events in their lives. The desired outcome of a life history interview is a personal narrative, what Hart describes as "analogous to a story with a beginning, middle and end; with a plot; with main characters, scoundrels and paragons; and with background settings" (1992: 634). Life history interviews are particularly well suited to scholarship in which narrative is "both object and method of analysis" (Ewick and Silbey 1995: 198). This includes research on identity construction and on how actors justify their social movement activity.

Life history interviews can be fairly unstructured. The researcher simply asks the interviewee to tell the story of her/his life, how s/he came to participate in the movement, the nature of her/his participation, and how it influences who s/he is today. Interviewers generally do not intervene in the informant's life story narration to suggest particular directions or questions, but make comments to encourage more complete expositions of events, to develop aids to respondents' memories by pegging recollections to historical events or life transitions, or to direct respondents to finish relevant stories that were incompletely narrated (see Connell 1995: 89–92). Researchers then analyze the narrative to understand what events were selected as sufficiently significant or pivotal to respondents' lives to be included in their life stories and how respondents connect experiences in social movements in causal sequences.

In Blee's study of women members of the contemporary U.S. racist movement (1996, 2001), she used life history interviewing to explore how women—most from stable, secure, and politically moderate backgrounds— came to be committed to the violent and extremist agendas of organized racism. Blee elicited the women's own life stories rather than posing questions about their beliefs in order to avoid the parroting of organizational propaganda that is so typical of members of racist groups. Her decision to use life history interviewing was also shaped by her theoretically informed interest in understanding racist activism as a constructed identity whose meaning changes with increased exposure to a racist group.

A life history approach was critical in Blee's research for eliciting information about the intersection of identity and ideology in the racist movement. In this narrative, racist women used conspiratorial teachings of the racist movement to describe events and turning points in their lives, for example, describing the loss of a job or a failed love affair as the consequence of Jewish power. Over time, they identified more closely with racist group ideas until, as one woman declared, "It is not that I am in the Klan. It is that the Klan is in me."

Although revealing how social movement participants make sense of their lives, life histories need to be used with caution since they can be highly unreliable indicators of autobiographical change. For example, virtually all of Blee's racist informants spoke of their decision to participate in an organized racist group as the result of a "conversion." Yet it was clear from their responses to a structured questionnaire that few became converted to racism before joining a racist group. Most joined through a personal connection to a current member and only then learned intensely racist ways of thinking. Mills's (1940) insight that vocabularies of motive are often furnished "after the act" is a useful reminder that it is problematic to take at face value a respondent's articulated reasons for joining a social movement. For this reason, social movement researchers need to weigh life history accounts against data from other sources.

Key Informant Interviewing

Key informant interviewing, originally derived from anthropological fieldwork, is used to gain access to insider understandings of a social movement (Lofland and Lofland 1995: 61). In key informant interviewing, the researcher questions a few well-placed informants, sometimes over an extensive period of time, to obtain descriptive information that might be too difficult and time-consuming to uncover through more structured data-gathering techniques, such as surveys, or through conducting multiple semi-structured individual interviews (Tremblay 1957). The researcher might be interested, for example, in social psychological questions, such as how members are recruited to a movement, the level of commitment participants invest in a movement, the emotions associated with participation, the evolution of a movement's collective action frame, or the biographical consequences of a social movement. Or the research question might pertain to organizational considerations, such as a movement's structure, strategies, and culture (Johnston and Klandermans 1995; Staggenborg 1991; Taylor 1996).

The most important requirement for selecting a key informant is the interviewee's position or role in the social movement being studied. The criteria for choosing key informants are the amount of knowledge he or she has about a topic and his or her willingness to communicate with the researcher. Social movement researchers have used key informant interviewing to delineate the organizations and networks that comprise a movement (Rupp and Taylor 1987); obtain descriptive data about social movement strategies, cultures, and internal dynamics (Whittier 1995); and map out the relationships between social movement organizations in a larger social movement industry (Morris 1984; Fantasia 1988).

Key informant interviews played a major role in Rupp and Taylor's research documenting the continuity of the American women's movement between 1945 and the early 1960s, a period in which both the scholarly and popular literature assumed that the women's movement had died (Rupp and

Taylor 1987). The archival evidence pointed to a continuance phase during which the women's movement was not a broadly based grassroots movement but was instead a small movement of elite women, primarily white, middle- or upper-class, well-educated professional women who had developed a commitment to feminism in the early decades of the twentieth century and for whom "feminism" and "women's rights" had come to have a rather narrow application.

Although the National Endowment for the Humanities, which funded the research, suggested that Rupp and Taylor limit the use of interviews to key informants who might fill in gaps in the written record, they conducted interviews also to check the validity of sources and interpretations. They interviewed twelve women who occupied leadership positions in the movement. To the extent that they interviewed women to find out about the features of a movement that existed in the past, the interviews could also be considered oral histories. Since Rupp and Taylor needed to obtain large amounts of data from these women, the average interview lasted four to six hours. The interviews were structured conversations, with the "experts" doing most of the talking. Many of the women, who ranged in age from their mid-sixties to early eighties, were reliving major events of their pasts, some of them reflecting on them for the first time. In many cases, the interview became a social event involving food and general conversation, during which, with the tape recorder off, some of the most sensitive information—about conflicts between personalities and women's sexual orientation—was shared.

These key informant interviews were essential to Taylor's (1989) conceptualization of movement abeyance structures, which she defines as activist networks that provide organizational and ideological bridges between different upsurges of activism by the same challenging group. Certainly, the ties between the major suffrage organizations of the 1910s and the National Woman's Party, which was the core feminist organization in the post-1945 period, were clear from the archival evidence. However, it was only through interviews with three key informants that Rupp and Taylor uncovered the connections between the women's rights movement of the 1940s and 1950s and the resurgent women's movement of the 1960s.

As this example illustrates, the crucial distinction between key informant interviews and respondent interviews is that in key informant interviews the interviewee's experiences and motivations are not the unit of analysis; rather the interviewee is being asked to serve as an expert to inform the researcher about various aspects of the movement. At times, researchers treat interviewees as both informants and respondents, in which case it is advisable to group questions in the interview guide according to the role of the interviewee to enhance the flow of the interview (see the interview guide published in the appendix of Rupp and Taylor 1987 for an example). Although Rupp and Taylor did individual interviews of key informants, in some research it may be more efficient or productive to do group interviews with key informants (Melucci 1988).

Focus Group Interviewing

Focus group interviews are discussions between a small group of participants guided by a moderator to obtain information about a particular topic of interest to the researcher. There is some disagreement in the literature about the optimum size of a focus group; some writers recommend six to ten members as the ideal size (Morgan 1997), and others suggest that it is more effective to have smaller size (five to seven people) focus groups (Berg 1998). Focus group interviewing is relatively new to social movement research. Focus groups are less novel, however, to social movements, who sometimes use them to devise collective action frames and other strategies that reflect the interests of their constituencies.

There are several advantages to group interviews. In contrast to individual interviews, focus group sessions allow researchers to observe interactions about a discussion topic, which can illuminate the way social movement activists collectively frame issues and construct group solidarity. For example, Gamson (1992) held discussions among small groups of working-class people to probe the way people form collective opinions about current political issues, such as affirmative action and nuclear power. Focus groups "provide a window into how others think and talk" with the particular advantage of mimicking natural conversations and interactions, and creating an active, dynamic "process of sharing and comparing among participants" (Morgan 1997). Focus groups can also provide insight into the way a social movement's targets interpret the movement. To generate information about the way viewing audiences make sense of gay and lesbian activists' appearances on television talk shows, Gamson (1998) conducted focus groups with talk show audiences. Finally, like semi-structured individual interviews, focus groups allow the researcher to probe the meaning or interpretation of verbally expressed individual views, opinions, and experiences and to obtain naturally arising glimpses into people's biographies.

Focus groups are becoming a powerful tool among social movement scholars working from a "tripartite" model of cultural investigation in which data about texts, production, and reception are collected and the intersections between them analyzed. Focus group interviewing is particularly useful for studying the cultural outcomes of social movements, such as how people understand and incorporate the ideas, goals, practices, and identities of protest groups (Gamson 1992). To the researcher's disadvantage, however, focus groups provide only fragments of individuals' biographies. They are further limited by the fact that the data generated by this method are essentially group data derived from interactions that distort individual expressions of opinion. Nevertheless, used in combination with other types of data, such as individual interviews, participant observation, and documentary evidence, focus groups can produce data about the individual and collective social realities of social movement participants and the way audiences apprehend and interpret a movement.

As an offshoot of a larger project (Rupp and Taylor 2002), Taylor, Rupp, and Joshua Gamson are interested in drag performances as a form of protest that promotes some of the goals of the larger gay and lesbian movement. Treating drag performances as an example of the variety of cultural and discursive protest repertoires intended to enunciate new cultural codes, they are investigating the role that drag performances play in undermining gender and sexual dichotomies and fostering the construction of a collective identity by inscribing community among the seemingly diverse audiences (straight and gay, male and female) who attend the performances. Over a period of five months, they conducted ten focus groups ranging in size from four to twelve participants comprised of audience members who attended drag performances at a cabaret in a major resort area in the United States. Taylor, Rupp, and Gamson obtained participants by distributing invitations at the evening shows and conducted the focus group sessions in the cabaret the next evening prior to the show. Typically there were two researchers present at each focus group, one to facilitate the group and the other to observe the group, take field notes about group dynamics, and assist with tape-recording the groups and identifying voices later during transcription. The discussions were moderately structured to allow participants' interpretations to emerge through a process that resembles everyday conversation. Taylor, Rupp, and Gamson also administered a questionnaire to participants after the group session, covering basic demographic information as well as questions on income, education, religion, sexual identity, and political identification.

Taylor, Rupp, and Gamson had two rationales for using focus groups rather than individual interviews. First, they wanted to observe participants' interactions as they were asked to interpret collectively the meaning of the gender displays used in the performances. Second, they were interested in observing how participants would interact when placed in a situation that, like the shows themselves, required the construction of a collective identity that bridged different genders and sexualities. The focus groups were generally mixed in terms of class, race, education, income, and sexual identity. It was not unusual for a group to be composed of same-sex and heterosexual couples, working-class and upper-class individuals, and transsexual and transgendered participants, as well as people who embrace traditional gender and sexual categories. While the audience's diversity sometimes made it tricky to facilitate the groups, the heterogeneity of the groups and the interactions that took place in them revealed insights into the way the race, gender, class, ethnic, and sexual identities of audience members' shaped their political consciousness, as well as the complex negotiations that take place in the construction of a collective identity. Focus group participants were not only willing to express unconventional identities and sexual attractions, but they openly questioned other members of the group about their sexual identities and reactions to the gender performances of the drag queens. For example, in one group, which included two heterosexual-identified married couples and a lesbian couple, a married woman expressed her sexual attraction to one of the drag queens even though "I'm not a lesbian." In another, a heterosexual-identified married man admitted getting sexually aroused by one of the drag queens, who fondled him after he gave him a tip, and a gay male participant questioned him about how that led him to interpret his sexual orientation. Such openness was due in part to the sociopolitical climate of the drag shows—the drag queens deliberately use audience participation strategies in their shows to foster the contestation of gender categories and meanings and the construction of community—which spilled over to the discussion groups.

Although focus groups are just beginning to be used by students of social movements, they could become a powerful tool for generating data and building new theoretical perspectives about the cultural outcomes of social movements. In contrast to individual interviews, they allow the researcher to observe the group interactions that underlie the construction of collective identity, collective action frames, and the emotional dynamics involved in the creation of oppositional communities.

Interpreting and Analyzing Interview Data

In his textbook on social research, Ragin (1994) notes that a primary difference between quantitative and qualitative methods is that quantitative data-gathering techniques are data condensers: they condense data to reveal the big picture. Qualitative methods, by contrast, are data enhancers: they enhance data to make it possible to see aspects of their subjects that might otherwise be missed. If obtaining in-depth detailed knowledge of social movements is one of the strengths of qualitative interview studies, this is also one of its drawbacks. When it comes to analyzing qualitative interview data, researchers find that they spend more of their time engaged in file work than in fieldwork. This is one of the reasons that studies based on semi-structured interviews are generally based on a fairly small number of interviews.

In semi-structured interviewing, *analysis and interpretation are ongoing processes.* As opposed to quantitative research, which depends on the completion of data collection to begin analysis, designs based on semi-structured interviews require researchers to begin analyzing data as it is being collected, and these initial analyses may provoke changes in the study. Based on their interpretations of earlier interviews, for example, researchers decide whom to select for subsequent interviews, what questions to ask, and what additional topics are worth exploring. The interpretation of initial interviews can also reshape the direction of the study. Social movement researchers may find the need to study different groups or activist networks, or to interview other types of respondents (followers as well as leaders), or to alter the questions and topics raised in subsequent interviews to reflect the understandings garnered in early waves of interpretation of interviews. Such flexibility allows researchers both to incorporate new avenues of inquiry suggested by respondents' interviews and to abandon areas that turn out to be unproductive or to correct theoretical misrepresentations in the original research design (Rubin and Rubin 1995).

In analyzing semi-structured interviews, researchers make an effort to clarify concepts and categories through *successive, alternating waves of data collection and interpretation.* In this iterative process, the first set of interviews are allowed to be wide-ranging in scope, with broad questions and little effort to limit the direction of interviewees' narratives (see Rubin and Rubin 1995 for further discussion of this technique). Through these interviews, the researcher seeks to develop a sense of important themes and directions. By interpreting and analyzing these initial interviews, the range and topics of successive waves of interviewing and analysis can be narrowed to focus on particular themes or topics that emerge as central or critical. Both the questions addressed to subsequent interviewees and the sampling of later respondents reflect these more tightly focused topics and interpretations. Oral and life history interviews and focus groups may also be organized in this fashion or, as in the case of research that seeks broad information about a social movement or detailed understanding of participants' self-understandings, may remain very open-ended and free-ranging throughout the project. In either case, interpreting interview data involves working both up from data and down from existing ideas, propositions, concepts, theories, and hypotheses in the social movement literature.

While we have emphasized the advantages of semi-structured interviewing in social movement research, it is important to keep in mind that even the most nondirective interviews ultimately produce data derived from artificially constructed realities. Interviews are highly situational conversations, respondents can engage in retrospective interpretation, the interviewer can fail to establish the level of rapport necessary to obtain accurate data, and interviewees can conceal or distort information. Because semi-structured interviews, like every method, reveal slightly different facets of social life, most scholars of social movements use *a combination of several data-collection techniques* (typically interviews, observation, and documentary evidence) to investigate the same question. *Triangulation* is the term used to refer to the combination of different kinds of data (usually three). Triangulation both increases the amount of detail about a topic and counteracts threats to validity associated with any one of the single methods (Denzin 1989).

Researchers develop interpretations of interview data through systematic procedures of *coding, categorizing, and analyzing.* Qualitative methods are used in social movement research to uncover the essential features of a case or number of cases, and the qualitative researcher typically uses the case or cases to exemplify one or more general theoretical processes pertaining to social movements. Coding transcribed interview narratives depends, therefore, on the objectives of the study. Passages in interviews can be coded descriptively for topics such as movement goals and strategies, names of individuals or organizations, chronologies of protest events, style and emotional content of narration, and any other meaningful dimensions. Linking coded interview passages together makes it possible to trace the history of the movement, activists networks and organizations, biographies of leaders or members, and chronologies of events.

In analyzing data derived from semi-structured interviews, researchers also pay attention to more abstract issues, including underlying themes, central ideas, core meanings, and the structures of narration, and use these to reexamine interview transcripts to check that the data are being represented accurately (see Denzin 1989; Lofland and Lofland 1995; and Berg 1998 for more detailed discussion of techniques for analyzing qualitative interview data). By coding, categorizing, and analyzing semi-structured interviews, researchers thus develop concepts that are increasingly abstracted from, but consistent with, individual accounts. At the same time, qualitative methods are holistic, which means that aspects of the movements are viewed in the context of whole movements. And, in analyzing the data, qualitative researchers make every effort to anchor their interpretations in the everyday understandings and language of their subjects.

Until recently, the process of coding, categorizing, and analyzing was largely done by hand, but the availability of computerized software packages has reshaped how scholars manage and interpret qualitative interviewing data. A detailed description of computer software goes beyond the scope of this chapter, but there are two common types of computerized data handling for semi-structured interviews. (An excellent overview of relevant software is found in Dohan and Sanchez-Jankowski 1998.) First, many word-processing programs make it possible to code efficiently qualitative interviewing data by allowing researchers to search for key words or word patterns, although retrieval procedures for this type of coding can prove cumbersome (Richards and Richards 1994). Second, there are a number of computerized software packages written specifically for managing and analyzing qualitative data such as that generated by semi-structured interviewing. One of the more popular of these is NUDIST, which can manage various kinds of text data such as interview transcripts, allowing text to be coded, indexed, retrieved, and grouped through a number of searching methods, including Boolean, context, proximity, and sequencing searches.

Conclusion

In recent years scholars have made good use of semi-structured interviewing techniques to illuminate new areas of social movement mobilization, develop new theories and questions about social movements, and understand a broad range of social movement types. These methods offer significant advantages for emerging research agendas on the cultural and emotional dynamics of social movements and on the construction of meanings and identities by social movement participants. They offer the potential for much-needed longitudinal studies of social movements and their organizations and members. Triangulation of methods in social movement research offers particular promise as a means of increasing analytic comprehensiveness and complexity. For example, semi-structured interviewing can be combined with research strategies that allow more systematic comparisons between comparable response categories, such as structured questionnaires or network analysis to link participants' descriptions of meaning with characteristics of social movement organizations. Similarly, the combination of participant observation or document analysis with semi-structured interviewing can be a useful means of analyzing the specific contexts within which participants in social movements construct their understandings of these movements.

It is important to consider the ethical obligations of researchers when employing semi-structured interviewing. Some social movement researchers have a preference for data generated from qualitative interviews because they lend themselves to the construction of representations of social movements couched in the language that ordinary people use to observe and describe their world. However, researchers who solicit the stories of social movement participants—perhaps to a greater extent than researchers who rely on observational or documentary methods—can find themselves privy to very intense and private emotions and experiences. The scholarly obligation to protect research subjects from harm may necessitate guarantees of confidentiality that ensure that material gained in interviews will not be made public in such a way that individuals can be identified (Blee 1999). It may also involve broader and more vague measures, such as taking care that the process of interviewing itself does not exploit the emotional vulnerabilities of respondents simply to gain data or does not provoke unnecessarily painful or troubling emotions or memories on the part of the interviewee (Taylor 1996). The ethical obligation of scholars who operate according to feminist or other emancipatory principles may extend to including interviewees as research collaborators, even to according interviewees input into the interpretation of their stories. Such efforts seek to reduce the interpretive authority of researchers and expand those of participants in the analysis of social movements.

Social movements scholars who use semi-structured interviewing techniques must present interviews in sufficient detail that a reader can judge the strengths and limitations of their interpretation. That means taking care to avoid using dramatic data that may not be the most significant. Moreover, the presentation of such work should be consistent with inconsistencies in the interviews, which, if possible, should be explained, not omitted. To the extent that social movement researchers often focus on interpreting historically or culturally significant events, a high-quality analysis should communicate to the readers a full and accurate feel for the specific context and everyday world of the activist group, no matter how atypical (see Rubin and Rubin 1995). And, finally, qualitative researchers should strive for a balance between clarification of the underlying character of the movement under investigation and the theoretical concepts it exemplifies. These principles can be used to guide social movement interviewing projects toward a rich and complex presentation of research.

Note

For their insightful comments and criticisms, we would like to thank Bert Klandermans, Leila Rupp, Suzanne Staggenborg, and Mayer Zald.

114 BLEE AND TAYLOR

References

Berg, Bruce L. 1998. *Qualitative Research Methods for the Social Sciences.* Boston: Allyn and Bacon.

Blee, Kathleen M. 1991. *Women of the Klan: Racism and Gender in the 1920s.* Berkeley: University of California Press.

———. 1993. "Evidence, Empathy and Ethics: Lessons from Oral Histories of the Klan." *Journal of American History* 80: 596–606.

———. 1996. "Becoming a Racist: Women in Contemporary Ku Klux Klan and Neo-Nazi Groups." *Gender and Society* 10: 680–702.

———. 1998. "Managing Emotion in the Study of Right-Wing Extremism." *Qualitative Sociology* 21: 381–99.

———. 1999. "The Perils of Privilege." *Law and Social Inquiry* 24: 993–96.

———. 2001. *Inside Organized Racism: Women in the Hate Movement.* Berkeley: University of California Press.

Burawoy, Michael, Alice Burton, Ann Arnett Ferguson, Kathryn J. Fox, Joshua Gamson, Charles Kurzman, Leslie Salzinger, Joseph Schiffman, and Shiori Ui. 1991. *Ethnography Unbound: Power and Resistance in the Modern Metropolis.* Berkeley: University of California.

Cochrane, Raymond, and Michael Billig. 1984. "I'm Not National Front Myself, But . . ." *New Society* 17 (May): 255–58.

Collins, Patricia Hill. 1991 "Learning from the Outsider Within: The Sociological Significance of Black Feminist Theory." In *Beyond Methodology: Feminist Scholarship as Lived Research,* edited by M. M. Fonow and J. A. Cook, 35–59. Bloomington: Indiana University Press.

Connell, R. W. 1995. *Masculinities.* Berkeley: University of California Press.

Dalton, Russell J. 1995. "Strategies of Partisan Influence: West European Environmental Groups." In *The Politics of Social Protest: Comparative Perspectives on States and Social Movements,* edited by J. C. Jenkins and B. Klandermans, 296–323. Minneapolis: University of Minnesota Press.

della Porta, Donatella. 1995. *Social Movements, Political Violence and the State: A Comparative Analysis of Italy and Germany.* Cambridge: Cambridge University Press.

Denzin, Norman K. 1989. *The Research Act: A Theoretical Introduction to Sociological Methods.* Englewood Cliffs, N.J.: Prentice-Hall.

Dohan, Daniel, and Martin Sanchez-Jankowski. 1998. "Using Computers to Analyze Ethnographic Field Data: Theoretical and Practical Considerations." *Annual Review of Sociology* 24: 477–98.

Ewick, Patricia, and Susan S. Silbey. 1995. "Subversive Stories and Hegemonic Tales: Toward a Sociology of Narrative." *Law and Society Review* 29: 197–226.

Fantasia, Rick. 1988. *Cultures of Solidarity: Consciousness, Action, and Contemporary American Workers.* Berkeley: University of California Press.

Gamson, Joshua. 1998. *Freaks Talk Back: Tabloid Talk Shows and Sexual Nonconformity.* Chicago: University of Chicago Press.

Gamson, William. 1992. *Talking Politics.* New York: Cambridge University Press.

Goodwin, Jeff, James M. Jasper, and Francesca Polletta. 2000. "Return of the Repressed: The Fall and Rise of Emotions in Social Movement Theory." *Mobilization* 5: 65–84.

Hart, Janet. 1992. "Cracking the Code: Narrative and Political Mobilization in the Greek Resistance." *Social Science History* 16: 631–68.

Jenness, Valerie, and Kendal Broad. 1997. *Hate Crimes: New Social Movements and the Politics of Violence.* New York: Aldine de Gruyter.

Johnston, Hank, and Bert Klandermans, eds. 1995. *Social Movements and Culture.* Minneapolis: University of Minnesota Press.

Klatch, Rebecca. 1999. *A Generation Divided: The New Left, The New Right, and the 1960s.* Berkeley: University of California Press.

Lofland, John. 1977. *Doomsday Cult: A Study of Conversion, Proselytization, and Maintenance of Faith.* New York: Irvington.

Lofland, John, and Lyn H. Lofland. 1995. *Analyzing Social Settings: A Guide to Qualitative Observation and Analysis.* 3d ed. Belmont, Calif.: Wadsworth.

McAdam, Doug. 1988. *Freedom Summer.* New York: Oxford University Press.

Melucci, Alberto. 1988. "Getting Involved: Identity and Mobilization in Social Movements." In *From Structure to Action: Comparing Social Movement Research across Cultures,* edited by Bert Klandermans, Hanspeter Kriesi, and Sidney Tarrow, 329–48. Greenwich, Conn.: JAI Press.

———. 1989. *Nomads of the Present: Social Movements and Individual Needs in Contemporary Society.* Philadelphia: Temple University Press.

Meyer, David S. 1990. *A Winter of Discontent: The Nuclear Freeze and American Politics.* New York: Praeger.

Mills, C. Wright. 1940. "Situated Actions and Vocabularies of Motive." *American Sociological Review* 5: 404–13.

Morgan, David. L. 1997. *Focus Groups as Qualitative Research.* 2d ed. Newbury Park, Calif.: Sage.

Morris, Aldon D. 1984. *The Origins of the Civil Rights Movement: Black Communities Organizing for Change.* New York: Free Press.

———. Forthcoming. "Reflections on Social Movement Theory: Criticisms and Proposals. *Contemporary Sociology.*

Naples, Nancy A. 1999. *Grassroots Warriors: Activist Mothering, Community Work, and the War on Poverty.* New York: Routledge.

Naples, Nancy A., with Emily Clark. 1996. "Feminist Participatory Research and

Empowerment: Going Public as Survivors of Childhood Sexual Abuse." In *Feminism and Social Change,* edited by H. Gottfried, 160–86. Urbana: University of Illinois Press.

Passerini, Luisa. 1992. "Lacerations in the Memory: Women in the Italian Underground Organizations." *International Social Movement Research* 4: 161–212.

Portelli, Alessandro. 1997. *The Battle of Valle Giulia: Oral History and the Art of Dialogue.* Madison: University of Wisconsin Press.

Potter, Jonathan, and Margaret Wetherell. 1988. "Accomplishing Attitudes: Fact and Evaluation in Racist Discourse." *Text* 8: 51–68.

Raeburn, Nicole C. 2000. "The Rise of Lesbian, Gay, and Bisexual Rights in the Workplace." Ph.D. diss., Ohio State University.

Ragin, Charles C. 1994. *Constructing Social Research.* Thousand Oaks, Calif.: Pine Forge Press.

Ray, Raka. 1999. *Fields of Protest: Women's Movements in India.* Minneapolis: University of Minnesota Press.

Richards, Thomas J., and Lyn Richards. 1994. "Using Computers in Qualitative Research." In *Handbook of Qualitative Research,* edited by Norman K. Denzin and Yvonna S. Lincoln, 445–63. Thousand Oaks, Calif.: Sage.

Robnett, Belinda. 1996. "African-American Women in the Civil Rights Movement, 1954–1965: Gender, Leadership, and Micromobilization." *American Journal of Sociology* 101: 1661–93.

Rochon, Thomas R. 1988. *Mobilizing for Peace: The Antinuclear Movements in Western Europe.* Princeton, N.J.: Princeton University Press.

Rubin, Herbert J., and Irene S. Rubin. 1995. *Qualitative Interviewing: The Art of Hearing Data.* Thousand Oaks, Calif.: Sage.

Rupp, Leila J., and Verta Taylor. 1987. *Survival in the Doldrums: The American Women's Rights Movement, 1945 to the 1960s.* New York: Oxford University Press.

———. 2002. *What Makes a Man a Man: Drag Queens at the 801 Cabaret.* Chicago: University of Chicago Press.

Snow, David A., Robert Bedford, and Leon Anderson. 1986. "Fieldwork Roles and Informational Yield: A Comparison of Alternative Settings and Roles," *Urban Life* 14 (4): 377–408.

Staggenborg, Suzanne. 1991. *The Pro-Choice Movement.* New York: Oxford University Press.

Tarrow, Sidney G. 1977. *Between Center and Periphery: Grassroots Politicians in Italy and France.* New Haven, Conn.: Yale University Press.

Taylor, Verta. 1989. "Social Movement Continuity: The Women's Movement in Abeyance." *American Sociological Review* 54: 761–75.

———. 1996. *Rock-a-by Baby: Feminism, Self-Help and Postpartum Depression.* New York: Routledge.

————. 1998. "Feminist Methodology in Social Movements Research." *Qualitative Sociology* 21: 357–79.

————. 2000. "Emotions and Identity in Women's Self-help Movements." In *Self, Identity, and Social Movements,* edited by Sheldon Stryker, Timothy J. Owens, and Robert W. White. Minneapolis, University of Minnesota Press.

Taylor, Verta, and Leila J. Rupp. 1991. "Researching the Women's Movement: We Make Our Own History, But Not Just as We Please." In *Beyond Methodology: Feminist Scholarship as Lived Research,* edited by Mary M. Fonow and Judith A. Cook, 119–32. Bloomington: Indiana University Press.

————. 1996. "Lesbian Existence and the Women's Movement: Researching the 'Lavender Herring.'" In *Feminism and Social Change: Bridging Theory and Practice,* edited by Heidi Gottfried, 143–59. Urbana: University of Illinois Press.

Taylor, Verta, and Nancy Whittier. 1992. "Collective Identity in Social Movement Communities: Lesbian Feminist Mobilization." In *Frontiers in Social Movement Theory,* edited by Aldon Morris and Carol McClurg Mueller, 104–29. New Haven, Conn.: Yale University Press.

Thompson, Paul. 1988. *The Voice of the Past: Oral History.* 2d ed. Oxford: Oxford University Press.

Thorne, Barrie. 1978. "Political Activist as Participant Observer: Conflicts of Commitment in a Study of the Draft Resistance Movement of the 1960s." *Symbolic Interaction* 2: 73–88.

Tremblay, Marc-Adélard. 1957. "The Key Informant Technique: A Non-Ethnographic Application." *American Anthropologist* 59: 688–701.

Whittier, Nancy E. 1995. *Feminist Generations: The Persistence of the Radical Women's Movement.* Philadelphia: Temple University Press.

5

Seeing Structure Happen: Theory-Driven Participant Observation

Paul Lichterman

The group I had been studying wanted to celebrate a victory, and I wanted to help. For months, members of Airdale Citizens for Environmental Sanity (ACES) had stood unassumingly outside of discount drugstores and, ever so politely, invited weekend shoppers to sign petition sheets on ironing boards—an appropriately homey touch in a family-oriented suburban town. Being an activist in Airdale was scary, and ACES members hoped their neighbors would not lump them together with young, loud protestors from the urban center. ACES managed to coax ten thousand Airdalers to sign the petition against a toxic waste incinerator that Microtech wanted to build. Microtech eventually shelved the plan. ACES threw itself a party. The loyal participant-observer brought along a homemade strawberry pie, hoping to show ACES how much he appreciated them both for preserving environmental sanity and for letting him tag along with the group.

The pie contributed more humor than culinary grace. One activist ribbed me mercilessly that its crust broke our plastic forks. The party table's centerpiece was a square sheet cake decked out in day-glo yellow and white frosting: A conventional dessert from a local grocery store had been quite good enough for this celebration. The pie, on the other hand, was becoming an unwelcome conversation-starter, and the conversation two men started having about it in front of me ended in a long exchange about the muscle cars that the two of them used to fix up when they were younger. I was getting the picture: Bringing a homemade strawberry pie made me look out of place—too precious, too unconventional, maybe even gender bending.

Participant observation promises many insights to a student of activism who does not mind being offended and can live with the possibility of offending others frequently, if inadvertently. The pie episode turned out to be valuable for more than ethnographic color; it helped me grapple with the central puzzle of my research on ACES (see Lichterman 1996): How could such an informal, mild-mannered group sustain activism so long in such a threatening milieu? Activism in a suburban town like Airdale, I was learning, depended on a style of activism different from the culturally unconventional (or less charitably, "politically correct") style often associated with grassroots activists. These suburban activists were fighting the same battles as their tie-dyed, sandal-clad urban allies. But they did not politicize their personal lives as much. They did not make a virtue of eating organic or homemade foods instead of standard grocery store fare. They did not seem to think it was sexist for the men at a party to go off in a corner to talk man-talk. They did not hash out political controversies for fun; they did not talk about their activism when they did not "have to." The differences between ACES and the other environmental activists I had been studying had implications for larger questions—about the cultural underpinnings of social movements, about putative differences between "newer" and "older" forms of activism, about underappreciated differences in styles of political commitment. This chapter will outline a participant-observation methodology that we can use to address theoretical questions that matter far beyond the particular groups we study.

There is more than one way to do participant observation. Instead of one, exclusive model for a "good" research design, participant observation encompasses several, evolving models of inquiry. Participant observation lends itself much less to standardized concepts, instruments, and measures than other research methods (Harper 1992; see also Snow and Anderson 1991). So at the very outset, participant-observers must make choices: How do we know what to look for when we are "in the field"? What counts as a finding? How do we know a study is finished? When we answer these questions, we do not typically rely on the hypothesis testing and statistical logic familiar to many sociologists. We must be explicit, then, about the logics we do follow. Doing participant observation means deciding how to conceptualize what we see and hear in the field, and not simply applying a set of "nuts and bolts" observation techniques.

For these reasons, this chapter highlights a logic of inquiry and conceptualization. My presentation is greatly indebted to two sets of writings on participant observation. Burawoy's statements on the "extended case method" (Burawoy 1998; Burawoy et al. 1991) define the main logic of inquiry that this chapter will explicate. The name of this logic is a bit confusing. The "extended case method" is not a logic of inquiry for case studies in general—that is a large and separate topic.[1] Rather, it is a method for treating "cases" in a particular way. It "extends" them by synthesizing participant observation evidence with theories of large social or cultural forces. My presentation will also fold in a few analytic techniques originally developed for a different logic, that of Glaser and Strauss's constant-comparative method (Glaser and Strauss 1967; Strauss 1987; Strauss and Corbin 1991). I will borrow a few of their terms, occasionally renaming them for simplicity's sake. In selectively combining these techniques with the extended case method, I part with some of Burawoy's argument about the distinctiveness of extended case methodology.[2] But to emphasize, I draw on Glaser and Strauss only to show how a few of their analytic techniques can assist a project that follows extended case logic.

In what follows, I define participant observation and briefly distinguish "field-driven" from "theory-driven" versions of the method. This section describes the kinds of research questions that each version can address, and the strengths and weaknesses of each. Then I introduce the theory-driven, extended case method that this chapter will highlight in detail. Before going on to illustrate the logic of the extended case method, I offer some brief guidance on establishing relations with the people we study, and making initial observations. The next sections introduce the sequence of steps in a project that follows the extended case method: starting with a theme and some expectations, discovering "problems in the field," and making a theoretical contribution with evidence from the field. Examples from my study of environmental activists will illustrate the process. The last two sections treat the special value, and the distinctive limits, of participant-observation research. The first shows how participant observation is especially useful for uncovering everyday meanings in movements. The other section points out the kinds of questions that participant observation, especially the theory-driven version, would not address well. The section describes how a participant-observer's focus on everyday life may address some researchers' questions about the impacts of movements. And it suggests ways to enhance a project by using other methods in conjunction with participant observation. A few parting words highlight the main themes in the chapter.

What Is Participant Observation?

Participant observation is research in which the researcher observes and to some degree participates in the action being studied, as the action is happening. Participant-observers study one or more *field sites*. A field site may or may not have one geographical location. Commonly, participant-observers in social movements choose to study an activist group that has regular meetings at a regular time and place; the group and its office are easy to identify as a "site." But we can imagine a team of direct action protestors who communicate mainly through phone trees and the Internet, who organize to block entrances to business parks all over a county; the participant-observer who talks to other researchers about the team refers to the team as one "site," in a project that may also include other sites. The participant-observer's prime source of evidence about a site is *field notes*. Field notes are detailed accounts of people, places, interactions, and events that the researcher experiences as a participant-observer.

Sociologists often refer to "qualitative methods," having in mind both participant observation and interviewing, and sometimes other methods. It is easy to associate participant observation and interviewing closely because qualitative research projects often depend on both methods in varying degrees. Both methods open a window on lived experience, on the meanings embedded in everyday life, on motives and emotions. At the same time, each form of research produces a different kind of evidence with its own strengths and weaknesses. Each will be more appropriate for some research questions than others, a point to which I will return at the end. Participant observation is distinct from other methods because it produces the most direct evidence on action as the action unfolds in everyday life.

Sociologists value participant observation for different reasons. For some researchers, the method produces rich descriptive accounts of everyday life. For others, participant observation has been the prime method for building on the edifice of interactionist sociology. It shows us how groups shape selves, how definitions of situations shape groups. Outside the interactionist tradition, participant observation has taught researchers about how organizational dynamics shape individual behavior. Participant-observers can learn a great deal about how different groups—men and women, for instance—respond to organizational rewards and sanctions, even without an intensive focus on the qualities of interaction. Of course, some sociologists have done preliminary participant observation for projects that rest mostly on interview or survey evidence (e.g., Luker 1984.). But this chapter treats participant observation as a primary method of inquiry, an end in itself. And I will highlight participant observation work that focuses closely on interaction. Doing so, I still need to distinguish between two modes of the method.

Two Modes of Participant Observation

Field-Driven Participant Observation

Many treatments, and many criticisms, of participant observation speak mainly to what I will call the "field-driven" mode of the method. Field-driven participant-observers write up projects intended to elucidate an empirical unit or subject matter—a labor union, a network of antinuclear affinity groups, a gay community—given that the boundaries of the subject matter may take work to discern. A given subject matter "in the field" directs the goals of research. A "theory-driven" project, in contrast, aims to address a theory, rather than to elucidate a substantive topic or field site with perhaps several theories. In theory-driven participant observation, a field site or subject matter is meaningful only in the categories of a theory, from the very beginning.[3]

In the conventional view, participant observation studies are valuable for describing relatively small groups or local settings, or helping us understand how groups and settings shape people's thoughts, feelings, and interactions. This view applies especially to the field-driven mode. On this view, participant observation can advance social movement scholarship at the interactional (micro) and organizational (meso) levels of analysis. It helps researchers ask "how" questions, and to distinguish different interactional processes—different "hows."

From the predominant reference point of statistical logic, social scientists often identify two limitations of participant observation. And like the strengths just named, these limitations are best understood in relation to the field-driven mode.[4] One is that participant observation evidence seems hard to generalize beyond the site under study. How can we know that activists in Airdale are like environmental activists elsewhere, or suburban activists elsewhere?[5] A second limitation arises from the level of analysis that social scientists have often imputed to the method. Participant observation, goes the claim, is appropriate for an interactionist or organizational focus but will tell us little about social-structural forces or historical change.

Theory-Driven Participant Observation: The Extended Case Method

This chapter emphasizes theory-driven participant observation in part because the theory-driven mode can answer back to these criticisms of the field-driven mode. Also, a theoretically driven study can offer powerful insights on questions that interest scholars who may not be concerned otherwise with the participant-observer's subject of study. Many social movement scholars have wanted to integrate macro and micro levels of analysis.[6] Here I will outline a type of theory-driven participant observation that advances just that goal.

The extended case method bids a participant-observer in the field "to extract the general from the unique, to move from the 'micro' to the 'macro'" (Burawoy 1998: 5). The researcher "extends" his view of a case by theorizing it as a very specific instance of social and cultural structures or institutional forces at work.[7] Participant-observers make these analytic moves into the macro by building on preexisting theory.

The extended case method highlights everyday processes—the "how"—just as field-driven participant observation does, but for different purposes. In the extended case method, we want to learn, ultimately, "how" institutional forces, social and cultural structures, shape action in our particular field sites. We conceive our groups and settings in macro-sociological categories, aiming to elucidate those categories, rather than elucidating a discrete, empirical subject matter as an end in itself. We study a group's collective identity, for instance, not to develop a general theory of collective identity but to theorize better how institutional forces enable and constrain the collective identities that a group affirms. Or to use the example I will elaborate throughout this chapter, my ultimate goal in studying ACES was not to develop a new theory of "suburban activism." My goal was to refine an existing, macro-level theory of American political culture by understanding ACES as an instance of that culture at work. I conceptualized my discoveries in the field—like the discovery of suburban activism—in relation to this larger theoretical goal.

To "extract the general from the unique," as Burawoy puts it, participant-observers must start with preexisting theories of the macro. We write theory into our field notes, from the very start. To practice the extended case method, we must accept the notion that we always are bringing tacit, if not explicit, concepts to even our first observations in the field. Our observations will never be completely raw, innocent of concepts. So we try to make our conceptual presuppositions as explicit as possible, instead of trying to rid ourselves of them altogether. We part with the assumption in some writings on participant observation that data emerge spontaneously from pure observation. Certainly, we must stand ready to reject our initial theories in light of our particular sites—only to propose revised, better theories. The empirical field of observation is central just as it is in field-directed participant observation, but in this theory-driven mode, we keep in mind that a field site could always get theorized in many different ways. The interaction about my pie was interesting because it helped me grasp a certain style of activism, and beyond that an enduring cultural structure. Another researcher might have conceptualized the pie incident differently, for a project about gender and politics, for instance. Neither focus would be more intrinsic to the site. Theoretical goals explicitly drive the observing and conceptualizing, and they determine what the "subject" is in our site.

In the extended case method, discoveries happen when repeated observation reveals an "anomaly" (Burawoy et al. 1991) that a preexisting theory would misapprehend, or miss altogether.[8] Having begun with explicit pre-suppositions and theories, the participant-observer stands ready for surprises in the field that challenge conceptual starting points. In this logic, discoveries in the field always get made in relation to one or more theories. And the ultimate conceptual goal of the extended case method is to *reconstruct pre-existing theory*, so that the general theory can accommodate the particular, the anomalous case along with the other cases the theory rests on already. In my study, ACES was anomalous in relation to a theory of political commitment that holds that individualism weakens commitment and turns people away from public life. ACES was an enduring, successful group that brooked a lot of individualism. I reconstructed the theory by arguing that individualism has different consequences for commitment in different settings, and that the consequences are not always bad. Conceiving an anomaly is perhaps the greatest challenge of the extended case method, and below I will outline a coding process we can use to advance the quest.

Social movement studies that incorporate key aspects of case extension logic, implicitly if not explicitly, include Fantasia's study of working-class consciousness and activism (1988), Ginsburg's study of pro-life and pro-choice activists (1989), and Ray's study of Indian women's movements (1998). Fantasia, for instance, began his study with an eye toward theories that define class consciousness as a set of ideas that American workers seemingly lack, ideas that survey research can tap. His research encountered anomalies in relation to this understanding of class consciousness and its supposed absence. Fantasia extended his view of his cases outward, conceiving the particular strikes and labor-organizing campaigns he studied as shaped by a larger context of national labor policy and corporate management strategies. With this view of his cases, Fantasia reconstructed the static, idea-centered notion of class consciousness, arguing that we should conceive of dynamic "cultures of solidarity." The concept highlights a group's or community's shared, temporary sense of working people's unity that a participant-observer may capture even if survey questions do not. Such cultures are oppositional; by definition, they emerge against and are shaped by a wider context of corporate and state power.

With the logic of the extended case method, then, participant-observers can speak back to the criticisms of participant observation that have usually assumed a field-driven version of the method. In regard to the criticism that participant observation suits micro-level questions only, the extended case method makes participant-observers into students of structural and institutional realities as well as interactional dynamics, simultaneously. As for the problem of generalization, we generalize our findings to other sites in that those findings are theoretical as well as empirical. They are conceived in the (now improved) categories of a theory that describes macro forces at work in many sites. In the same vein, an extended case project may even address causal questions, because it can show *how* the causal relations work, through everyday relationships we study in the field.

The weaknesses of theory-driven participant observation are the field-driven mode's strengths. It can become too easy to give short shrift to the diversity of people and situations in our site when our eyes are, ultimately, on a theoretical prize. We might press on with a conceptual argument when we have but few empirical instances of it in our field notes. We might miss a pattern or misconstrue an absence of a pattern that is itself theoretically valuable. I learned that ACES members, for instance, did not agree on what would count as a "good activist." Though it seemed an inconvenience for my theoretical categories at first, this diversity became a major focus of the study.

We need to balance theoretical relevance with empirical groundedness and interpretive validity. Mindful of this challenge, now we can examine the stages of a theory-driven project in detail. But first I want to discuss the initial steps that any participant-observer of social movements, field-driven or theory-driven, should take.

Getting Started: How Do I Get Activists to Let Me Study Them?

Many handbooks on participant observation discuss the challenges of getting permission to study people; I will not review this literature here.[9] But participant-observers who study social movements face a few special challenges worth discussing briefly. One challenge is to manage the logistical, and perhaps political, inconvenience a participant-observer may pose for a movement. Few movement groups have lots of extra time to spend on outside researchers no matter how unobtrusive they are. And in the past decade, more and more movement groups have worried about surveillance; groups may wonder whether the researcher is really a spy.

It is best to tell the truth about your research intentions, as early as is practical and fair. Rarely can covert research be justified ethically. And being discovered by surprise may only encourage an immobilizing fear among the activists you want to "protect." You need to seek out a good moment to introduce your research hopes early in a project. Get on a meeting agenda after you have decided you do in fact want to study the group; talk to a contact person and find out when is the earliest good time to ask a group's permission to study it.

There are intellectual as well as ethical reasons to seek permission early.

A participant-observer might otherwise cheat herself out of the opportunity to see how a group responds to an outsider. Do not assume you already know how the activists relate to a wider public world just because you agree with the group's cause or have read about activists like them. When I asked a radical, queer activist group if I could observe and participate alongside them, I was surprised to find out that the group considered itself very open, even to a researcher who did not identify as queer. Having read about radical identity politics, I had wondered whether I would be laughed out of the room. The group's public-spiritedness in fact became a central theme of my study (Lichterman 1999).

Participant-observers have entered social movement groups in various ways. Fantasia (1988) already had a job at what later became one of his field sites. Ginsburg (1989) had been a journalist producing a documentary about abortion activism in the locale she would later study; pro-life as well as pro-choice activists considered Ginsburg's portraits of them to be fair, and her reputation eased her entry as a researcher into groups on both sides. Participant-observers, in other words, do not always enter sites with but one researcher's "hat." We do not always join a movement group with the goal of studying it from the start. Like Fantasia, some participants in collective action later become scholars researching the movement they first came to know wearing a different hat. How we first enter the movement does not affect the logic we use to study it, if we are using the extended case method; how we first enter could very well affect our assessment of which theories are interesting and worth reconstructing, though. But however we enter, it is best to make clear, as soon as we are sure of our own research hopes, that we want permission to participate with a researcher's hat on.

Another challenge of participant observation in social movements is more personal. Sympathizing with your activist group, you may disdain your academic hat and prefer to take your place in struggle alongside "real" people "in the trenches." Participant-observers have discussed at length the politics of our relationships with the researched—how we should talk about our unfolding projects, how we should write about the people we study, how we should fashion our relationships with them. I agree with Bourdieu's (Bourdieu and Wacquant 1992) and Gouldner's (1973) arguments to the effect that participant-observers may not be helping people they write about by casting them as noble underdogs, or writing as if they are "really just like them underneath."

Do not overidentify with the people you are studying. It is entirely possible for you to do what activists in the group under study are doing, and believe sincerely in the cause, without implying that you are therefore no different from any other member. Of course, participant-observers do not have to identify personally with the movements they study in order to be good researchers. Whether researching a movement whose victories we publicly cheer or a movement whose very existence we privately disdain, I would argue that writing about the movement in scholarly terms gives the researcher a "hat" that other members are not wearing unless they too are writing scholarly accounts of the group. The mental and social distance created by wearing a researcher hat, among others, may be a welcome space for reflection—for the researcher and for group members. In my experience, at least some activists appreciate a respectful researcher who can offer a sympathetic outsider's reflection on the group. Participant-observers need to think through the political and moral issues at stake in the researcher-researched relationship, during the project as well as beforehand. In the debates over these issues, feminist and postmodern perspectives compete with a universalism like Gouldner's, which may sound almost quaint in the contemporary intellectual environment.

Here I offer only a simple point to which participant-observers from diverse perspectives can subscribe: We learn more when we are willing to keep an analytic lens focused on the groups we study. We learn less if we surrender that lens on the notion that we already agree with the group's cause and therefore understand what they are doing, or we already disagree with the group's cause and therefore understand—to our chagrin—what they are doing. Keeping the conceptual lens at hand hardly precludes other lenses, other relationships to the group that arise during a project: occasional helper, fellow activist, friendly critic.[10]

Getting Started: What Do I Write in Field Notes?

Start with a Theme, a Theory, and Some Expectations

Practically any field site offers up clues to a variety of sociological questions. Theory-driven participant observation requires that we come to a field site informed by a theme; a very general theme is fine. Whether the theme is "constructing identity," or "expressing emotions," or "mobilizing resources," we usually know our themes through preexisting concepts and theories we have already read. Maybe we have chosen the theme because previous studies seem inadequate. So it is crucial to be self-conscious about concepts and theories that inform our themes. What preexisting theories do you think your site is going to help you refine, or challenge?

As Burawoy directs (Burawoy et al. 1991), the most important thing to do at the start of a theory-driven project is to write down some expectations about the site. How will the theme or theory apply in your case? And less conceptualized expectations are just as important. What will the people be like? What will they talk about? What will the people themselves think they are doing, and why? No expectations are too trivial to write at this stage; force yourself to write guesses, hunches, preliminary musings that are as detailed as possible.

This rule of thumb will be jarring to researchers who have learned that participant observation means trying to enter a site with a mental blank slate. Accepting that our slates can never be blank, the theory-driven mode makes a virtue of our embeddedness in presuppositions, especially the ones we develop from reading research literatures. It asks us to make those presuppositions as explicit as possible. Some participant-observers (Glaser and Strauss 1967; Strauss 1987) emphasize the value of "memos" that we write to ourselves about our projects in progress, even if the content of those memos never makes it into a finished book or article. A first memo that details your sensitizing theme, your theories (whether formal or folk), and your expectations is the most important memo you can write.

"Expectations" are not formal hypotheses. They need not be based on any prior research or theory, although it is important to note as much if they are. Participant-observers usually do not claim to test hypotheses with a limited "sample" of one or several field sites. Our goal is not to establish statistical relationships between variables. "Hypothesis testing" in the conventional sense belongs to a different—statistical—logic of inquiry that makes sense in conjunction with other methods. Instead, participant-observers work through a cycle of *generating* and substantiating hypotheses in the field. When substantiated with observation, those hypotheses lead to theoretical innovation, as we will see below. Researchers in a statistical, hypothesis-testing mode of inquiry usually hope that a hypothesis is correct. We will see that we theory-driven participant-observers, in contrast, hope that at least some of our preliminary expectations will be wrong! Rarely are we disappointed.

Take Notes at the Start of the Study

After writing a memo about a theme, theories, and expectations, you need to write accounts of your experiences during the first contacts with a field site. These first notes will help you identify the salient people and relationships to keep in mind as you try to find a place for yourself as a researcher in the site. You can always augment these first, descriptive notes later when you have learned more about people in the site, but observation starts with the first exploratory phone call or visit to a site.

The study proper begins after a group gives you permission to observe and participate alongside them. For the first few sessions in the field site, it is best to represent as much of the session as possible in field notes. If the "field session" is a group meeting for instance, then field notes about the session should describe people and places in as much detail as possible. Just as important, field notes should reconstruct as much conversation as possible. A detailed record of conversation, with lots of direct quotes, will be far more useful than a summary statement that "they argued about whether or not to block corporate headquarters." Pay attention not only to which people talk and what they say, but how they say it. What style of meeting are they trying to sustain—an informal gathering, a carefully ordered progression guided by *Robert's Rules,* a consensus process? Are they living up to their stated goals for interaction? Notes on the first few sessions, in other words, should recapitulate as much of the form and content of those sessions as possible. But this "tell all" style of field-note writing should give way after those first few sessions to a more focused inquiry in which you are looking and listening for particular things, as I describe in the next section.

Finding "Problems in the Field"

Coding

Participant-observers need to know what they are looking for in the field. We must keep checking out expectations and developing new ones, in efforts to find an anomaly. But identifying anomalies is rarely so straightforward. People you study will not come up and tell you that your theories are wrong, nor will what they say or do signal theoretical consequences unambiguously. How can you organize a mass of field notes and organize your own observation in the field to tell if an anomaly is forthcoming?

A simple analytic strategy will help. Glaser, Strauss, and Corbin have developed a number of techniques as part of the "constant-comparative" method of analysis. These researchers' ultimate goals differ from those dictated by the extended case method (Burawoy et al. 1991). But both methods call for research in which, as Strauss and Corbin succinctly put it, "data collection and data analysis are tightly interwoven" (1991: 59). Participant-observers do not wait until the end of a project to sit down with field notes and look for findings. Here I will describe how a coding-and-observing strategy from Glaser, Strauss, and Corbin can help an extended-case field study progress toward a problem, and ultimately an interesting anomaly for a theory. I will demonstrate this strategy with some of the earlier field notes I wrote about the ACES group.

Coding begins when you peruse your first field notes with your initial theme (and theory, if you have one) and expectations in mind. You are looking for anything that might be interesting and relevant: something about what people say, how they say it, or about the setting itself. And you flag these interesting items—descriptions of people, snippets of conversation, sequences of action—with a term that you make up yourself. This search-and-flag exercise is *coding*. Coding simply means naming the item you have "flagged" in your notes and applying the name consistently, wherever you find that item in your notes. Borrowing loosely from Glaser and Strauss, we can call that name a *concept*.[11] You mark every instance you can find of that concept in your notes, writing the concept name in the margin, or perhaps on a separate memo sheet. More often than not, some of the different concepts turn out to be related; they are all aspects of some larger concept, some type of activity, or setting, or person. Concepts help you decide what to look for during the next field session.

Having constructed one or more concepts, you generate simple "hypotheses"—or to use a more suitably informal term from Burawoy, *expectations*—about why these concepts matter. How do the concepts relate to your very first expectations and your theme? *Keeping those expectations in mind at your next field session,* you observe different settings, or different people, or different activities, to see if those concepts continue to be relevant in the next set of notes: Now you are practicing what Glaser and Strauss have called *theoretical sampling*. That is, you are looking for ("sampling") more and more examples of your concepts in your field site.

To summarize, coding not only documents what you have found but suggests what to look for next. Coding is very dialogical. It does the most work for a project when you sustain an ongoing dialogue with yourself about which concepts and expectations are working out, and which are not helpful and ought to be dropped.

Coding to Identify a Problem in the Field: An Illustration

A Theme and a Theory to Challenge

When I first talked to the ACES contact person on the phone, I had a theme in mind, as well as a theory and a rough concept, that I carried over from fieldwork I had been doing in the U.S. Green movement. I had chosen the Green movement because I was interested in the *theme* of political commitment. I expected early on that this movement, among others, might be an anomaly for some influential writings on political commitment. These writings propound a *theory,* popular in sociology and in common-sense thinking too, that American individualism turns people away from political commitments.[12] The theory claims that a rising emphasis on self-expression and personal feelings in American culture weakens Americans' sense of obligation—to communities, to political struggle, to the public good. I have called this theory the "seesaw model" of commitment: as the quest for individuality rises, a sense of commitment beyond the self declines. Personal expressiveness and true, long-lasting political commitment work at cross-purposes, goes the theory. The seesaw model would expect that people steeped in the culture of personal expression, people who value individuality highly, would have a difficult time sustaining political commitments at all. They would make for undependable activists. Given their emphasis on individual empowerment and their dedication to long-term, fundamental social change, the Greens were already an anomaly for the seesaw model. But my fieldwork with the Greens did not make clear enough what exactly in the seesaw model needed to be revised. Precisely how were the Greens an anomaly? And what made individualism work differently in different groups?

The seesaw model—the theory—interested me at the outset, as a means to understanding political commitment. Having now seen that the case of the Greens challenged the theory, I hoped that further comparison could further refine my critique of the theory. The following scenarios represent how I continued following the constant-comparative logic, in conjunction with the extended case method.

Round One

My emerging critique of the seesaw model suggested that activist groups have different styles of commitment, not just more or less commitment. So I began a rough *concept*: "commitment style." The next step was to choose an activist group, my *theoretical sample,* for which I could generate a few *expectations* about commitment style, and advance a comparative perspective on the Greens. For the sake of a good comparison, I chose ACES, located in a suburban locale dozens of miles from the Greens' urban office. The ACES group's ideologies on paper looked somewhat similar to those of the Greens, but I expected its commitment style would be different. I imagined that the Greens' radical, personal expressiveness thrived more in culturally "hip" urban centers than in placid suburbs like Airdale. I expected the commitment style in ACES would differ also from the style upheld by critics of individualism—a tradition-bound, tightly unified style of collective action that we might associate more with labor unions or long-established racial or ethnic minority communities than with middle-class suburbs. So continuing on the theme of political commitment, and armed with a concept and some expectations, I was ready to ask ACES members to let me observe and participate alongside them.

ACES gave me a friendly welcome. Eager to do whatever other members were doing, I volunteered for several weekend stints of gathering signatures on petitions against the toxic waste incinerator. A week later I had field notes from a fascinating, sometimes anxiety-provoking petitioning stint with Edie, a part-time student and homemaker who had just recently joined the group. Several things struck me in this set of notes. One was the number of times that Edie said or implied that petitioning was quite all right to do. I was struck at Edie's efforts to convince other people, and herself, that activism could be reasonable. I could code these notes by writing in the margins "it's ok" or "reasonability" wherever a conversation or description of action in the notes fit one of these designations.

Recall that the coding process requires that you be in dialogue with yourself about how your project is progressing. I argue that it is helpful to write commentaries on field notes after *every* session in the field. I wrote comments at the end of these first notes in which I proposed for myself a new concept that could guide my observations in the next field session. I decided for now that perhaps Edie enacted a distinctive commitment style, and one that differed from that of most Greens. I called the style "citizen activism," and I posed myself a question to keep in mind as I observed ACES members the next time around. Here is an excerpt from this commentary:

> Citizen activism—taking the role of concerned citizen, not radical personhood . . . putting on a public mask . . . working within the constraints of public decorum. Is Edie weird, or are the other ones citizen activists too? Do they talk about it the way she does? In their context it is very daring to do what they are doing. More daring than doing "political" things in [city where my Green group was located].

Some researchers attach commentaries like these to the end of one session's field notes; others write them as memos and keep them in a separate log. It is helpful, too, to write commentaries with a longer perspective, ones that pull concepts or nascent arguments out from a number of field visits (see Strauss 1987). In any event, you should write commentaries that help you keep track of a project's overall direction, as well as more particular coding notes or hypotheses that you insert within the text of field notes or in the margins. I realized not long after writing these comments that "citizen activist" could be a confusing tag, since some sociologists have used that term for community organizing groups that did not look much like ACES. I settled on the concept "suburban activist" instead.

Round Two

With the first set of notes and commentary to guide me, I returned to the field with a new expectation to try out in the field: that other ACES members would be "suburban activists" like Edie. They, too, would sound like they needed to assure people, and reassure themselves, that activism could be a reasonable thing to do. With this new hunch it only made sense to "sample" other members of ACES, and so I paid special attention to two members with longer histories in the group than Edie's.

Reviewing field notes after several more field sessions, I did not see much evidence of the "reasonability" and "it's OK" concepts. Those two other members did not talk as if they needed to justify their activism or defend their reasonableness. I looked through my notes for examples of how other ACES members presented themselves, and still did not find much use for my two initial concepts. In fact it struck me that members of this group did not have that much in common at all. I puzzled, how could these activists be so different in their approach to activism? How could their group hang together, in a chilly, unwelcoming milieu no less, when the members did not even relate to activism in the same way?

Now I had a *problem in the field*.[13] I was wrong to expect members to share a common approach to activism. The suburban activist concept would not be very valuable if it did not illuminate much about most ACES members. It was time to discard the "suburban activist" concept and find some other concept to drive my observations of ACES, or else to rework the concept. In the extended case method, puzzles and failed expectations like these are tremendous opportunities. They signal that it is time to revisit preexisting theory in search of clues.

Toward Theoretical Innovation

Making a Problem in the Field into an "Anomaly"

I reminded myself that studying ACES was supposed to help me learn more about political commitment—and about what exactly was wrong with the seesaw model. I was surprised that ACES was turning out to be an effective, harmonious group, and yet it not only brooked a lot of individuality but was solicitous of members' privacy in a way the Greens were not. ACES never goaded individual members to take more risks than they wanted to. Members did not need to share the same definitions of what a good activist was. Yet, ACES had been pursuing its cause steadfastly for years. They were talking about protecting "the community" even when few in the community seemed interested in listening. A loose group with lots of leeway for individual participation, cautious respect for privacy, and yet lots of staying power: that was the problem in the field.

Following the extended case method, I puzzled over whether this problem might be an anomaly for the seesaw model, or for some other preexisting theory. Several different theories could have helped me "extend" the case of ACES. During my study, for instance, some prominent social movement theories were emphasizing the collective identity, or the strategic frames, that empowered movement groups. These theories might have been interesting to critique and extend in light of the variety in ACES members' activist identities and ideologies. Alternatively, some theories of "new social movements" have assumed that grassroots environmentalists are cultural radicals rebelling against the conventional values of industrial society. I might have used my findings on the very culturally conventional ACES group to challenge and specify the sweeping generalization. The finished study does engage some of this theoretical work. In the extended case method, there is no natural reason to choose one theory over another to engage with evidence from the field. Engaging a theory with relevant evidence is a matter of intellectual craft more than statistical logic.

But the seesaw model had interested me initially, so I would continue working with it *unless* it simply had little relation, either positive or negative, to my field sites. Already critical of the seesaw model, I had chosen ACES on the expectation that it could teach me more about what was inadequate about this theory. So why was I surprised that a group with leeway for different amounts of participation and risk could be effective? Even when we force ourselves to write down expectations at the outset of a study, our assumptions do not all become transparent to us. And I had been assuming that members of a group would be pretty uniform in their commitment style—even if that meant they *all* practiced a deeply "personalized" politics like that of the Greens. This assumption was itself an "expectation" I only now recognized. But ACES members did not all want to participate intensively the way Greens did. Different individuals in the group defined the role of a good activist in very different ways. Now aware of my implicit, and failed, expectation, I could see that the problem in the field might be a new and interesting anomaly for the seesaw model. I did not need to find another preexisting theory to try out in the field just yet, much less drop the ACES case from my study.

I decided that ACES's regard for members' fears of going public might be part of a commitment style in itself. In other words, respect for members' privacy was not incompatible with public commitment. So perhaps I had found another false dichotomy in the seesaw model. Maybe the only way people could be members of an activist group in Airdale without scaring other Airdalers, or themselves, was to practice activism in a way that did not threaten the privatized, "family-oriented" way of life in Airdale.

Reading through other studies helps participant-observers advance an emerging dialogue between a problem in the field and a theory. In the extended case method, preexisting studies do not "bias" observation; they inform observation, as long as we keep in mind that preexisting studies have but provisional value for our own, depending on how the conceptual contours of our study are shaping up. In my case I found that writings on suburban culture supported the dialogue between my problem and the seesaw model. I culled from these writings (for instance, Baumgartner 1988) that privatism is one of the most distinctive features of residential enclaves that are called "suburban." That is, suburbanites are no less morally engaged or politically principled *as individuals* than other citizens, but suburban, *everyday public settings* tend to lack a strong sense of shared cultural authority. Those settings encourage people to keep moral or political principles to themselves rather than sharing them with local neighbors, shoppers, or club members. While the Greens, as well as low-income, largely African American anti-toxics activists in my study, felt no compunction about talking about corporate greed, or earth spirituality, or the will of God, the suburban activists were more comfortable keeping their motivations private, respecting other people's "space," in efforts to avoid sounding presumptuous about principles that might not be shared after all. In Airdale's civic milieu, no one had the authority to make someone else take a lot of risks for a public cause. It made sense that an activist group in the suburban milieu could succeed only if it was not too "groupy," and let individuals participate in their own way.

I was ready to review my notes again, with a new concept in mind. It was more clear now that I was really studying a *setting*—one that produces suburban activ*ism*—not the individual "suburban activ*ist*."

Round Three

With the category of "suburban activism" now in mind, I tried out the new expectation that ACES members could have different individual styles while all showing signs of adapting to, struggling with, a privatized civic culture that frowned on speaking out. I would look through my notes, and listen while in the field, for examples of conversation about what it was like to be an activist in Airdale. Instead of looking for a type of person, I was looking for evidence of a situation—the situation, or predicament, of activism in a privatized milieu.

Evidence was easy to find. Many, many conversations and situations recorded in my field notes fit the "suburban activism" concept as I was now using it: a member's wariness about being perceived as "the nut fringe," another member's refusal to talk about her activism with her softball team, the group leader's reticence about being called an "activist" at all, most members' habit of cutting short or squirming uncomfortably through the long political excursuses of the old-time union organizer in the group. The new conceptualization worked. It named something the group shared. From a field-driven perspective, "suburban activism" was a contribution in itself, the more so if I had spent even more time describing its characteristics, the kinds of people likely to practice it, the kinds of settings likely to welcome it.

While I did aim to describe suburban activism in more than bare, skeletal terms, my theory-driven goals lay in linking it to the larger theory, the seesaw model of commitment, with which I had started. ACES was an anomaly for a theory that holds not only that individuality weakens groups, but that a respect for privacy always detracts from collective efforts on behalf of communities. I did not have to say that the seesaw model was therefore entirely wrong or that previous research supporting it was invalid. The point, rather, was to make a theoretical innovation that could cover the case of ACES (and the case of the Greens) as well as others already covered in the previous theory.

Specifying the Macro and Answering a Sociological Question

In the extended case method, we use an anomalous case to improve on theories of institutional and structural forces. The force at work in this case was a cultural structure, a kind of individualism that both enables and constrains the ways that Americans go public as activists. Challenging but not simply rejecting the seesaw model, I argued that individualism might not always weaken public commitment, that individualism as a moral culture could have varying meanings and varying consequences, *depending on the setting* in which people spoke and acted individualistically.

In some settings, like those of Green or ACES meetings, activists related their efforts to reference points in the wider world—a town or city, other social movements, political traditions, religious faiths, government agencies. They were not turning away from the public world just because they practiced their activism in an individualistic or privacy-respecting way. In other settings, people's main reference points might be their own psyches. I studied one such group as a comparison case, a spiritually oriented monthly gathering.[14] Members of Planethelpers talked about the earth's seasons, about global environmental dangers. But most of all, they talked about themselves: identifying deeply with the earth itself, they held that working on oneself therapeutically would help "heal" the planet. Group therapy with like-minded souls was the truest means to a better environment. In the setting of a Planethelpers meeting, people encouraged each other to refer to themselves, even if some of those people (including one Green activist) expressed other concerns about the political world in other settings. In Planethelpers, people only rarely, fitfully, talked about how their group might relate to cultural or political change. They rarely talked about their own locale; it was as if their meetings did not take place anywhere in particular. The group did not participate in demonstrations, town meetings, hearings, public education workshops, or campaigns. In this instance, the seesaw model was perfectly adequate to the interaction I observed.

With a specific understanding of settings, participant-observers improve on a preexisting theory of macro forces. Of course, researchers can conceptualize settings in many different ways. And settings are not always coextensive with single groups. In my study, what mattered greatly about an activist setting was the way that activists would imagine relationships with a larger world within their own meetings. I heard those relationships through the reference points that came up in everyday discussions; those reference points were stable over time. This understanding of settings led to an improvement on the seesaw model of commitment, in a way that could also cover cases in which individualism really does turn activists toward their navels and away from public causes.

There is a final, rhetorical step in a case extension. As Lareau (1989) has argued, participant-observers can use understandings of the "how," the everyday processes, to answer straightforward theoretical questions. We can answer the question, Is the preexisting theory of those processes adequate? Addressing that question, we highlight that our studies make theoretical, not simply descriptive, contributions. My study had described how the culture of individualism worked in social movements. Now I could come back to the question, Is the seesaw model adequate? The study challenged the preexisting seesaw model with an improved theory.

Researchers more familiar with the logic of hypothesis testing and statistical sampling may ask why a participant-observer can critique theory on the basis of just one group. After all, researchers usually want a large sample for testing their claims. But participant-observers who use extended case logic do not "reject" theories on the basis of one or a few field sites. We aim to *improve* preexisting theories so that they can cover our anomalous case as well as the others that have already supported the theory as is. The "improvement" may involve substantial reconceptualization.

In Search of Everyday Meanings

Listening to people talking in their own settings, on their own time, participant-observers have the opportunity to glean the everyday meanings, tacit assumptions, ordinary customs, practical rules of thumb that organize people's everyday lives. Social scientists read participant observation studies, whether theory-driven or field-driven, partly to get a close view of these meanings, a good interpretation. In this section, I want to point out the value of participant observation for accessing everyday meanings, and provide two practical pointers.

Everyday meanings may be harder to derive using interview or survey methods that ask the researched to respond in terms of the researcher's categories. Unquestionably, other methods teach us a great deal about activists' everyday lives. And we participant-observers must be vigilant, as Emerson, Fretz, and Shaw (1995) point out, not to impose "exogenous" meanings inadvertently on the people we study. That is, before theorizing people and settings in sociological terminology, we usually want to see how people understand themselves and their world in their own, everyday terms. My point is simply that a participant-observer is particularly well positioned to pick up the everyday meanings that organize group life, because participant observation takes place in the group settings and time frames dictated by the researched and not by sociologists. My question about the meaning of activist commitment in Airdale, for instance, got a different kind of answer with participant observation evidence than it did from interviewing the activists.[15] Much as these interviews were essential for other research questions, including "cultural" questions, I needed to do participant observation to answer the question about the meaning of activism in Airdale.[16]

During an interview, ACES member Barb told me that as a nurse, she had seen a lot of cancer patients; ACES's opposition to the toxic waste incinerator made sense to her on health grounds. As movement scholars are finding (Polletta 1998), we can learn a lot from stories, including things we certainly cannot learn through participant observation. But I would have been wrong to assume Barb's interview story, one I never heard her tell in a group setting, could tell us a lot about the meaning of being an activist *in Airdale*. It took participant observation in the group's own settings to find out that Barb and other members shared a reticence about speaking out—even in the group itself. Listening to stories group members told each other in those group settings was tremendously valuable. I learned these Airdalers' *shared meaning* of activism. Everyday meanings are easiest to find when we study everyday interaction. Two pointers facilitate the search.

Focus carefully on words. This deceptively simple directive is easiest to follow when field notes have direct quotes, reconstructions of verbatim conversation. What distinctive terms, names, in-group jargon does the group seem to share? Are there stories, sayings, rules of thumb that members tend to repeat to one another, or tell new members? I would hear ACES members telling each other short stories with a common theme: Airdalers' skewed perceptions of activists. The leader recounted more than once that a local woman approached her and said, "I'm willing to lie down in the street with you now"; the woman assumed that being an activist meant practicing civil disobedience, something ACES members had never done. Stories like these tell us a lot about everyday meanings. Frequently used terms are important to decode too, even if they sound familiar or unremarkable to the researcher. ACES member Edie joked repeatedly that ACES was not a "radical leftist organization." It took time for me to figure out that she was not referring to socialist ideology. She meant that the group was civil, polite, eager to talk with Airdalers as fellow citizens; it was not a group of fire-breathing "wide-eyed radicals."

Listen for categories of person, setting, or action that people use in contrast with other categories. Listen for the dichotomies of good and bad that organize a group's view of itself and the world. One ACES activist said that ACES members were not "radical anarchists" but "concerned about our families." She said on another occasion that group members were not "flaky" but rather "raising families and trying to live responsible lives." These dichotomies say a lot about the predominant ways of imagining public and private worlds in Airdale. In Airdale, one could be either irrational (radical anarchist, flaky), or responsible (at home, in private). No wonder activism felt so uncomfortable! Understanding the everyday meaning of activism in Airdale ultimately helped clarify what was wrong with a widely accepted understanding of political commitment, the seesaw model.

The Limits of Participant Observation and the Potential of Multiple Methods

Of course, theory-driven participant observation will not answer all questions worth asking about social movements. Some of the limits are intrinsic to participant observation: It would be unwise to expect a participant observation study to tell us why movements arise in some historical periods but not others. In my study, I wanted to find out *how* grassroots environmentalists defined and practiced political commitment, not *why* grassroots environmentalism grew in the 1980s. Neither would participant-observers want to use evidence from one or a few field sites to make strong claims about the extent of variety in a nationwide movement. I discovered that different American environmental groups defined and practiced political commitment differently. But I did not need to claim that I had studied all existing types of American grassroots environmentalism, nor that I had discovered all types of political commitment.

Some limits are particular to the theory-driven mode. Participant-observers often want to elucidate a substantive topic as an end in itself, rather than aim to revise a theory that cuts through many substantive topics. If we want to develop an in-depth portrait of environmental activism in one city, for instance, we will not want to be constrained by the selective sampling and observing that goes with reconstructing an existing theory. We may want to observe all the environmental groups we can, and employ many theories to illuminate the subject of local environmentalism. I knew there were other interesting grassroots environmental groups in the region of my study. Researching them would have added a lot to a picture of grassroots environmentalism, but it would not have advanced my goal of refining a theory of political commitment.

Some participant-observers may want to describe the everyday meanings or practices of one activist group in great detail. Perhaps the group earns scholarly interest because it is controversial, or confounds common sense, or represents a kind of movement that is little studied. Again, this is a goal that would not sit well with a method that bids researchers to look closely at everyday interaction in order to see larger social forces at work. Theory-driven goals are not better or worse than field-driven goals; they produce different kinds of stories about everyday life.

Doing participant observation, a researcher does assume that a close look at everyday life will be worthwhile. That should not be a troublesome assumption, given a lot of the questions that motivate research on social movements: How do activist groups develop collective identities? What motivates activists? How do movements express or manipulate emotions? What makes movement organizations strong or weak? How does the personal become political? How do movements use and perpetuate cultural and political traditions? If the question is about what movements accomplish in the wider society, it might be easy to assume that participant-observation will not be a promising method. If we want to know why national movements succeed or fail, or what policy changes they produce, surely it helps to have the broad overview of a survey researcher or social historian.

Participant-observers can learn at least one thing very relevant to questions about movement impacts, however: In everyday life, activists can define "success" very differently, even within the same movement. The U.S. Green groups that I studied used to say at meetings that they did not want to get into the trap of "putting out fires" with single-issue advocacy. They wanted to alert people to more fundamental, social-structural problems smoldering beneath any single issue. They wanted to keep alternative visions alive by living them out in their own lives and by educating the public. Willingly, they limited their own immediate impact on local environmental conflicts because of their commitment to a broader vision of social and cultural change. Compared to a group like ACES that scored many concrete victories in its locale, the Greens looked like failures to some local activists; the Greens were less politically visible than other environmental groups and had few concrete victories to chalk up to their credit. Their definition of success differed from that of activists more committed to conventional, interest-group advocacy. *Meaningful* impact, or success, might take a lifetime of activism, Greens would say. No doubt many were smiling, if not cheering wildly, when anticorporate consumer activist Ralph Nader ran for president on the Green Party ticket, sixteen years after the Green movement's beginnings in the United States.

Combining participant observation findings with survey or historical research findings, we can enrich our understanding of movements' impacts. We can learn more about why some movements affect policies while others do not. We can learn more about the range of impacts. Over time, movements may change many people's ways of looking at the world, their definitions of a good life, their ways of defining what politics is, as well as changing national or local policies. Combined with other kinds of research, participant observation can reveal the enduring influence of a movement on everyday life, years after the movement's height of visibility and political influence.

Understanding a movement's impacts is just one of a variety of reasons for using participant observation in conjunction with other methods. When researchers combine participant observation with another method, that method is often interviewing: We may want to learn more about the biographies of the people we have watched and listened to in the field, or the histories of the groups we have followed. We may want to ask different people to retell the same event, and see how and why the stories differ. We may want to find out about the more private selves people harbor outside the group contexts we have studied. Bearing in mind that interview evidence and participant observation evidence are not simply interchangeable, we can combine them judiciously to create a richer account of lived experience.

Conclusion: From Small Sites to Big Theories

This chapter has shown how participant observation research, even in relatively small sites, can address theoretical questions about social or cultural structures. Participant-observers can use the extended case logic to understand social movements in their ongoing relations to larger contexts. We can bring "large-scale" terms of sociological analysis, such as power, culture, hegemony, professionalization, globalization, directly to bear on our questions about how social movements evolve, institutionalize, or fragment. And given the difficulties in defining exactly where a social movement begins and ends, we gain an added benefit from research that starts with a theoretical, macrosociological imagination rather than a substantive category alone. The extended case method helps us study groupings that define themselves in political terms, and may be the fruit of or fertile soil for social movements, but may confound the substantive category "social movement": culturally alternative child-care centers and state-funded organizations for AIDS victims are but two examples.[17]

It is worth keeping in mind the limits as well as potentials of theory-driven participant observation for studying social movements. Descriptive studies of movements, field-driven studies that bring varied frameworks to bear on a site of interest—these have crucial contributions to make on their own terms. Social movement scholarship benefits from a diversity of research questions, and the extended case method broadens that diversity. I still cringe at the Airdale activists' response to my strawberry pie. But all told, I think the embarrassment was worth it.

Notes

1. See, for instance, Ragin's comprehensive typology of case studies (1992); see also Feagin, Orum, and Sjoberg 1991; and Snow and Trom's contribution to this volume.

2. I will not take space in this chapter to justify my selective synthesis. I want to keep my discussion of the logic to a minimum sufficient for a practically oriented introduction. But I note that Burawoy (Burawoy et al. 1991: 17) bids that participant-observers return to their field sites each time with fresh hypotheses developed after thinking through the field notes from the last visit. The simple coding scheme I derive from Glaser and Strauss's constant-comparative method reflects and facilitates just this process. Lareau (1989) also combined the extended case method with a coding technique—a much more complex one than offered here.

3. The field-driven/theory-driven distinction is fairly similar to the distinction between empirical units and theoretical constructs in Ragin's (1992) typology, and I borrow the phrase "empirical unit" here. But my dichotomy emphasizes the goal of the study rather than the definition of a case—much as the two are related. And I intend my terms only for participant observation research design. It is best to think of theory-driven and field-driven modes as goals on a spectrum; participant-observers quite often combine aspects of both logics, not always self-consciously.

4. This section is especially indebted to Burawoy et al. 1991, and Burawoy 1998, though I have stated the limitations in slightly different terms.

5. Generalization can take other forms besides the most common, statistical one I am noting here. See "theoretical generalization" in Glaser and Strauss 1967; see also Snow and Anderson 1991.

6. See, for instance, Klandermans, Kriesi, and Tarrow 1988; McAdam, McCarthy, and Zald 1995. Integrating macro and micro was explicitly the theme of the 1998 miniconference sponsored by the Collective Behavior/Social Movements Section of ASA.

7. While Burawoy implies that the "macro" is social structure, I have argued that a participant-observer can "extend" out to cultural structure, too. See Eliasoph and Lichterman 1999.

8. I use *anomaly* loosely, to denote any observation that would trouble a theory. Burawoy has named several kinds of problems that could prompt reconstruction of a theory (Burawoy et al. 1991: 10). Sometimes a theory needs to be reconstructed because observations in the field directly contradict the theory. Other times, observations show that a theory suffers internal contradictions, or unbearable silences.

9. A wonderfully sensible guide to the process is Bogdan and Taylor 1978.

10. My short treatment here highlights the value of achieving some analytic distance from the activists we study. Other researchers would emphasize what we can learn from identifying closely with the researched. Reinharz (1988) makes a compelling case for closeness. See also Snow, Benford, and Anderson 1986 on taking the "ardent activist" role and becoming a leading activist of the movement under study. I emphasize that closeness and analytic distance are not mutually exclusive. The "hats" metaphor breaks down: one can wear more than one at the same time.

11. Glaser and Strauss (1967) distinguish *concepts* from *categories* in their introduction to coding. For our purposes, one term will suffice.

12. For complete references to this debate about individualism and political commitment, see Lichterman 1995a, 1996.

13. This term is my own. While following Burawoy's attention to "anomalies," "surprises," or "problems," I use this term in conjunction with *anomaly*, not as a substitute. I want to highlight that participant-observers discover problems that might not translate so directly or obviously into anomalies for the theory we have brought to the field.

14. I did not treat the Planethelpers in my book, mostly for fear that the book would become too long. I reasoned that the book's argument could stand well enough without this group, but studying the group helped me sharpen my presentation of the argument.

15. See the distinction between "perspectives in action" and "perspectives of action," from Gould et al. 1974, described in Snow and Anderson 1991.

16. For more elaboration on this point, see Lichterman 1996, 1998.

17. See Brown 1997; Eliasoph 1998.

References

Baumgartner, M. P. 1988. *The Moral Order of a Suburb.* New York: Oxford University Press.

Bogdan, Robert, and S. Taylor. 1978. *Introduction to Qualitative Research Methods.* New York: Wiley and Sons.

Bourdieu, Pierre, and L. Wacquant. 1992. *An Invitation to Reflexive Sociology.* Chicago: University of Chicago Press.

Brown, Michael. 1997. *RePlacing Citizenship.* New York: Guilford Press.

Burawoy, Michael. 1998. "The Extended Case Method." *Sociological Theory* 16 (1): 4–33.

Burawoy, Michael, et al. 1991. *Ethnography Unbound.* Berkeley: University of California Press.

Eliasoph, Nina. 1998. "Politics by Other Means: The Case of the Child-Focussed Civil Society." Paper given at "Social Movements and Society," a conference sponsored by the Collective Behavior/Social Movements Section of the American Sociological Association, Davis, Calif., August.

Eliasoph, Nina, and Paul Lichterman. 1999. "'We Begin with Our Favorite Theory': Reconstructing the Extended Case Method." *Sociological Theory* 17 (2): 228–34.

Emerson, Robert, R. Fretz, and L. Shaw. 1995. *Writing Ethnographic Fieldnotes.* Chicago: University of Chicago Press.

Fantasia, Rick. 1988. *Cultures of Solidarity.* Berkeley: University of California Press.

Feagin, Joe R., Anthony M. Orum, and Gideon Sjoberg. 1991. *A Case for the Case Study.* Chapel Hill: University of North Carolina Press.

Ginsburg, Faye. 1989. *Contested Lives: The Abortion Debate in an American Community.* Berkeley: University of California Press.

Glaser, Barney, and Anselm Strauss. 1967. *The Discovery of Grounded Theory.* Chicago: Aldine.

Gould, Leroy C., Andrew L. Walker, Lansing E. Crane, and Charles W. Lidz. 1974. *Connections: Notes from the Heroin World.* New Haven, Conn.: Yale University Press.

Gouldner, Alvin. 1973. "The Sociologist as Partisan: Sociology and the Welfare State." In *For Sociology: Renewal and Critique in Sociology Today,* 35–69. New York: Basic Books.

Harper, Douglas. 1992. "Small N's and Community Case Studies." In *What Is a Case?* edited by Charles Ragin and Howard Becker, 139–58. Cambridge: Cambridge University Press.

Klandermans, Bert, Hanspeter Kriesi, and Sidney Tarrow. 1988. *From Structure to*

Action: Comparing Social Movement Research across Cultures. Greenwich, Conn.: JAI Press.

Lareau, Annette. 1989. *Home Advantage.* London: Falmer Press.

Lichterman, Paul. 1995a. "Beyond the Seesaw Model: Public Commitment in a Culture of Self-Fulfillment." *Sociological Theory* 13 (3): 275–300.

———. 1995b. "Piecing Together Multicultural Community: Cultural Differences in Community Building among Grassroots Environmentalists." *Social Problems* 42 (4): 513–34.

———. 1996. *The Search for Political Community: American Activists Reinventing Commitment.* New York: Cambridge University Press.

———. 1998. "What Do Movements Mean? The Value of Participant Observation." *Qualitative Sociology* 21 (4): 401–18.

———. 1999. "Talking Identity in the Public Sphere: Broad Visions and Small Spaces in Sexual Identity Politics." *Theory and Society* 28 (1): 101–41.

Luker, Kristin. 1984. *Abortion and the Politics of Motherhood.* Berkeley: University of California Press.

McAdam, Doug, John McCarthy, and Mayer Zald. 1995. *Comparative Perspectives on Social Movements.* New York: Cambridge University Press.

Polletta, Francesca. 1998. "Contending Stories: Narrative in Social Movements." *Qualitative Sociology* 21 (4): 419–46.

Ragin, Charles. 1992. "Introduction: Cases of 'What Is a Case?'" In *What Is a Case?* edited by Charles Ragin and Howard Becker, 1–17. Cambridge: Cambridge University Press.

Ray, Raka. 1998. *Fields of Protest: A Comparison of Women's Movements in Two Indian Cities.* Minneapolis: University of Minnesota Press.

Reinharz, Shulamith. 1988. *On Becoming a Social Scientist.* New Brunswick, N.J.: Transaction Books.

Snow, David A., and Leon Anderson. 1991. "Researching the Homeless: The Characteristic Features and Virtues of the Case Study." In *A Case for the Case Study,* edited by Joe R. Feagin, Anthony M. Orum, and Gideon Sjoberg, 148–73. Chapel Hill: University of North Carolina Press.

Snow, David, Robert Benford, and Leon Anderson. 1986. "Fieldwork Roles and Informational Yield: A Comparison of Alternative Settings and Roles." *Urban Life* 14 (4): 377–408.

Strauss, Anselm. 1987. *Qualitative Analysis for Social Scientists.* Cambridge: Cambridge University Press.

Strauss, Anselm, and Juliet Corbin. 1991. *Basics of Qualitative Research.* Newbury Park, Calif.: Sage.

6

The Case Study and the Study of Social Movements

David A. Snow and Danny Trom

We have three primary objectives in this chapter: to identify the central characteristics of the case study so as to provide a basis for distinguishing it from other methods and research strategies relevant to the study of social movements, to elaborate a number of procedural and analytic principles relevant to conducting case studies, and to elaborate and illustrate the empirical and theoretical utility of the case study as a research strategy in relation to the study of social movements.[1]

Since most studies of social movements derive their data from research on a particular movement or a stretch of time in a movement's career, one could conclude that the case study method and the study of social movements are almost one and the same. Yet, technically speaking, we know that not all studies of social movements are case studies, as the case study is but one research strategy for examining social movements and movement-related processes.[2] It therefore is necessary to unpack and then reconstitute that relationship to acquire a better understanding of the utility of the case study as but one strategy for studying social movements. Thus, we begin by identifying the central characteristics of the case study and then elaborate a number of procedural and analytic guidelines, including consideration of the different types of cases, that are pertinent to planning and conducting a case study. We then assess the principal contributions and weaknesses of the case study as it applies to social movements, focusing in particular on the relationship between the case study and the process of theoretical generalization. Throughout our discussion, we refer to relevant movement research that illustrates and illuminates our observations. We do so selectively, however, so we make no claims about this being an exhaustive overview and integration of all movement case studies.

Specification of the Defining Characteristics of the Case Study

To begin a discussion of the case study by specifying its defining characteristics may appear, at first glance, as an exercise in rendering unnecessarily problematic what is self-evident: that a case study is a study that focuses empirically and analytically on a case of something, that is, on a single instance or variant of some empirical phenomenon rather than on multiple instances of that phenomenon. But to conceptualize a case study as such is to approach it in a narrow, simplistic, textbook fashion. So we begin by elaborating what we consider as the core defining characteristics of the case study. These characteristics, which are derived from examination of a number of conceptual works focusing specifically on the case study (Lofland 1996; Orum, Feagin, and Sjoberg 1991; Snow and Anderson 1991; Yin 1989), include (a) investigation and analysis of an instance or variant of some bounded social phenomenon that (b) seek to generate a richly detailed and "thick" elaboration of the phenomenon studied through (c) the use and triangulation of multiple methods or procedures that include but are not limited to qualitative techniques.

A Case of What?

To note that a case study is a detailed study of a case of something is, of course, a truism. But it begs the question of what constitutes "a case." In exploring this issue, Ragin suggests that the best way to proceed is to ask, "What is this (the object of study) a case of?" (1992: 6).[3] Yet, when this is done, almost any study can be thought of as a case study because all studies are defined in part by one or more of at least four considerations. First and foremost, all studies are bounded in time and place (Ragin 1992: 2; Sjoberg et al. 1991: 48), thus making the results of any study temporally and spatially contingent. This is true even for random, cross-sectional surveys inasmuch as they provide a picture of a population's opinions, attitudes, and/or self-reports that is bounded by time and place (Ragin 1992: 2; Sjoberg et al. 1991: 48). Second, the primary phenomenon investigated in most studies can be classified as "a member of a larger set of broadly defined objects" (Ragin 1992: 2; Sjoberg et al. 1991), especially since most of what is studied, whatever the substantive area of inquiry, is a subset or species of an encompassing genre. Third, oftentimes the object of study is "an instance of an important theoretical concept or process" (Ragin 1992: 2). And fourth, sometimes the focus of inquiry is "an intrinsically interesting historical or cultural entity in its own right" (Ragin 1992: 2; Sjoberg et al. 1991: 54–55).

Applying these observations to the study of social movements, it is instructive to ask, for any movement study that might be classified a case study, such questions as the following: Is the object of study a particular analytic type or representative of a genre of movements, such as reform, religious, or revolutionary movements? Is it a particular social movement process, such as recruitment, framing, tactical innovation, diffusion, or emergence? Does it illustrate a particular theory or perspective, such as Smelser's value-added theory (1963) or McCarthy and Zald's variant of resource mobilization theory (1977)? Or is it an instance of an especially interesting social phenomenon, such as the civil rights movement, homeless mobilization, or the seemingly unlikely union of labor and environmentalists in a common cause?

Are affirmative answers to such questions sufficient to classify a study as a case study? Consider, for example, Capek and Gilderbloom's study of tenant mobilization in the United States. By their own admission, it is "a case study of the tenants movement in the 1980s" (1992: 7). But other than the claim that it is a case study, what makes it such? Is it the fact that it focuses on a single movement, or movement industry, nationwide? Is it the goal of facilitating understanding of the character and significance of tenants' movements in relation to modern urban life?

If a movement case study is defined in terms of focus on a broad, single type of movement, a single instance or variant of that genre, or the use of the object of empirical inquiry to illuminate a larger empirical reality or theoretical process, such as individual recruitment and participation, then do not most, and maybe all, studies of social movements constitute case studies? Take, for example, Jenness and Broad's study of "how gay/lesbian and feminist antiviolence projects across the United States have responded, or failed to respond, to hate-motivated violence against gays/lesbians . . . and girls/women" (1997: 13); McAdam's study (1988) of the precipitants and consequences of participation as volunteers in the 1964 Mississippi "Freedom Summer" campaign; Rochford's (1985) study of the Hare Krishna movement in America in the mid-1970s; Snow's study (1993) of recruitment to and participation in the Nichiren Shoshu Buddhist movement in the United States; Staggenborg's (1991) study of the development and operation of the pro-choice movement in the United States; Taylor's study (1996) of the postpartum self-help movement in the United States; Trom's (1999) study of two local mobilizations against facilities to obstruct and degrade visually the proximate environment; or Wagner's study (1993) of the resistance and collective action associated with a single homeless community in Maine. Each of these studies can be construed as a case study in terms of the above criteria; that is, like the Capek and Gilderbloom study, they focus on and seek to illuminate a particular movement (e.g., gay/lesbian/feminist antiviolence movement) and/or a set of movement processes (e.g. recruitment and participation) by studying the movement as a whole or instances of it.

Thus, case studies, whatever the substantive or theoretical area, are constituted in part by empirical and analytical focus on an instance or variant of some more generic phenomena, a particular theoretical concept or process, or a social event or happening that is interesting in its own right. But such foci alone do not make for a case study. As previously noted, case studies are also defined in terms of two other criteria.

Detailed, Thick, and Holistic Elaboration of the Case

The second defining feature is the generation of a richly detailed, "thick" elaboration of the phenomenon under study and the context in which it is embedded. This characteristic feature is mentioned and accented in various discussions of the case study. For example, Yin (1989: 23) notes that the objective of the case study is to investigate empirically phenomena within their "real-life context."[4] Similarly, Orum and colleagues (1991: 2) indicate that a case study is "an in-depth, multifaceted investigation" of social phenomena. And Snow and Anderson's (1991) conceptualization of case studies as "holistic analyses of cultural systems of action" focuses attention even more concretely on the contextualized and embedded character of the social actions, events, and/or processes that are the objects of analysis.[5] More concretely, holistic analysis of cultural systems of action involves the development of a rich and intricate understanding of "sets of interrelated activities and routines engaged in by one or more networks of actors within a social context that is bounded in time and space" (Snow and Anderson 1991: 152).[6] While systems of action may vary considerably in scope, as between a street corner clique and a state government, and in regulative or normative formality, as between a tightly or loosely regulated audience or group, the unit of analysis for the case study "is typically some system of action rather than a cross section of individuals, as in a survey" (Snow and Anderson 1991: 152).

Thus, in the case of social movements, the system of action may be highly focused and microscopic in terms of level of analysis, as with the recruitment activities and processes associated with one or more movements; or more meso-oriented in scope, as when assessing the characteristics of and links between movement organizations within the same industry; or even broader and more macroscopic, as when examining a protest cycle or the nature of movement activity within a city or society over a period of time.

Whatever the scope, the research objective of the case study is to understand and illuminate how the focal actions, events, and/or processes "are
produced and reproduced or changed by examining their ongoing interaction with other elements within the particular context" (Snow and Anderson
1991: 153). To do this is to attempt to produce a holistic—that is, a richly
or thickly contextualized and embedded—understanding of the phenomenon or system under investigation.

Use and Triangulation of Multiple Methods

If the principal objective of case study is to develop thick, detailed, holistic
elaborations of selected cases or systems of action, the question arises as to how
it differs from other procedures, such as ethnography, that also seek to produce richly and thickly detailed accounts of the phenomenon studied. The answer is that case studies, if done appropriately, generate analyses and understandings that are more multilayered and nuanced because of their third
defining feature: the triangulation of multiple methods or procedures that
include but are not limited to qualitative techniques such as ethnography.

The centrality of such procedural triangulation to conceptualization of
the case study is suggested by a number of works that highlight the use and integration of multiple methods as one of its defining features (Lofland 1996;
Orum et al. 1991; Snow and Anderson 1991; Yin 1989). Although triangulation encompasses broadly the use of multiple methods, data sources, investigators, and even theoretical perspectives in the course of a study (Denzin
1989b), it has been associated traditionally more with the use of multiple,
overlapping methodologies (McGrath, Martin, and Kulka 1982; Webb et al.
1981), which are generative, in Yin's words, of the kinds of "multiple sources
of evidence" that are fundamental to the development of richly and thickly
contextualized, holistic analyses. The underlying logic of such triangulation

is rooted in the complexity of social reality and the limitations of all
research methodologies. The basic argument is that social reality is too
complex and multifaceted to be adequately grasped by any single method.
Consequently, rather than debate the merits of one method vis-à-vis
another . . . one does better to combine the multiple strategies so that they
complement and supplement one another's weakness. (Snow and Anderson
1991: 158)

Not only is a mix of methods a fundamental feature of the case study,
but typically included in this mix, as previously noted, are one or more qualitative procedures. These qualitative procedures may include ethnography
and participant observation (see Lichterman, this volume); various forms of

qualitative interviewing, ranging from semi-structured interviewing (see Blee and Taylor, this volume) to unstructured conversational interviewing; and the use of various documents and archives, particularly those that are indigenously generated, such as social movement fliers, pamphlets, and newspapers. The relevance of such qualitative procedures to the case study is that they are grounded in real-life situations and settings, and are therefore more likely to generate the kinds of data that allow for the development of a richly detailed and holistic understanding of the phenomenon of interest.

To illustrate, let us turn to Snow and Cress's study of homeless social movement mobilization and collective action across U.S. cities (Cress and Snow 1996, 2000). The study involved the generation of three different but overlapping data sets, each of which was associated with a different methodology. At the city level of analysis, data were collected on movement-sponsored homeless protests in seventeen cities, as well as on aspects of the cities themselves, through structured content analysis of relevant articles in seventeen local daily newspapers during a twelve-year period. At the organizational level, ethnographic and conversational interview data were gathered on fifteen homeless social movement organizations and the various organizations making up the organizational fields in which they were embedded in eight cities. And at the individual level, questionnaire interviews were conducted with four hundred homeless individuals in three cities to assess what accounts for differential participation in collective action among the homeless. All told, this three-pronged, multifaceted methodology generated three overlapping sets of data on homeless social movement organizations and their protest activities across U.S. cities that would not have been possible to assemble via any single method.[7]

By accenting procedural triangulation as a defining feature of the case study, we have suggested as well that a case study is not a method per se, as are ethnography, survey research, laboratory experimentation, and historical/comparative research. Rather, we argue that the case study is more appropriately conceptualized as a research strategy that is associated with a number of data-gathering methods or procedures. Thus, the case study cannot be distinguished by a particular method, although it is likely to include one or more qualitative procedures in the mix of methods used to excavate and understand any particular case.

To summarize the foregoing, we have identified what we regard as the three central, defining features of the case study. Taken together, we can conceptualize the case study as *a research strategy that seeks to generate richly detailed, thick, and holistic elaborations and understandings of instances or* *variants of bounded social phenomena through the triangulation of multiple methods that include but are not limited to qualitative procedures.* The virtues of this conceptualization are threefold: first, it captures what most case studies with which we are familiar actually do; second, it clearly suggests that a case study is constituted not only by its focus (e.g., on an instance of some more generic phenomenon, a particular theoretical concept or process, or an interesting social event) but also by two additional sets of overlapping characteristics—the generation of holistic analyses by means of procedural triangulation—that together congeal into a distinctive research strategy; and third, it distinguishes the case study from other research procedures and methods. Indeed, given the conceptualization proffered here, it should be clear how the case study differs from the other methods and data-generating strategies, such as survey research, ethnography, in-depth interviews, focus group research, and experimental research.

Guidelines for Conducting a Case Study

How does one proceed in conducting the case study as conceptualized above? Although there are no consensual procedures clearly articulated in the case study literature, it is unlikely that any of its proponents would take exception with the basic steps outlined by Lofland (1996) for conducting case studies of social movement organizations. These steps include (1) selecting a case, (2) collecting data on the case, (3) asking questions about the case, and (4) answering the questions raised (Lofland 1996: 25). The first two steps focus attention on the *procedural guidelines* associated with case studies, such as acquiring a good sense of what the case is a case of and the extent to which it is an appropriate empirical venue for pursuing one's research interests, and then determining the existence and accessibility of pertinent data sources and the kinds of methods necessary to tap and mine those data caches. The second two steps constitute *analytic guidelines* by directing attention to the articulation of generic questions about aspects of the case or cases, and then to the development of empirically grounded answers to or propositions about those focal questions. Rather than reiterate in summary form Lofland's discussion of each step, we elaborate a number of procedural and analytic guidelines that we regard as fundamental to conducting case study research that generates a richly detailed, thick, and holistic understanding of the case or system of action in question. We illustrate each of these sets of guidelines with reference to social movement research.

Procedural Guidelines

In describing procedural guidelines, we refer to a number of underlying principles that are most relevant throughout the case selection and data collection phases of the case study research process, and that enhance the prospect of conducting an empirically compelling case study. We think there are at least four such procedural guidelines, although we do not claim that they are exhaustive. Listed in the form of research directives, case study research should be conducted so that it is (1) open-ended and flexible, (2) multiperspectival, (3) longitudinal, and (4) triangulated in terms of researchers as well as methods.

Open-ended and Flexible Research

As an orienting procedural principle, case study research should be open-ended and flexible in terms of both the design and execution of the research. This is not only because case study researchers are generally on the lookout for multiple and varied data sources, but also because there rarely is reason to be wedded to a particular method at the outset of the research. Instead, it is more common to adapt the methodology to the exigencies of the field, that is, to new data sources and data-gathering opportunities as they arise. The reason for this flexibility and eclecticism is rooted, in large measure, in the tendency for case studies to

> begin with a broad, general set of questions or understandings about the phenomena under investigation and then become more focused as the research progresses. Initially, they are rather like exploratory geological expeditions, with more focused probes occurring after the contours of the landscape have been mapped. Consequently, new or unanticipated events, relations or processes, as well as data sources, frequently surface with the turn of the corner. And these unexpected observations often lead, in turn, to the formulation of new questions and foci for investigation, thus making for a dynamic, recursive research process. (Snow and Anderson 1991: 162)

McAdam's case study of the 1964 Mississippi Freedom Summer campaign aptly illustrates this open-ended, recursive process. In the prologue to his book *Freedom Summer* (1988), McAdam recounts how he "stumbled" on to a data cache that was not only different from what he was looking for but that led to a study that was different in focus and substance from what he initially planned to pursue. So what was it that McAdam stumbled upon that prompted him to shift his focus from the links between Freedom Summer participants and the later movements of the 1960s and 1970s to the precipitants and consequences of participation in the Freedom Summer campaign? It was the discovery of "the original five-page applications filled out" not only "by the volunteers in advance of the summer" but also "by an additional 300 persons who had applied to the project, been accepted, but for whatever reason had failed to go to Mississippi" (McAdam 1988: 7–8). Prior to this unanticipated discovery, he was looking for a list of all summer volunteers who also indicated the college or university they were attending. What he found, however, was far better. As he put it:

> I had serendipitously stumbled onto the makings of a kind of naturalistic experiment. Here were two groups—volunteers and no-shows—that presumably looked fairly similar going into the summer. One had the experience of Freedom Summer. The other did not. (McAdam 1988: 8)

And thus was born his in-depth examination of the correlates and consequences of participation in the Freedom Summer campaign.

The important point of such research experiences for our purposes is that they not only underscore the open-ended character of the case study, but they highlight its utility or payoff as well: the discovery of novel data sources and the not infrequent generation of unexpected findings.

Multiperspectival Orientation

A second procedural guideline, in terms of the design and execution of case study research, is the development and maintenance of a multiperspectival orientation. What this means in practice is heightened realization that a grounded understanding of the object of analysis—be it a social entity, a social process, or a set of events—and its embedding context requires consideration of the array of relevant actors and voices. This realization of the importance of accessing different but interacting perspectives that constitute, in part, the phenomenon under investigation is consistent with the "polyphonic" sensibilities of the recent interpretative approaches associated with strands of postmodernism and cultural studies (Denzin 1989a: 113–15; Rosaldo 1989), as well as with Schutz's (1964) earlier emphasis on "multiple realities."[8] As well, this multiperspectival orientation is called for within the study of social movements by the recognition that any particular movement organization is embedded within a "multiorganizational field" consisting of at least three sets of actors or subfields: supporters or protagonists, antagonists, and bystanders or an audience (Curtis and Zurcher 1973; Hunt, Benford, and Snow 1994; Klandermans 1992). Thus, to understand the operation of one or more social movement organizations within the same movement calls for consideration of not only the perspectives and concerns of movement leaders and activists but also the views and concerns of antagonists (e.g., countermovements), targets (e.g., those from whom concessions are sought), allies (e.g., supportive friends within the broader movement or the political system), and constituents (e.g., individuals/groups who are the beneficiaries of the movement's collective action campaigns).

Illustrative is Cress and Snow's ethnographic examination of fifteen homeless social movement organizations (SMOs) in eight U.S. cities, in which they attempted to map the organizational field in which each SMO was embedded and discern patterns of interaction within each field, such as resource flows and goal attainment outcomes (1996, 2000). To do this necessitated that they secure information from the various sets of actors within each organizational field. Toward that end, they employed an "onion-snowball strategy" that began with a homeless SMO in each city and then moved outward within the field in a layered fashion contingent on the information and referrals received (Cress and Snow 2000: 1074). In general, this involved moving from interviews with SMO leaders and activists to facilitative or supportive organizations, such as churches and some service providers, to the targets of the SMOs and their collective actions, such as mayors' offices and police departments. By proceeding in this fashion, not only were the perspectives of relevant actors secured but patterns of interaction and influence were identified and mapped as well.

Whatever the focus of analysis or the issue(s) in question, to conduct multiperspectival research is to attempt to access, secure, and link together analytically the perspectives or voices of the range of relevant actors.

Longitudinal Research

The third procedural guideline for conducting case studies is that the research should be conceived as longitudinal, in the sense that it is conducted over a period of time. Making longitudinality a feature of the research enhances the prospect of capturing and analyzing social processes as they emerge and evolve. This characteristic is not peculiar to the case study, as comparative/historical research, ethnography, in-depth interviewing, and the longitudinal panel survey all lend themselves to discerning various social processes. But there is no question about the utility of the case study for grasping and monitoring social processes. Additionally, the case study enables one to get a handle on the mechanisms and interactions that affect the processes in question. Both of these utilities are readily evident in case-based research on various social movement processes, such as differential recruitment (e.g., McAdam 1986; Rochford 1982; Snow, Zurcher, and Ekland-Olson 1980), framing processes (e.g., Benford 1993a, 1993b; Capek and Gilderbloom 1992; Jenness and Broad 1997), conversion processes in the context of religious movements and "cults" (e.g., Downton 1979; Lofland and Stark 1965; Snow and Phillips 1980), processes inhibiting or facilitating the development of commitment and solidarity (e.g., Goodwin 1997; Hirsch 1990), and in the conjunction of various events and activities that shape and expand social movements and their influence (e.g., Boltanski 1987; Boltanski and Thevenot 1991; Cefai and Trom 2001; Cress and Snow 2000; Trom 1999). Even at the meso or organizational level, understanding of movement organizational fields and organizational dynamics, including resource acquisition processes and flows, has been advanced by case study research (e.g., Cress and Snow 1996; Staggenborg 1991).

Researcher Triangulation

The final procedural guideline we accent refers to the use and coordination of multiple researchers, what can be thought of as team field research or researcher triangulation. We argued earlier that procedural or methodological triangulation is a defining feature of the case study. But we noted that there are other forms of triangulation, one of which is the use and coordination of multiple researchers. This type of triangulation, although not a characteristic feature of the case study, clearly facilitates attainment of its general research objectives. This is because it is often difficult for a single researcher to acquire a detailed, holistic understanding of the context in which the phenomenon of interest operates. Thus, the use of multiple researchers attends to two problems endemic to the "lone ranger" case study or research design: it increases the prospect of gaining a variety of angles of vision and perspectives by allowing for the assumption of a greater variety of positions or roles in relation to the objects of research, and, in turn, it increases access to and facilitates retrieval of relevant data, in terms of both variety and depth. While many, and perhaps most, case studies are of the "lone ranger" variety, both within and outside of the study of social movements, the advantages of conducting a project that is triangulated in terms of investigators should be evident.

Illustration of the utility of researcher triangulation is provided by returning to Snow and Cress's study of the case of homeless social movement mobilization in selected U.S. cities. As noted earlier, the research involved the generation of three different data sets derived through a number of different methodologies: ethnography, archival and newspaper research, and face-to-face questionnaire interviewing. While one researcher might have been able to assemble one of the data sets, it would have been nearly impossible for a single researcher to conduct the research associated with all three data sets. Hence, five researchers were involved in various aspects of the study, with no fewer than two involved with each of the three components.

Thus, the study was triangulated in terms of research investigators as well as methods and data.

Analytic Guidelines

In describing analytic guidelines, we refer to a number of general principles that focus and sharpen empirically, conceptually, and theoretically the kinds of conclusions that can be derived from the research findings. These guidelines refer to general characteristics about the case in relation to other cases rather than to the empirical particulars of the case as a system of action. They focus attention on a number of ways in which cases can vary and the analytic implications of these dimensions of variation. We elaborate two such dimensions of variation. The first concerns the character of the case in relation to the subset of cases or larger phenomenon with which it is associated. Specifically, what kind of case is it? And second, it is useful to know whether the study is based on detailed examination of a single case or a comparison of multiple cases within the same set or genre of phenomena. Hence the question: How many cases is the study based on and what is the relationship of the case(s) to the encompassing entity?

Kinds of Cases

Situating a case in relation to other instances of the phenomenon of interest is a necessary condition for exploring analytically the conceptual and theoretical implications of one's findings. This can be done by addressing two issues. One is specifying what the phenomenon of interest is a case of. Is it a variant of a particular type or category of movement? Is it a particular theoretical concept or process? Or is it an interesting event or happening that merits investigation in its own right? Since this issue was discussed earlier in relation to conceptualization of the case study, we focus here on the second issue, which concerns the kind of case represented by the object of investigation. Sjoberg et al. (1991) and Yin (1989), among others, suggest that cases are generally one of four kinds: they are relatively typical or normal and thus constitute a representative case; they may be a critical case in the sense of constituting an ideal assessment of some observed or theorized principle; they are a deviant or negative case in that they constitute an exception to the expected pattern, be it observed or theorized; or they may be an extreme or unique case in the sense of not being fully comparable to other, seemingly similar cases. Whatever the ideal type of case represented by the actual case, there is implied familiarity with the set of phenomena of which it is a particular instance, such that the case for investigation can be situated in some fashion in relation to other phenomena that exhibit certain similarities.

Normal or Representative Cases

In actuality, few case studies of social movements clearly specify what kind of case they represent. Most imply typicality, but it is rarely stated explicitly or demonstrated empirically in a compelling fashion. This is not to say, however, that researchers do not sometimes acknowledge and struggle with this issue, devising ways to "normalize" their case or cases both strategically and rhetorically. Illustrative is Staggenborg's discussion of her focus on seven local pro-choice movement organizations in Chicago and Illinois, along with six national organizations, in her study of the movement nationally:

> The focus on a single state and local movement does raise the question of how typical the movement's activity in Illinois is, a problem shared by other case studies. In this book, however, the problem is mitigated in several ways: First, the national-level analysis reveals many processes parallel to those found locally, which suggests that the local findings are likely to be generalizable. Moreover, in studying the national movement as well as the state and local movements, some information pertaining to other states besides Illinois was obtained from knowledgeable movement leaders. . . . Finally, in the case of the pro-choice movement, there are published accounts of movement activity in several other states. . . . [which] I draw on . . . wherever possible to compare the Illinois movement with those in other states. (Staggenborg 1991: 9)

The clear implication of such case-normalizing discussions is that the case is fairly or reasonably representative of the larger social movement with which it is associated, and thus provides a basis for some sort of descriptive and/or theoretical generalization, a point to which we will return later.

Critical Cases

Although the case typicality presumption is operative in most movement case studies, some researchers highlight the critical character of their cases, emphasizing that they are ideal for getting a clear fix on the relevant empirical and theoretical issues. In their study of the tenant movement in the United States, for example, Capek and Gilderbloom (1992) suggest that their case-based comparison of Santa Monica and Houston was ideal in the critical sense because the former was a rent-controlled city whereas the later was not. As they explain:

> As "ideal types," or polar contrasts, of the regulated versus "the free enterprise" city . . . Santa Monica and Houston serve as important illustrative examples for a study of social movements. While Santa Monica experienced one of the most significant urban social movements in the 1970s

and 1980s, Houston was devoid of any significant social movements since the 1950s. By examining data from a city with a tenant's social movement (Santa Monica) and a city without a movement (Houston), we can probe the broader implications of such movements for urban policy. (Capek and Gilderbloom 1992: 7)

Their even more detailed case study of the tenant movement in Santa Monica is justified as well because it constituted a critical case in the sense that it facilitated the development of a program of progressive urban reform that, among other things, made Santa Monica "a national symbol of the heated debate over the place of regulation in the United States" (Capek and Gilderbloom 1992: 8–9). Thus, the Santa Monica case, particularly in conjunction with Houston, was regarded as a critical case for the examination and understanding of progressive urban movements and reform in the United States. In such cases, the issue of the typicality or representativeness of the case is essentially irrelevant, since it is particular features or characteristics of the case that make it an ideal or critical one for the set of issues or concerns in question.

Negative and Extreme Cases

We have just seen how some movement case studies are justified methodologically in terms of the "normality" or "typicality" of the cases, while others are rationalized in terms of the "criticality" of the cases. As noted previously, cases can also be justified methodologically on the grounds that they are "negative" or "deviant" in relation to other cases of the same genre or some set of principles,[9] or on the grounds that they are "extreme" cases in that they stand outside of or beyond the genre of cases with which they are typically associated.[10] Few, if any, movement case studies with which we are familiar claim to fall into either of these two typological categories, although the findings and theoretical implications of some movement case studies are or can be presented as negative cases with respect to existing movement theories and related hypotheses. A case in point is Snow and Phillips's (1980) assessment of the Lofland and Stark conversion model (1965) with data derived from Snow's case study (1993) of the growth and spread of the Nichiren Shoshu Buddhist movement in the United States. Lofland and Stark proffered a universal theory of conversion. The theory was grounded empirically in Lofland's case study (1977) of recruitment and conversion to a small, offbeat religious cult, dubbed the "doomsday cult," and articulated a set of seven conditions (acutely felt tension, religious problem-solving perspective, religious seekership, experiencing a turning point, development of cult affective bonds, neutralization of extracult attachments, and intensive interaction with moment members) that were deemed to be necessary and sufficient for the occurrence of conversion. However, Snow and Phillips's analysis of data focusing on conversion to and participation in Nichiren Shoshu revealed that only two of the seven posited conditions were necessary (formation of cult affective bonds and intensive interaction), thus suggesting modification of the theory through the process of what is variously referred to as negative case analysis or analytic induction (Becker 1998; Lincoln and Guba 1985).

Although a close reading of the methodological procedures underlying most movement case studies is suggestive of the kind or type of case they represent, this is too rarely clearly articulated. We say too rarely because articulating the type of case one's case is provides the reader with a kind of signpost for evaluating the claims and merits of the study. More explicitly, to know whether a case is "normal," "critical," "deviant," or "extreme" suggests different evaluative criteria and expectations because, as we have suggested, different types of cases have different uses and limitations.

Number of Cases and Their Relationships

The second dimension of contrast that has analytic implications concerns whether the study focuses on a single case or a comparison of multiple cases within the same set or genre of phenomena. This is an important distinction, since the case study is sometimes narrowly conceived as the study of a single phenomenon or a single instance of a broader category. This conceptualization is contrary to ours, however. As suggested earlier (see note 7), we contend that the case study can be both, a study of a single case or of multiple cases, so long as the cases share some attributes in common and are variants of some larger, encompassing category as, for example, in the case of the relationship between social movement organizations and the broader movement of which they are a part. This position is consistent with Yin's (1989: 46–60), whose discussion of various case study designs includes both analyses of single cases and multiple cases embedded within a larger case. There are examples of both in the study of social movements, as well as studies that fall between the single and multiple case prototypes by examining the relationship between a single case, such as an SMO, and the larger movement in which it is embedded and presumably revelatory and illustrative. We briefly discuss and illustrate each of these variants.

Single Cases

Analyses of single cases are exhibited by studies of single movements that are not based on studies of one or more subcases. Such studies typically take one of two forms. The first is characterized by studies that provide a primarily descriptive overview of a single, usually national-level movement. The case is the movement as a whole, and the objective is to situate it in time and place, in history that is, and to say something about its beliefs or ideology, its appeal and diffusion, and its operation. The discussion is framed in terms of extant, and typically fashionable, theoretical perspectives and issues pertinent to social movements, but the primary contribution is descriptive rather than analytic in the sense of refining or extending movement-related theoretical arguments or conceptualizations. Illustrations of this variety of movement case study include Bromley and Shupe's (1979) analysis of "the Moonies" (the Unification Church) in the United States, and Eve and Harrold's (1991) examination of the creationist movement in modern America.

The second form taken by single case studies makes the analysis of major movement processes and issues the centerpiece of the inquiry. A holistic, highly contextualized, descriptive understanding of the movement is still provided, but it is secondary to elaborating empirically how these focal processes, which typically are presumed to operate across movements, operate within the context of the movement studied and how these more specific findings extend and/or refine the relevant theoretical or conceptual understandings within the field. Illustrative of this type of case analysis are Lofland's (1977) previously discussed study of a small religious movement, with emphasis on the processes of proselytization and conversion, and Goodwin's (1997) study of the Huk rebellion in the Philippines, with its emphasis on affective ties and their implications for understanding the solidarity and discipline of the participants. In each case, the author's work is acknowledged as much, and perhaps more so, for its theoretical and conceptual contributions as for its descriptive accounts of the movement or movement events studied. Lofland's research (1977), for example, provided the empirical grounding for Lofland and Stark's influential theory of conversion (1965), and Goodwin's research (1997) helped to resuscitate both empirically and theoretically the role of emotion and passion in relation to the operation and functioning of social movements.

Multiple Cases

Case study analyses of multiple cases embedded within a larger, encompassing case also appear to take two forms in the study of social movements. In one form, the cases, typically movement SMOs or events, are taken to be "normal cases" that are arguably representative of the broader movement. Staggenborg's (1991) use of thirteen social movement organizations (six national and seven local organizations in Chicago and Illinois) as the basis for understanding the pro-choice movement in America is illustrative of this use of multiple cases, as is Wright's (1997) study of homeless protest in San Jose and Chicago to gain descriptive and analytic leverage on homeless mobilization more broadly.

In the second form of multiple case analysis, the cases are examined in a comparative framework that allows for a more nuanced assessment of variation among the cases with respect to the broader movement and processes or conceptual issues examined. Cress and Snow's (1996, 2000) study of homeless social movement mobilization is illustrative. As previously mentioned, the ethnographic/qualitative segment of the study involved an examination of fifteen homeless SMOs in eight U.S. cities. Based on the data gathered for each of the SMOs and using the analytic technique of qualitative comparative analysis,[11] Cress and Snow were able to discern differences in resource mobilization, benefactors, organizational viability, and outcomes that not only contributed to an understanding of the homeless movement in general, but to detailed understanding of local variations and to the factors that accounted for those variations.

Whether the multiple case study is basically illustrative or comparative, it appears to be especially useful for extending and refining relevant theoretical perspectives, as illustrated by the implications of Staggenborg's study (1988) for understanding leadership professionalization and SMO formalization, and of Cress and Snow's study for a more textured understanding of the dynamics of resource mobilization on the margins (1996) and movement outcomes (2000).

Synecdochical or Revelatory Cases

We noted a third form of movement case study, which does not fit neatly into either the single case or multiple case study category. Instead, a detailed, holistic study of a specific case is used as a springboard, in almost a synecdochical fashion, for gaining insight into and understanding of the larger movement of which it is a part, and is presumably revelatory as either a representative or critical case. We refer to this as a synecdochical or revelatory case study in that a part or segment of the larger movement is used as the major conduit for grasping the whole.[12] Illustrative is Capek and Gilderbloom's (1992) previously mentioned case study of the tenants' movement in the United States during the 1980s, which was based in part on the use of Santa Monica as a critical case. Rochford's (1985) study of the Hare Krishna movement also exemplifies this type of case study. Although Rochford does not refer explicitly to his study as a case study, he uses his ethnographic fieldwork experience, primarily with the Krishna commune in Los Angeles, as the basis for his account of the development and transformation of the Krishna movement in the United States.

In this section we have elaborated how case studies can vary in terms of the kinds of cases they constitute, the number of cases on which the study is based, and the relationship between the case and what it is taken to illustrate or represent. The rationale for exploring these dimensions of contrast among cases is that they can have significant analytic implications for the empirical, conceptual, and theoretical reach of the research. Thus, we discussed these dimensions of contrast in terms of analytic guidelines that the researcher should have in mind throughout the entire case study research process, and particularly when considering the implications of the research findings.

Contributions, Limitations, and Theoretical Generalization

The strengths and major contributions of the case study are suggested by our very conceptualization of it as a research strategy for generating thick, in-depth, holistic understandings of cases as cultural systems of action, and by the procedural and analytic guidelines for conducting case studies that have significant empirical, conceptual, and theoretical implications. Unpacked and decoded, the upshot is that insofar as case studies approximate this conceptualization and are conducted in terms of the accented procedural and analytic guidelines, they should generate richly detailed and holistic accounts of the social entities, activities, events, or processes that are the focus of study. Moreover, it is arguable that because of the methodologically triangulated character of the case study, it should be able to generate richer, more detailed, and more multivocal analyses than any single methodology. If so, then the contributions of movement case studies to understanding particular movements and the dynamics and processes linked to those movements should be considerable. Hence, the case for conducting case studies.

But is that it? Can or do case studies yield more than rich, detailed, contextualized accounts of social phenomena that are interesting in their own right, as with the Civil Rights movement, the women's movement, and the homeless movement, for example? "No" or "probably not" is the likely stereotypic, textbook answer to this question, in large part because of the presumption that the case study is bound up in itself in a fashion that does not allow for or facilitate generalization. Indeed, this presumed lack of the generalizability of the case study constitutes the major stereotypic weakness or shortcoming attributed to it. This is not a particularly troublesome shortcoming for methodologies associated with the more ideographic, interpretive disciplines or perspectives, but when the encompassing discipline is one that places a premium on generalization, as does sociology, then this weakness is especially damning. However, like most stereotypic characterizations, this one is neither absolutely true nor false. Rather, the relationship between the case study and generalizability is contingent on the kind of generalization at issue and the type of case study.

Regarding the kind of generalization, the knee-jerk, elementary presumption is that there really is only one kind: statistical, or enumerative, generalization. This is the kind of generalization associated, for example, with the projection of national election outcomes based on a survey of 1,500 randomly selected adults. Clearly the case study is inappropriate for this kind of generalization. But such statistical generalization is not the only form of generalization. There is also analytic, or theoretical, generalization, which is the kind of generalization case studies are most likely to pursue. As Yin, among others, has noted, one of the goals of the case study "is to expand and generalize theories (analytic generalization) and not to enumerate frequencies (statistical generalization)."[13] And in this respect, case studies are more like experiments than surveys in that "they are generalizable to theoretical propositions and not to populations or universes" (Yin 1989: 21).

But how is such theoretical generalization accomplished via the case study? We think it occurs through three forms of theoretical development that have been associated with, but are not peculiar to, qualitative research strategies: theoretical discovery, theoretical extension, and theoretical refinement.[14] *Theoretical discovery*, in the context of more inductive, qualitative research, entails the generation of what Glaser and Strauss (1967) referred to as "grounded theory." Examples of such discovery among movement case studies include Lofland and Stark's (1965) theory of conversion grounded in Lofland's earlier ethnographic case study of a small religious "cult," and Snow and his colleagues' (Snow et al. 1986; Snow and Benford 1992) contributions to the development of a framing perspective on movements that evolved from their respective qualitative case studies of the Nichiren Shoshu Buddhist movement, the peace movement, and anti-homeless neighborhood movements.

Theoretical extension, rather than generating new theory, extends existing theoretical formulations to new or different social categories, contexts, or processes, or even to other levels of theory, as say between substantive and formal theory.[15] Examples of movement case studies that have contributed to theoretical development via extension fall into two categories: those that extend or generalize from a case study of a specific movement to the broader, more general category of social movements, as in the case of most analytic, rather than primarily descriptive, movement case studies; and those that

broaden the application of a theoretical principle or argument from one domain of analysis to another, as in the case of Goodwin's (1997) borrowing
from and extending aspects of psychoanalytic social theory to the problem
of the relationship between affectual ties and solidarity in high-risk social
movements.

Theoretical refinement, the last of the mentioned avenues to theoretical
generalization, involves the modification of an existing theoretical perspective, or aspects of it, with new case material. Examples of this form of theoretical development are fairly abundant in the social movement arena. Illustrative are Staggenborg's (1988, 1991) suggested refinements of aspects of
resource mobilization theory derived from her case-based findings regarding
leadership professionalization and organizational formalization in the pro-
choice movement, the modifications to the Lofland-Stark conversion theory
(1965) suggested by Snow's case study of recruitment and conversion to a
different religious movement (Snow and Phillips 1980; Snow 1993), and the
modifications to various examinations of the determinants of movement
outcomes suggested by Cress and Snow's (2000) investigation of the factors
accounting for variation in the outcomes of fifteen homeless SMOs in eight
U.S. cities. More specifically, Cress and Snow's research highlights the importance of conjunctural/interactive explanations of outcomes rather then
single-theory explanations. As they conclude, upon examining the relative
influence of hypothesized organizational, tactical, political, and framing determinants of movement outcomes,

> our findings identify the importance of organizational viability and fram-
> ing activities for obtaining targeted outcomes by homeless SMOs. When
> these conditions are present and occur in conjunction with political me-
> diation, the particulars of which affect the types of tactics that are associ-
> ated with successful outcome attainment, we found that the homeless
> SMOs are likely to have their greatest impact. While it is an empirical
> question whether this conjunction of conditions holds for other move-
> ments, the findings and analysis suggest that attempts to understand
> movement outcomes that focus on the ways in which different conditions
> interact and combine are likely to be more compelling and robust, both
> theoretically and empirically, than efforts that focus on the conditions
> specified by a single perspective or that pit one perspective against another.
> (Cress and Snow 2000: 1101)

Taken together, these three avenues to theoretical development indicate
that the utility of movement case studies is not limited to the generation of
richly detailed, thick, holistic descriptive accounts of the movements or

processes investigated, but that case studies can also function as an important mechanism for theoretical generalization. This is more likely to be so for some types of case studies than others, however. As noted previously, different types of case studies—those with a focus on selected social processes or theoretical principles, and those based on the analyses of multiple cases rather than single cases—are likely to have a higher yield in terms of theoretical development and generalizability.

These observations suggest at least three ways in which the prospective conceptual/theoretical reach and yield of movement case studies can be enhanced: the first is to not only be sensitized to the various forms of theoretical development but design the study with at least one of these pathways (discovery, extension, and refinement) as an objective; the second is to try to conduct case studies that illuminate selected movement-related processes and theoretical issues as well as provide detailed, holistic analyses; and the third is to broaden the study to include for comparative purposes, insofar as it is possible, additional cases or comparison groups.

In light of the foregoing, three general conclusions seem warranted: first, that case studies are not inimical to conceptual and theoretical generalization; second, that movement case studies can be designed to enhance their theoretical yield; and third, that contributions of the case study as a research strategy within the social movement arena are more varied and potentially far-reaching than generally presumed.

Notes

The initial draft of this chapter was written while the first author was a fellow at the Center for Advanced Studies in the Behavioral Sciences, Stanford. Gratitude is expressed for the financial support provided by the center's general funds. We also wish to acknowledge the editors of this volume, Doug McAdam, and an anonymous reviewer for their constructive and helpful comments on an earlier draft of the chapter.

1. We conceptualize social movements broadly to include all collectivities acting with some degree of organization outside of institutional channels for the purpose of promoting or resisting change in the group, society, or world order of which it is a part (for an elaboration of this conceptualization, see McAdam and Snow 1997: xviii–xxvi). This conceptualization is sufficiently broad to include movements that range organizationally from informal networks of collective actors to an interconnected set of social movement organizations, that may use various tactics including but not limited to standard protest, and that seek various kinds of changes or transformations, ranging from personal to religious to political.

2. Throughout the chapter, we refer to the case study as both a research strategy

and as a method. We use the latter advisedly, however, as we emphasize that the case study is a research strategy rather than a particular method.

3. The injunction to ask repeatedly, "What is this a case of?" suggests that the answer to the question may not be known with certitude at the outset of a study. This is because empirical and theoretical understanding of what the object of study is a case of is likely to emerge, and even change, during the research process. This suggests, then, that answers to the question "What is this a case of?" that are proffered at the outset of actual research can only be provisional and tentative at best, and thus have an almost propositional character to them. See Ragin 1992 for further discussion of this issue.

4. Yin contends that the object or phenomenon of study be "contemporary," but we find this stipulation too inelastic and narrow in that it precludes consideration of cases that have already run their course. Within the collective action/social movement arena, for example, we would argue that there are numerous studies that constitute case studies even though they focus on concrete instances of collective action that have already occurred, as with McAdam's (1988) study of the Freedom Summer campaign of 1964, Goodwin's (1997) study of affective ties and solidarity in relation to the Huk rebellion in the Philippines, and Piven and Cloward's (1977) compilation of studies of four poor people's movements. This may suggest that the line between case studies and historical/comparative studies is often a blurred, hazy one, but we do not find such ambiguity to be particularly troublesome inasmuch as we suspect that there are often points of overlap among methods.

5. The phrase "cultural systems of action" is borrowed from Znaniecki (1934) to distinguish human systems from other systems that exist independent of human activity and experience.

6. The terms *activities* and *routines* are used broadly to include various kinds of interactional episodes, relationships, events, and performances that may congeal or cluster into a movement and thus constitute important aspects of a movement. See, for example, Tilly's (1994) discussion of movements as a "historically specific cluster of political performances," and Olzak's (1989) overview of collective action event analysis. Obviously the analyses of events differ depending on whether they are the object of a case study rather than an event history analysis.

7. One might reasonably question whether this study, with data on homeless SMOs and movement activity in multiple cities, stretches the concept of the case study beyond recognition. Obviously, we think not, for the various data points (e.g., fifteen SMOs) are all instances of a broader, encompassing category, in this case, the homeless movement in the United States. Thus, the critical consideration in determining whether a study of multiple cases constitutes a case study depends on whether those multiple cases are instances of a broader, more generic category. If they are, then examination and comparison of a subset of the variant cases are likely

to yield a much more detailed and nuanced understanding of the broader category as a case than is study of a single instance of it. We discuss this issue further later in the chapter.

8. To acknowledge that there may be an array of relevant voices and realities associated with any given movement or movement activity does not presume that all voices are equally influential or relevant, as often implied in some variants of postmodernism. Just as sets of social actors are arrayed hierarchically in social life, so are the perspectives associated with them, as Becker's (1998) concept of "hierarchy of credibility" makes clear.

9. Although the concepts of the negative case and the deviant case are customarily used interchangeably, Emigh (1997) has argued that they are distinctive.

10. There is debate among students of genocide and the Holocaust as to whether the latter can be compared with other instances or cases of the former. If not, the Holocaust constitutes an extreme or unique case that may not be explicable in terms used to account for seemingly similar cases. For a discussion of the extreme case, with reference to the Holocaust, see Sjoberg et al. (1991: 62–63).

11. Qualitative comparative analysis is an analytic technique based on Boolean algebra that facilitates identification of the necessary and sufficient conditions for an event to occur when comparing a relatively small number of cases, as typically occurs with cases studies based on the analysis of multiple cases. See Ragin 1987 for a detailed discussion of this analytic technique.

12. The term *revelatory* is used by Yin to refer to case studies that allow for the observation and analysis of "a phenomenon previously inaccessible to scientific investigation" (1989: 48). We regard this as a more general function or utility of case studies, especially when based on qualitative fieldwork. Thus, our use of the term *revelatory* here is somewhat more specific and concrete, as when a particular case— a movement SMO, for example—is used as the basis for gaining insight into and illuminating the larger movement.

13. For further discussion of the distinctions between statistical generalization and the generalization potential of the case study, see Desrosieres 1998. Also, see Stake 1978 for discussion of the link between the case study and what he calls "naturalistic" generalization, which refers to the tendency of case study research to facilitate understanding of the phenomenon in question because it is more likely to resonate with readers than most other kinds of research with the exception of studies based on ethnography and in-depth interviewing.

14. See Snow and Morrill 1995 for a more detailed discussion of these forms of theoretical development, particularly as they relate to qualitative and ethnographic research.

15. Burawoy (1998) provides a detailed and persuasive discussion of the connection between theoretical extension and the case study method in his elaboration

of what he calls "the extended case method." We clearly agree with his coupling of theoretical development and "reconstruction" via the extended case method, although we contend that extension is only one of several ways in which the case study can facilitate theoretical generalization and development.

References

Becker, Howard S. 1998. *Tricks of the Trade: How to Think about Your Research While You're Doing It.* Chicago: University of Chicago Press.

Benford, Robert D. 1993a. "Frame Disputes within the Nuclear Disarmament Movement." *Social Forces* 71: 677–701.

———. 1993b. "'You Could Be the Hundredth Monkey': Collection Action Frames and Vocabularies of Motive within the Nuclear Disarmament Movement." *Sociological Quarterly* 34: 195–216.

Boltanski, Luc. 1987. *The Making of a Class: Cadres in French Society.* Cambridge: Cambridge University Press.

Boltanski, Luc, and Laurent Thevenot. 1991. *De la justification. Les Economies de la grandeur.* Paris: Gallimard.

Bromley, David G., and Anson D. Shupe. 1979. *The Moonies in America.* Beverly Hills: Sage.

Burawoy, Michael. 1998. "The Extended Case Method." *Sociological Theory* 16: 4–33.

Capek, Stella M., and John I. Gilderbloom. 1992. *Community versus Commodity: Tenants and the American City.* Albany: State University of New York Press.

Cefai, Daniel, and Danny Trom. 2001. "Action collective et mouvements sociaux." *La Mobilisation dans des arenes publiques,* Raisons Pratiques N. 11. Paris: Editions de l'EHESS.

Cress, Daniel M., and David A. Snow. 1996. "Mobilization at the Margins: Resources, Benefactors, and the Viability of Homeless Social Movement Organizations." *American Sociological Review* 61: 1089–1109.

———. 2000. "The Outcomes of Homeless Mobilization: The Influence of Organization, Disruption, Political Mediation, and Framing." *American Journal of Sociology* 105: 1063–1104.

Curtis, Russell L., and Louis A. Zurcher. 1973. "Stable Resources of Protest Movements: The Multi-organizational Field." *Social Forces* 52: 53–61.

Denzin, Norman K. 1989a. *Interpretive Interactionism.* Newbury Park, Calif.: Sage.

———. 1989b. *The Research Act.* 3d ed. Englewood Cliffs, N.J.: Prentice Hall.

Desrosieres, Alain. 1998. *The Politics of Large Numbers: A History of Statistical Reasoning.* Cambridge, Mass.: Harvard University Press.

Downton, James V. 1979. *Sacred Journeys: The Conversion of Young Americans to Divine Light Mission.* New York: Columbia University Press.

Emigh, Rebecca. 1997. "The Power of Negative Thinking: The Use of the Negative Case in the Development of Sociological Theory." *Theory and Society* 26: 649–84.

Eve, Raymond A., and Francis B. Harold. 1991. *The Creationist Movement in Modern America*. Boston: Twayne Publishers.

Feagin, Joe R., Anthony M. Orum, and Gideon Sjoberg, eds. 1991. *A Case for the Case Study*. Chapel Hill: University of North Carolina Press.

Glaser, Barney G., and Anselm L. Strauss. 1967. *The Discovery of Grounded Theory.* Chicago: Aldine.

Goodwin, Jeff. 1997. "The Libidinal Constitution of a High-Risk Social Movement: Affectual Ties and Solidarity in the Huk Rebellion, 1946–1954." *American Sociological Review* 62: 53–69.

Hirsch, Eric L. 1990. "Sacrifice for the Cause: The Impact of Group Processes on Recruitment and Commitment in Protest Movements." *American Sociological Review* 55: 243–54.

Hunt, Scott A., Robert D. Benford, and David A. Snow. 1994. "Identity Fields: Framing Processes and the Social Construction of Movement Identities." In *New Social Movements: From Ideology to Identity,* edited by Enrique Laraña, Hank Johnston, and Joseph R. Gusfield, 185–208. Philadelphia: Temple University Press.

Jenness, Valerie, and Kendal Broad. 1997. *Hate Crimes: New Social Movements and the Politics of Violence*. New York: Aldine De Gruyter.

Klandermans, Bert. 1992. The Social Construction of Protest and Multiorganizational Fields." In *Frontiers in Social Movement Theory,* edited by Aldon D. Morris and Carol McClurg Mueller, 77–103. New Haven, Conn.: Yale University Press.

Lincoln, Yvonna S., and Egon G. Guba. 1985. *Naturalistic Inquiry.* Beverly Hills, Calif.: Sage.

Lofland, John. 1977 [1966]. *Doomsday Cult: A Study of Conversion, Proselytization, and Maintenance of Faith*. Enlarged ed. New York: Irvington.

———. 1996. *Social Movement Organizations: Guide to Research on Insurgent Realities*. New York: Aldine De Gruyter.

Lofland, John, and Rodney Stark. 1965. "Becoming a World Saver: A Theory of Conversion to a Deviant Perspective." *American Sociological Review* 30: 862–74.

McAdam, Doug. 1986. "Recruitment to High-Risk Activism: The Case of Freedom Summer." *American Journal of Sociology* 92: 64–90.

———. 1988. *Freedom Summer.* New York: Oxford University Press.

McAdam, Doug, and David A. Snow. 1997. *Social Movements: Readings on Their Emergence, Mobilization, and Dynamics.* Los Angeles: Roxbury.

McCarthy, John D., and Mayer N. Zald. 1977. "Resource Mobilization and Social Movements: A Partial Theory." *American Journal of Sociology* 82: 1212–42.

McGrath, Joseph E., Joanne Martin, and Richard Kulka. 1982. *Judgment Calls in Research.* Beverly Hills, Calif.: Sage.

Olzak, Susan. 1989. "Analysis of Events in the Study of Collective Action." *Annual Review of Sociology* 15: 119–41.

Orum, Anthony M., Joe R. Feagin, and Gideon Sjoberg. 1991. "Introduction: The Nature of the Case Study." In *A Case for the Case Study,* edited by Joe R. Feagin, Anthony M. Orum, and Gideon Sjoberg, 1–26. Chapel Hill: University of North Carolina Press.

Piven, Francis Fox, and Richard A. Cloward. 1977. *Poor People's Movements: Why They Succeed, How They Fail.* New York: Random House.

Ragin, Charles C. 1987. *The Comparative Method: Moving beyond Qualitative and Quantitative Strategies.* Berkeley: University of California Press.

———. 1992. "Introduction: Cases of 'What Is a Case?'" in *What Is a Case: Exploring the Foundations of Social Inquiry,* edited by Charles C. Ragin and Howard S. Becker, 1–17. New York: Cambridge University Press.

Rochford, E. Burke, Jr. 1982. "Recruitment Strategies, Ideology, and Organization in the Hare Krishna Movement." *Social Problems* 29: 339–410.

———. 1985. *Hare Krishna in America.* New Brunswick, N.J.: Rutgers University Press.

Rosaldo, Renato. 1989. *Culture and Truth: The Remaking of Social Analysis.* Boston: Beacon Press.

Schutz, Alfred. 1964. *Collected Papers II: Studies in Social Theory.* The Hague: Martinus Nijhoff.

Sjoberg, Gideon, Norma Williams, Ted R. Vaughan, and Andree F. Sjoberg. 1991. "The Case Study Approach in Social Research: Basic Methodological Issues." In *A Case for the Case Study,* edited by Joe R. Feagin, Anthony M. Orum, and Gideon Sjoberg, 27–79. Chapel Hill: University of North Carolina Press.

Smelser, Neil. 1963. *Theory of Collective Behavior.* New York: Free Press.

Snow, David A. 1993. *Shakubuku: A Study of the Nichiren Shoshu Buddhist Movement in America, 1960–1975.* New York: Garland.

Snow, David A., and Leon Anderson. 1991. "Researching the Homeless: The Characteristics and Virtues of the Case Study." In *A Case for the Case Study,* edited by Joe R. Feagin, Anthony M. Orum, and Gideon Sjoberg, 148–73. Chapel Hill: University of North Carolina Press.

Snow, David A., and Robert D. Benford. 1992. "Master Frames and Cycles of Protest." In *Frontiers in Social Movement Theory,* edited by Aldon D. Morris and Carol McClurg Mueller, 133–55. New Haven, Conn.: Yale University Press.

Snow, David A., and Calvin Morrill. 1995. "Linking Ethnography and Theoretical Development: Systematizing the Analytic Process." Unpublished manuscript.

Snow, David A., and Cynthia L. Phillips. 1980. "The Lofland-Stark Conversion Model: A Critical Assessment." *Social Problems* 27: 430–47.

Snow, David., E. Burke Rochford Jr., Steven K. Worden, and Robert D. Benford. 1986. "Frame Alignment Processes, Micromobilization, and Movement Participation." *American Sociological Review* 51: 464–81.

Snow, David A., Louis A. Zurcher, and Sheldon Ekland-Olson. 1980. "Social Networks and Social Movements: A Microstructural Approach to Differential Recruitment." *American Sociological Review* 45: 787–801.

Staggenborg, Suzanne. 1988. "The Consequences of Professionalization and Formalization in the Pro-Choice Movement." *American Sociological Review* 53: 585–606.

———. 1991. *The Pro-Choice Movement: Organization and Activism in the Abortion Conflict.* New York: Oxford University Press.

Stake, Robert E. 1978. "The Case-Study Method of Social Inquiry." *Educational Researcher* 7: 5–8.

Taylor, Verta. 1996. *Rock-a-by Baby: Feminism, Self-Help, and Postpartum Depression.* New York: Routledge.

Tilly, Charles. 1994. "Social Movements as Historically Specific Clusters of Political Performances." *Berkeley Journal of Sociology* 38: 1–30.

Trom, Danny. 1999. "De la réfutation de l'effet NIMBY considérée comme une pratique militante." *Revue Française de Science Politique* 1: 31–50.

Wagner, David. 1993. *Checkerboard Square: Culture and Resistance in a Homeless Community.* Boulder, Colo.: Westview Press.

Webb, Eugene J., Donald T. Campbell, Richard D. Schwarz, Lee Sechrest, and Janet Belew. 1981. *Nonreactive Measures in the Social Sciences.* 2d ed. Boston: Houghton Mifflin.

Wright, Talmadge. 1997. *Out of Place: Homeless Mobilizations, Subcities, and Contested Landscapes.* Albany: State University of New York Press.

Yin, Robert K. 1989. *Case Study Research: Design and Methods.* Rev. ed. Newbury Park, Calif.: Sage.

Znaniecki, Florian. 1934. *The Method of Sociology.* New York: Farrar and Rinehart.

7

Network Analysis

Mario Diani

Social Movements and Social Networks

For many years, researchers have studied the network nature of social movements, both interorganizational and political networks (Curtis and Zurcher 1973; Zald and McCarthy 1987) and subcultural and countercultural ones (Gerlach and Hine 1970; Melucci 1996). Recently, however, systematic empirical analyses of movement networks have grown substantially (Diani and McAdam forthcoming). Most have focused on recruitment processes and participation (Fernandez and McAdam 1989; Kitts 2000; Knoke and Wisely 1990; McAdam 1988; McAdam and Fernandez 1990; McAdam and Paulsen 1993; Snow, Zurcher, and Ekland-Olson 1980). Others have addressed interorganizational dynamics (Diani 1995; Rosenthal et al. 1985; 1997). Still others have investigated how the structure of a given social system shapes collective action on the basis of either historical evidence (Gould 1995) or simulation data (Marwell and Oliver 1993; Oberschall and Kim 1996). Some have even maintained that network forms of organization represent the distinctive trait of social movements (Diani 1992b). Attention to network dynamics has also been strong among those studying individual participation or interorganizational processes among voluntary organizations at large (Galaskiewicz 1979; McPherson and Rotolo 1996).

Social network analysis enables us to conduct systematic investigations of network processes within social movements from two main perspectives. First, it helps us to analyze how collective action is affected by the actors' embeddedness in preexisting networks. Questions addressed so far include, among others: How does the network location of individuals shape their decisions to act as well as their overall behavior (Fernandez and McAdam 1989)? How does the network location of social movement organizations (SMOs) relate to their influence, visibility, or capacity to act as movement representatives (Diani 1995)? How do properties of the social structure in which a movement operates affect its performance (e.g., Gould 1995)? However, social ties originate from action as much as they constrain it (Emirbayer and Goodwin 1994; Sewell 1992). Second, then, we may use network analysis to illustrate how social movement actors create new linkages that in turn will constrain the subsequent development of protest and/or subcultural activities. The shape of networks may be regarded as the outcome of network-building strategies, which in turn can tell us a lot about the nature of a movement at a given point in time (Diani 1995).

Although network analysis is often associated with a set of formal, heavily mathematical tools, it is best conceived as a broader approach to social processes, which may also be conducted through qualitative studies. Here I present guidelines for a quantitative network analysis, but the concepts I introduce may also be subject to qualitative treatment. As the interpretation of action hardly derives straightforwardly from network properties, networks require careful investigation in order to reconstruct the meaning of certain ties (Emirbayer and Goodwin 1994; Somers 1994). To this purpose, triangulation strategies, combining qualitative and quantitative evidence, are most useful.

The chapter addresses issues of data construction first, and then moves to data analysis. The next section, "Defining Network Data," deals with a crucial topic. For analytical purposes, social movement networks may consist of individuals, organizations, or an integration of both. Criteria are required to identify their boundaries in order to have a meaningful unit of analysis and to differentiate between movements and their social environment (who is part of a movement and who is simply an ally?). The linkages between movement actors—as well as between them and other actors—may be direct or indirect; that is, they may imply concrete interaction or be mediated through actors' shared participation in specific events or through joint affiliations to third parties. Analysts may focus on specific linkages, for example, those based on joint promotion of action campaigns, or on multiple linkages, accounting for any type of tie between two movement organizations or activists. Having identified the constitutive elements of a network, I next discuss the issues of data collection and organization. I present several data sources (interviews, archival data, and other unobtrusive measures) and then show how to organize data in matrix forms, making them suitable for analysis.

The second part of the chapter outlines two broad approaches to data analysis. It is often interesting to measure the position of individual movement actors (be they activists or organizations) within their networks to explain their behavior (e.g., the length and intensity of their commitment to a specific SMO), or to assess their potential influence over a given movement. The section "Analyzing Individual Positions in Movement Networks" introduces indicators appropriate to that purpose. At the same time, though, focusing on specific actors may conceal the broader patterns of exchanges within a movement. Such exchanges are far from random but take a form that may be subject to meaningful interpretation. Looking at overall patterns of exchanges in a movement may tell us about the logic of alliance building dominant in that movement, and even about its identity. The final section is therefore devoted to techniques allowing us to reconstruct the structure of a network as a whole.[1]

This presentation pays more attention to data construction and data collection than to specific analytical techniques, which are restricted to the simplest available options.[2] Devoting more space to data construction should prove most helpful to researchers interested in translating the network metaphor in some specific, if limited, research procedure. Having developed an understanding of how network data may be collected and organized, readers will be able to stretch their analyses as far as their technical competence and theoretical imagination allow. Excellent treatments of network analysis are now available, from the introductory (Scott 1992) to the advanced and encyclopedic (Wasserman and Faust 1994), and readers should refer to them for a more comprehensive grasp of this perspective.

Defining Network Data

A network can be defined as a set of actors or, in the language of graph theory, nodes, connected by a specific type of relation (Knoke and Kuklinski 1982: 12). Network analysis offers us the tools to interpret the structure of the network, that is, the patterns of ties between the nodes. To this purpose, however, we must first identify both the nodes and the ties between them.

Nodes

In the specific case of social movements, network nodes consist mostly of individual or collective actors. One may be interested in the relationships between people who are active in and/or sympathize with a given movement, and in the impact of their network location on their behavior. Or one may want to look for subcultural networks, exploring the personal linkages among activists of a given movement. For example, Fernandez and McAdam

(1989) found that the differential involvement of individuals in political and associational networks on American university campuses significantly affected their chances to join the Freedom Summer campaign.

Alternatively, one may focus on the linkages between groups and organizations with different degrees of formalization in order to identify the main lines of fragmentation within a social movement, or to explore the substantive influence of the most central organizations in the network. When studying Milanese environmentalism, for example, I tried to find out to what extent traditional divisions between conservation and political ecology, embedded in the deeper left-right cleavage, still shaped ties between organizations that broadly identified with the same cause (Diani 1995).

Boundaries

Whatever the main focus, identifying the boundaries of the network is one of the most difficult problems for any social movement (and indeed any social network) analyst. In principle one can distinguish between a *nominalist* and a *realist* strategy (Laumann, Marsden, and Prensky 1983). From a *nominalist* point of view, "network closure is imposed by the researcher's conceptual framework that serves an analytic purpose" (Knoke and Kuklinski 1982: 22): the researcher identifies a set of criteria defining membership in a given network, selects the network nodes on this basis, and then proceeds to look at the interactions between those nodes. One may focus on all organizations that define themselves as environmentalist or mobilize primarily on environmental issues (e.g., Diani 1995), on movement organizations that operate in a given territory (e.g., Carroll and Ratner 1996), or on organizations that operate in a given policy domain (e.g., Laumann and Knoke 1987, in their broader study of networks in the energy and health policy domains in the United States).

Alternatively, one may prefer a *realist* approach, in which "the network analyst adopts the presumed subjective perceptions of system actors themselves, defining the boundaries of a social entity as the limits that are consciously experienced by all or most of the actors that are members of the entity" (Knoke and Kuklinski 1982: 22). This general guiding principle may be specified in different ways. The boundaries of a movement network may be defined by actors' identities, namely, by the process through which individuals or organizations recognize each other as part of a specific type of community, linked by a specific type of solidarity. A more relaxed version of this approach may focus on actual interactions. Membership in a movement network does not result from actors' traits, such as their interest in certain issues, or their acceptance or refusal of certain action repertoires. Instead, it depends on their concrete interorganizational and interpersonal linkages. One particular version of this approach is snowball sampling, that is, starting with a certain group of nodes, then proceeding to include in the network all their contacts (adjacencies, in the language of network analysis), and then the latter's contacts, until no additional actors are mentioned.

Each of these strategies may or may not make sense, depending on the questions addressed, and each presents some shortcomings. A nominalist approach may lead the researcher to identify the movement with a category of groups with certain traits, forgetting about the concrete relationships between them and about processes of identity. For example, identifying the environmental movement as the set of all organizations mobilizing on environmental issues may result in the inclusion of groups with little in common and no shared identities. A realist approach may present other problems; for example, emphasis on identity may lead to the exclusion from a network of those groups that play an important role in certain mobilization campaigns but do not define their identities around them. For example, recent studies of environmentalism in Spain (Jimenez 1999) and Italy (Diani and Forno forthcoming) found that many groups mobilizing on environmental issues are not primarily environmentalist but are still heavily connected to environmental groups. Likewise, the more relaxed version of realism may be impractical in all those cases where additional groups keep being mentioned by interviewees, and networks are spread over a vast territory.

In most cases, researchers will ultimately use a combination of different strategies. When studying the Milanese environmental network, I started with a nominalist approach (groups focusing on environmental issues and operating in Milan or the neighboring towns; see the appendix in Diani 1995 for further details), but then I supplemented it with a realist approach, as I conducted most of my analysis on those actors who recognized each other as part of the environmental movement. Had my focus been on any group campaigning on environmental issues rather than on groups sharing a specific environmental identity, then I would have adopted a relaxed version of the realist criterion, starting with those actors who were concretely involved in alliances and joint campaigns.

Ties

Having identified nodes, the next step is to establish what represents a linkage between them. We can distinguish between interpersonal linkages and interorganizational linkages, as well as between direct and indirect linkages.

Direct Linkages between Persons and Organizations

Direct linkages are all those instances in which a nonmediated interaction occurs between two actors. Individuals active in or sympathizing with a social movement may be connected through relationships of personal kinship, friendship, or acquaintanceship; exchanges of information; or joint participation in movement activities (or even nonmovement ones, e.g., membership of bodies ranging from a scientific advisory board or a parliamentary committee to a parent-teacher association or community group). Linkages may also consist of more ideational, cognitive, and emotional exchanges, for example, when actors identify each other as sharing similar values and ideals or as parts of the same side in a given conflict.

Organizations mobilizing in movements are similarly connected in a variety of ways. Ties may include alliances and joint promotion of mobilization events or campaigns, circulation of information and sharing of expertise and other members' skills, and provision of practical support, from financial help to shared offices. Both core and grassroots members of different organizations may eventually come to develop a shared understanding of their action. Emotional bonds and shared identity may then result, which go beyond the specific individuals and constitute part of the organizational cultures, thus facilitating further interaction at later stages.

Indirect Linkages Based on Shared Activities

Direct ties concretely connect two individuals or movement organizations (see below on problems of data collection). There are also instances, however, when the existence of a linkage is not directly assessed but may be reasonably inferred from the joint participation of two actors in the same set of events or activities (when, of course, this does not entail face-to-face interaction, in which case we have a direct tie). For the purpose of specific investigations, for example, studies of submerged movement networks (Melucci 1996), interpersonal linkages between activists may be assumed from their attendance at the same protest rally, their membership in similar or even the same organizations, or their involvement in the same countercultural scene. Similar remarks apply to organizations. They may be assumed to be linked by their adhesion to protest initiatives originally promoted by third parties, their comembership in umbrella organizations, or their ties to the same public agencies.

The relationship between individuals and organizations represents a particular version of the interplay of actors and activities, which has been referred to as "the duality of persons and groups" (Breiger 1988): organizations may be expected to be connected when they share key activists (similar to the argument emphasizing the contribution of interlocking directorates to interfirm relations; Mizruchi 1996); conversely, individuals may be expected to be linked if they share membership—especially active membership—in specific organizations. This is just a version of the broader argument that shared activities generate linkages, yet one worth special attention, given its fruitfulness for our area of investigation (Diani 1995; Fernandez and McAdam 1989).

In general, however, shared activities—even more, shared traits—do not necessarily imply concrete relations. In some cases, it is sensible to assume the existence of a tie, for example, when two organizations are named in press reports as involved in the same protest event. In other cases, for example, when organizations or individuals share an interest in broad issues, the same assumption is more disputable. At the very minimum, this approach identifies the potential for direct relations stemming from similarity in key activities and traits, which may be expected to facilitate direct linkages.

Properties of Relations

Relations may be *binary* or *valued*. In the first case, the mere presence or absence of a linkage is recorded, regardless of its intensity. In the second, the strength of the tie is taken into account. The strength of a tie can either be conceived as frequency of interaction, or as the amount of emotional investment attached to it, regardless of the actual number of contacts. For social movement organizations, strength of a tie may be measured by the number of protest events they jointly promote, the number of joint activists, or their members' subjective perceptions of the importance of the link. For individuals, strength of a tie may again be a combination of subjective measures, such as affection, solidarity, personal closeness, and ideological proximity, and objective ones, such as the amount of shared memberships.

Likewise, relations may be *symmetric* or *directed*, depending on whether or not a mutual, balanced flow of resources and exchanges is assumed. Some indicators of relations inevitably imply symmetric ties. For example, when two organizations share a key member, their linkage is treated as symmetric unless additional information suggests otherwise. In contrast, ties identified on the basis of sociometric choices (i.e., when actors are asked to nominate their closest links) may generate both symmetric or asymmetric connections, depending on whether two respondents nominate each other or not. This difference is important because some of the technical procedures outlined below—in particular, centrality and prestige indices—fit only one data type.

Although most network analyses of collective action focus on cooperative ties (but see Franzosi 1999; Tilly and Wood forthcoming), one should also consider, where appropriate, other types of relations. These include *competitive relations,* which may or may not be compatible with cooperative ones, and occur when two or more SMOs compete for the same pool of potential support, or for recognition from the same public bodies, and so on. They also include *conflictual relations,* when ideological and practical differences and the resulting factionalism lead to open conflict. On occasion, it may also make sense to study instances of *neutrality* or *indifference* between actors. These occur when two or more actors regard each other as outsiders to their relevant social space—defined here in terms of both alliance and oppositional fields (della Porta and Diani 1999: 125).

Collecting and Organizing Network Data

When choosing a strategy of data collection, the first and major choice is whether one wants to analyze data providing some objective measure of the interaction, or data reflecting instead the cognitive and/or emotional perceptions of actors, regarding their closest or most distant alters (Marsden 1990: 437). To some extent the choice is driven by our research questions. If we are interested in the extent to which movement organizations depend on different types of actors (institutions, public agencies, charities, political parties, etc.) for practical support like monetary contributions or legal and technical information, then we should look for objective measures of linkages (e.g., records of donations made to other organizations, or records of attendance at meetings of consultation bodies, or membership in umbrella organizations). If, however, we intend to treat network ties mainly as indicators of movement identities, then we should focus on measures that reflect the attitudes and emotions of movement actors to each other, and on subjective perceptions rather than objective measures of interaction. Preference for subjective measures will encourage recourse to surveys, questionnaires, and eventually in-depth interviews, while objective measures will be obtained more easily from available data records such as archives or newspapers.

Survey Data

The shortage of easily accessible data sets is a major problem for analysts of social movement networks.[3] Major surveys focusing on political behavior, like Eurobarometer or World Values Surveys, may provide some very limited evidence on the extent of individuals' involvement in personal and associational networks. Other surveys, like the British Household Panel, may also provide data on individual behavior and its changes over time suitable to network analysis. However, the information generated in this way is usually generic and unable to address the most interesting network questions. In most cases, movement analysts will have to resort to ad hoc surveys among the members of a given network, contacted either as individual activists (e.g., McAdam 1988), as organization representatives (e.g., Knoke and Wood 1981), or in both capacities (Diani 1995). In this case, most network data are usually generated through sociometric choice questions, as respondents are asked either to nominate a limited number (normally three to five) of their most liked/close/frequent partners, or to identify their contacts from lists of all the individuals/organizations one respondent (or his/her organization) could in principle be connected to. Information about activities by respondents can also be used to generate case-by-affiliation matrices, which should later be subjected to network analysis. Some of these surveys may also include questions about the evolution of types of participation over time.[4]

In general, questions based on lists of names have been found to generate more ties than those encouraging unprompted recollection of ties, even when the number of possible mentions was not capped (Marsden 1990: 440–43). This difference could mean that respondents tend to focus on their most important ties when answering open questions, and to include less important and less obvious ties when confronted with a list; it might also reflect, however, the unreliability of unguided recollections of ties. Whatever the case, respondents' accounts of network ties tend to be less accurate, the more detailed the information required (Marsden 1990: 445–50). In our terms, while the identification of the main allies of a given SMO may be fairly reliable, attempts to chart changes in the intensity of the relationship may be expected to be more hazardous.

There are different ways to deal with this problem. We may look exclusively at measures of global perceived proximity/distance rather than at detailed accounts of exchanges. Or we may focus on reciprocated ties, where both respondents mutually and separately identify each other as relevant partners. This approach may be appropriate for ties between partners of comparable organizational strength/influence but not in other cases. For example, a tie to a major national SMO may be very important for a small group but not vice versa, and still represent a meaningful relationship when it comes to identifying exchanges of information or mechanisms. Once again, the best response is probably triangulation, namely, combining as many different sources of information as possible.

When planning a survey focusing on network data, *issues of access* should be carefully considered. This may be more problematic with radical groups than with conventional political groups or actors because network data may be particularly sensitive. In general, all the prescriptions for the analysis of protest and radical actors also apply here. Particular attention should be paid to the definition of the project goals, reassurances about the confidentiality of the information received, and the development of an explicitly contractual relationship between researchers and respondents (Kriesi 1992; Melucci 1992: 244–46). In this particular case, the sensitivity of network questions suggests that an interview be contemplated even if the format of the questions might in itself fit a less demanding, and cheaper, postal questionnaire.

Archival Data

When available, archives or similar sources provide another answer to the search for "objective" linkages (Burt 1983a). Archives are a desirable source of network data for at least three reasons: they are cost effective, they are more reliable than personal recollection at tracing changes in networks over time, and they minimize problems of access. Unfortunately, systematic *archives of social movement activity* are rare: social movements are transient phenomena, and their members are often uninterested in keeping systematic records of their activities. Nonetheless, some remarkable studies have indeed drawn upon archival records. For example, McAdam's (1988) analysis of recruitment networks of activists in the Freedom Summer campaign relies heavily on the organization's own records of prospective applicants (see also Duffhues and Felling 1989; Rosenthal et al. 1985, 1997). *Court records* are another important source of network data. Della Porta (1988) uses them to account for recruitment patterns of Italian left-wing terrorists in the 1970s. Similar data have also been used to generate ties between actors in historical examples of contention (Barkey and Van Rossem 1997; Gould 1999).

Newspaper reports offer a possible alternative, which has not yet been extensively explored. Jimenez (1999) has mapped networks of environmental organizations in Spain based on press reports for the 1988–97 period. From a different perspective, Franzosi (1999) has used newspaper reports to trace interactions between the actors involved in the social and political conflict that led to the advent of fascism in Italy in 1922. If data obtained in this way were a valid measure of actual ties, use of these sources would represent a major step forward toward network analysis of movements over long time spans. However, there are several reasons for caution. Newspaper sources have been found to be inadequate to chart maps of grassroots organizations because only the best-known groups tend to be mentioned in reports (Diani 1992a). They might perhaps provide a more reliable account of alliances developing on the occasion of the most visible and politically salient campaigns, although this remains to be seen.[5]

Sampling → Not a good idea

The size of networks, which may easily reach hundreds of nodes, poses recurrent problems to analysts. If we are interested in the structure of direct ties within a given movement—e.g., in order to map alliances between specific actors—then we have to cover the totality of the population or at least approximate it. Moreover, in general, analyses of global networks do not allow for sampling as individual-level survey data do—although the latter may be useful when analyzing data on individual involvement in networks. As a rule of thumb, Burt (1983b) estimated the amount of ties lost through sampling as approximately $100 - p$, where p is the proportion of nodes in a network for which we have been able to collect data. For example, if we contact 10 percent of movement actors in a given area, we are likely to miss 90 percent of the ties in the whole network. This means that network sampling should be fairly limited, unless, of course, we base our analysis on actor-by-affiliation data, where ties derive from shared affiliations or co-occurrences rather than direct connection. In this case sampling is a possibility worth exploring.[6]

Data Matrices

Data about both direct and indirect linkages are organized in matrix form. Most network analysis procedures are conducted on square M × M matrices, which record the linkages between the M actors in a given network. In these *actor-by-actor* matrices, rows and columns coincide since the nodes (i.e., the individuals or the organizations) reported in the rows are the same as in the columns; any cell M_{ij} (i.e., the cell defined by the intersection of the ith row and jth column) records the presence, absence, or intensity of a tie between nodes i and j. In my own research on the Milanese environmental movement in the mid-1980s I recorded information mainly in this way: I asked each organization to identify their contacts to other environmental organizations and recorded this information in a square matrix where rows and columns consisted of the same forty-two groups. Table 7.1 provides an example of such a matrix, reporting alliance ties between four Milanese environmental groups.

While an actor-by-actor matrix records direct connections between nodes, an *actor-by-event* matrix (also referred to as *actor-by-affiliation* matrix) records connections based on shared activities. These are M × N (usually rectangular) matrices, where rows correspond to the nodes of the network, and columns report any meaningful affiliation. Two environmental groups may be linked by their collaboration with the same umbrella organization

Table 7.1. Square actor-by-actor matrix, showing major alliances and asymmetric ties between environmental SMOs in Milan in 1985

Actors	Legambiente	WWF	LIPU*	Milan Green List
Legambiente	–	1	0	0
WWF	1	–	0	0
LIPU*	0	1	–	0
Milan Green List	1	1	0	–

*Italian League for the Protection of Birds

Source: Diani 1995.

or by their joint participation in specific protest events. For example, in Table 7.2 WWF and the Milan Green List have a strong potential linkage because they share an involvement in four out of five campaigns reported. We might have a similar matrix with activists in the rows, and the activities they might share (e.g., membership in the same organizations, participation in specific campaigns, etc.) in the columns.

Although actor-by-event matrices organize important information, they usually provide the basis for network analysis only once they are transformed into square M × M matrices through elementary matrix algebra.[7] In such matrices, cells report the number of joint affiliations/events linking two actors. Table 7.3 shows, for example, the number of campaigns that different Milanese environmental organizations were jointly involved in. Remarkably, this procedure generates a different network than the one shown in Table 7.1, based on SMOs' identification of each other as major allies.[8]

Sometimes, *event-by-event,* N × N matrices, rather than actor-by actor,

Table 7.2. Rectangular actor-by-event matrix, showing involvement of SMOs in main single-issue campaigns in Milan in 1985

Actors	Traffic	Pollution	Urban decay	Green areas	Animal rights
Legambiente	1	1	1	0	0
WWF	1	1	1	1	1
LIPU*	0	1	0	1	1
Milan Green List	1	1	0	1	1

*Italian League for the Protection of Birds

Source: Diani 1995.

Table 7.3. Square actor-by-actor matrix, showing number of joint campaigns linking SMOs in Milan in 1985

Actors	Legambiente	WWF	LIPU*	Milan Green List
Legambiente	–	3	1	2
WWF	3	–	3	4
LIPU*	1	3	–	3
Milan Green List	2	4	3	–

*Italian League for the Protection of Birds

Source: Diani 1995.

M × M ones, may also be meaningful. In this case, actors participating in several events constitute linkages between them. For example, we could use data recording the involvement of M movement organizations in N issue campaigns not only to estimate the linkages between these organizations, as we did in Table 7.3, but also to assess the linkages between main issue campaigns. Table 7.4 illustrates the extent of the overlap between different issue campaigns in Milan 1985, measured as the number of core SMOs who were involved in them.

When organizing network data, it is important to allow for their *multiplexity.* As a rule, each type of linkage should be recorded independently. For example, when researching networks of SMOs, we should build distinct matrices based on joint campaigning and information exchange, rather than collapsing all ties from the very beginning into a single matrix of interorganizational relations. If substantively and theoretically meaningful, combination of different types of ties may always be done at a later stage.

Table 7.4. Square event-by-event matrix, showing number of SMOs linking different campaigns in Milan in 1985 through their participation

Single-issue campaigns	Traffic	Pollution	Urban decay	Green areas	Animal rights
Traffic	–	3	2	2	2
Pollution	3	–	2	3	3
Urban decay	2	2	–	1	1
Green areas	2	3	1	–	3
Animal rights	2	3	1	3	–

Source: Diani 1995.

Analyzing Individual Positions in Movement Networks

Research has pointed at two important areas where the network position of individuals may have substantial implications for their role in social movements. On the one hand, individuals' differential network positions have been found to affect their overall commitment to a cause. For example, activists who are centrally located in flows of communication and exchanges within a movement may in general be expected to maintain their identification with it for longer than people who are marginal in the same networks (McAdam and Paulsen 1993; Passy forthcoming).

On the other hand, network position may also be expected to affect movement actors' influence both within and outside a movement. This assumption is consistent with attempts to identify the network bases of power and influence in a variety of organizational domains (Laumann and Pappi 1976; Laumann and Knoke 1987; Mizruchi 1996; Nohria and Eccles 1992). From this perspective, measures of network position might therefore be used as independent variables in analyses attempting to explain movement actors' uneven political influence. However, the very same measures may also be the object of explanatory attempts; that is, they may be the dependent variables in analyses relating differences in individual actors' position to other properties. Admittedly, the relation between network position and power is still ambiguous and disputed. Scholars adopting a structural approach to the study of power and influence also disagree regarding its best structural indicators (Bonacich 1987; Freeman 1979; Knoke 1990).

Centrality Measures

A popular way to measure the position of specific actors (individuals or organizations) in a network is by looking at their *centrality*, that is, at the extent to which they are located in core positions in a web of exchanges. In this section I present a set of centrality measures, which reflect different specific properties of the interaction (Freeman 1979; Scott 1992: ch. 5; Wasserman and Faust 1994: ch. 5). The simplest way to measure centrality is by looking at the number of ties that actors send to and receive from other actors in a network. These measures are usually referred to as *out-degree* and *in-degree*, respectively (or simply *degree* in the case of symmetric ties). Figure 7.1 shows the network consisting of four major environmental SMOs in Milan, which I introduced in Table 7.1. The Milan branch of WWF has an in-degree of three, as it is identified as an alliance partner by all the other actors in the network, but an out-degree of one, as it only identifies Legambiente as a partner. Degree measures reflect first of all the global involvement of a node in a network. However, in-

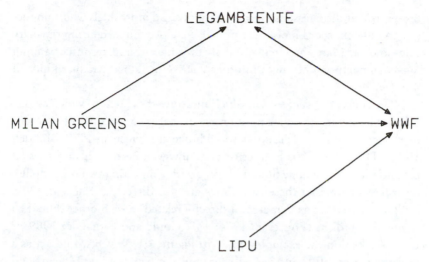

Figure 7.1. Elementary network structure in Milan, 1985.

degree (i.e., the number of times that an actor is identified by other actors as a partner) may also be regarded as an elementary indicator of leadership. For example, in-degree has proved a useful indicator of SMOs' capacity to attract support for their own strategies and projects from other groups (Diani 1995: ch. 5; Diani forthcoming), as well as of the visibility of certain individuals as spokespersons of an aggrieved community (Schou 1997).

Measures like in-degree suffer, however, from being "local measures"; they fail, in other words, to take into account that while the number of ties in which a SMO or a leader is involved obviously matters, the linkages and the structural position of the actors to whom they are connected are also crucial. For example, in terms of mobilization capacity it makes a difference if one SMO is connected to actors that are also central in the network, or not. This view is reflected in the concept of *prominence* (Bonacich 1972; Knoke and Burt 1983). Being related to alters who in turn control a large number of ties, prominent actors may be expected to have easier access to crucial resources and information.[9]

Instead of looking at movement actors' capacity to attract support—eventually from contacts who are also central, as in the case of prominence—we may focus on their effectiveness in creating bridges between different sectors of a movement. Social movements are highly differentiated phenomena, whose cohesion and unity cannot be taken for granted, and are constantly redefined and renegotiated (Melucci 1996). Factionalism is one of their recurrent features, and one with damaging consequences for their impact and prospects. For these reasons, the organizations and individuals who enjoy access to different social movement milieus may play important intermediary roles and facilitate the circulation of information and resources among movement actors. They may, in other words, operate as peculiar kinds of *social brokers.*

The concept of *betweenness,* which measures the extent to which a node is located in an intermediate position on the paths connecting other actors, may be regarded as an indicator of social brokerage (Freeman 1979; Marsden 1982). The concept has been criticized, however, because it measures all instances in which a node finds itself on a path connecting two other nodes, regardless of whether these two nodes are also directly connected. Only bridges between actors that are not directly related to each other should be regarded as brokers (Boissevain 1974: 148; Gould and Fernandez 1989).[10] By this token, in the example shown in Figure 7.1, WWF would act as a broker between LIPU and Legambiente but not between Legambiente and the Milan Green List, as these SMOs are also communicating directly.

Another way to look at social brokerage is through Burt's (1992) concept of *structural hole.* Structural holes in a network are filled with non-redundant linkages, that is, linkages without which two actors could not be connected even through intermediaries. For example, dropping the linkage between LIPU and WWF in Figure 7.1 would generate a structural hole, as the two SMOs could not access each other through third parties. In contrast, the tie between the Milan Green List and Legambiente is a redundant tie, as the two could access each other through their liaison with WWF (see also Diani forthcoming).

Extensions to Global Network Properties

The principles behind individual measures of centrality (in particular, degree measures) also allow us to identify some basic properties of global networks. We may want, for example, to assess the extent to which members of a given movement are densely connected to each other, and by doing so, formulate some hypotheses about the strength of identity and mutual commitment in that movement. To this purpose we may measure that network's *density.* We obtain a basic density measure by dividing the sum of the degree scores of its n members (in simpler words, the number of linkages actually in place between the network members) by the number of potential linkages ($n \times n$-1). For example, in the Milanese environmental movement in 1984–85, the density of the network where ties between SMOs consisted of shared core members was .06, while it was .05 in the networks based on alliance or regular exchange of information. In other words, only 5 percent to

6 percent of the possible 1,721 (42 × 41) ties among the forty-two SMOs analyzed were actually in place (Diani 1995).

It may also be interesting to assess how centralized certain movement networks are, for example, to compare patterns of circulation of different types of resources or to evaluate the solidity of their activists' claims to grass-roots democracy. The *centralization* of a network corresponds to the ratio of the actual difference between the centrality of the most central point, and that of all the other points, and the highest possible difference (Scott 1992: 93). While certain movements may be perceived as more or less centralized,[11] even networks in the same movement, based on different types of linkage, have been found to display different degrees of centralization. In the Milanese environmental movement, for example, the network based on ties consisting of friendship between core activists of two different groups had a centralization measure of .153, which increased to .196 for the network based on multiple memberships, .229 for the alliance network, and .266 for the information exchange network.

Even these elementary indicators may highlight important aspects of the functioning of a movement. In the Milan case, for example, the highest centralization of the information network suggests that fewer SMOs were the focus of information exchanges than of attempts to establish alliances. One can easily imagine a situation of neighborhood SMOs promoting joint campaigns at the local level while also supporting campaigns promoted by national SMOs, but referring only to the latter when they needed specific technical, legal, or political information. However, both networks based on interorganizational linkages were more centralized than those where linkages were created by single activists' individual choices. The latter linkages were scattered more evenly among activists, with the network based on personal friendships between core members being more decentralized than the network based on multiple memberships.

Analyzing Social Movement Structures

Social movements consist of a myriad of exchanges (of mobilization resources, information, activists, etc.) between the actors identified with a given cause. Despite the popular image of networks as loose phenomena, precariously integrated, and deprived of any internal logic, movement networks are far from unpatterned. To the contrary, available evidence suggests that exchanges between pairs of actors tend to combine in meaningful forms, open to substantive interpretation, and also capable of some stability over time (Diani 1995). Looking at those patterns, and finding out how movement actors build and reproduce linkages among them, may reveal to us precious information about the nature of a movement, its identity and its internal fragmentation.

This section outlines two major ways to analyze the overall structure of a network. One is conventionally referred to as *social cohesion,* the other, as *structural equivalence* (Knoke and Kuklinski 1982; Scott 1992). The former focuses on direct ties between actors, and on the sectors of a network where density is particularly high; the latter focuses on those subsets of actors in a network that are involved in similar patterns of exchanges to third parties. The choice between the two ultimately depends on the specific research questions.

Social Cohesion

When studying a network of movement activists, we may, for instance, want to identify within them the densely knit circles based on personal linkages (friendship, kinship, professional ties, etc.). If looking at organizations, we may want to identify those subsets of the network that are strongly connected by alliance ties. We may also apply the same logic within specific movement organizations, and look at how their members relate (or do not relate) to each other. In each case, emphasis is on subsets of actors in a network, which are directly connected. A social cohesion approach is most useful when we are interested in the specific exchanges and collaborations taking place within a movement network.

In this perspective, *clique* is the key concept, defined as a "sub-set of points in which every possible pair of points is directly connected by a line and the clique is not contained in any other clique" (Scott 1992: 117). This concept is also known as *strong clique,* to emphasize the strictness of its defining requirement. Figure 7.2 maps the whole alliance network in the Milanese environmental movement in the mid-1980s. We can identify a few strong cliques in that network, for example, the one consisting of nodes N1 (Legambiente Milan), N8 (WWF Milan), N16 (Milan Green List), and N17 (South Park Campaign), located at the very center of the graph. In most cases, however, it may be convenient to adopt a looser criterion and focus on so-called *n*-cliques, where a tie between two nodes is assumed if the two are connected through no more than *n* steps. For example, a 2-clique is a clique consisting of all the nodes connected either directly to or through one intermediate node. On the right of Figure 7.2, we can, for example, identify a 2-clique consisting of Legambiente Milan plus several organizations active in the Northern Milan periphery (N2, N3, N7, N9, and N20). The clique-based approach has inspired a few important studies of social movements dynamics, most notably Rosenthal and colleagues' analysis of the structure of women's movements in New York State between 1840 and 1920 (Rosenthal et al. 1985, 1997).

Structural Equivalence

Alternatively, we might not be interested in the specific nodes our SMOs or movement activists are linked to, but we would rather identify subsets of actors who have similar patterns of linkages to third parties. The larger the size of a movement network, the less meaningful it becomes to focus only on direct ties to assess identity and fragmentation. After all, movement actors might simply lack the resources necessary to keep active ties to all the actors they feel close to. Accordingly, to identify nodes occupying the same—or a similar—structural position within a network, it may be advisable to drop the cohesion criterion and pay most attention to whether or not certain nodes are involved in similar ties to other actors. More specifically, two actors in a network are *structurally equivalent* if they have similar ties to the same set of alters, and they are *regularly equivalent* if they are related to different sets of alters who, however, occupy similar structural positions (Scott 1992: 142–45; Degenne and Forsé 1999: 86–92).

Figure 7.2 provides a preliminary illustration of these principles. At the bottom of the figure, nodes N19, N21, and N22 (local informal groups in

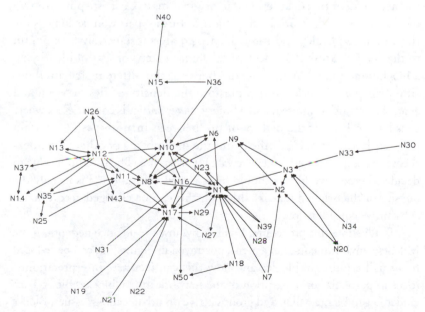

Figure 7.2. The Milan environmental alliance network.

the southern Milanese periphery) are in a structurally equivalent position as they are all linked to the same actor, the South Park Campaign, and have no interorganizational linkages to other actors. Let us also look at two other SMOs who are also involved in one tie only, Democratic Geology (N28), connected to Legambiente Milan, and libertarian group Oblum (N31), connected to the Milan Green List. These nodes are regularly equivalent in that their contacts are both highly central in the network and occupy a similar structural position within it.

As structural equivalence is the most popular approach, I will focus my presentation on it. Structural equivalence relies on a variety of classificatory techniques, in particular, different types of cluster analysis (Scott 1992: ch. 7). Although their specific methods and algorithms are different, they all aim at identifying subsets of nodes in a network, with similar scores on a number of variables (I talk of "scores on variables" instead of "ties to other nodes" because one may apply this approach to both M × M actor-by-actor matrices and M × N actor-by-affiliation matrices). Among clustering techniques, the first developed explicitly for network analysis is Concor (standing for Convergence of Iterated Correlations; Breiger, Boorman, and Arabie 1975; White, Boorman, and Breiger 1976).

Concor partitions a network into a number of blocks, the incumbents of which have similar—if not strictly identical—patterns of ties to the rest of the network. In practical terms, the original matrix is first split into two blocks, which may in turn be the object of further partition, as long as the structurally equivalent positions identified are substantively meaningful to the analyst (Scott 1992: 134–40). The next step consists of identifying a blockmodel, summarizing the ties between the different structural positions of the network. To this purpose the density of ties between and across blocks are computed, and a binary *image matrix* is constructed, where cells have value 1 if the density of ties between incumbents of a certain position/block, or between them and the incumbents of other blocks, exceeds a certain threshold, and have value 0 otherwise. The threshold value to decide whether two blocks should be regarded as connected is usually the density of the original matrix, although this can be changed according to substantive considerations.

To illustrate this procedure, I will show how the alliance network in the Milanese environmental movement, portrayed in Figure 7.2, can be reduced to a small number of blocks, and how this can facilitate interpretation. I focus in particular on a partition of the network in five blocks. Block 1 includes Legambiente Milan and groups active on urban ecology issues; Blocks 2, 4, and 5 consist of neighborhood associations and local branches of major

Table 7.5. Image matrix of the alliance network in the Milanese environmental movement, 1985

	Block 1	Block 2	Block 3	Block 4	Block 5
Block 1	1	0	0	0	0
Block 2	0	1	0	0	0
Block 3	1	0	1	0	0
Block 4	1	0	0	0	0

national SMOs active respectively in the North, South, and West Milanese periphery, plus—in block 4—the Milan Green List; Block 3 hosts conservation groups active on both urban and natural protection issues (among them, WWF and Italia Nostra).

Concor also computed the intensity of the ties within and between the five blocks. The image matrix, showing the simplified structure of the movement, is reported in Table 7.5. If the density of ties within a block or across two blocks exceeds the overall density of the alliance network (in this case, .05), value 1 is assigned to the corresponding cell in the image matrix; otherwise value 0 is assigned. Figure 7.3 shows the relationships between the five blocks (blocks that are internally connected—i.e., with a density of ties among their incumbents par or above the average—have their names in capital letters). It illustrates much more clearly than the original network reported in Figure 7.2 the centralized nature of environmental alliances in Milan in

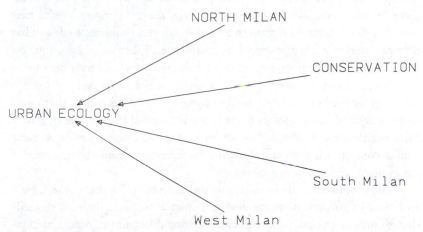

Figure 7.3. Alliances between blocks in Milan, 1985.

the mid-1980s, and the priority assigned by peripheral actors to neighbor-hood and conservation issues.

One should be aware that clustering procedures are subject to instability in their results and that the allocation of specific nodes to specific blocks might be different depending on the method adopted. It is therefore advisable to adopt triangulation strategies to check for the robustness of the clusters. Dimensional methods such as principal component analysis or multidimensional scaling (MDS) constitute a convenient option (see Scott 1992: ch. 8, for details; see also Burt 1991: 124–49). Principal component analysis locates variables in n-dimensional space depending on the strength of their correlation to each other and to a smaller number of underlying dimensions; multidimensional scaling locates cases in n-dimensional space depending on their proximity/distance. Both methods, however, are equally applicable to square actor-by-actor matrices, as cases and variables coincide. MDS in particular has often been used to this purpose, in combination with Concor (Breiger, Boorman, and Arabie 1976; Diani 1995: 116 and 127) or other clustering procedures (Laumann and Knoke 1987: 394). For example, nodes in Figure 7.2 have been located spatially with a multidimensional scaling routine. If we encircled the nodes that Concor allocated to the same block, we would note a substantial degree of consistency between the two procedures.

Conclusions

In this chapter, I have introduced some key steps that anyone interested in a systematic analysis of movement networks has to go through, and a few basic options for data analysis. Focusing on the constitutive elements of a network has highlighted a set of issues, the relevance of which goes beyond those interested in quantitative analysis. Even those willing to look at networks from a qualitative perspective need to address problems such as what defines a movement network and its boundaries. Likewise, the sections on individual and global network measures should hopefully have reminded everyone, and not just the number crunchers, of the importance of the dynamics these measures are supposed to capture. The mechanisms that result in some individuals or groups being more influential than others in movement politics are—or should be—of interest to the broad social movement studies community, as should those mechanisms that shape the structure of a movement and its internal cleavages.

One should be aware of some obvious limitations to the method. First and most important, meaning does not stem automatically from ties. Although some hypotheses may be made, relating different network configurations to varying degrees of internal solidarity and cohesion among movement members (Diani 1995: chapters 1 and 7), the specific meaning assigned by movement actors to their linkages requires specific investigation. As a result, qualitative data from a variety of sources are needed to supplement and enrich the more formal ones. Second, recent attempts notwithstanding (Franzosi 1999; Jimenez 1999; Osa forthcoming; Tilly and Wood forthcoming), the dynamic element in the network analysis of movements is still weak, and this type of analysis is problematic to conduct, given the lack of diachronic data, which we have discussed earlier in this chapter. Despite these shortcomings, however, the potential contribution of network analysis—and structural approaches in the broadest sense—to social movement research remains significant. Social movements are internally heterogeneous and diversified phenomena whose components are involved in complex relations to each other. Network analysis may help us disentangle this complexity.

Notes

I am grateful to Bert Klandermans, David Knoke, and Suzanne Staggenborg for their comments on an earlier draft of this chapter.

1. Throughout the text, I refer to output generated by Ucinet, a package developed by Linton Freeman, Steve Borgatti, and Martin Everett. Scott (1992: 176–82) offers a succinct description of Ucinet as well as of two other popular options among network analysts, Structure and Gradap. Information on how to procure these and other network analysis packages may be found on the Web site of INSNA, the International Network for Social Network Analysis, at http://www. heinz.cmu.edu/project/INSNA/soft_inf.html.

2. For more sophisticated applications of network concepts to collective action, see, among many others, Marwell and Oliver 1993 and Gould 1991.

3. See Marsden 1990 for a thorough discussion.

4. For example, McPherson and Rotolo (1996) analyze participation in voluntary associations with data collected from 1,050 individuals in ten Nebraska towns in 1989, which record respondents' past and present involvement in seventeen types of associations.

5. A comparison of my 1990 survey data (Diani 1995: ch. 6) with press reports in Milan in 1988–90 actually yields very different networks.

6. For a thorough discussion of these and related issues, see Burt 1983a and Marsden 1990.

7. More specifically, they are transformed by the multiplication of a matrix by its transpose, namely, the same matrix with rows and columns swapped. For example, the 4×4 matrix in Table 7.3 is obtained by multiplying the 4×5 matrix in Table 7.2 by its 5×4 transpose. See Namboodiri 1984 for an introduction to matrix algebra.

8. One can, of course, apply the same logic to a M × M matrix, where cases in rows and columns do coincide, and which represents a specific case of the general M × N matrix. By multiplying a M × M matrix by its transpose, one will obtain a new matrix reporting the number of actors in the specific network to which two nodes are both related.

9. However, even high prominence is not always and necessarily evidence of power; under certain conditions, power in a network may actually stem from semi-peripheral positions. When a network is segmented and consists mainly of sub-groups with high density of internal linkages and low density of ties to external actors, then centrality in the global network may not translate into power (Bonacich 1987: 1182).

10. Fernandez and Gould (1994) also differentiate between brokerage within and across specific social and/or interest groups. The most interesting cases are those where the actors connected by the broker belong to two different subgroups, for example, two different factions in a political movement.

11. For example, despite the role of independent local action groups, environmental movements have usually been portrayed as more centralized than women's movements (Rucht 1989).

References

Barkey, Karen, and Ronan Van Rossem. 1997. "Networks of Contention: Villages and Regional Structure in the Seventeenth-Century Ottoman Empire. *American Journal of Sociology* 102: 1345–82.

Boissevain, Jeremy. 1974. *Friends of Friends*. Oxford: Blackwell.

Bonacich, Phillip. 1972. "Factoring and Weighting Approaches to Status Scores and Clique Identification." *Journal of Mathematical Sociology* 2: 13–120.

———. 1987. "Power and Centrality: A Family of Measures." *American Journal of Sociology* 92: 1170–82.

Borgatti, Steve, Martin Everett, and Linton Freeman. 1992. *UCINET IV Version 1.0 Reference Manual*. Columbia, S.C.: Analytic Technologies.

Breiger, Ronald L. 1988. "The Duality of Persons and Groups." In *Social Structures: A Network Approach*, edited by B. Wellman and S. D. Berkowitz, 83–98. Cambridge: Cambridge University Press.

Breiger, Ronald L., Scott A. Boorman, and Philip Arabie. 1976. "An Algorithm for Clustering Relational Data with Application to Social Network Analysis and Comparison with Multidimensional Scaling." *Journal of Mathematical Psychology* 12: 328–83.

Burt, Ronald. 1983a. "Network Data from Archival Records." In *Applied Network Analysis*, edited by R. Burt and M. Minor, 158–74. London: Sage.

———. 1983b. "Studying Status/Role Sets Using Mass Surveys." In *Applied Network Analysis,* edited by R. Burt and M. Minor. London: Sage.

Burt, Ronald. 1991. *Structure. Reference Manual 4.2.* New York: Columbia University.

Burt, Ronald S. 1992. *Structural Holes.* Cambridge: Harvard University Press.

Carroll, William K., and R. S. Ratner. 1996. "Master Framing and Cross-Movement Networking in Contemporary Social Movements." *Sociological Quarterly* 37: 601–25.

Curtis, Russell L., and Louis A. Zurcher. 1973. "Stable Resources of Protest Movements: The Multi-Organizational Field." *Social Forces* 52: 53–61.

Degenne, Alain, and Michel Forsé. 1999. *Introducing Social Networks.* London: Sage.

della Porta, Donatella. 1988. "Recruitment Processes in Clandestine Political Organizations: Italian Left-Wing Terrorism." In *From Structure to Action: Comparing Social Movement Research across Cultures,* edited by Bert Klandermans, Hanspeter Kriesi, and Sidney Tarrow, 155–72. Greenwich, Conn.: JAI Press.

della Porta, Donatella, and Mario Diani. 1999. *Social Movements.* Oxford: Blackwell.

Diani, Mario. 1992a. "Analysing Social Movement Networks." In *Studying Collective Action,* edited by M. Diani and R. Eyerman, 107–35. Newbury Park, Calif.: Sage.

———. 1992b. "The Concept of Social Movement." *Sociological Review* 40: 1–25.

———. 1995. *Green Networks. A Structural Analysis of the Italian Environmental Movement.* Edinburgh: Edinburgh University Press.

———. Forthcoming. "'Leaders' or Brokers? Positions and Influence in Social Movement Networks." In *Social Movements and Networks,* edited by Mario Diani and Doug McAdam. Oxford: Oxford University Press.

Diani, Mario, and Francesca Forno. Forthcoming. "The Evolution of Environmental Protest in Italy 1988–1997." In *Environmental Protest in Western Europe,* edited by Christopher Rootes. Oxford: Oxford University Press.

Diani, Mario, and Doug McAdam, eds. Forthcoming. *Social Movements and Networks.* Oxford: Oxford University Press.

Duffhues, Ton, and Albert Felling. 1989. "The Development, Change, and Decline of the Dutch Catholic Movement." In *Organizing for Change,* edited by B. Klandermans, 95–116. Greenwich, Conn.: JAI Press.

Emirbayer, Mustafa, and Jeff Goodwin. 1994. "Network Analysis, Culture, and the Problem of Agency." *American Journal of Sociology* 99: 1411–54.

Fernandez, Roberto, and Roger Gould. 1994. "A Dilemma of State Power: Brokerage and Influence in the National Health Policy Domain." *American Journal of Sociology* 99: 1455–91.

Fernandez, Roberto, and Doug McAdam. 1989. "Multiorganizational Fields and Recruitment to Social Movements." In *Organizing for Change,* edited by B. Klandermans, 315–44. Greenwich, Conn.: JAI Press.

Franzosi, Roberto. 1999. "The Return of the Actor: Interaction Networks among Social Actors during Periods of High Mobilization (Italy 1919–1922)." *Mobilization* 4: 131–49.

Freeman, Linton C. 1979. "Centrality in Social Networks. I. Conceptual Clarifications." *Social Networks* 1: 215–39.

Galaskiewicz, Joseph. 1979. *Exchange Networks and Community Politics.* Beverly Hills, Calif.: Sage.

Gerlach, Luther, and Virginia Hine. 1970. *People, Power and Change.* Indianapolis: Bobbs-Merrill.

Gould, Roger. 1991. "Multiple Networks and Mobilization in the Paris Commune 1871." *American Sociological Review* 56: 716–29.

———. 1995. *Insurgent Identities.* Chicago: University of Chicago Press.

———. 1999. "Collective Violence and Group Solidarity: Evidence from a Feuding Society." *American Sociological Review* 64: 356–80.

Gould, Roger, and Roberto Fernandez. 1989. "Structures of Mediation." *Sociological Methodology* 19: 89–126.

Jimenez, Manuel. 1999. "Ten Years of Environmental Protest in Spain." Paper for the workshop "Environmental Protest in Comparative Perspective." ECPR Joint Sessions, Mannheim.

Kitts, James. 2000. "Mobilizing in Black Boxes: Social Networks and Participation in Social Movement Organizations." *Mobilization* 5: 241–57.

Knoke, David. 1990. *Political Networks.* Cambridge: Cambridge University Press.

Knoke, David, and Ronald S. Burt. 1983. "Prominence." In *Applied Network Analysis,* edited by Ronald S. Burt and Michael Minor, 195–222. Beverly Hills, Calif.: Sage.

Knoke, David, and James H. Kuklinski. 1982. *Network Analysis.* Newbury Park, Calif.: Sage.

Knoke, David, and Nancy Wisely. 1990. "Social Movements." In *Political Networks,* edited by D. Knoke, 57–84. Cambridge: Cambridge University Press.

Knoke, David, and James R. Wood. 1981. *Organized for Action: Commitment in Voluntary Associations.* New Brunswick, N.J.: Rutgers University Press.

Kriesi, Hanspeter. 1992. "The Rebellion of the Research Objects." In *Studying Collective Action,* edited by M. Diani and R. Eyerman, 194–216. Newbury Park, Calif.: Sage.

Laumann, Edward O., and Franz U. Pappi. 1976. *Networks of Collective Action: A Perspective on Community Influence Systems.* New York: Academic Press.

Laumann, Edward O., and David Knoke. 1987. *The Organizational State: Social Choice in National Policy Domains.* Madison: University of Wisconsin Press.

Laumann, Edward O., Peter V. Marsden, and David Prensky. 1983. "The Boundary Specification Problem in Network Analysis." In *Applied Network Analysis:*

A Methodological Introduction, edited by R. S. Burt and M. Minor, 18–34. Beverly Hills, Calif.: Sage.

Marsden, Peter V. 1982. "Brokerage Behavior in Restricted Exchange Networks." In *Social Structure and Network Analysis,* edited by Peter Marsden and Nan Lin, 201–18. Beverly Hills, Calif.: Sage.

————. 1990. "Network Data and Measurement." *Annual Review of Sociology* 16: 435–63.

Marwell, Gerald, and Pamela Oliver. 1993. *The Critical Mass in Collective Action: A Micro-Social Theory.* Cambridge: Cambridge University Press.

McAdam, Doug. 1988. "Micromobilization Contexts and Recruitment to Activism." In *From Structure to Action,* edited by B. Klandermans, H. Kriesi, and S. Tarrow, 125–54. Greenwich, Conn.: JAI Press.

McAdam, Doug, and Roberto Fernandez. 1990. "Microstructural Bases of Recruitment to Social Movements." In *Research in Social Movements, Conflict and Change,* vol. 12, edited by L. Kriesberg, 1–33. Greenwich, Conn.: JAI Press.

McAdam, Doug, and Ronnelle Paulsen. 1993. "Specifying the Relationship between Social Ties and Activism." *American Journal of Sociology* 99: 640–67.

McPherson, J. Miller, and Thomas Rotolo. 1996. "Testing a Dynamic Model of Social Composition: Diversity and Change in Voluntary Groups." *American Sociological Review* 61: 179–202.

Melucci, Alberto. 1992. "Frontier Land: Collective Action between Actors and Systems." In *Studying Collective Action,* edited by M. Diani and R. Eyerman, 238–58. Newbury Park, Calif.: Sage.

————. 1996. *Challenging Codes.* Cambridge: Cambridge University Press.

Mizruchi, Mark S. 1996. "What Do Interlocks Do? An Analysis, Critique, and Assessment of Research on Interlocking Directorates." *Annual Review of Sociology* 22: 271–98.

Namboodiri, Krishnan. 1984. *Matrix Algebra: An Introduction.* London: Sage.

Nohria, Nitin, and Robert G. Eccles, eds. 1992. *Networks and Organizations: Structure, Form, and Action.* Boston: Harvard Business School Press.

Oberschall, Anthony, and Hyojoung Kim. 1996. "Identity and Action." *Mobilization* 1: 63–85.

Oliver, Pamela. 1989. "Bringing the Crowd Back In: The Nonorganizational Elements of Social Movements." In *Research in Social Movements, Conflict and Change,* vol. 11, edited by L. Kriesberg, 1–30. Greenwich, Conn.: JAI Press.

Osa, Maryjane. Forthcoming. "Troublemakers and Counter-Revolutionaries: Network Development and Protest Cycles in Authoritarian Regimes." In *Social Movements and Networks,* edited by Mario Diani and Doug McAdam. Oxford: Oxford University Press.

Passy, Florence. Forthcoming. "Social Networks Matter. But How?" In *Social*

Movements and Networks, edited by Mario Diani and Doug McAdam. Oxford: Oxford University Press.

Rosenthal, Naomi, Meryl Fingrutd, Michelle Ethier, Roberta Karant, and David McDonald. 1985. "Social Movements and Network Analysis: A Case Study of Nineteenth-Century Women's Reform in New York State." *American Journal of Sociology* 90: 1022–54.

Rosenthal, Naomi, David McDonald, Michelle Ethier, Meryl Fingrutd, and Roberta Karant. 1997. "Structural Tensions in the Nineteenth Century Women's Movement." *Mobilization* 2: 21–46.

Rucht, Dieter. 1989. "Environmental Movement Organizations in West Germany and France: Structure and Interorganizational Relations." In *Organizing for Change,* edited by B. Klandermans, 61–94. Greenwich, Conn.: JAI Press.

Schou, Arild. 1997. "Elite Identification in Collective Protest Movements." *Mobilization* 2: 71–86.

Scott, John. 1999. *Social Network Analysis: A Handbook.* 2d ed. London: Sage.

Sewell, William H., Jr. 1992. "A Theory of Structure: Duality, Agency, and Transformation." *American Journal of Sociology* 98: 1–29.

Snow, David A., Louis A. Zurcher, and Sheldon Ekland-Olson. 1980. "Social Networks and Social Movements: A Microstructural Approach to Differential Recruitment." *American Sociological Review* 45: 787–801.

Somers, Margaret. 1994. "The Narrative Constitution of Identity: A Relational and Network Approach." *Theory and Society* 23: 605–49.

Tilly, Charles. 1994. "Social Movements as Historically Specific Clusters of Political Performances." *Berkeley Journal of Sociology* 38: 1–30.

Tilly, Charles, and Leslie Wood. Forthcoming. "Contentious Connections in Great Britain, 1828–1834." In *Social Movements and Networks,* edited by Mario Diani and Doug McAdam. Oxford: Oxford University Press..

Wasserman, Stanley, and Katherine Faust. 1994. *Social Network Analysis: Methods and Applications.* Cambridge: Cambridge University Press.

White, Harrison, Scott A. Boorman, and Ronald L. Breiger. 1976. "Social Structure from Multiple Networks. I. Blockmodels of Roles and Positions." *American Journal of Sociology* 81: 730–80.

Zald, Mayer N., and John McCarthy. 1987. *Social Movements in an Organizational Society.* New Brunswick, N.J.: Transaction.

8

Recovering Past Protest: Historical Research on Social Movements

Elisabeth S. Clemens and Martin D. Hughes

The past is full of protest, but only some protests have left footprints. Throughout the Middle Ages, Europe was swept by a series of popular religious mobilizations (Kaelber 1995; Ladurie 1978). We know something of this resistance to the Roman Catholic Church because it was persecuted as heresy. Villagers in the Ottoman Empire used the courts to articulate their grievances (Barkey and Van Rossem 1997), while English soldiers and merchants presented a stream of petitions to Parliament and demanded redress of their grievances (Zaret 1996). We can reconstruct these mobilizations because they produced official documents archived by government institutions. To a far greater extent than contemporary social movement research, historical research is shaped by the politics, practices, and events that selectively document protest.

Deprived of the opportunity to distribute a survey, conduct interviews, or embark on a spell of participant observation, researchers interested in social movements of the past must discover evidence originally collected by others and make that evidence speak to core theoretical questions. The questions that can be asked may be constrained by the material that is available for constructing answers. But despite the challenges of finding and mining evidence, the questions are vitally important: When and how and why have people resisted authority? What visions of other worlds and possible futures motivate challengers? How does social change happen?

For social movement researchers, the most basic question is whether social movements existed in past societies. If one takes some of the leading figures in the field literally, then historical research on social movements has a horizon of only two centuries or so. Based on his studies of contention in France and England, Tilly argues that the "national social movement" was an innovation of the early nineteenth century (1995a: 61). Tarrow (1998: 2) concurs that "mounting, coordinating and sustaining [confrontations with elites, authorities, and opponents] are the unique contribution of the social movement—an invention of the modern age and an accompaniment to the rise of the modern state." Consequently, much research on past protest explores social formations that are not quite movements in the contemporary sense. But these conflicts and mobilizations reveal modern polities in the process of becoming.

In turning to the past, social movement research begins by questioning its core concept. Many of the basic elements of social movement theory have emerged from studies of particular places at particular times, most significantly, the advanced industrial democracies in the decades following World War II. Consequently these concepts are history-laden in ways that may not be evident until one ventures to apply them to protest in very different settings.[1] What is an opportunity in a polity where representative democracy is not yet even thinkable? What is a resource in a preindustrial society? For earlier periods, research on protest addresses events and processes that bear a family resemblance to contemporary social movements while lacking some defining features such as orientation to the state or modularity of the forms of protest.

A researcher looking for evidence of past protest with a checklist drawn from the present may easily miss—or misrepresent—evidence of other forms of resistance or mobilization. Rather than assuming that past protest took the same form as contemporary social movements, historical research should begin by identifying the distinctive components of "movement-like" processes: identities and networks, events and repertoires, grievances and frames, organizations and resources. Even when past protest diverges from the taxonomies of contemporary movement research, many of these constitutive elements will speak to basic theoretical questions. The challenge is to avoid anachronism, to apply contemporary concepts to past protest without ignoring the otherness of the past.

With these conceptual issues on the table, we turn to some of the nuts and bolts of historical research. How do you locate archives and other resources for historical research? How can one assess the authenticity, representativeness, and interpretation of historical documents? What are possible strategies for linking theoretical concepts and different kinds of evidence? Because there is no single "historical method," we survey exemplary studies that illustrate the creative and persuasive use of different kinds of evidence.

Whereas many of the other chapters in this volume present a specific method, this chapter provides a set of exemplars. Given a research question and available evidence, what combinations are possible?

In light of these challenges and possibilities, historical research on social movements is best approached with a measure of opportunism. The most careful research design may falter if the critical data cannot be located; innovative contributions often stem from unanticipated discoveries in the archives. Good historical research is essentially detective work; this chapter is intended to help researchers recognize when a clue is a clue.

Finding Sources

Assuming an interesting topic and a general theoretical question, the next challenge is to find out whether there is any relevant evidence. Begin by knowing enough about your topic to make effective use of these reference tools. In the relevant secondary literature, what are the key terms, places, and names? What are the major sources of evidence in published studies of the topic? If formal organizations were involved in protest, pull together a preliminary list. Do the same for individuals who seemed to have played an important role. Such basic preparatory work will facilitate a more effective search for available materials. Before committing to a specific research design, it is wise to get a sense of your options.

Although work in the archives is often the most fun, take some time to survey what can be gathered from standard sources used in other related research. Beyond a standard literature review on a particular topic, the constitutive components of past protest—organizations, individuals, events, and frames—provide a guide to research strategies based on primary documentation. Sources of evidence are inevitably peculiar to particular topics. In this discussion, we emphasize sources useful for research on U.S. history; for those embarking on research in other settings, this discussion may provide a checklist for scavenging the footnotes and methodological appendixes in other literatures.

Organizations

Organizations provide a useful starting point because they tend to produce documents (although this is far less likely under repressive regimes). To judge whether a project is feasible, you will want to know whether any of the organizations involved left records. Organizations that still exist—such as the Women's Christian Temperance Union or the American Federation of Labor—may have their own collections; contact information for associations in the United States is available in the *Encyclopedia of Associations*

(Gale). Documents produced by many associations, both defunct and on-going, have been deposited in archives around the country. *ArchivesUSA* (Chadwyck-Healey; also available online in many research libraries) is a source for bibliographic records and indexes for approximately one hundred thousand archives and manuscript collections in the United States. The American Association for State and Local History publishes a directory of historical societies in the United States. For the old-fashioned bibliophile, the *National Union Catalog* (available in the reference section of many research libraries) is a valuable source for organizational records such as conference proceedings, serial publications, and official histories.

Organizational documents are often a treasure trove for research, but they may also omit or distort crucial information in order to present the organization more favorably, for the sake of present legitimacy or future legacy. For example, internal turmoil may be downplayed or excluded completely. The conference proceedings of nineteenth-century voluntary associations often printed only those resolutions that were adopted; defeated proposals left only a trace in the skipped numbering of resolutions (Clemens 1997). Consequently, researchers should be alert for signs of the internal politics of documentation as well as the (self-imposed) constraints associated with government surveillance or repression.

The fruitfulness of beginning with formal movement organizations is likely to decline as topics become more distant in time. Historically, the right of association or the ability to establish a durable formal organization has been tightly controlled under a wide variety of regimes. Consequently, the success of many studies of past protest will depend on finding evidence of the individuals and networks engaged in some form of contention.

Individuals

It is also possible to begin your search by following individuals. In some cases, organizational documents will provide a framework for research on individual activists; in the United States, for example, many movement organizations published lists of officers or members, souvenir volumes featuring prominent members, and obituaries. *ArchivesUSA* can be used to search for individual names; manuscript collections may include personal correspondence, published essays, newspaper clippings, and various memorabilia. When assessing such sources, remember that not everyone is an equally good or diligent correspondent; it is always possible that the most valuable troves will be found in the files of someone slightly off to one side of your investigation.

For relatively prominent individuals, published sources are also available:

Who's Who in America (Marquis), the *Dictionary of American Biography* (Scribner), and the *National Cyclopedia of American Biography* (White). The *Biographical and Genealogical Master Index* (Gale) acts as a search engine for these volumes as well as a number of others. Finally, the *New York Times Names Index* (1851–1974) and *Obituary Index* (1858–1968) are valuable sources for reconstructing careers of organization and activism. Research in other national settings can be aided by comparable sources (e.g., Stenton 1976).

It is likely, however, that only prominent leaders and political celebrities will be included in such volumes and sources. For the rank-and-file membership of social movements, consider genealogical records. The U.S. Genealogy Web Project (http://usgenweb.org), a free service maintained by a national network of volunteers, is an electronic gateway for genealogical research. Oral histories are another valuable resource. The Oral History Association (http://omega.dickinson.edu/organizations/oha) maintains a directory of oral history centers and collections. When relying on such sources and collections, be clear about the criteria that were used to compile a biographical dictionary or to invite individuals to produce an oral history. The categories employed in constructing these resources will shape what can be learned from them.

Beyond these resources compiled by researchers and associations, a wide variety of historical records can be treated as sources of individual-level data. In Europe, historical demographers have made extensive use of parish records; Bearman and Deane (1992: 35) explore the links between social mobility and radicalization using "a register reporting the occupations of the 7,654 men who, from 1548 to 1689, obtained the freedom of the city of Norwich." Note that in both these cases, evidence is available because some institution—itself potentially the target of protest—created a list or registry. Consequently, the forms of resistance and precursors of protest that are generated in "hidden spaces" (Scott 1990) rarely leave traces recoverable by researchers—and then often only in police files or the reports of spies. Given the limited evidence of the private or covert side of protest, much historical research focuses on those moments when protest becomes public.

Events and Outcomes

Whereas tracing organizations and individuals focuses on the movement itself, other research strategies mine the intersection of protest with important institutions: the press and the government. Newspapers, whether a local "sheet" or a "newspaper of record," are a staple for research on past protest. Many research libraries have microfilmed holdings of some newspapers. The

New York Times is among the most widely available and is, conveniently, indexed from the 1850s. Other guides to newspaper holdings include the *History and Bibliography of American Newspapers, 1690–1820* (American Antiquarian Society 1947) and *American Newspapers, 1821–1936: A Union List of Files Available in the United States and Canada* (H. S. Wilson 1937). For periodicals, see the *Union List of Serials in Libraries of the United States and Canada.*

All the problems of selection bias widely discussed in contemporary research (McCarthy, McPhail, and Smith 1996) are as great—and probably even greater—for earlier periods. In the United States, most nineteenth-century newspapers were explicitly partisan and cannot be read as even attempting to produce an objective record of "all the news that is fit to print." This partisanship can be turned to advantage, however, by reconstructing the multiple claims and frames linked to different political camps (Ellingson 1995).

Reconstruction of past protest can also begin at the state. In some cases—notably in France—a highly developed system of government surveillance has left a rich lode of records on protest and subversion (Gould 1995; Tilly 1986). In the United States, police records are less centralized and accessible (although they have been used in rich studies of crime, vagrancy, and domestic abuse), but movement outcomes may be addressed through evidence of legislation or court challenges. At this time, the Library of Congress, the world's largest library, is making increasing portions of its holdings available electronically; the National Archives and Records Administration, which houses documents from all three branches of the federal government, is in the midst of a similar process. States and localities are also expanding their electronic presence, although the lower the level of government, the more uneven the progress. In many cases, old-fashioned library work will still be in order, starting with the designated "federal depository" in each state (often the main university library), which should have holdings of state legislation and legal proceedings for most of the twentieth century.

Government documents and newspapers have distinctive advantages and disadvantages. The former include the consistency and range of data gathered every year, every decade, or at every occurrence of a particular type, such as a strike or an arrest. So long as one checks that data collection procedures have not changed significantly over time, these sources provide rarely rivaled sequences of evidence over time. For example, 150 years of data from the U.S. Census is now available from the Integrated Public Use Microdata Series. This advantage, however, brings with it potential dangers. Government agencies and newspapers collect and publish data in accordance with their own interests and their own procedures. Although official documents are often the best sources of systematic evidence, a researcher must always asked who collected the data, by what procedures, and for what purposes?

Evaluating Evidence and Interrogating Sources

The preceding discussion of sources has been full of caveats. Documentary research requires particular attention to questions of authenticity, representativeness, genre, and interpretation (for an excellent discussion, see Platt 1981). To the extent that challenges involve claims-making, the resulting documents must be read as arguments rather than "objective" representations. Much of the available evidence is the product of the targets of protest, a problem that increases with distance from the present. Religious authorities documented heresy trials; judicial authorities produced records of arrests, trials, and executions. Public expressions of grievances were often carefully tailored to evade censors and repression. Other sources of evidence may be colored by the perceptions of earlier commentators or the conventions of genres such as newspapers. The capacity to create and to preserve documents was typically more closely held by elites than in many contemporary societies. And when an individual account of resistance is preserved, the absence of formally recognized organizations makes it difficult to link the statements of a single person to some broader pattern of subversion or mobilization.

The danger lies in reliance on a simple "reflection" model that takes a text or account as evidence of what "really" happened or what people "really" believed or how society "really" was. Inasmuch as archives are collections of cultural artifacts, historical research should attend to issues developed in the sociology of culture. As the art historian Michael Baxandall explains, "The maker of a picture or other historical artefact is a man [or woman] addressing a problem of which his product is a finished and concrete solution. To understand it we try to reconstruct both the specific problem it was designed to solve and the specific circumstances out of which he was addressing it" (1985: 14–15). Religious authorities are trying to solve a problem with a heresy trial; the resulting documents are shaped by the institutional politics of the church, by the conceptions of orthodoxy, by established conventions of argument, and so on. Newspapers present "stories" that are shaped by events, interpretations of events, journalistic conventions, assessments of what will attract audiences and please powerful sponsors. Contemporary evidence, of course, is beset by similar problems. But to the extent that we study social movements in our own society in our own time, we are less likely (although not guaranteed) to make howling errors in our assumptions about evidence.

When research relies on documents produced by others for other purposes, it is particularly critical to be skeptical. First, is a document authentic? Look for evidence of authorship, the circumstances of production, and the typical features of a document produced in that particular time and place. Is it credible? (Platt 1981; for an extended treatment of the use of evidence in historical description, see McCullagh 1984). Even if the author was an eyewitness, he or she may have been unreliable or intentionally deceptive. Who was the intended audience, and what were the conventions of a particular genre—letter, petition, public speech? What seems surprising to a modern reader may have been utterly predictable to a member of the intended audience; similarly, contemporary researchers may well fail to be surprised by what is most novel or unusual in a particular document. Questions of authenticity, credibility, genre, and representativeness are central to the craft of the historian, and historical sociologists are now expected to meet their fellow discipline's standards of research.

Historical sociologists also face particular challenges with respect to interpretation and theoretical explanation. While questions of the completeness and representativeness of archival holdings are a major concern for research designs that involve counting events or mapping ties, analyses that address meanings and motives face challenges more closely linked to the sociology of culture. In a virtuoso essay, "Workers Revolt: The Great Cat Massacre of the Rue Saint-Séverin," Darnton (1985) elegantly dissects one particular text: a former apprentice printer's memoir of a particularly gruesome joke played on his master and the master's wife some two or three decades earlier. Darnton transforms one text infused with particularities into a window on the past by locating the memoir's specifics in historical knowledge of broader fields of practice: patterns of conflict among apprentices, journeymen, and masters; the state of the eighteenth-century printing industry; and the peculiar uses of cats in early modern festivities and rituals. This strategy does not rest on the "representativeness" of the document (for this is a rather extraordinary memoir) but rather on the consistency of the account with knowledge derived from many other sources.

Of course, virtuoso performances are often poor exemplars for discussions of methods—one is a virtuoso or one isn't. In a discussion of methodology in the sociology of culture, Griswold (1987) offers a more attainable guide for the interpretation of cultural objects. Cultural objects, including archival documents, may be *comprehended* in light of the "symbols, patterns of symbols or relations, and formal structures" (24) that characterized the context of production or reception by some audience. An abolitionist pamphlet is to be comprehended in terms of antebellum constructs of race, religion, and rights, not in those of a post–civil rights researcher. The cultural object may then be *explained* with reference to the agent, to the mentality or situation of the social group(s) to which the agent belongs, and, finally, to social and cultural experience both proximate and remote (23). Appropriated by historical sociologists, this methodology provides a discipline for ensuring that you understand your sources.

Bearing these challenges of documentary research in mind, one can find much in the archives to illuminate key theoretical concerns in social movement research. In the sections that follow, we survey how social movement researchers have located and analyzed data relevant to a series of core theoretical concepts: identities, networks, and careers; events and repertoires; resources and organizations; framing; movement attributes and outcomes; and social change.

Linking Theory, Concepts, and Evidence

Social movement theory offers a rich selection of theoretical concepts linked to particular units of analysis. Consequently, the process of developing a research design is inevitably iterative: given the questions that you want to ask, is there evidence to answer them? Given the evidence available in the archives (see Figure 8.1), what sorts of theoretical questions can be addressed? Of the various methodologies surveyed in this volume, which can be adapted for historical or archival research? Although one cannot interview the dead or expect them to return completed surveys, many of the standard questions on those instruments can be answered using archival evidence. Although participant observation strategies are obviously precluded, to what extent can one make use of first-person accounts found in letters or diaries? In the discussion that follows, we identify exemplars of historical research that link diverse sources of evidence to the constitutive elements of past protest: identities, networks, and careers of activism; protest events and repertoires; resources and organizations; and framing and grievances.

Identities, Networks, and Careers of Activism

One of the most basic questions in social movement research is, Who participates? This question calls for individual-level evidence that is rare in newspaper accounts, which are as likely to invoke a collective actor—"farmers" or "metalworkers"—as to enumerate specific individuals with identifiable social characteristics. To answer the question of participation, some researchers have turned to documents produced by movement organizations themselves. Membership lists provide a starting point for names and sometimes additional information such as occupation or residency (Schwartz 1976). In

Identities, Networks, and Careers of Activism

Organizational archives	Rosenthal et al. 1985, on joint membership Anheier and Neidhardt 1998, on membership
Government documents	Gould 1995, on arrest records for participation and marriage certificates for network ties
Newspapers	Clemens 1999, on obituaries for careers
Biographical dictionaries	Clemens 1999, on careers of activism

Protest Events and Repertoires

Newspapers	Tilly 1995a; Fransozi 1987, 1998 (both for protest events)
Organizational archives	Kniss (1997: 197–202), for conflict events Clemens 1997, on convention proceedings for repertoires
Government documents	Shin 1998, on agrarian tenancy disputes Munger 1991, on litigation as a tactic

Framing and Grievances

Newspapers	Babb 1996; Gould 1995
Government documents	Barkey and Van Rossem 1997, on court cases Markoff 1996, on *cahiers de doleance*
Organizational archives	Brustein 1996, on party platforms

Organizations and Resources

Organizational archives	Aminzade (1993: 75), on budgets Banaszak (1996: 74–81) Clemens (1997: 90), on budgets Conell and Voss 1990, on organizational forms Redding 1992, on size

Figure 8.1. Linking concepts and evidence: exemplary studies.

some cases, membership followed an application process, and surviving documents can provide much richer information about individuals, their history of other memberships or activism, and the identity of their sponsors for membership. Anheier and Neidhardt (1998) constructed a rich portrait of members of the Nazi party in Munich based on newly available membership archives. In other cases, membership lists may provide only names, but these can then be used to link membership to information in municipal directories, biographical dictionaries, *Who's Who,* other membership lists, and virtually any other source of data at the level of individual participants. Given that such sources are more likely to provide information on social elites, this has been a particularly effective strategy for reconstructing the social identity of a movement's leadership (Beisel 1997: 49–53; Schwartz 1976: 116).

By tracing these linkages across social identities, the analysis of individuals who participate can lead to an examination of the social networks that sustain participation and mobilization. In some cases, individual-level data can reconstruct interorganizational ties and the migration of activism across movements and through individual careers. In research on the U.S. woman suffrage movement, Rosenthal and colleagues (1985, 1997) exploited the organizational convention of publishing membership lists. Given that many nineteenth-century associations compiled such lists, the joint membership of individuals in organizations can be used to reconstruct the interorganizational field of the woman suffrage movement. To the extent that the same individuals belonged to both the Women's Christian Temperance Union and the suffrage organization, those organizations are held to be closely tied to one another, and the changing strength of interorganizational ties can be traced over time.

To reconstruct movement networks, Clemens (1999) exploited organizational documents in a different way. Over the course of the struggle for the vote, suffrage leaders documented their own efforts and accomplishments. Of the six volumes that resulted, two include reports on activities in each of the different states. Using these reports to construct a concordance of names, Clemens constructed a list of active suffragists; some, however, are never mentioned elsewhere in the official narrative of the movement since they had been effectively purged, usually for excessive partisanship or inappropriate behavior. In this way, the movement's own documents can be used to reconstruct the divergence of patterns of activism from the "official story" of the winning faction. Supplemented by evidence from biographical dictionaries, newspapers, and archives, this collective biography of activists also uses the principle of "joint membership" to document how the suffrage movement was embedded in a broader organizational field and how that embedding contributed to patterns of movement schism and decline.

In the absence of evidence of "individual joint membership," diverse indicators of social connectedness can be aligned to suggest the interlocking networks that generated activism. Gould's (1995) study of Paris during the 1848 revolution and the Commune of 1871 exemplifies the creative pursuit of this approach. Individual records of membership in the National Guard or arrest provide evidence of where participating individuals lived. To assess what types of social networks organized these neighborhoods, Gould sampled marriage licenses, which required a number of witnesses, each also identified by residence. Adding evidence on occupation gathered from these records and other directories, Gould concludes that in some neighborhoods individuals were embedded in occupation- or trade-based networks that crossed neighborhoods, while others (those most involved in the uprisings) were more likely to be embedded in cross-class networks within a neighborhood. The two sources of evidence are linked by claims of typicality; given that most residents of a neighborhood were married in front of witnesses with diverse class backgrounds, residents of the same neighborhood would be mobilized into politics through economically diverse networks. These claims were then tested against individual accounts drawn from trial records, newspaper reports, and other sources of evidence. Resting on the dogged construction of systematic evidence for quantitative analysis, Gould's argument also invokes criteria of triangulation and sufficiency in order to test his interpretation.

For the more recent past, the absence of extensive membership lists or individual records can be circumvented in additional ways. In *Women of the Klan* (1991: 4–5), Blee combined evidence of individual participation gleaned from organizational records, from obituaries, and from interviews generated by public notices and connections with local historical societies. As this tool kit of research strategies suggests, however, one of the key factors that distinguishes historical research on social movements is the difficulty of collecting systematic individual-level data. Consequently, whereas much contemporary research has focused on processes of micromobilization, historical research has tended to emphasize dimensions of social movement activity that are more readily available in archival sources, notably protest itself.

Protest Events and Repertoires

In important respects, social movements are like icebergs with much of the action happening below the surface. This is particularly true of past movements that developed in societies lacking rights of association or petition, in regimes that actively suppressed political challenge and protest. But because the authorities were troubled by protest, they tended to keep track of it. Consequently, one extremely productive strategy has been to reconstruct social movements by tracking *protest events,* the moments when movements break through the veils of conspiracy and private grievances into public protest (for a more extensive discussion, see the chapter by Koopmans and Rucht, this volume).

Exemplified by the work of Tilly, this strategy builds on institutional-ized practices of recording protest events. In a setting with a well-developed press, the media provide one source of such accounts. To trace the transfor-mation of popular contention in Great Britain, Tilly and colleagues created data sets by coding "contentious gatherings" mentioned in a number of pub-lications as well as in parliamentary records (1995a: 393–405). For other settings, notably France (Tilly 1986), police and judicial archives have been mined to reconstruct a record of extralegal, or at least disruptive, protest. Barkey and Van Rossem (1997) argue that court cases were an important form of contention in the Ottoman Empire and used judicial records to reconstruct both the social identities and grievances that typified struggles over economic development. Munger (1991) used court cases to illuminate the grievances and tactics of coal miners in West Virginia. Shin (1998) relied on government documentation of agrarian conflicts in Korea.

Reliance on either newspapers or government documents offers the benefit of relatively consistent documentation of protest; both sources pose the challenge of interpreting the evidence in light of the institutional biases in documentation. For news publications, what constitutes a "newsworthy event" (Franzosi 1987; Gitlin 1980: 27–30), and how do these cultural understandings shape the silences and emphases of the records left for his-torical researchers? In the case of official police archives, how did the inter-ests and ideologies of state actors shape when action was deemed "illegal" and how it was understood?[2]

With protest event or court case data in hand, one can ask a number of different questions. One line of research addresses the composition of the population of events: what forms of contention (Tilly 1995a), grievances and targets (Markoff 1986), or tactics (Munger 1991) predominate? How do these patterns of protest change over time? These questions speak to the core understanding of the development of the form of the social movement as a part of the process of social change that also produced capitalism and modern nation-states. Records of protest events provide one tool for recon-structing *repertoires* of protest or organization. In cases where movements themselves published newspapers or convention proceedings, these docu-ments provide evidence of which tactics and models were *considered* as well as actually deployed: "A close reading of such proceedings reveals two sets of available models: those already used by group members (or traditionally identified with 'this sort of group') and those used by other groups in society. Both are analytically important. First, familiar models were one way in which a group defined its identity, both for its own members and for others. Second, the known but not yet used organizational models were both recipes for innovation and symptoms used to diagnose social problems" (Clemens 1997: 60).

A second approach explores the ecological covariates of protest (e.g., Soule 1992): what are the economic or demographic or cultural characteristics of communities or districts where protest is more or less frequent? In this case, the research design is often doubly dependent on institutionalized practices of documentation, for both the event data and for the statistics compiled by government agencies.

A further, potentially complementary strategy mines the event data for more information about the character and unfolding of protest itself. Markoff (1986) coded the character of protest in revolutionary France, finding that mass literacy is not associated with the frequency of revolt but with its targets. Both Tilly (1995a: 87–105) and Franzosi (1989, 1998) exploit the narrative structure embedded in accounts of protest: *who* (workers, peasants, etc.) engaged in *what action* (petition, food riot, etc.) directed at *what target* (parliament, employers, etc.). Examining lynching in the American South, Griffin (1993) analyzed the "event-structure," or sequence of particular actions, of a narrative to develop a generalizable causal interpretation. Through these methods, data on events can do much more than track the incidence of protest. Event data can reconstruct the relational and temporal dynamics of protest and response.

Whereas event data focus research on the sporadic eruptions of protest into public visibility, this turn to the processual dimensions of protest raises questions about the mobilization of insurgency, the organization of challenges, and the framing of grievances. To address these issues, historical research turns to strategies different from the analysis of protest events.

Resources and Organizations

Membership lists cross levels of analysis: they provide evidence of individual participation but also document the role of formal organization in the mobilization of protest. Where individual-level data are either unavailable or hopelessly unsystematic, organizational evidence can provide the foundation for historical research on social movements. As with government documents and newspaper reports, however, organizational documents (or their absence) should not be interpreted uncritically. In many cases, oppositional politics takes the form of protest precisely because the rights of association are severely limited and, at times, entirely suppressed. Under such conditions, extensive organization may fuel mobilization without leaving a trace in the archives; secret societies are an important element in the history of organized protest. Finally, even where the right of association is guaranteed, movement organizations may seek to hide information about their assets or activities from the authorities. Organizational documents tend to reflect the perspective of the movement leadership and may suppress internal debates or purge dissidents and losers from the official history of the movement (Clemens 1999). Consequently, such sources will tend to overstate the degree of consensus within movement organizations.

With these caveats in mind, organizational evidence provides some of the most fertile material for the historical analysis of social movements. In addition to the membership data discussed earlier, organizational documents can illuminate many issues theoretically central to social movement research: the mobilization of resources (McCarthy and Zald 1977), the perception and exploitation of opportunities (Banaszak 1996), and the repertoire or deployment of frames (Snow et al. 1986) and organizational forms (Buechler 2000: 204–9; Clemens 1996).

Perhaps the most prominent line of research asks about the consequences of the presence (and sometimes the size or resources) of organizations for either the formation or outcomes of social movements. In a study of a nineteenth-century labor association, the Knights of Labor, Conell and Voss (1990) explore how variations in local labor organizations ("trade" versus "mixed" or quasi-industrial) influenced subsequent mobilization into the Knights of Labor. Their analysis combined organizational evidence published by a historian with demographic and economic data available from the U.S. Census and other government studies. Exploring the consequences of the presence of an organized Farmers Alliance on voting for the People's Party in North Carolina in the 1890s, Redding (1992) similarly combined organizational data drawn from the Alliance's own records with demographic, economic, and electoral data collected and published by government agencies.

The proliferation of studies on nineteenth-century France, Britain, and the United States is not accidental. These analyses rest on multiple processes of archiving evidence that researchers deem reliable: organizational archives, government documents, and other public sources such as city directories. As always, the quality of historical research turns on the researcher's judgments about the quality and character of evidence.

Framing and Grievances

Inasmuch as archives shelter cultural artifacts, historical researchers frequently pursue cultural analyses of movement activity. In recent years, "framing" (Snow et al. 1986) has been among the most important theoretical guides to such research. Drawing on Goffman (1974), the core argument is that frames constitute "'schemata of interpretation' that enable individuals 'to locate, perceive, identify, and label' occurrences within their life space and the world at large. By rendering events or occurrences meaningful, frames function to organize experience and guide action, whether individual or collective" (Snow et al. 1986: 464). This theoretical orientation has an affinity with methods of literary analysis long used to interpret texts: analyzing narratives, tropes, images, and metaphors. With a few exceptions (e.g., Ansell 1997; Ellingson 1995), however, social movement researchers have emphasized the presence/absence of key themes and arguments rather than appropriating more complex forms of literary interpretation.

In a study of the U.S. greenback movement, Babb (1996) provides an exemplary combination of frame analysis and the construction of a quantitative data set. Unlike many early modern mobilizations where evidence was produced largely by the targets of protest, the greenbackers organized in a society characterized by universal male suffrage (outside the South), relatively high literacy, and a vibrant newspaper industry. In this case, analysis can be based on documents produced by members of the movement (if disproportionately by leaders and the more literate) and largely for the members of the movement. Babb focused on two newspapers, the *Workingman's Advocate* and the *National Labor Tribune,* that are recognized by historians as important publications of the labor movement in the decades after the Civil War.

In this case, the problems of "representativeness" are different from those faced by contemporary researchers relying on the *New York Times* for a record of protest events; these earlier newspapers were explicitly allied with a cause rather than aspiring to "objectivity." Babb began with orienting themes related to political cleavages and programs; using these as guides, she identified a total of almost 250 relevant articles. Articles were coded by content: by the invocation of identity, either of the enemy or the movement/ author; by the definition of problems and proposed solutions. Her analysis then focused on responses to "anomalies" or exceptions to the ideologies of labor-greenback advocates; the result is a rich illumination of the interplay of events and frames, of the robustness of frames in confrontation with evidence or experience.

This systematic approach to frame analysis depends on a particular set of historical conditions: relatively continuous publication by the same sources in a relatively open polity. Working with more diverse sources— pamphlets, newspapers, records of meetings—and a more contested polity, Gould employed a threshold criterion to identify salient frames in a series of contentious mobilizations in Paris: "it would not be terribly useful to go further and present a systematic accounting of the locutions used in public discourse in 1848, 1871, and the intervening years, even if such an enterprise were practical. The reason is that appeals based on a specific collective identity need not numerically swamp other sorts of appeals to be regarded as significant for mobilization: what is necessary is that they be sufficiently widespread to make plausible the claim that large numbers of people might have responded to them" (1995: 31). Such arguments rest on the researcher's documentation of a wide, at times exhaustive, reading of available sources; this wide reading undergirds claims to expert interpretation (Carruthers and Babb 1996).

Here again, it is critical that any analysis of frames rest on an appreciation of the social organization of cultural production and reception (Griswold 1987). Elite representations of workers' motives are evidence—indeed important evidence—of something, but they are not an unproblematic documentation of the grievances or narratives that fueled participation in popular protest. An individual diary or testimony may or may not illuminate "typical" understandings of the situation; this depends on the ways in which the individual author was "typical" of his or her times. In such cases, criteria of dependability and triangulation developed by qualitative researchers (Erlandson et al. 1993: 28–35) are useful guides to deciding when a judgement of what is "typical" is warranted.

To gain more leverage on the variation of frames over time and between places, many historical researchers have turned to creative uses of comparison: across time periods, across groups, across settings, and across conflict events.[3] Gould's elegant study of insurrections in nineteenth-century Paris is organized around a comparative question: "the very clarity and robustness of the class awareness permeating the events of 1848 make its faintness in 1871 a puzzle in need of resolution" (1995: 4). In a comparison of nineteenth-century labor movements in the United States and Britain, Voss (1996) suggests that differences in "fortifying myths" can explain why models of organizing used in a first wave of mobilization were not revived in the United States but were resurrected in Britain a few decades later. Banaszak (1996) uses a comparison of the U.S. and Swiss movements for woman suffrage to isolate causally important differences in the opportunities—and perceptions of opportunity—that distinguished the early success of the former from the belated enfranchisement of Swiss women. In all these examples, the argument rests on comparisons in the set of frames—dominant, typical, or simply present—that characterized movement mobilization and conflict in different times or settings.

Other studies hold time and place constant in order to gain leverage from comparisons across groups or social settings. In a comparative study of labor, agrarian, and women's organizations at the turn of the twentieth century, Clemens (1997: 59–62) relies on extensive readings of convention proceedings, movement publications, and archival sources to identify the distinctively different ways in which members of these groups tended to answer the question, How shall we organize? Based on patterned relationships between the "organizational repertoires" of different kinds of political challengers and the kinds of political outcomes these challengers secured, she argues that understandings of legitimate models of mobilization had important consequences for trajectories of institutional change.

Focusing on the employers of the same period, Haydu (1999) argues that a "case for frame correspondence requires demonstrating that some of the same individuals and organizations were active on multiple fronts, shaping managerial, civic, and status group identities. Such personal and organizational networks provide mechanisms for harmonizing frames across institutional spheres. They also render more plausible the claim that specific frames prevailed in fighting unions *because* they replicated those deployed in other battles" (1999: 319). Although in this particular study Haydu relies on a thick analysis of primary and secondary historical sources, this argument could easily inform a systematic design contingent on the existence of evidence for a matrix of multiple individuals or organizations participating in multiple conflicts (Clemens 1996, 1997).

A further approach to frame analysis involves tracking changes in episodes or moments within a sequence of conflicts. As in Babb's study of the labor-greenbackers, Ellingson (1995) relies on nineteenth-century newspapers to document the discursive struggle over slavery and antiabolition violence in antebellum Cincinnati. This research addressed "three discrete periods of public debate . . . separated by two episodes of collective violence. . . . After each episode, speakers altered their discourses by framing new diagnoses and solutions according to the real and perceived outcomes of collective violence and formed new discursive alliances in order to gain legitimacy and support for their positions" (1995: 115–16). Complementing Haydu's research on the consistency of frames across settings, Ellingson demonstrates how events changed the frames deployed by the same (collective) actors across a series of conflicts.

In her study of the anti-vice movement in three nineteenth-century American cities, Beisel (1997) uses a still finer-grained approach. Here the goal is to delineate what was at stake in a conflict for different contenders, what precisely constituted vice or a threat to the virtue of American children? Were museum exhibitions of paintings of nude women pornography? Etchings of paintings of nude women? Photographs of such paintings? Or what of photographs of nudes themselves? Through close comparison of the controversy around different methods and venues of presentation, Beisel specifies the specific understandings of the problem of vice that motivated participants in the anti-vice movements of the time.

Finally, some studies have harnessed frame analysis to the questions of network-based mobilization that motivate many individual-level studies. In the absence of evidence on individual-to-individual ties or comemberships, Ansell (1997) demonstrates how distinct discourses mobilized and realigned French labor organizations in voting to support a general strike in 1894.

From Movement Attributes to Outcomes: Developing Explanatory Arguments

Historical research on participation, events, organizations, and resources is typically motivated by the underlying assumption that "movements matter," that protest makes things happen. Those studies that concentrate more directly on the causal relationships between movement attributes or actions and various historical outcomes typically rely on the demonstration of correlations; the greater requirements for systematic quantitative evidence result in this area of research being concentrated on the relatively recent past of collective protest in nation-states with extensive systems of social documentation, whether through newspapers or government agencies.

Two distinct patterns emerge from a review of recent quantitative analyses of social movements prior to World War II (for a few examples, see Table 8.1). First, some quantifiable attribute of the movement in question invariably appears, either as a causal or as an outcome variable. The attribute may be movement size, measured by counts of individuals (Redding 1992) or number of groups (Amenta and Zylan 1991; Kaufman 1999); number of movement activities, such as strikes or other protests (Ragin, Coverman, and Hayward 1982; Markoff 1986); or number of outcomes associated with the movement. Examples of the latter include Townsend memorials endorsed by state legislatures (Amenta, Carruthers, and Zylan 1992), and Townsend-endorsed candidates for Congress (Amenta and Zylan 1991). Studies of countermovements (e.g., Griffin, Wallace, and Rubin 1986; Jenkins and Brents 1989) are no exception to this pattern. Griffin and colleagues measure countermovement size by the expenditures and number of members in the National Association of Manufacturers. Jenkins and Brents (1989) measure a single type of countermovement event: congressional testimony concerning the Social Security Act of 1935.

In most of these studies, note how issues central to a resource mobilization perspective influence the existence of evidence. Formal organizations create lists of members and formal budgets; organizations with some social

Table 8.1. From movements to outcomes in U.S. politics, 1880s–1950s

a. Electoral Outcomes

Redding 1992: Did the strength of the Farmers' Alliances translate into electoral strength for the People's Party?

Unit of analysis	Movement data	Selected correlates
North Carolina counties, 1890–1900	Dues-paying members/ county (Farmers Alliance Archives)	Votes/county (U.S. Census)
		Tenancy/crops (U.S. Census)
		Commercialization/ increase in cotton (U.S. Census)
		Economic, racial, and religious composition (U.S. Census)

b. Public Policy and Spending

Kaufman 1999: Did the presence of different kinds of associations influence patterns of municipal spending?

Unit of analysis	Movement data	Selected correlates
U.S. cities over 50,000 (1890)	Presence of different types of civic associations (city directories, 1879–81)	Municipal expenditures (U.S. Census)
		Voting, party competitiveness, and third parties (U.S. Census)
		Population, economic, and regional controls (U.S. Census)

Amenta, Carruthers, and Zylan 1992: Did movement strength influence the generosity of state-level old-age pensions?

Unit of analysis	Movement data	Selected correlates
48 U.S. states (1939–48)	Union density, membership in the Fraternal Order of Eagles, Townsend clubs per capita, Townsend-endorsed members of U.S. House (secondary sources, organizational publications, U.S. Census)	Aged population (U.S. Census)
		Employment and industrialization (U.S. Census and other government reports)
		Party strength and voting rights (U.S. Census and secondary sources)

standing are invited to testify as "representatives" of different political constituencies. Protests by the relatively unorganized or less literate are much less likely to leave an evidentiary trace. In all of these cases, the significant primary research involves collecting systematic data on some aspect of a "movement" (presence of a type of association, occurrences of strikes or protests, number of members, etc.), which is then related to other evidence available from standard government sources or other studies.

The second pattern emerges from a visual examination of the second and third columns in Table 8.1. In most instances, data come from records kept either by governments or by social movement organizations themselves. Secondary literature is cited only where earlier scholars have already assembled the data from such primary sources. It is noteworthy that almost all the studies discussed in this section involve Western industrializing nations (United States, U.K., and France) where governments are characterized by extensive record-keeping. Consequently, this type of research design will be much more challenging when used to understand protests in earlier periods or in national settings where government collection of data was less extensive or systematic.

This interplay of case selection and standard research strategies helps to define the state of the art in historical research on social movements and to identify opportunities for innovation. As represented by publications in major journals, sociological research on past protest converges on a limited set of cases and research strategies. Substantively, almost three-quarters of the historical research literature (which we defined as anything up to World War II) published in the *American Journal of Sociology* and the *American Sociological Review* over the past two decades addressed either the United States (especially the period between the Civil War and the New Deal) or France between the Revolution of 1789 and World War I. A survey of research published in other journals or in books or in other languages, as well as the important contributions by historians, political scientists, and anthropologists to the study of past protest, would add to the list of topics covered without erasing the prominence of a limited set of cases. Because of this combination of patches of dense inquiry with vast stretches of unexplored territory, research strategies will be strongly conditioned by one's initial choice of topic. An examination of the class basis of protest in France requires grappling with an extensive, rich, and sophisticated research literature (e.g., Aminzade 1993; Gould 1995; Markoff 1996; Tilly 1986). The same question posed in another setting at another time may well be a voyage into the unknown. In these cases, research questions will be guided by general theoretical expectations or by comparisons with better-documented cases.

Is Historical Research Different?

The discussion so far has proceeded as if the only distinctive challenge of historical research is that the evidence is harder to find, more likely to provoke dust allergies, and less likely to generate the hoped-for adventures of a participant-observer. But this pragmatic approach to finding evidence and linking evidence to theoretical concepts has, thus far, blithely ignored a host of questions about the entire project of historical research.

In recent years, there has been a spirited, sometimes heated debate over the theoretical standing of historical sociology. Kiser and Hechter advance one line of argument, contending that causal explanations in historical research require attention to causal relations and mechanisms specified in general theory. This argument contrasts the use of "general, transhistorical" theoretical concepts with the purported retreat of historical sociology to particularism and purely inductive inquiry (1991: 4–5; 1998). For movement researchers, this manifesto calls for historical research to test theoretical generalizations established in work on contemporary movements: do opportunities or resources produce higher rates of mobilization or protest in early modern Spain as well as in late-twentieth-century Germany? In response, Somers (1998) and others have argued for alternative understandings of theory as profoundly historical.

In an extreme simplification, this second position requires social movement researchers to remember that they necessarily study "opportunities" or "resources"—rather than opportunities or resources—since each of these is constituted and understood in distinctive ways in different historical settings. For an understanding of popular protest, the division among elites constituted by a struggle among early modern courtiers is not the same as the sharing of control by different parties in a constitutional democracy. To the extent that research necessarily involves translating theoretical concepts into empirical measures or observations, historical research demands particular care in thinking about how to transport modern theories to past settings.

While this debate continues to rage, a set of less contentious guidelines for historical research have emerged calling for "different forms of explanatory principles, differently emphasizing the role of initial conditions, general laws and path dependency" (Goldstone 1998: 829; on comparative research design, Mahoney 1999). From the literature on revolution, Tilly draws practical implications that are equally applicable to social movement research: "Students of revolution have imagined they were dealing with phenomena like ocean tides, whose regularities they could deduce from sufficient knowledge of celestial motion, when they were actually confronting phenomena like great floods, equally coherent occurrences from a causal perspective, but enormously variable in structure, sequence, and consequences as a function of terrain, previous precipitation, built environment, and human response" (1995b: 1601). So how does this directive translate into social movement research?

One strategy is to be particularly sensitive to changes in relationships among factors over time. Delineating methods attentive to both general theory and historical specificity, Isaac and Griffin argue that "much conventional quantitative time-series research is 'ahistorical' . . . [insofar as] critical contingencies of social change, understood as the sudden or gradual temporal conditioning of historical-structural relationships are generally ignored in quantitative explorations of historical processes" (1989: 873). Using time-series data on unionization and strikes, they demonstrate methods for detecting "historical contingencies" that may significantly alter relationships among factors such as organizational foundings and protest events. Haydu (1998) also uses research on labor organizing to illustrate methods for delineating causal mechanisms that link events across different periods, contributing to either the reproduction or change of theoretically important structural relationships.

Other researchers have developed methods for addressing the most basic characteristic of historical research: attention to sequence or temporality (Abbott 1984) as well as the "event-structure" of historical narratives, specifically lynchings in the American South (Griffin 1993). Finally, any historical researcher needs to be constantly on guard for inadvertent anachronisms: the absence of published grievances in the heavily censored newspapers of eighteenth-century France is not evidence of quite the same thing as the absence of published grievances in the vibrantly partisan press of the nineteenth-century United States or in the increasingly monolithic corporate press of the late twentieth century.

As this brief sketch of metatheoretical debates and methodological innovations suggests, historical research can lead into extraordinary complex puzzles. Although the prospect of such conceptual thornbushes may be daunting, there remains one exceptionally good reason to venture into this thicket: the explanation of social change.

Social Movements and Social Change

Perhaps the most important contribution of historical research on social movements is the demonstration that "social movements" are themselves the historical accomplishment of particular kinds of societies (Buechler 2000: 3–11). All sorts of people have engaged in widely varying sorts of protest throughout history. But, as Tarrow (1998: 2) argues, "mounting, coordinating and sustaining [confrontations with elites, authorities, and opponents] are the unique contribution of the social movement—an invention of the modern age and an accompaniment to the rise of the modern state."

In keeping with this insight, historical researchers have begun to document the transition from earlier forms of protest—bread riots, *charivari*—to the more sustained mobilizations that identify "the social movement." This research is most advanced in the case of Western European nations, anchored by Tilly's studies of France (1986) and England (1995a). Other research has explored the conditions that facilitated this transition from one repertoire of protest to another; Markoff (1986), for example, addresses the transitional moment of the French Revolution, discovering that in less literate regions protest was more likely to take traditional forms such as food riots, whereas greater literacy was associated with attacks on government buildings and symbols of national authority.

In historical settings after the appearance of recognizable social movements, research has explored how early forms of protest and organization gave way to new forms. Gould (1995) asks why the class-based character of the 1848 insurrection in Paris was not evident in the Commune of 1871. Conell and Voss (1990) investigate the consequences of labor organization for mobilization into the Knights of Labor. Clemens (1997) traces how movement activity based in large voluntary associations gave rise to interest-group lobbying a few decades later. Addressing the history of social movements themselves, the growing body of research documents the complex sequence and succession of forms of mobilization, although a great deal of research remains to be done outside the most-studied cases of France, England, and the United States.

A second goal of historical research on social movements is more daunting. To what extent has historical research answered the question of whether and how "movements matter"? The challenge of documenting the *outcomes* of social movements is shared by contemporary movement research, yet it is here that the longer time horizon of historical research offers potential advantages. Most historians would agree that the heretical movement now known as the Protestant Reformation "mattered," although there is a lively debate over precisely how and why, over whether it should be understood as a cause, an effect, or both of modernization. Most would also concur that the abolitionist movement, both in the United States and abroad, "mattered" in some way for the economic and political development of the United States and the global economy. Again, however, there are fierce debates over the extent to which movement activity was a central cause or merely a banana peel on the bottom step of a trajectory defined by economic, technological, and institutional conditions.

Recovering Past Protest

These debates underscore the difficulties faced by those embarking on archival research. But historical research also possesses distinctive advantages, particularly with respect to movement outcomes. Such studies can explore the impact of movement involvement on individual lives through biographical data, the influence of movements on changes in political institutions or discourse, and the perpetuation of cultures of activism through personal networks or institutionalized "abeyance structures." Many are drawn to social movement research out of a belief that social movements (sometimes) matter; historical research provides an opportunity to explore when and how and why they do.

Many of the challenges in historical research turn on questions of evidence: finding it, interpreting it, and using it. But as the research discussed throughout this chapter amply illustrates, movement researchers have met these challenges with considerable creativity and success. If necessity is the mother of invention, historical scholarship on social movements will continue to generate methodological innovation and advances in the use of a wide range of sources.

Notes

For their insightful comments and criticisms, we would like to thank Bert Klandermans, Suzanne Staggenborg, and Mayer Zald.

1. We discuss current debates over the status of historical sociology in the final section of this chapter.

2. For well-researched and extensively documented cases, such as the French Revolution, it may be possible to construct a data set of protest events by relying on the secondary literature. For an example, see Markoff 1985.

3. Mahoney (1999) provides an extremely useful analysis of strategies of causal assessment—nominal (presence or absence of a factor), ordinal (more or less), and narrative—in comparative history.

References

Abbott, Andrew. 1984. "Event Sequence and Event Duration: Colligation and Measurement." *Historical Methods* 17: 192–204.

Amenta, Edwin, and Yvonne Zylan. 1991. "It Happened Here: Political Opportunity, the New Institutionalism, and the Townsend Movement." *American Sociological Review* 56: 250–65.

Amenta, Edwin, Bruce Carruthers, and Yvonne Zylan. 1992. "A Hero for the Aged? The Townsend Movement, the Political Mediation Model, and U.S. Old-Age Policy, 1934–1950." *American Journal of Sociology* 98: 308–39.

Aminzade, Ronald. 1993. *Ballots and Barricades: Class Formation and Republican Politics in France, 1830–1871.* Princeton, N.J.: Princeton University Press.

Anheier, Helmut K., and Friedhelm Neidhardt. 1998. "The Nazi Party and Its Capital: An Analysis of the NSDAP Membership in Munich, 1925–1930." *American Behavioral Scientist* 41: 1219–37.

Ansell, Christopher K. 1997. "Symbolic Networks: The Realignment of the French Working Class, 1887–1894." *American Journal of Sociology* 103: 359–90.

Babb, Sarah. 1996. "'A True American System of Finance': Frame Resonance in the U.S. Labor Movement, 1866 to 1886." *American Sociological Review* 61: 1033–52.

Banaszak, Lee Ann. 1996. *Why Movements Succeed or Fail: Opportunity, Culture, and the Struggle for Woman Suffrage.* Princeton, N.J.: Princeton University Press.

Barkey, Karen, and Ronan Van Rossem. 1997. "Networks of Contention: Villages and Regional Structure in the Seventeenth-Century Ottoman Empire." *American Journal of Sociology* 102: 1345–82.

Baxandall, Michael. 1985. *Patterns of Intention: On the Historical Explanation of Pictures.* New Haven, Conn.: Yale University Press.

Bearman, Peter S., and Glenn Deane. 1992. "The Structure of Opportunity: Middle-Class Mobility in England, 1548–1689." *American Journal of Sociology* 98: 30–66.

Beisel, Nicola. 1997. *Imperiled Innocents: Anthony Comstock and Family Reproduction in Victorian America.* Princeton, N.J.: Princeton University Press.

Blee, Kathleen M. 1991. *Women of the Klan: Racism and Gender in the 1920s.* Berkeley and Los Angeles: University of California Press.

Brustein, William. 1996. *The Logic of Evil: The Social Origins of the Nazi Party, 1925–1933.* New Haven, Conn.: Yale University Press.

Buechler, Steven M. 2000. *Social Movements in Advanced Capitalism: The Political Economy and Cultural Construction of Social Activism.* New York: Oxford University Press.

Carruthers, Bruce G., and Sarah Babb. 1996. "The Color of Money and the Nature of Value: Greenbacks and Gold in Postbellum America." *American Journal of Sociology* 101: 1556–91.

Clemens, Elisabeth S. 1996. "Organizational Form as Frame: Collective Identity and Political Strategy in the American Labor Movement, 1880–1920." In *Comparative Perspectives on Social Movements: Political Opportunities, Mobilizing Structures, and Cultural Framings,* edited by Doug McAdam, John D. McCarthy, and Mayer N. Zald, 205–26. New York: Cambridge University Press.

———. 1997. *The People's Lobby: Organizational Innovation and the Rise of Interest Group Politics in the United States, 1890–1925*. Chicago: University of Chicago Press.

———. 1999. "Securing Political Returns to Social Capital: Women's Associations in the United States, 1880s–1920s." *Journal of Interdisciplinary History* 29: 613–38.

Conell, Carol, and Kim Voss. 1990. "Formal Organization and the Fate of Social Movements: Craft Association and Class Alliance in the Knights of Labor." *American Sociological Review* 55: 255–69.

Darnton, Robert. 1985. *The Great Cat Massacre and Other Episodes in French Cultural History.* New York: Vintage.

Ellingson, Stephen. 1995. "Understanding the Dialectic of Discourse and Collective Action: Public Debate and Rioting in Antebellum Cincinnati." *American Journal of Sociology* 101: 100–144.

Erlandson, David A., Edward L. Harris, Barbara L. Skipper, and Steve D. Allen. 1993. *Doing Naturalistic Inquiry: A Guide to Methods*. Newbury Park, Calif.: Sage.

Franzosi, Roberto. 1987. "The Press as a Source of Socio-Historical Data: Issues in the Methodology of Data Collection from Newspapers," *Historical Methods* 20: 5–16.

———. 1989. "From Words to Numbers: A Generalized and Linguistics-Based Coding Procedure for Collecting Textual Data." *Sociological Methodology* 19: 263–98.

———. 1998. "Narrative Analysis—Or Why (and How) Sociologists Should Be Interested in Narrative." *Annual Review of Sociology* 24: 517–54.

Gitlin, Todd. 1980. *The Whole World Is Watching: Mass Media in the Making and Unmaking of the New Left*. Berkeley and Los Angeles: University of California Press.

Goffman, Erving. 1974. *Frame Analysis: An Essay in the Organization of Experience*. Cambridge: Harvard University Press.

Goldstone, Jack A. 1991. *Revolution and Rebellion in the Early Modern World*. Berkeley and Los Angeles: University of California Press.

———. 1998. "Initial Conditions, General Laws, Path Dependence, and Explanation in Historical Sociology." *American Journal of Sociology* 104: 829–45.

Gould, Roger V. 1995. *Insurgent Identities: Class, Community, and Protest in Paris from 1848 to the Commune*. Chicago: University of Chicago Press.

Griffin, Larry J. 1993. "Narrative, Event-Structure Analysis, and Causal Interpretation in Historical Sociology." *American Journal of Sociology* 98: 1094–1133.

Griffin, Larry J., Michael Wallace, and Beth Rubin. 1986. "Capitalist Resistance to the Organization of Labor before the New Deal: Why? How? Success?" *American Sociological Review* 51: 147–67.

Griswold, Wendy. 1987. "A Methodological Framework for the Sociology of Culture." *Sociological Methodology* 17: 1–35.

Haydu, Jeffrey. 1998. "Making Use of the Past: Time Periods as Cases to Compare and as Sequences of Problem Solving." *American Journal of Sociology* 104: 339–71.

———. 1999. "Counter Action Frames: Employer Repertoires and the Union Menace in the Late Nineteenth Century." *Social Problems* 46: 313–31.

Isaac, Larry W., and Larry J. Griffin. 1989. "Ahistoricism in Time-Series Analyses of Historical Process." *American Sociological Review* 54: 873–90.

Jenkins, J. Craig, and Barbara Brents. 1989. "Social Protest, Hegemonic Competition, and Social Reform: A Political Struggle Interpretation of the Origins of the American Welfare State." *American Sociological Review* 54: 891–909.

Kaelber, Lutz. 1995. "Other- and Inner-Worldly Asceticism in Medieval Waldensianism: A Weberian Analysis." *Sociology of Religion* 56: 91–119.

Kaufman, Jason. 1999. "Three Views of Associationalism in Nineteenth-Century America: An Empirical Examination." *American Journal of Sociology* 104: 1296–1345.

Kiser, Edgar, and Michael Hechter. 1991. "The Role of General Theory in Comparative-Historical Sociology." *American Journal of Sociology* 97: 1–30.

———. 1998. "The Debate on Historical Sociology: Rational Choice Theory and Its Critics." *American Journal of Sociology* 104: 785–816.

Kniss, Fred. 1997. *Disquiet in the Land: Cultural Conflict in American Mennonite Communities.* New Brunswick, N.J.: Rutgers University Press.

Ladurie, Emmanuel Le Roy. 1978. *Montaillou: The Promised Land of Error.* Trans. Barbara Bray. New York: George Braziller.

Mahoney, James. 1999. "Nominal, Ordinal, and Narrative Appraisal in Macro-causal Analysis." *American Journal of Sociology* 104: 1154–96.

Markoff, John. 1985. "The Social Geography of Rural Revolt at the Beginning of the French Revolution." *American Sociological Review* 50: 761–81.

———. 1986. "Literacy and Revolt: Some Empirical Notes on 1789 in France." *American Journal of Sociology* 92: 323–49.

———.1996. *The Abolition of Feudalism: Peasants, Lords, and Legislators in the French Revolution.* University Park: Pennsylvania State University Press.

McCarthy, John, Clark McPhail, and Jackie Smith. 1996. "Images of Protest: Dimensions of Selection Bias in Media Coverage of Washington Demonstrations, 1982 and 1991." *American Sociological Review* 61: 478–99.

McCarthy, John, and Mayer N. Zald. 1977. "Resource Mobilization and Social Movements: A Partial Theory." *American Journal of Sociology* 82: 1212–41.

McCullagh, C. Behan. 1984. *Justifying Historical Descriptions.* New York: Cambridge University Press.

Munger, Frank. 1991. "Legal Resources of Striking Miners: Notes for a Study of Class Conflict and Law." *Social Science History* 15: 1–33.

Platt, Jennifer. 1981. "Evidence and Proof in Documentary Research, 1 and 2: Some Specific Problems, and Some Shared Problems, of Documentary Research." *Sociological Review* 29: 31–52, 53–66.

Ragin, Charles, Shelley Coverman, and Mark Hayward. 1982. "Major Labor Disputes in Britain, 1902–1938: The Relationship between Resource Expenditure and Outcome." *American Sociological Review* 47: 237–52.

Redding, Kent. 1992. "Failed Populism: Movement-Party Disjuncture in North Carolina, 1890–1900." *American Sociological Review* 57: 340–52.

Rosenthal, Naomi, Meryl Fingrutd, Roberta Karant, Michele Ethier, and David McDonald. 1985. "Social Movements and Network Analysis: A Case Study of Nineteenth-Century Women's Reform in New York State." *American Journal of Sociology* 90: 1022–54.

Rosenthal, Naomi, David McDonald, Michele Ethier, Meryl Fingrutd, and Roberta Karant. 1997. "Structural Tensions in the Nineteenth-Century Women's Movement." *Mobilization* 2: 21–46.

Rubin, Beth. 1986. "Class Struggle American Style: Unions, Strikes and Wages." *American Sociological Review* 51: 618–33.

Schwartz, Michael. 1976. *Radical Protest and Social Structure: The Southern Farmers' Alliance and Cotton Tenancy, 1880–1890.* Chicago: University of Chicago Press.

Scott, James C. 1990. *Domination and the Arts of Resistance.* New Haven, Conn.: Yale University Press.

Shin, Gi-Wook. 1998. "Agrarian Conflict and the Origins of Korean Capitalism." *American Journal of Sociology* 103: 1309–51.

Snow, David, E. Burke Rochford Jr., Steven K. Worden, and Robert Benford. 1986. "Frame Alignment Processes, Micromobilization, and Movement Participation." *American Sociological Review* 41: 464–81.

Somers, Margaret R. 1998. "'We're No Angels': Realism, Rational Choice, and Relationality in Social Science." *American Journal of Sociology* 104: 722–84.

Soule, Sarah A. 1992. "Populism and Black Lynching in Georgia, 1890–1900." *Social Forces* 71: 431–49.

Stenton, Michael. 1976. *Who's Who of British Members of Parliament: A Biographical Dictionary of the House of Commons Based on Annual Volumes of Dod's Parliamentary Companion and Other Sources.* Atlantic Highlands, N.J.: Humanities Press.

Tarrow, Sidney. 1998. *Power in Movement: Social Movements and Contentious Politics.* 2d ed. New York: Cambridge University Press.

Thornton, Russell. 1981. "Demographic Antecedents of a Revitalization Movement: Population Change, Population Size, and the 1890 Ghost Dance." *American Sociological Review* 46: 88–96.

Tilly, Charles. 1986. *The Contentious French*. Cambridge, Mass.: Belknap.

———. 1995a. *Popular Contention in Great Britain, 1758–1834*. Cambridge, Mass.: Harvard University Press.

———. 1995b. "To Explain Political Processes." *American Journal of Sociology* 100: 1594–1610.

Voss, Kim. 1994. *The Making of American Exceptionalism: The Knights of Labor and Class Formation in the Nineteenth Century*. Ithaca, N.Y.: Cornell University Press.

———. 1996. "The Collapse of a Social Movement: The Interplay of Mobilizing Structures, Framing, and Political Opportunities in the Knights of Labor." In *Comparative Perspectives on Social Movements: Political Opportunities, Mobilizing Structures, and Cultural Framings,* edited by Doug McAdam, John D. McCarthy, and Mayer N. Zald, 227–58. New York: Cambridge University Press.

Zaret, David. 1996. "Petitions and the 'Invention' of Public Opinion in the English Revolution." *American Journal of Sociology* 101: 1497–1555.

9

Protest Event Analysis

Ruud Koopmans and Dieter Rucht

Protests are messages directed to political adversaries, sympathizers, decision makers, and the wider public. Besides more conventional activities, such as voting and lobbying, they are important tools for various actors, most notably social movements, to attract attention, to appeal or to threaten, to make claims heard and visible, and eventually to have an impact on politics and society. Protest can be studied by focusing on individual cases, broader campaigns or conflicts, or the universe of all contentious actions in a given society.

In the past few decades, protest event analysis (PEA) has been developed to systematically map, analyze, and interpret the occurrence and properties of large numbers of protests by means of content analysis, using sources such as newspaper reports and police records. These protest data, in turn, can be linked to other kinds of data in order to study the causes and consequences of protest. In contrast to much earlier work in the areas of contentious politics, social movements, riots, revolutions, and the like, PEA provides a more solid empirical ground for observing protest activities in large geographical areas over considerable spans of time. It is a method that allows for the quantification of many properties of protest, such as frequency, timing and duration, location, claims, size, forms, carriers, and targets, as well as immediate consequences and reactions (e.g., police intervention, damage, counterprotests).

Whereas earlier studies of protest as an aggregate of many individual events tended to rely on impressions and speculative generalizations, PEA, if properly conducted, can provide valid and reliable information that can be subjected to a wide range of statistical procedures. To give just a few examples, PEA allows one to identify in which geographical and thematic areas protest concentrates, to study whether the composition of the government has an influence on the volume of protest, and to determine whether protest radicalizes in phases of declining mass mobilization.

It is important to note, however, that PEA does not mirror in a representative way the universe of all protests that actually take place. For example, very small and very moderate protests tend to be strongly underreported by the mass media, whereas virtually all very large and very violent protests are covered. Yet, as we will argue, such biases are not necessarily detrimental to understanding protest as a social phenomenon, and may even to some extent be considered advantageous.

PEA, understood in this way, began with a few scattered studies in the 1960s and 1970s and has since gained significance and recognition. Social scientists worldwide, although mostly in the United States and Western Europe, have studied protest generally or more particular forms or domains of protest in one or several countries. More recently, cooperation among some of these scholars has intensified and has resulted in conferences[1] and joint publications devoted to PEA (Rucht, Koopmans, and Neidhardt 1999; Koopmans and Rucht 1999). Moreover, ambitious cross-national comparative studies by joint research teams are under way. In addition to its mere quantitative spread, PEA has also become more refined and sophisticated, as we will see in the following brief overview.

Approaches to Protest Event Analysis

The early practitioners and pathbreakers of PEA were political scientists in search of various social and political indicators (Russett et al. 1964; Taylor and Hudson 1972), students of riots (Gurr 1968; Spilerman 1970; Danzger 1975), and historical sociologists interested in explaining long-term trends of strikes or political violence (Snyder and Tilly 1972; Tilly, Tilly, and Tilly 1975). From a methodological viewpoint, these data collections were not yet very sophisticated. The basic idea was to cover many countries (as in the case of the *Handbook for Social and Political Indicators,* by Russett [1964]), long time periods (as in the case of *The Rebellious Century,* by Tilly, Tilly, and Tilly [1975]; and in Snyder and Tilly 1972), or a particular wave of extraordinary events (as in the case of riot studies). It appears that relatively little attention was paid to the selectivity of the sources, the creation of fine-grained coding categories, and the development of well-documented rules and procedures. At the same time, however, based on more focused studies, a number of researchers had begun to engage in a methodological discussion, particularly where newspapers were used as a source to identify and code protest events (Lieberson and Silverman 1965; Danzger 1975; Snyder and Kelly 1977).

A second generation of research is marked by the studies of Kriesi and colleagues (1981) on "political activation events" in Switzerland from 1945 to 1978, Jenkins and Perrow (1977) and Jenkins (1985) on farmers' protest in the United States, McAdam (1982) on civil rights protest in the United States, and Tarrow (1989) on the protest cycle in Italy from 1965 to 1975. In methodological terms, these studies built on the earlier work mentioned above. However, they made more extensive use of protest data by breaking them down according to various analytical criteria, which was only possible, of course, because of a greater variety and differentiation of the underlying categories for data collection. Other work along similar lines followed and gradually evolved into a small research industry. It paralleled, and was partly inspired by, the growing area of social movement studies, which, on the whole, moved toward more detailed, more sophisticated, and in part more quantitatively oriented empirical research.

PEA now has spread to, or been applied to, diverse countries such as South Africa (Olzak and Olivier 1999), Japan (White 1995), Ireland (White 1999), Denmark (Mikkelsen 1999), Greece (Kousis 1999), early nineteenth-century England (Tilly 1995), the former USSR (Beissinger 1999), Poland (Ekiert and Kubik 1999), and Hungary (Szabó 1996). Given the potential explanatory and interpretative power of cross-national comparison, it was quite logical to also engage in cross-national PEA based on a common research design and research instrument. Probably the most influential example of this approach is the study by Kriesi and colleagues (1992, 1995), which focuses on new social movements in France, Germany, the Netherlands, and Switzerland from 1975 to 1989 (see also Koopmans 1995; Duyvendak 1995; Duyvendak et al. 1992; Giugni 1993). The second and more recent cross-national PEA study covers Hungary, East Germany, Poland, and Slovakia in the period from 1989 to 1993 (Ekiert and Kubik 1998; Lemke 1997). All these studies relied on newspapers as their main or even exclusive source of information, but the authors did not spend much effort qualifying the properties and biases of their sources.

Finally, a number of projects, most of them still unfinished, in one way or another considerably refined, systematized, and/or expanded PEA. One stream was to more systematically study the selectivity biases of the sources by (1) using different sources of the same kind, for example, more than one national newspaper in a given country (Fillieule 1996), (2) comparing national and regional/local newspapers (Hocke 1999), (3) comparing different media sources, for example, newspapers and television news (McCarthy, McPhail, and Smith 1996; McCarthy et al. 1999), (4) comparing newspapers from different countries in their coverage of the same events (Mueller 1997), and (5) comparing media data with extramedia data such as police records (McCarthy, McPhail, and Smith 1996; McCarthy et al. 1999; Fillieule 1996, 1999; Hug and Wisler 1998; Barranco and Wisler 1999; Hocke 1999, 2000; Oliver and Myers 1999).

The Prodat project (the name stands for protest data), which will be presented in more detail below, combined aspects (1), (2) and (5). It covers all protests in Germany over a long period, from 1950 to (currently) 1995. Unlike Prodat, the TEA project ("Transformation of Environmental Activism"), a study comparing seven EU countries in the period from 1988 through 1997, draws on only one newspaper per country (Rootes 1999). However, it also puts much emphasis on studying selectivity biases, for example, by covering in some countries local sections of the same newspaper and by interviewing in all countries journalists about practices and structures that may influence the selectivity of newspaper reports. The Merci (Mobilisation on Ethnic Relations, Citizenship and Immigration) project, which, too, will be presented in more detail below, also included several checks for selectivity biases. This project's methodological innovation is to broaden the unit of analysis by including not only all actors but also all forms of claims-making that appear in media coverage in this particular issue field.

Finally, a number of researchers have used the advanced possibilities of electronic search procedures to identify protests, such as those offered by Reuters Textline service, which is available online within *Lexis Nexis* from 1980 onward (Bond et al. 1997; Imig and Tarrow 1999, 2001; Reising 1999). The promise of this approach is to identify with a reasonable degree of accuracy classes of events in a huge body of English-language text, thereby allowing for immediate cross-national analysis without working with different coding teams in different countries speaking different languages. The advantages and disadvantages of this method relative to conventional hardcopy coding still need to be investigated. Because it uses the machine-assisted coding based on the Kansas Event Data System (Schrodt 1996), the search so far refers only to the headlines and the first sentence of Reuters online news reports.

Devices, Problems, and Solutions

Researchers engaging in PEA face a number of crucial decisions. Some of these, though appearing merely technical, can have a considerable impact on the needed resources and the quality of the data (validity and reliability). Therefore, these decisions should be made with much caution and based on pilot work. It is also important to acquire a body of practical knowledge and skills that for the most part are not to be found in method books. Only a few hints can be provided here.

Unit of Analysis

Probably the most consequential aspect of PEA is the choice of the unit of analysis. According to their interests and theoretical background, researchers have used different concepts and different labels, such as "political activation event," "contentious gathering," "protest event," and, most inclusively, "political claims-making." Narrow concepts are easier to identify and provide lower numbers of cases, whereas broad concepts allow one to address a wider range of questions but may require substantially more coding work. Much depends here on the kind of research questions one wants to tackle, and it is therefore difficult to provide general guidelines. For example, if one is interested in interactions between police and movements, or the radicalization of movement repertoires, there is little need to extend the range of events to be included beyond the classical range of "unconventional" mobilization forms such as demonstrations, civil disobedience, and violence. However, if one wants to investigate institutionalization processes, it may be advisable to extend the range of events to include more "conventional" forms such as press statements, petitions, participation in hearings, and litigation. Otherwise, one may be unable to see important parts of institutionalization processes simply because more institutionalized forms of action are excluded from the sample. For such purposes, one may also consider coding such events not just when they are sponsored by social movement organizations, but also when they are organized by institutional actors. After all, one form in which institutionalization of social movements may take place is when their aims are taken up or their representatives co-opted by institutional actors and thus carried into the political system. Similarly, if the framing of protest is to be studied, the unit of analysis should be defined broadly to include discursive forms of protest, most importantly press conferences and public statements. These forms usually provide more information on the argumentative structure behind movement demands than the coverage of street protests, which usually focuses on aspects such as action forms, violence, police intervention, or numbers of participants.

Needless to say, such extensions of the range of events come at a considerable cost, and one should consider carefully whether one really needs them to answer one's research questions. However, when setting up a project, one should also be aware that it is difficult to extend the range of events during the coding process (e.g., because a new research question may emerge that one had not thought of before the investigation), since extensions would require going through again all the source material that has been already coded. Whatever the unit chosen, it must be defined in operational terms by specifying its characteristics and drawing boundaries to similar but analytically separate phenomena. Such a delineation can best be done by relying not just on a brief definition but on a detailed explanation of its components and a discussion of various borderline cases. Important dimensions of a definition of the unit of analysis may include the nature of the actor (individual vs. collective, private vs. state), the nature of the action or claims (degree of specificity, conventionality, disruptiveness, action and/or rhetoric), and the context of the action (public space, specific arenas).

Once a range of types of events to be included in the analysis has been chosen, the delimitation of events in time and space has to be decided. This involves more than just determining the period and geographical area of the study. Apart from isolated events that are clearly delimited in time and space, there are more complicated cases of series of connected events dispersed in time and place, large numbers of which are sometimes covered in a few lines in newspaper coverage. For example, in the Prodat study discussed below, an article in the 1980s on a Sunday rally by opponents of the construction of a new runway for Frankfurt Airport mentioned that similar rallies had taken place every Sunday for four years. In the Dutch case study of the Kriesi et al. (1995) project, an article on an "Action Week" of the Dutch peace movement in 1984 described a few events in detail and then mentioned that similar events had taken place during that week in four thousand (!) other localities. Obviously, the decision to count each of these events separately, to summarize them into one aggregate event, or even to disregard them altogether because of too much missing information may have an enormous impact on event counts.[2] General rules on how to deal with these problems are again difficult to specify. At any rate, it is advisable to take care that such special cases are easily identifiable within the data set, thus allowing one to exclude or include them in data analysis.

In view of purported tendencies of globalization and "de-territorialization" of politics, even formerly simple questions of territorial delimitation must be problematized. If Kurdish immigrants living in Germany demonstrate before the European Parliament in French Strasbourg to protest against the persecution of their ethnic group by the Turkish government, should this event be part of a German case study on immigrant mobilization? Or, alternatively, should it be included in a study of French immigrant mobilization? If the

American Jewish Committee writes an open letter to the German Chancellor Kohl to protest racist attacks in Germany, is this to be included in a study of antiracist claims-making in Germany, in a U.S. case study, or in both? Although, as Koopmans and Statham (1999a) have demonstrated, such transnational claims-making is as yet not a massive phenomenon, it is too important to be ignored. Researchers should therefore carefully consider whether they should stick to the standard procedure of delimiting the unit of analysis on the basis of where the event takes place, or whether they also want to take into account the territorial "location" of the authorities and policies that are addressed by the event.

Finally, we must briefly mention that other basic units of analysis are possible as an alternative, or as an addition to the event. Franzosi (1999), for instance, emphasizes the need to code individual instances of interaction between actors instead of events. This implies unpacking a protest event by separately coding movement-police, movement-countermovement, and movement-bystander interactions that may otherwise be summarized into one event. Going one step further, McPhail and Schweingruber (1999) unpack events in even more detail, coding each change of behavior by one of the protagonists in the event as a new sequence. Moving in the opposite direction, Kousis (1999) codes campaigns (or "protest cases," as she calls them somewhat vaguely) that may consist of hundreds of events with a specific thematic focus (e.g., all protests against a particular nuclear power station) instead of events, and compares their characteristics with those of other campaigns. Again, to an important extent the choice among these alternatives depends on the research questions. To some extent, however, the different options may also be combined, for example, by keeping protest events as the unit of analysis but having the coders assign them to campaigns, thus allowing aggregation of the data to compare campaign characteristics, as has been done in the case of Prodat.

Specific Variables

Regarding the unit of analysis, one has to specify the variables to be coded, as well as their categories, providing rules of operationalization along similar lines as for the basic unit of analysis. When it comes to the choice of variables to be coded, it is important not just to create a shopping list of items of interest. First, mass media and the police often do not record the kind of information that would be of interest to the researcher. Second, information on some variables, particular regarding "hard" news (e.g., place, time, form of action), is more reliable than information on "soft" aspects (e.g., the social composition of the participants or the dynamics of the event as it evolves over time). For an important variable, namely the number of participants, information is missing in about 40 to 60 percent of the cases in different PEA projects (Olzak 1992; Rucht and Neidhardt 1999). Nonetheless, this variable should not be dropped, since for most large protests—say those with more than one thousand participants—information is usually provided in media reports. These events are precisely the ones that account for a very large proportion of overall participant numbers.[3] When different numbers of participants are provided by different sources (organizers, police, journalists), one solution is to code the sources of information and/or to use the mean number as a proxy.

Sources

As we have seen, PEA can rely on different kinds of sources, each having their own strengths and weaknesses. Most frequently used are newspapers, which, in most cases, are easily accessible and provide better and more detailed coverage than radio and television news (Rucht and Ohlemacher 1992; Olzak 1989). News agency reports are generally more inclusive but draw a different picture than what is seen by the average citizen as a consumer of mass media. Moreover, news agency reports are difficult to obtain for more distant periods. As we will discuss below, police records tend to be more inclusive than national and local newspapers but, as a rule, are difficult to access and may differ in their selection criteria and quality from country to country and from one locality to another. Some countries have a permitting system for protests that can be used as an additional source of information (e.g., for the identification of the organizers), but this information is collected prior to the protest and is therefore of limited value for studying the actual event (McCarthy, McPhail, and Smith 1996; McCarthy et al. 1999).

Generally, of course, the use of multiple sources (media and nonmedia, several newspapers instead of just one) is preferable. However, cost and time considerations should again be taken into account. For example, taking two newspapers generally more than doubles the time required for coding, because in addition to coding additional events, information on the same events in both sources has to be identified, matched, and combined. Quantitatively, the amount of extra events gained by adding a second source is significantly less than the increase in coding time. In the Prodat project, for instance, the two sources combined contain only about one-quarter to one-third more events than each single source. Of course, controlling for qualitative source biases is generally a more important reason for taking multiple sources than just increasing the number of events. This issue will be discussed in the next section when we present some reliability and validity tests drawn from the Prodat and Merci projects.

Sampling

Depending on the amount of resources, the accessibility and nature of the sources, and the (expected) numbers of cases and variables, a sampling procedure may be required. Sampling can drastically reduce the workload without great losses of information as long as the total number of recorded events is large enough to allow meaningful analysis, and the sample is representative for the population of recorded events.[4] To be sure, individual events of great significance or the continuity of certain chains of events may be missed when a sampling procedure is applied.[5] When sampling newspaper issues of particular days, Monday issues of newspapers that do not appear on Sundays have the advantage that they report on two event days. Relying only on Mondays, however, creates the risk of under- or over-reporting certain types of events. For instance, workers and students tend to protest less on weekends than many other groups. Protests that break daily routines (e.g., traffic blockades) also tend to occur on weekdays rather than weekends. Therefore, for most purposes the sample should be based not only on Monday issues but also on a systematic sample of other issues (see the examples in the section "Illustrations of the Use of Protest Event Analysis").

Coding Process

Coding proceeds in several steps. First, candidate articles that may contain events to be coded are identified, copied, and read more closely and in conjunction with other reports on the same event or campaign. In a second step, the events thus identified and delimited are coded according to a standardized scheme, and finally archived. It is best to enter data directly into a simple matrix or a more sophisticated computerized grid that, for example, provides menus and submenus for particular variables and values, and assigns codes automatically when a particular category is clicked. All relevant coding rules should be documented in a codebook. Arbitrary cases must be discussed among the coders and may lead to additional rules or the specification of existing rules. It is important, however, to elaborate the rules as far as possible in a training and test period prior to the actual coding because any substantial changes afterward may result in the recoding of hundreds or thousands of events for which data have been already entered. Intra- and interreliability tests of all coders should be carried out to identify, document, and improve data reliability, both for the primary selection (to which degree are candidate articles retrieved and events contained in them identified?), and for the secondary selection of categories within key variables (e.g., action form or claim content). Reliability tests should be conducted not only at the beginning but also at regular intervals during the process of data entry. In such a test, all coders should scan the same set of, say, ten newspaper issues, identify protest events, and code them. The comparison of the results allows one to identify flaws, errors, and misinterpretations of existing coding rules.

Problems of Comparability in Cross-National Studies

Standardization of all rules and practices relating to the coding process is particularly important in cross-national comparison. When coding is done by various teams of different nationality and language, there must be a master template from which all translations are derived. Particular attention should be paid to linguistic and legal differences that may affect coding decisions. Problems with different political and judicial systems may arise, for instance, if forms of action are legal in one country but illegal in another. For example, in Germany demonstrations in front of governmental and parliamentary buildings are generally prohibited (the so-called *Bannmeile*) as is the covering of the face by protesters to prevent identification by police cameras. These actions that are illegal in Germany are legal in other contexts. It is therefore preferable to keep the illegal/legal distinction separate from the action form variable to avoid confounding the two dimensions in cross-national comparison. Linguistic differences and nuances may similarly affect coding. For instance, in German and English there exists a clear distinction between a *Kundgebung* or rally (a protest gathering at one particular place), on the one hand, and a *Demonstration* or march, on the other. In Dutch and French, by contrast, both forms tend to be denoted by the same words, for example, *manifestation, demonstratie,* or *betoging*. Linguistic differences that may affect coding can best be identified and dealt with if there is at least one bilingual coder on each team. These coders should code sample material from the respective other team, and the results should be compared.

Covariates

It is advisable not only to code protest events but to also collect data on relevant covariates (potential causes or outcomes that can be linked to protest data) from the very beginning. Otherwise, the uses of PEA will remain largely descriptive. In some cases, covariates are easily available, for example, public opinion data. Relying on such secondary sources, however, has a number of disadvantages. First, while such data tend to be readily accessible for some variables (especially socioeconomic ones such as unemployment, mobility, or income levels), suitable data are difficult to obtain for many variables that play a key role in current theorizing on social movements (e.g., political opportunities, alliance and conflict structures, discursive framing). Further, secondary covariates are usually measured on higher spatial and temporal levels of aggregation than the protest event data, or they are discontinuous. Third, such problems are magnified when one attempts to include secondary covariates in cross-national comparative contexts, because different national institutions often employ highly divergent definitions and methods for collecting data. While such problems already hamper comparisons regarding seemingly "objective" variables such as unemployment levels, they especially affect central theoretical variables of interest such as agenda setting or elite support.

Primary gathering of covariate data is therefore often preferable, although their collection can sometimes be as time-consuming and difficult as the coding of protest events. Two strategies are available here. First, one may code primary data from other sources, for example, Senate roll calls or data on organizational populations (e.g., Soule et al. 1999). If one is interested in a large number of contextual variables and actors, however, this strategy may quickly exceed the resource capabilities of even the most ambitious research program, since the coding of each single source can be practically a project in its own. A second strategy, then, may be more economical—though it still involves a considerable amount of work—namely, to use the same media sources that are used for gathering protest events to gather information on contextual variables, for example, elite debates and conflicts, legislative activity, or court rulings (e.g., Koopmans and Statham 1999b). Of course, there are limits to this method, too, since not all relevant covariates can be reliably drawn from newspaper coverage.

Resources and Infrastructure

Unlike carrying out a handful of interviews or a small group experiment, quantitative PEA tends to be time-consuming and costly. The coding of large numbers of events can hardly be accomplished by one person in a few months. Taking into account all the additional work such as training, archiving, discussing problematic cases, correcting errors, and so on, the identifying and coding of one event may easily take thirty to forty minutes on average. This implies that more ambitious protest event studies that are not limited to a clearly circumscribed issue field and a relatively small temporal and spatial scope require not only substantial financial resources but also a solid research infrastructure. Ideally such projects should be situated in a research setting that can provide for continuity and where funding is not exclusively dependent on short-term contracts. Beyond material resources, these projects need committed and tenacious principal investigators who can survive nervous breakdowns, fluctuation of personnel, the succession of different generations of computer software, and so on. This does not mean that PEA is only possible with plenty of money and time. Data collection on a particular issue domain covering a decade can be managed by a small team in two years, as the TEA project has demonstrated with its focus on environmental issues, resulting in up to fourteen hundred events per country.

Illustrations of the Use of Protest Event Analysis

In the following, we will describe two ambitious projects in order to highlight some of the practices, strengths, developments, and limitations of PEA. The projects, Prodat and Merci, have been initiated at the Social Science Research Center Berlin (WZB) under the auspices of Rucht and Koopmans, respectively. To some extent, we will be also able to compare results from both projects to investigate the degree to which they differ in their descriptive findings.

The Prodat Project

Prodat, though standing on the shoulders of the work of Tarrow and Kriesi, goes beyond earlier studies in several respects. First, it is inclusive in that it covers all forms of protest by all nongovernmental collective actors on every conceivable issue in West Germany since 1950, and in East Germany since 1989. However, the underlying definition of protest does not include purely verbal claims, nor does it include individuals as actors.[6]

Second, Prodat relies on two national "quality" newspapers, the *Süddeutsche Zeitung* and the *Frankfurter Rundschau,* which, according to pretests, were best suited among the four available national quality papers that have been in existence since 1950. Each of these two newspapers contributes about 25 percent of exclusively reported events to the full sample (i.e., 50 percent of events in the full sample were reported by both papers). Even in those cases where both papers reported on a particular event, they often include information on specific aspects of the event that are not mentioned by the other paper. The use of two papers also allows one to identify discrepancies or errors in factual information. Because of the reliance on two newspapers and the resulting considerable increase in the time required for reading and coding, our resource restrictions made sampling necessary. The sample chosen includes all Monday issues, as well as all remaining issues of each fourth week.[7]

Third, the project includes a sizable number of events (currently about 13,500), a large number of variables,[8] and detailed categorizations of these variables. For a few variables, multiple values can be coded, taking into account the combination of various claims or forms of action in the same event. Obviously, valid information on all variables is not always available (see Rucht and Neidhardt 1999: 82), and in a few instances variables had to be dropped because of too much missing information. On the whole, however, the collection of detailed information allows for studying rather specific aspects, particularly since the overall number of protests is high, and thus disaggregation to low levels of analysis is possible.

Fourth, a considerable investment was made to study the selectivity of national newspapers. One approach was to collect information for one issue area, namely antinuclear protests, from a wide range of sources other than newspapers. Another and more important step was to conduct a study to control for the main sources' selectivity by using police records and a local newspaper in one particular geographical area (see below).

Fifth, when considering the range and level of detail of the collected information, it should be stressed that Prodat was never conceived to answer one single overriding question. On the contrary, it was designed to serve diverse and partly unpredictable needs of the scientific community. Besides offering the possibility to study protest in itself by analyzing, for example, correlations between various properties of protest, the protest data can be also used as a dependent or independent variable, that is, in analyses of protest as the result of a range of causal factors (e.g., deprivation, repression, increase of resources) or as a cause for social and political changes (e.g., reform bills, attitudinal shifts among the population). Obviously, this requires access to other sets of data. Only more recently, an effort was made to collect such data to be linked to protest events. So far, this search has been mainly restricted to the issue areas of women, peace, and environment.

First analyses of the protest data have highlighted the great variety of questions that they can help to address. For example, the data allow one to answer the question of whether left governments are confronted with more or less protest than right and mixed governments (Koopmans and Rucht 1995), whether protest radicalizes when mass mobilization declines (Rucht 1996), whether the type of carriers of protest changes over time (Rucht 1999), and whether there is an increase in EU-related protests as a response to ever closer European integration (Rucht forthcoming). Some of the descriptive findings have surprised even close observers of protest in Germany, who, as it appears now, cherished some striking misperceptions. For example, contrary to common assumptions, there was no decline in the aggregate of protest since the early 1980s, nor was there a decline in environmental protest in particular. Also, protest in Germany has not become more moderate over time (Neidhardt and Rucht 1999). Probably less a surprise, but still a remarkable finding, is that xenophobic protest is less widespread in West Germany when compared to East Germany (relative to the size of the population) in spite of the fact that the percentage of immigrants is about five times higher in the West than in the East.

Overall, Prodat is a data source that allows for both broad and detailed analyses of a wide range of questions, answers to which, at least in the German case, had previously been based only on more or less informed speculation. The adoption of major parts of the project design and all essential elements of the coding scheme by a U.S. team (Doug McAdam, John McCarthy, Susan Olzak, and Sarah Soule), who study protest in their home country, will enhance possibilities for analyses and hopefully contribute to a better understanding of the patterns and dynamics of protest.

Beyond Protest Events: Political Claims Analysis in the Merci Project

One way of meeting the challenge of linking protest events more systematically to contextual data has been developed in the context of the project Mobilisation on Ethnic Relations, Citizenship and Immigration (Merci), a five-country comparative study of political contention over issues of migration and ethnicity.[9] Koopmans and Statham (1999b) criticize traditional protest event analysis on two grounds. First, protest event studies tend to limit attention to certain types ("extra-institutional," "disruptive," "unconventional," or "non-routine") of political contention carried by certain types ("noninstitutional," "nongovernmental," "challenger," or "non-elite") of actors. Despite considerable variation among protest event studies in the ranges of action forms and actors included, and thus regarding the inclusiveness of the protest definition used, each of them reflects the dichotomy between "members" and "challengers" of the political system (Gamson 1968; Tilly 1978) that has become typical for political process approaches to social movements. Koopmans and Statham argue that this polarized distinction between included, settled elites and excluded groups rattling at the gates of the polity is no longer a valid image of modern democratic polities, which are characterized by cross-cutting alliances between polity members and challengers, and a mutual interpenetration of institutional and noninstitutional politics.

The Merci project therefore extends the primary coding from newspapers to include not only protest—in whichever way defined—but *all forms* of contentious claims-making by *all types of actors* relating to the issues of interest, that is, immigration and ethnic relations. Thus, the data include such diverse forms of claims-making as legislative decisions to limit asylum rights, violent attacks against asylum seekers, public statements by Muslim groups to extend multicultural rights, as well as government-sponsored public demonstrations against racism. Each instance of contentious claims-making is considered as an event, and thus all of these different types of claims-making by different actors are available on the same temporal and spatial levels of analysis and can be systematically related to each other. This allows researchers to investigate directly such questions as the impact of ethnic violence on elite action on the immigration issue (and vice versa; see Koopmans 1996, 1998), conflict and alliance structures within the migration field (Koopmans and Statham 1999a, 2000), and the framing of antiracism by different collective actors (Koopmans 2001). For the comparative purposes of the project, it is particularly important that the reliance on primary coding implies that variables have been coded in cross-nationally comparable ways on the basis of inclusion rules and classification schemes developed by the researchers themselves.

The point made above about the problematic nature of limiting the data gathering to unconventional protest forms and/or noninstitutional actors can be illustrated with the Merci data (for further details, see Koopmans and Statham 1999b: 208–10). Of all the claims against racism and the extreme right in the Merci sample, only 35 percent were made by noninstitutional actors; the remaining two-thirds stemmed from political parties, churches, labor unions, government representatives, and other institutional actors. Moreover, only 27 percent of these claims involved the use of typically "unconventional" protest forms such as demonstrations, rallies, or violence. Even of those claims made by explicit antiracist or pro-minority organizations, less than half were typical protest events: 55 percent consisted of press statements and other discursive forms.

The point here is, of course, not the fact as such that limiting protest event data to some combination of unconventional forms and noninstitutional actors results in a quantitatively less inclusive database. More important, this approach offers truncated views of the action repertoire of noninstitutional groups, as well as of the penetration of social change claims into institutional politics. Such truncations are unfortunate since they preclude many kinds of theoretically interesting analysis, not only considering the interaction among institutional and noninstitutional actors but also relating to shifts in repertoires and particularly the question of institutionalization of protest. In addition, truncated protest data may lead to serious misinterpretations concerning levels of social movement activity, particularly in temporal or spatial comparisons. For instance, on the basis of unconventional protest events only, the Merci data would lead us to conclude that German antiracist groups display a much higher level of mobilization than their British counterparts. However, when we include conventional forms of claimsmaking, we find a larger number of claims in Britain, suggesting a higher level of institutionalization of the British movement but certainly not a lower level of overall activity.

Testing the Selectivity and Robustness of Data

It can hardly be overemphasized that protest event data derived from mass media reports should not be equated with the universe of protests that occur daily in many places. Most of these events are not considered to be newsworthy by the national press. They are therefore covered by local media only or remain completely unreported, thus existing just for the participants and the immediate bystanders. If we blindly followed the media reports, we might be totally misguided when making inferences to the universe of all protests for a given place and time. Media do not mirror this universe in any representative way. They select according to their own criteria and follow issue attention cycles which, however, can be empirically investigated. Assessing, or even quantitatively testing, the selectivity of the sources from which information is drawn is crucial to all kinds of PEA. Other and probably equally important problems are those of the validity and reliability of the search and coding procedures. In this section, we will address these issues, using the Prodat and Merci projects as reference points.

What Media Present and What They Ignore: Lessons from Prodat

From the outset, Prodat included the idea of undertaking selectivity studies from various perspectives. Not all these ideas have materialized,[10] and not all possible selectivity tests will be presented here. However, some results of the most interesting and most detailed selectivity study in the Prodat context will be reported.

Hocke (1999, 2000)[11] has conducted a detailed study to investigate media selectivity, focusing on protests in the city of Freiburg in southwestern Germany in the period from 1983 to 1989. The location was chosen for a combination of reasons: (1) Freiburg is characterized by a relative high level of protest, (2) it has a good local newspaper holding a monopoly, and (3) it has a local police department that not only was willing to provide access to its files but also has excellent and detailed records of certain categories of protests.

Hocke produced two sets of data on selected types of events:[12] one data set was drawn from the police archive, and the other from the local news-paper, which he then matched with the Freiburg protests reported by the two nationwide newspapers included in Prodat's core data set. The study was theoretically guided by the concept of news values, an aspect we have to largely neglect here. Hocke differentiated between two kinds of selectivity. Primary selection refers to whether or not a protest was reported by local and/or national media. Secondary selection refers to the extent and the way in which certain aspects or properties of the reported protest were presented (or omitted).

The police data, though in themselves not without minor biases, proved to be an extremely inclusive and reliable source, particularly for "hard" news such as place, time, form of action, and the number of participants. These data from police files represent the first and most inclusive layer with a total of 196 events for the event days chosen according to the Prodat sample and the categories of protest for which the police data proved to be reliable. The local newspaper reported only a proportion (37.8 percent) of the events reg-istered by the police. (The other way round, only few protests reported in the local newspaper were not covered by the police). Finally, the Prodat data drawn from national newspapers included only nine protests, which were re-ported by both the local newspaper and the police. Measured against the po-lice data as the most inclusive source, Prodat represents only a small fraction (4.6 percent) of all events in Freiburg. This low percentage is in line with what McCarthy et al. (1996) found for protests in Washington, D.C., and Fillieule (1999) for France. Given this extreme selection, one might con-clude that protest event data drawn from national newspapers are a useless source. However, these data represent what is considered as newsworthy by the media and therefore reaches a broad audience. Moreover, even the very limited sample of events recorded by the national press includes virtually all large protests and all violent events. Finally, one should keep in mind that for many analytic purposes, it is not so much the actual level of protest but its composition and trends over time that are of interest.

Another important finding of Hocke is that the different sources follow a hierarchy of news values, with the lowest average value for the protests cov-ered by the police, a medium value for protests in the local newspaper, and the highest value for protests in the national newspapers.[13] Among the news values of which the impact on primary selection was tested by logistic regres-sion analysis, the most important single factor accounting for the probabili-ty of local press coverage was the size (number of participants), followed by duration and the innovative character of the event. For the national news-papers, the participation of an established actor in the protest was the best predictor of coverage, followed by the innovative character of the event, whereas size did not play a significant role. Moreover, Hocke found that the combination of certain news values dramatically increased the likelihood that an event would be reported.[14]

A number of conclusions of more general significance can be drawn from this study. First, local newspapers are much more inclusive than national papers but still very selective when compared to the universe of protest for which the police data in this particular community provided a proxy. Second, the higher the news value, the greater the likelihood that an event would be reported in the local and eventually the national press. Third, a combination of certain news values was the strongest predictor of media coverage, though these combinations were not completely identical in the case of local and national newspapers.

The Robustness of Event Data: A Comparison of Newspaper and Police Data on Extreme Right Violence in Germany

Given the high degree of selectiveness of media coverage of protest events, it is warranted to ask how valid newspapers are when compared to more encompassing sources such as police statistics, and if the results of newspaper-based studies do not depend strongly on which newspapers, samples, and event definitions one chooses. An opportunity to test the robustness of protest event data in view of these questions is offered by the overlap between the Prodat and Merci data for the years 1990–94 regarding xenophobic mobilization. In addition, for this period, official statistics on xenophobic and extreme right violence gathered by the German Office for the Protection of the Constitution (*Bundesamt für Verfassungsschutz,* BfV) are available, thus allowing for a comparison with police sources.

There are important differences between Prodat and Merci regarding coding rules and sampling methods, for example, regarding the newspapers used, the sample of issues that was coded, rules for inclusion and separation of events, as well as entirely different codebooks with sometimes strongly diverging category systems for core variables. Finally, of course, the coding in the two projects was done by different coders. This implies that any differences we find between the data sets of the two projects must be interpreted as a result of the sum of intercoder and "interproject" unreliabilities. Given these important differences in sampling and coding rules, comparing the two projects' coding of the same event population allows for a powerful test of the robustness of protest event studies. Adding the BfV data allows us in addition to investigate the selectivity and validity of newspaper sources compared to police data.

First, we compare the three sources regarding the targets of violence. Here, we can distinguish three types of aims: anti-Semitic targets (e.g., destruction of Jewish graveyards), other xenophobic targets (e.g., physical attacks on foreigners or asylum-seeker centers), and other extreme right targets and aims (e.g., violence against left-wing groups, against the police, or related to a glorification of the Nazi regime). Figure 9.1 shows that the distribution of acts of violence across these three categories was highly similar in the three sources. This result is surprising, since one might have expected that in the German context violence with explicit neo-Nazi aims, and particularly with anti-Semitic aims, would draw disproportional newspaper attention. The way in which newspapers are coded in protest event studies turns out, however, to be quite insensitive to such media sensibilities. Anti-Semitic and neo-Nazi violence did in fact draw disproportionate media attention, affecting the ways in which the media covered such violence, for example, by treating such violence more prominently (e.g., on the front page) and by elaborating the article beyond a mere description of the event to include moral condemnations by politicians, journalists, and editors. However, since protest event analysis completely ignores placement, size, and other aspects of the journalistic treatment of events, the only thing that matters is the rate at which different types of events are mentioned at all, and in this there were, as Figure 9.1 shows, no substantial differences among the different types of extreme right violence.

For one of the potentially most promising applications of protest event data, time series analysis, the degree of bias affecting the distribution of events across temporal units is of particular importance. Figure 9.2 shows

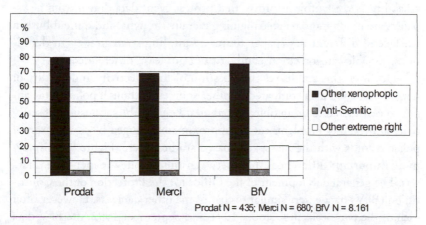

Figure 9.1. Targets of xenophobic and extreme right violence, 1990–94.

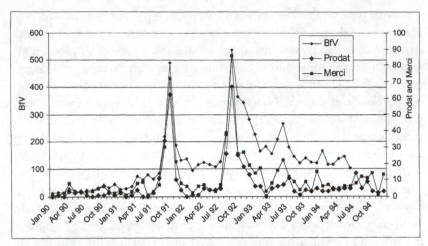

Figure 9.2. Xenophobic and extreme right violence in three data sets.

the development of the monthly number of violent xenophobic and extreme right events in the three data sets from January 1990 to December 1994. To be sure, there are some divergences in the periods of lower extreme right activity, in which error and noise components are likely to exert a relatively stronger influence on the data than in periods with strong trends in the level of protest activity. However, the general temporal trends in the two newspaper-based data sets are remarkably similar. So similar in fact that the correlation coefficient between the two data sets is as high as .96 ($p < .001$). If we consider that reliability coefficients of .90 (or even .80) are generally judged to be satisfactory regarding intercoder reliability *within* projects, this figure for reliability *between* projects proves that protest event data drawn from newspapers are much more reliable than is generally thought, and quite robust in the face of different newspaper sources, sampling strategies, event definitions, variable categorizations, and, last but not least, different coders.[15]

However, this still leaves the question of the selectivity and validity of newspaper-based data compared to other sources. Although police data cannot be considered to be an objective standard either, the seriousness of selectivity and validity problems can be approximately gauged by comparison of police records with the newspaper-based studies. Here, Figure 9.2 displays more important differences than between the two newspaper-based data sets. The general development of the Office for the Protection of the Constitution (BfV) data is very similar to that of the other data sets. However, after each of the two peaks in October 1991 and September 1992, the BfV data stabilize on a relatively high level compared to the initial level of activity in

1990, while the drops in levels of violence after these peaks are much more pronounced in the newspaper data. This difference may be explained in two ways. First, we may argue that the difference is due to media attention cycles focused around the peaks in xenophobic and extreme right violence, after which newspapers quickly lost interest in the topic and returned to a low rate of coverage of such events. Alternatively, the rising long-term trend in the BfV data may be due to increased police attentiveness to xenophobic and extreme right violence, which, in view of widespread public criticism of the police's inattentiveness to the issue of xenophobia, is not an implausible hypothesis. We may safely assume that both processes have played a role and that both types of sources are affected by selectivity problems, albeit of a different nature.

The important question, however, is to what extent such problems might affect the usefulness of protest event data for the purpose of time series analysis. Correlating the BfV data with the other two data sets, we arrive at a coefficient of .84 for BfV-Prodat, and .88 for BfV-Merci. Although these correlations are not as high as the one between the two newspaper-based data sets, they are still within a range that would more than satisfy most researchers working with more conventional techniques, such as survey interviews or conventional forms of content analysis. All in all, then, this comparison of three very different sources of event data shows that while selectivity and bias issues need to be acknowledged and where possible addressed, protest event data, whether drawn from newspapers or from other sources, are much more reliable and valid than is sometimes thought.

Conclusion

PEA is still a relatively new tool that, compared to more established methods such as interviewing, has not yet become part of the standard methodological repertoire. In many respects it is a demanding but also a rewarding enterprise that we suggest to adopt, adapt, and refine. Though there is still ample room for creativity in further developing the method, there is neither a need to reinvent the wheel in each PEA project nor to make each project so unique that comparison across projects becomes virtually impossible.

The main advantages of PEA are obvious. It provides us with a detailed map of the occurrence and patterns of large numbers of protest events that can be analyzed in their own right but can also be used for more complex analyses linking protest to other events, structures, and developments. PEA provides a solid ground in an area that is still often marked by more or less informed speculation. Before any meaningful attempt can be undertaken to study and interpret both the causes and effects of protest, we first have to get a grasp of its occurrence and patterns. PEA is a tool to accomplish this on a broad scale and in a systematic way.

Nevertheless, we should not ignore the limits and problems of PEA. Apart from the practical problems that have to be surmounted and the resource investments required, it provides us with information on a limited number of aspects of protest and social movements. For example, it tells us little if anything about the underlying mobilization structure, the motivation of the protesters, or the reactions of the wider public. Moreover, it reflects what others have considered worthy of recording on files and storing in archives, or of reporting in the mass media, and therefore shares all the problems that come along with such sources. However, the most frequent objection against the method, namely, that it does not represent reality, is, in our view, based on a misperception. Indeed, PEA does not mirror what some call "reality." It is based on a constructed reality. This constructed reality, however, is of extreme importance for both policymakers and the wider public. We observe our social and political world mainly through the mass media. In a certain sense, protests and other events that remain unreported are simply "nonexistent." Though we do not argue that is it meaningless to study this hidden and therefore for most people "nonexistent" realm of protest, we do not believe that the most energy should be invested in such an enterprise at the cost of what really matters in shaping the perceptions of policymakers and the general public, and thereby may eventually influence the course of social change.

Notes

1. International conferences on PEA were held at the Social Science Center Berlin in summer 1995 and summer 1998.

2. For example, the number of other peace movement events in the Kriesi et al. sample was less than one hundred for the year 1984; that is, inclusion of the four thousand events would have increased the number of events for that year forty times. The solution chosen in this project was to code such cases as one (dispersed) event, with a special "multiple" code for the locality variable.

3. Similarly, "missing" values for numbers of wounded or arrested usually mean "none" or "very few." Newspapers do not usually bother with reporting non-events unless they are unexpected; that is, if nothing is said about numbers of wounded or arrested, this usually means that there were none. One way of dealing with missing information on numbers of participants for the purpose of concrete analyses is to replace the missing value by the median value in the sample for the action form in question (see Kriesi et al. 1995: appendix).

4. In some cases even nonrepresentative samples (e.g., those based on Monday

issues) may be sufficient, as long as the form and extent of the bias are known, and the bias is constant across units of analysis (years, countries, cities, etc.); see Koopmans 1999.

5. This risk is greater when one codes only specific event days (e.g., Saturdays and Sundays if one uses the Monday paper) than when one simply includes all events mentioned in the issue, irrespective of when they occurred. Important events such as mass demonstrations or terrorist attacks often still receive media attention some time after the event, for example, in reports about subsequent counterdemonstrations, political consequences, police investigations, and so on.

6. But note that with a minimum of three people the threshold for "collective" actors is set low, and in some well-defined cases even an individual actor may qualify as an instigator of collective protest. The search was restricted to nonstate actors, thus including besides genuine protest groups also political parties, churches, unions, and so forth, but excluding government-initiated collective events.

7. This sample corresponds to 37.5 percent of the newspaper issues and 46.4 percent of the "event days," considering that Monday issues essentially refer to Saturday and Sunday events.

8. The most relevant variables for each single event are place, time, duration, size, issue, claims, form, social and organizational carriers, geographical level of mobilization, immediate objects, direct or indirect targets, immediate consequences (e.g., injuries, material damage, arrests), and related events (e.g., other events that are part of the same campaign, or counterprotests).

9. The study has been initiated by the Social Science Research Center Berlin and includes case studies of Germany, the UK, France, the Netherlands, and Switzerland. The participants are Ruud Koopmans (WZB), Paul Statham (University of Leeds), Florence Passy (University of Geneva), Thom Duyvené de Wit (University of Amsterdam), and Marco Giugni (University of Geneva).

10. For example, one plan was to use a good archive of a particular protest group or a distinct social movement and to compare this group's or movement's own documentation of protests with corresponding information from Prodat.

11. Hocke served, among other roles, as a trainer and supervisor of the coders in the project.

12. These are rallies, demonstrations, blockades, and vigils.

13. However, both the local and the national newspaper also included protests with a very low news value.

14. For both the local and national newspapers, such a combination was size and disruptiveness, and participation of an established actor and specificity of the claim. For the national newspapers only, it was additionally the combination of temporal placement of the event and participation of an established actor.

15. For a similar comparison between data sets referring to the German anti-nuclear energy movement, with similar results, see Koopmans 1999.

References

Barranco, José, and Dominique Wisler. 1999. "Validity and Systematicity of Newspaper Data in Event Analysis." *European Sociological Review* 15 (3): 301–22.

Beissinger, Mark R. 1999. "Event Analysis in Transitional Societies: Protest Mobilization in the Former Soviet Union." In *Acts of Dissent: New Developments in the Study of Protest,* edited by Dieter Rucht, Ruud Koopmans, and Friedhelm Neidhardt, 284–316. Lanham, Md.: Rowman and Littlefield.

Bond, Doug, Craig J. Jenkins, Charles L. Taylor, and Kurt Schock. 1997. "Mapping Mass Political Conflict and Civil Society." *Journal of Conflict Resolution* 41 (4): 553–79.

Danzger, M. H. 1975. "Validating Conflict Data." *American Sociological Review* 40: 570–84.

Duyvendak, Jan Willem. 1995. *The Power of Politics: New Social Movements in France.* Boulder, Colo.: Westview.

Duyvendak, Jan Willem, Hein-Anton van der Heijden, Ruud Koopmans, and Luuk Wijmans. 1992. *Tussen verbeelding en macht. 25 jaar nieuwe sociale bewegingen in Nederland.* Amsterdam: SUA.

Ekiert, Grzegorz, and Jan Kubik. 1998. "Contentious Politics in the New Democracies: East Germany, Hungary, Poland, and Slovakia, 1998–93." *World Politics* 50 (4): 547–81.

———. 1999. "Protest Event Analysis in the Study of Democratic Consolidation: Poland, 1989–1993." In *Acts of Dissent: New Developments in the Study of Protest,* edited by Dieter Rucht, Ruud Koopmans, and Friedhelm Neidhardt, 317–48. Lanham, Md.: Rowman and Littlefield.

Fillieule, Olivier. 1996. "Police Records and National Press in France: Issues in the Methodology of Data-Collections from Newspapers." Working Paper No. 96/25 of the Robert Schuman Centre. Florence: European University Institute.

———. 1999. "'Plus ça change, moins ça change': Demonstrations in France during the Nineteen-Eighties." In *Acts of Dissent: New Developments in the Study of Protest,* edited by Dieter Rucht, Ruud Koopmans, and Friedhelm Neidhardt, 199–226. Lanham, Md.: Rowman and Littlefield.

Franzosi, Roberto. 1999. "The Return of the Actor: Interaction Networks among Social Actors during Periods of High Mobilization (Italy, 1919–1922)." *Mobilization, Special Issue: Protest Event Analysis* 4 (2): 131–49, edited by Dieter Rucht and Ruud Koopmans.

Gamson, William A. 1968. *Power and Discontent.* Homewood, Ill.: Dorsey.

Giugni, Marco G. 1993. *Entre stratégie et opportunité. Les nouveaux mouvements sociaux en Suisse.* Dissertation, University of Geneva.

Gurr, Ted Robert. 1968. "A Causal Model of Civil Strife: A Comparative Analysis Using New Indices." *American Political Science Review* 62: 1104–24.

Hocke, Peter. 1999. "Determining the Selection Bias in Local and National Newspaper Reports on Protest Events." In *Acts of Dissent: New Developments in the Study of Protest,* edited by Dieter Rucht, Ruud Koopmans, and Friedhelm Neidhardt, 131–63. Lanham, Md.: Rowman and Littlefield.

———. 2000. *Massenmedien und lokaler Protest. Empirische Fallstudie zur Medienselektivität in einer westdeutschen 'Bewegungshochburg'.* Unpublished Ph.D. diss., Free University Berlin.

Hug, Simon, and Dominique Wisler. 1998. "Correcting for Selection Bias in Social Movement Research." *Mobilization* 3 (2): 141–61.

Imig, Doug, and Sidney Tarrow. 1999. "The Europeanization of Movements? A New Approach to Transnational Contentions." In *Social Movements in a Globalizing World,* edited by Donatella della Porta, Hanspeter Kriesi, and Dieter Rucht, 112–33. London: Macmillan.

———. 2001. "Mapping the Europeanization of Contention: Evidence from a Quantitative Data Analysis." In *Contentious Europeans: Protest in an Emerging Polity,* edited by Doug Imig and Sidney Tarrow, 27–49. Lanham, Md.: Rowman and Littlefield.

Jenkins, Craig. 1985. *The Politics of Insurgency: The Farm Worker Movement in the 1960s.* New York: Columbia University Press.

Jenkins, J. Craig, and Charles Perrow. 1977. "Insurgency of the Powerless: Farm Workers' Movements 1946–1972." *American Sociological Review* 42: 249–68.

Koopmans, Ruud. 1995. *Democracy from Below: New Social Movements and the Political System in West Germany.* Boulder, Colo.: Westview.

———. 1996. "Asyl: Die Karriere eines politischen Konflikts." In *Kommunikation und Entscheidung. Politische Funktionen öffentlicher Meinungsbildung und diskursiver Verfahren,* edited by Wolfgang van der Daele and Friedhelm Neidhardt, 167–92. Berlin: Edition Sigma.

———. 1998. "Rechtsextremisus, fremdenfeindliche Mobilisierung und Einwanderungspolitik unter dem Gesichtspunkt politischer Gelegenheitsstrukturen." In *Paradigmen der Bewegungsforschung: Entstehung und Entwicklung von Neuen Sozialen Bewegungen und Rechtsextremismus,* edited by Kai-Uwe Hellmann and Ruud Koopmans, 198–212. Wiesbaden: Westdeutscher Verlag.

———. 1999. "The Use of Protest Event Data in Comparative Research: Cross-National Comparability, Sampling Methods and Robustness." In *Acts of Dissent: New Developments in the Study of Protest,* edited by Dieter Rucht, Ruud

Koopmans, and Friedhelm Neidhardt, 90–110. Lanham, Md.: Rowman and Littlefield.

———. 2001: "Better Off by Doing Good. Why Anti-Racism Must Mean Different Things to Different Groups." In *Political Altruism? Solidarity Movements in International Perspective,* edited by Marco Giugni and Florence Passy, 111–32. Lanham, Md.: Rowman and Littlefield.

Koopmans, Ruud, and Dieter Rucht. 1995. *Social Movement Mobilization under Left and Right Governments: A Look at Four West European Countries.* Discussion Paper FS III 95–106. Wissenschaftszentrum Berlin.

———. 1999. "Protest Event Analysis: Where to Now?" *Mobilization, Special Issue: Protest Event Analysis* 4 (2): 123–30, edited by Dieter Rucht and Ruud Koopmans.

Koopmans, Ruud, and Paul Statham. 1999a. "Challenging the Liberal Nation-State? Postnationalism, Multiculturalism, and the Collective Claims-Making of Migrants and Ethnic Minorities in Britain and Germany." *American Journal of Sociology* 105 (3): 652–96.

———. 1999b. "Political Claims Analysis: Integrating Protest Event and Public Discourse Approaches." *Mobilization, Special Issue: Protest Event Analysis* 4 (2): 203–22, edited by Dieter Rucht and Ruud Koopmans.

———. 2000. "Political Claims-Making against Racism and Discrimination in Britain and Germany." In *Comparative Perspectives on Racism,* edited by Jessika ter Wal and Maykel Verkuyten, 139–170. Aldershot: Ashgate.

Kousis, Maria. 1999. "Environmental Protest Cases: The City, the Countryside, and the Grassroots in Southern Europe." *Mobilization, Special Issue: Protest Event Analysis* 4 (2): 223–38, edited by Dieter Rucht and Ruud Koopmans.

Kriesi, Hanspeter, Ruud Koopmans, Jan Willem Duyvendak, and Marco G. Guigni. 1992. "New Social Movements and Political Opportunities in Western Europe." *European Journal of Political Research* 22: 219–44.

———. 1995. *New Social Movements in Western Europe. A Comparative Analysis.* Minneapolis: University of Minnesota Press.

Kriesi, Hanspeter, Rene Levy, Gilbert Ganguillet, and Heinz Zwicky. 1981 *Politische Aktivierung in der Schweiz, 1945–1978.* Diessenhofen: Regger.

Lemke, Christiane. 1997. "Protestverhalten in Transformationsgesellschaften." *Politische Vierteljahresschrift* 38 (1): 50–78.

Lieberson, S., and A. R. Silverman. 1965. "The Precipitants and Underlying Conditions of Race Riots." *American Sociological Review* 30: 343–53.

McAdam, Doug. 1982. *Political Process and the Development of Black Insurgency, 1930–1970.* Chicago: University of Chicago Press.

McCarthy, John D., Clark McPhail, and Jackie Smith. 1996. "Media Bias in the

Coverage of Washington, D.C. Demonstrations." *American Sociological Review* 61: 478–99.

McCarthy, John D., Clark McPhail, Jackie Smith, and Louis J. Crishock. 1999. "Electronic and Print Media Representations of Washington, D.C. Demonstrations, 1982 and 1991: A Demography of Description Bias." In *Acts of Dissent: New Developments in the Study of Protest,* edited by Dieter Rucht, Ruud Koopmans, and Friedhelm Neidhardt, 113–130. Lanham, Md.: Rowman and Littlefield.

McPhail, Clark, and David Schweingruber. 1999. "Unpacking Protest Events: A Description Bias Analysis of Media Records with Systematic Direct Observations of Collective Action—The 1995 March for Life in Washington, D.C." In *Acts of Dissent: New Developments in the Study of Protest,* edited by Dieter Rucht, Ruud Koopmans, and Friedhelm Neidhardt, 164–195. Lanham, Md.: Rowman and Littlefield.

Mikkelsen, Flemming. 1999. "Contention and Social Movements in an International and Transnational Perspective: Denmark 1914–1995." *Journal of Historical Sociology* 12 (2): 128–57.

Mueller, Carol. 1997. "Media Measurement Models of Protest Event Data." *Mobilization* 2 (2): 165–84.

Neidhardt, Friedrich, and Dieter Rucht. 1999. "Protestgeschichte der Bundesrepublik Deutschland 1950–1994: Ereignisse, Themen, Akteure." In *Eine lernende Demokratie: 50 Jahre Bundesrepublik Deutschland,* edited by Max Kaase and Günther Schmidt, 129–64. Berlin: Edition Sigma.

Oliver, Pamela E., and Daniel J. Myers. 1999. "How Events Enter the Public Sphere: Conflict, Location, Sponsorship in Local Newspaper Coverage of Public Events." *American Journal of Sociology* 105 (1): 38–87.

Olzak, Susan. 1989. "Analysis of Events in Studies of Collective Action." *Annual Review of Sociology* 15: 119–41.

———. 1992. *The Dynamics of Ethnic Competition and Conflict.* Stanford, Calif.: Stanford University Press.

Olzak, Susan, and Johan L. Olivier. 1999. "Comparative Event Analysis: Black Civil Rights Protest in South Africa." In *Acts of Dissent: New Developments in the Study of Protest,* edited by Dieter Rucht, Ruud Koopmans, and Friedhelm Neidhardt, 253–283. Lanham, Md.: Rowman and Littlefield.

Reising, Uwe K. H. 1999. "United in Opposition? Cross-National Time-Series of European Protest in Three Selected Countries, 1980–1995." *Journal of Conflict Resolution* 43 (3): 317–43.

Rootes, Chris. 1999. "The Transformation of Environmental Activism." *Innovation: The European Journal of Social Sciences* 12 (2): 187–206.

Rucht, Dieter. 1996. "Forms of Protest in Germany 1950–1992: A Quantitative

Overview." Paper prepared for the workshop "Europe and the United States: Movement Societies or the Institutionalization of Protest." Cornell University, Ithaca, N.Y., March 1–3.

———. 1999. "Linking Organization and Mobilization. Michels' 'Iron Law of Oligarchy' Reconsidered" *Mobilization* 4 (2): 151–169.

———. Forthcoming. "The EU as a Target of Political Mobilization: Is There a Europeanization of Conflict?" In *L'Europe des intérêts: lobbying, mobilisations et espace européen,* edited by Richard Balme, Didier Chabanet, and Vincent Wright. Paris: Presses de Sciences Politiques.

Rucht, Dieter, Ruud Koopmans, and Friedhelm Neidhardt, eds. 1999. *Acts of Dissent: New Developments in the Study of Protest.* Lanham, Md.: Rowman and Littlefield.

Rucht, Dieter, and Friedhelm Neidhardt. 1999. "Methodological Issues in Collection of Protest Event Data: Units of Analysis, Sources and Sampling, Coding Problems." In *Acts of Dissent: New Developments in the Study of Protest,* edited by Dieter Rucht, Ruud Koopmans, and Friedhelm Neidhardt, 65–88. Lanham, Md.: Rowman and Littlefield.

Rucht, Dieter, and Thomas Ohlemacher. 1992. "Protest Event Data: Collection, Uses and Perspectives." In *Studying Collective Action,* edited by M. Diani and R. Eyerman, 76–106. London: Sage.

Russett, Bruce M., et al. 1964. *World Handbook of Political and Social Indicators.* New Haven, Conn.: Yale University Press.

Schrodt, Philip A. 1996. KEDS: Kansas Event Data System. Version 0.9.B4.

Snyder, David, and William R. Kelly. 1977. "Conflict Intensity, Media Sensitivity and the Validity of Newspaper Data." *American Sociological Review* 42: 105–23.

Snyder, David, and Charles Tilly. 1972. "Hardship and Collective Violence in France, 1830 to 1960." *American Sociological Review* 37: 520–32.

Soule, Sarah A., Doug McAdam, John McCarthy, and Yang Su. 1999. "Protest Events: Cause or Consequence of State Action? The U.S. Women's Movement and Federal Congressional Activities, 1956–1979." *Mobilization, Special Issue: Protest Event Analysis* 4 (2): 239–56, edited by Dieter Rucht and Ruud Koopmans.

Spilerman, Seymour. 1970. "The Causes of Racial Disturbances: A Comparison of Alternative Explanations." *American Sociological Review* 35 (4): 627–49.

Szabó, Máté. 1996. "Politischer Protest im postkommunistischen Ungarn 1989–1994." *Berliner Journal für Soziologie* 6 (4): 510–15.

Tarrow, Sidney. 1989. *Democracy and Disorder: Protest and Politics in Italy 1965–1975.* Oxford: Clarendon.

Taylor, Charles L., and Michael C. Hudson. 1972. *World Handbook of Political and Social Indicators.* 2d ed. New Haven and London: Yale University Press.

Tilly, Charles. 1978. *From Mobilization to Revolution.* Reading, Mass.: Addison-Wesley.

———. 1995. *Popular Contention in Great Britain 1758–1834.* Cambridge, Mass.: Harvard University Press.

Tilly, Charles, Louise Tilly, and Richard Tilly. 1975. *The Rebellious Century, 1830–1930.* Cambridge, Mass.: Harvard University Press.

White, J. W. 1995. *Ikki: Social Conflict and Political Protest in Early Modern Japan.* Ithaca, N.Y.: Cornell University Press.

White, Robert W. 1999. "Comparing State Repression of Pro-State Vigilants and Anti-State Insurgents: Northern Ireland, 1972–75." *Mobilization, Special Issue: Protest Event Analysis* 4 (2): 203–22, edited by Dieter Rucht and Ruud Koopmans.

10

Macro-Organizational Analysis

Debra C. Minkoff

There is relatively widespread agreement among both academics and activists that a variety of organizations—community-based and national, formal and informal, civic and political—anchor processes of social movement emergence and development. Still, the organizational analysis of social movements remains relatively underdeveloped both theoretically and methodologically. In large part, this situation reflects the tendency of analysts to focus on specific social movements using the case study method, which privileges the histories of individual movements and/or what goes on within particularly prominent movement organizations. The resulting deep knowledge of singular movements and organizations has contributed a great deal to theory building, while at the same time limiting the vantage point from which we can comprehend social movements as historically variable collective mobilizations arising from "multiorganizational fields" (Curtis and Zurcher 1973; Klandermans 1992), "social movement families" (della Porta and Rucht 1995), and "social movement sectors" (McCarthy and Zald 1977; Garner and Zald 1987).

The purpose of this chapter is to demonstrate the promise of a dual shift in social movement analysis: to the level of social movement industries, families, and sectors and toward developing quantitative approaches for analyzing processes of change in movement populations over time. As I will suggest, to understand a social movement's or society's "protest potential" (Jenkins and Klandermans 1995), we need to understand its *organizational potential*, which means knowing "how mobilizing structural forms emerge and evolve; how they are chosen, combined, and adapted by social movement activists; and how they differentially affect particular movements as well as movement cycle trajectories" (McCarthy 1996: 141). To this end, it is necessary to develop a macro-organizational research program that builds on recent theoretical and methodological advances in organizational analysis. Organizational ecology (Hannan and Freeman 1989; Hannan and Carroll 1995) is especially useful in that it provides guidelines for research design and analysis.

In the next section I will clarify the rationale for shifting the level of social movement analysis toward the study of social movement industries, families, and sectors. I will then describe the kinds of research questions that can be most effectively addressed by such an approach and, by extension, the necessary types of data and methods of analysis. This will provide the opportunity to evaluate the strengths and limitations of available strategies for compiling and analyzing comprehensive data sets on social movement organizations (SMOs) and movement sectors. In addition, I will address the question of how the study of macro-organizational dynamics can inform the study of protest mobilization over time. This review will draw on my own research on the development of the contemporary civil rights and feminist movements in the United States, which is based on a synthesis of resource mobilization/political opportunity approaches and macro-organizational theories (Minkoff 1995). The chapter concludes with a discussion of the potential contributions—and limitations—of a macro-organizational approach to understanding social movement dynamics.

Shifting the Vantage Point: Why Macro-Organizational Analysis?

The starting point for a macro-organizational approach to studying social movements is the observation that although movements are comprised of more than the sum of their affiliated organizations, their organizational base fundamentally shapes the kinds and amounts of resources that activists are able to mobilize, the issues that come to dominate and identify their cause, and the strategies they adopt in interaction with authorities and opponents. Social movement organizations—in contrast to interpersonal networks, intermittent collective protests, and specific coalitional campaigns—are established specifically with the intent of routinizing (usually scarce) resource flows and stabilizing relationships between movements and their environments, constituted by mass and elite supporters, authorities, and opponents.

Importantly, movements are comprised of a variety of organizational forms, and their composite structure is a significant factor determining the movement's dominant trajectory over time. Take, for example, the pro-choice movement in the United States. As Staggenborg (1991) demonstrates, a characteristic of this movement has been its reliance on a combination of both professional SMOs, exemplified by the National Abortion Rights Action League, and more decentralized movement groups, such as the Chicago Women's Liberation Union. Whereas the former provided an institutionalized base of support as the movement unfolded in response to the pro-life opposition, the latter provided a source of innovation, flexibility, and continued protest and direct action. A similar range of organizational diversity has been noted in the American civil rights movement (McAdam 1982), in the environmental movement in Europe and the United States (Brulle 2000; Dalton 1994; Diani 1995), and within a range of left-libertarian and other new social movements in Western Europe (Kriesi 1996; Rucht 1996). Such diversity not only provides a potentially effective division of labor but also increases the likelihood of intramovement competition—over resources, tactics, activist identities, and dominant ways of framing the issues—that may ultimately contribute to movement decline (Zald and McCarthy 1980; McAdam 1982; Minkoff 1995).

The relationship between interorganizational competition and movement decline illustrates one possible mechanism of change in social movements. Researchers have also noted negative "radical flank" effects (Haines 1984), the channeling of funding toward more professional SMOs (Jenkins and Ekert 1986), and the "tangle of incentives" that provide advantages to SMOs that register with the state and conform to dominant institutional standards of organizational structure (McCarthy, Britt, and Wolfson 1991). These are all processes that promote the survival chances of more moderate organizations *at the expense of more confrontational ones* and thereby constrain the potential heterogeneity within the movement's organizational base. In turn, the composition of the organizational system determines the overall probability that confrontational tactics can be supported over more institutionalized forms of activity, for example. This illustration suggests that information on the range and diversity of movement organizational forms and, more importantly, the dynamics of SMO evolution is necessary for understanding the range and diversity of protest activity generated by movements over time.

Organizational dynamics cannot be observed or measured at the level of individual SMOs or even with a focus on a few key movement actors. As Garner and Zald (1987: 293) suggest, "to understand the course of social movements we have to understand them as a *configuration* and within a *determining environment*." Macro-organizational theory and research provide a powerful set of tools for studying the development of SMO forms and their relationship to their "determining environment." Organizational ecology, in particular, draws attention to the relationship between organizations and their environments and how this shapes the variety of available models of organization. As Hannan and Freeman (1989: 52) note, organizational ecologists "want to understand the dynamics of organizational diversity, *how social changes affect the mix of organizations in society*" (emphasis in the original). They go on to clarify that "diversity of forms has no counterpart at the level of single organizations. It is a property of a population or community of organizations. . . . It is in this sense that the population is the unit of analysis."

Elsewhere (Minkoff 1995) I have drawn on organizational ecology to argue that environmental selection and changes in the political and resource environment are central mechanisms that establish the legitimacy of organizational constituencies and forms and circumscribe how movement populations develop. As Tilly (1978: 125) notes in discussing the mechanisms by which government agencies, competition or coalition with established insiders, and sponsorship by powerful elites shape the development of the polity, "each new entry or exit redefines the criteria of membership in a direction favorable to the characteristics of the present set of members." Organizational entries and exits can be conceptualized in the same way. The targeting of different groups, either directly, through repression or the withholding of resources, or indirectly, through various forms of "institutional channeling" (McCarthy, Britt, and Wolfson 1991), influences the costs of SMO formation and maintenance and in the long run establishes the diversity or homogeneity of SMO forms. In the case of the contemporary American women's and civil rights movements, such dynamics are manifest in the increasing prevalence of national advocacy organizations after 1970, the subsequent replacement of service provision as a dominant mode of social change activity, and the creation of a relatively circumscribed niche for protest organizations (Minkoff 1994). This represents a significant change in the "organizational repertoire" (Clemens 1993) available to women and racial and ethnic minorities in the post–World War II period.

One implication of conceptualizing SMOs as carriers of movement strategies, resources, goals, and collective identities, then, is the proposition that changes in the organizational structure of social movements critically shape the dynamics of movement development. Thus, to understand the trajectories of specific social movements and cycles of protest more broadly, it is necessary to know how populations of movement organizations evolve over time. Here, again, the research program of organizational ecology is relevant:

An ecology of organizations seeks to understand how social conditions affect the rate at which new organizations and new organizational forms arise, the rates at which organizations change forms, and the rates at which organizations and forms die out. In addition to focusing on the effects of social, economic, and political systems on these rates, an ecology of organizations also emphasizes the dynamics that take place *within* organizational populations. (Hannan and Freeman 1989: 7)

Ideally, such a research program requires information on all organizations in the defined population and data on the external context over a meaningful period of time. Practically, this means (1) defining the population to be studied and (2) identifying data sources available for developing longitudinal censuses of movement organizations. Finally, a macro-organizational approach requires quantitative methods suitable for analyzing the central components of SMO population change—founding, disbanding, and organizational transformation—and linking them to changes in the external environment, focusing on such factors as resource conditions, the political opportunity structure, and cycles of protest. As I hope to illustrate, a macro-organizational approach provides empirical leverage on two central questions for movement analysis: (1) How do SMO populations change over time in response to political and resource conditions? and (2) What are the implications of changes at the level of SMO populations for protest mobilization?

Defining SMO Populations

The first conceptual task is to define the organizational population of interest. To this end, researchers need to specify (1) the movement or movement families of interest, (2) the scope of activity (e.g., transnational, national, local), and (3) the criteria for including organizations as members of the population. There is little consensus, however, about what distinguishes social movement organizations from other "movement mobilizing structures," such as traditional voluntary associations, informal networks, and community institutions (McCarthy 1996), or from traditional interest groups and political parties that may also promote movement objectives (Kriesi 1996; Rucht 1996; Burstein 1999). One familiar approach is to emphasize the use of extra-institutional protest as the central mode of SMO operation (McAdam 1982; Rucht 1996). More recently, researchers have also considered such organizational features as degree of reliance on and commitment to grassroots participation, orientation toward authorities or the mass base, and dominant structural arrangements (networks of informal groups versus formal organization) (Kriesi 1996; Rucht 1996).

Attempts to isolate the key features of SMOs represent an important advance in social movement analysis, but in terms of specifying organizational populations it is also necessary to provide a theoretical rationale for drawing boundaries around multiple organizations and treating this aggregate as the unit of analysis. Hannan and Carroll (1995: 34), for example, define populations in terms of their shared niche, which "consists of the social, economic, and political conditions that can sustain the functioning of organizations that embody a particular form." Organizational form is defined as "the core properties that make a set of organizations ecologically similar" (Hannan and Carroll 1995: 29). As Aldrich (1999: 37, 244) notes, this conceptualization hinges on the idea of common responsiveness to environmental change and implies considering organizational populations as sets of potential competitors. McCarthy and Zald (1977: 1228) illustrate this logic: "While various SMOs may compete for resources from isolated adherents to the 'justice for black Americans' SM, SMOs representing the 'justice for American women' SM may be competing for the same resources (to the extent that these two SMs have overlapping adherent pools)." One implication of using the criteria of shared resource dependencies is that, depending on the research question, population boundaries may need to be drawn more widely than at the level of isolated movements.

An alternative conceptualization, and one that is more common among social movement researchers, relies on common objectives or goals as the criteria for considering organizations as components of the same "social movement industry" (McCarthy and Zald 1977) or "social movement infrastructure" (Kriesi 1996). This approach is also implicit in della Porta and Rucht's (1995: 233) definition of a social movement family as a "nationally based, historical configuration of movements that—although they have different specific goals, immediate fields of struggle, and strategic preferences—share a common worldview, have organizational overlaps, and occasionally ally for joint campaigns." A further level of aggregation points to the concept of a "social movement sector" that comprises all social movement industries or infrastructures in a given society (McCarthy and Zald 1977; Kriesi 1996).

As is clear, there are no well-established criteria or sampling frames for delineating social movement organizational populations. Operationally, researchers tend to first define social movements with respect to the issues motivating collective action and then draw further distinctions with respect to which organizational forms are considered the appropriate focus of analysis, both in terms of their mode and scope of operation and challenge. I have suggested that the idea of shared resource dependencies and the potential for competition represents one useful approach to drawing population boundaries; alliance formations or cooperative linkages represent an alternative. Of course the two are not mutually exclusive empirically, and I would argue that a comprehensive view of the organizational system requires careful consideration of which organizational forms—regardless of their movement orientation—are embedded in shared resource and institutional environments and therefore subject to similar evolutionary dynamics. The important point is that macro-organizational analysis requires that researchers be explicit about how they define the organizational population of interest. Not only do such decisions influence the choice of available data sources, but they also fundamentally constrain the theoretical scope conditions and applicability of the research.

Enumerating SMO Populations: Data and Research Designs

The macro-organizational approach that I am advocating requires the collection of longitudinal data that enable researchers to document the size and changing composition of the SMO population of interest. Once the population (and, correspondingly, level of analysis) is defined, appropriate data sources must be identified that provide regularly updated information on the number of active SMOs and that provide a means of documenting population ecologies using dates of SMO founding, termination, and changes in form. Ideally, such information is available at regular time intervals in order to construct valid time series. I refer to this strategy as longitudinal data and design. Alternative approaches to enumerating SMO populations have relied on published directories, movement-based resources, and organizational surveys to develop panel designs that capture changes in the SMO population between longer time intervals. In this section I will provide examples of these different research strategies and offer an evaluation of their various strengths and limitations.

Longitudinal Data and Design

Modeling my own research on other studies in organizational ecology (see Aldrich 1999 for a useful review), I constructed a longitudinal database of 975 national women's, African American, Asian American, and Hispanic American organizations active between 1955 and 1985.[1] The primary data source was the *Encyclopedia of Associations,* vol. 1, National Organizations (published by Gale Research Company). This directory provides descriptive information on national membership associations, including such information as the year the organization was formed and organizational membership, objectives, and activities; entries are updated for each new edition based on information provided by the organizations. Groups that have become defunct or inactive since publication of the previous edition are noted in the index of subsequent editions, providing a means of coding organizational disbanding.

To obtain an over-time census of organizations, I coded each entry of the first twenty-three editions of the *Encyclopedia*, using national scope and constituency focus as the primary criteria for inclusion (see Minkoff 1995: Appendix A). Organizations could focus their activities in a number of institutional arenas (such as politics, education, the media), and their activities, while diverse, tended to fall into four general categories: social protest, institutional advocacy, service or resource provision, and cultural activities.[2] Because I wanted to map changes in organizational forms over time, such variation in strategies was a crucial component of the original research design. Additionally, the bulk of identified organizations were reform-oriented, which involves modifying existing institutional arrangements and social relations without demanding structural change in the prevailing social or political system, but I also included groups with more radical orientations and a handful that argued for maintaining the status quo or resisting social change as in the best interests of the group (such as a group active in the early 1970s called MOM/WOW—Men our Masters/Women our Wonders).

Although the *Encyclopedia* is the most comprehensive directory of U.S. national nonprofit membership associations in print (the current edition contains information on nearly twenty-three thousand organizations), it does have limitations. First, very small or short-lived organizations may not be consistently located. More significantly, protest groups are likely to be underrepresented, although those that are prominent in accounts of the civil rights, feminist, and Chicano movements, such as the Black Panthers and the Chicago Women's Liberation Union, are included in the directory, along with less visible groups that indicate some protest activity, such as Charter Group for a Pledge of Conscience and the Freedom Socialist Party. However, organizations may be reluctant to document involvement in more confrontational activities or to overstate their pursuit of more legitimate ones such as advocacy, which would also lead to an underestimation of the protest subsector.

Another set of limitations relates to the parameters established by the publication itself. For example, the *Encyclopedia* excludes government bodies and staff-run, not-for-profit organizations such as research centers and operating foundations. Although these structures are important elements of the entire field of women's and racial and ethnic minority activity, limiting analysis to membership organizations was justified since they face problems of organizational formation and maintenance that organizations not dependent on members do not share (Knoke 1989). In addition, the *Encyclopedia* reports organizational activity at the national level and does not provide information on local variation in organizational forms. A final issue is that a directory's publication date can set limits on the historical period covered by the study. In my case, the starting date of 1955 corresponded with the period McAdam (1982) identified as the emergent phase of the civil rights movement, and I was able to collect data through the mid-1980s, arguably capturing the surge and decline of the 1960s protest cycle that generated additional ethnic minority movements and contemporary feminist activism. Had there been substantive reasons for detailing organizational developments at an earlier period, however, the *Encyclopedia* would have been a much more limited resource.

Panel Data and Design

Other researchers have pursued different approaches to developing profiles of specific social movement industries and sectors, using published directories either to collect organizational-level data at set points in time (Smith 1997) or to derive a sampling frame for survey administration and subsequent tracking of active and defunct SMOs (Edwards and Marullo 1995).

Published Directories

Smith's (1997) research on the transnational social movement sector is exemplary with respect to using a directory of international organizations to map the quantitative expansion of transnational social movements after 1970, defined as those movements active in more than two national states (Smith 1997: 42). Smith collected data from the 1974, 1983/84, and 1993/94 editions of the *Yearbook of International Organizations,* published by the Union of International Associations. This directory includes information on organizations' founding dates, goals, membership, and formal consultative ties and informal links with international government organizations. The *Yearbook* uses UN records on nongovernmental organizations, self-reports, referrals, and the media to identify organizations and to compile organizational profiles; the editors also check the reported information against other sources, for example, periodicals, official documents, and the media. Smith reviewed each page of entries and included every nongovernmental organization whose primary aims included some form of social change, determined on the basis of the organization's name and reported aims.[3]

Smith's study provides a macro-organizational perspective on the development of the transnational social movement sector, representing "snapshots" at decade intervals. One drawback of this approach, however, is that it cannot account for interim changes in the organizational population. A well-documented finding is that new organizations and, more specifically, new organizational forms experience a "liability of newness" (Stinchcombe

1965) that exposes them to an increased risk of failure in their initial years of activity. For example, in my own research I found that organizations established after 1955 faced a significantly higher rate of failure until they survived their tenth year (Minkoff 1993). If the transnational SMOs studied by Smith are at all similar, turnover in the sector within a decade is likely to be substantial. Nonetheless, this research design captures broad sectoral trends over time.

Combining Published and Survey Data

An alternative way to take advantage of published directories for enumerating SMO populations is illustrated by a study of peace movement organizations (PMOs) that were active at both the national and local levels in the late 1980s and early 1990s (see Edwards and Marullo 1995). What is distinctive about this research design is that it relied on a published directory, the 1987 edition of the *Grassroots Peace Directory,* to draw a nationally representative stratified sample of groups working for peace, which were then surveyed by mail in 1988 and again in 1992 to update information and ascertain which PMOs were still active.[4] Edwards and Marullo (1995) report that the *Grassroots Peace Directory* is a comprehensive listing of peace movement groups compiled by the Topsfield Foundation, a key funder of peacemaking activities, that was updated bimonthly until it ceased publication in 1989. The foundation relied on extensive contacts with PMOs throughout the country and a network of state and regional coordinators to locate groups active at various levels. The 1987 edition listed over 7,700 local, state, and national PMOs, which ranged from informal groups of friends working together to large national organizations with local affiliates and extensive memberships, as well as peace task forces and committees of larger organizations. These groups were active on a number of issues, including arms control and disarmament, opposing U.S. policies in Central America, and promoting alternative methods of conflict resolution at the local level.

A significant strength of this research design is that it uses a directory that was established as a resource for peace activists by a foundation that was a major supporter of the movement. It is therefore not only more likely to be comprehensive but also accurate, especially with respect to small, more informal local peace groups. The fact that the *Directory* includes information on national, regional, and local groups, along with peace committees and task forces of national organizations, presents a valuable opportunity to inclusively map the contours of the movement and compare organizational distributions along different dimensions. A final feature of note is that because the *Directory* itself includes information on basic organizational features, it provides a means for constructing a stratified sampling frame and calculating response bias (see Smith 1997). Researchers are thus able to estimate population characteristics from a more delimited number of cases, which is especially useful when attempting to develop movement profiles for a very localized and dense movement industry. In terms of detailing over-time trends, however, survey methodology is relatively constrained since it can, at best, only rely on retrospective data reported by organizational officials (which the PMO study does not attempt) or be used for the analysis of short-term trends measured through follow-up surveys.

Movement-Based Information Sources

A final strategy for enumerating SMO industries over specific time periods is illustrated by the research conducted by McCarthy and his collaborators on the anti–drunken driving movement in the United States (McCarthy et al. 1988; McCarthy and Wolfson 1996). They relied on multiple sources, including roster lists from two national umbrella organizations (Mothers Against Drunk Driving [MADD] and Remove Intoxicated Drivers [RID]), periodical indices, organizational newsletters, and personal communication with local activists to build a list of the population of local anti–drunken driving citizen's groups in the United States in the mid-1980s (McCarthy and Wolfson 1996). At a preliminary stage of the research, founding dates were determined from reports of local groups or from umbrella group rosters. Using these data, McCarthy and colleagues (1988) derived population estimates based on the cumulative number of foundings between 1978 (the first founding date available) and 1985. Using the list of organizations compiled in 1985, the researchers distributed a mail survey in 1986. A follow-up survey of MADD groups was conducted at the end of 1988 after ascertaining from the current MADD chapter roster list which of the 1985 groups were still in existence. A related study by Weed (1991) relied on a random sample of local MADD chapters to conduct phone surveys in 1985. Weed subsequently used a list of inactive chapters or revoked charters to determine the number and percentage of groups that had ceased activity over a two-year period.

Enumerating Organizational Populations: Summary and Assessment

Taken together, these various research designs suggest a set of strategies for enumerating transnational, national, and local social movement organizational populations and tracking changes in these populations over time. Making use of organizational directories that are published at regular intervals and contain basic information on organizational characteristics has a clear advantage with respect to detailing over-time population trends. Longitudinal data sets can be compiled that capture both entries and exits from the population, thereby providing a relatively accurate picture of how the diversity and distribution of organizational forms develop over time. Two obvious limitations of such directories are that researchers are constrained to work with the reported information, and the boundaries of the organizational population are circumscribed by the scope of the publication, both in terms of the kinds of groups included (international, national; membership, nonmembership) and the period of coverage. Directories and information sources that originate within the movements of interest themselves are likely to be more inclusive, but often such resources do not span a significant period of time and thus have been more useful for developing sampling frames for more in-depth surveys. Here the benefit is that the researcher can collect a broader, and potentially more in-depth, range of organizational information, but the trade-off in terms of capturing over-time developments is fairly significant. At best researchers can use the same list of organizations to conduct follow-up surveys or use other sources to determine the persistence of the original set of organizations at a later point. Information on the number and diversity of organizations active throughout the movement's history, however, may not be available. Constructing time series data on population trends is also limited to detailing the cumulative number of new organizations established over time, which provides only a partial view of the development of the organizational structure of the movement or sector.

Analyzing SMO Population Change

As Edwards and Marullo note (1995: 910), "understanding which groups disband and which ones persist to struggle another day is crucial for analyzing and anticipating the agenda and repertoire of subsequent mobilizations." I would add that knowledge of which groups enter the movement arena and how political and resource conditions shape the prospects for SMO formation, survival, and change represents a key part of the story as well, since it provides the link between the meso-organizational and macro-political opportunity structures. In this section I will describe the quantitative techniques that I have used to analyze processes of organizational founding, failure, and change, and will illustrate the relationship between research design and analysis. I will also indicate alternative approaches that make use of the kind of panel data described in the last section (see Olzak and Olivier 1998 for a more comprehensive evaluation of quantitative methods available for analyzing event data).

Founding Rate Analysis: Poisson Regression

One approach to analyzing the relationship between organizational formation and changes in the social movement environment involves using Poisson regression, which is a regression strategy appropriate for use with yearly count data (Cameron and Trivedi 1984). The dependent variable is the number of organizations formed each year, and aggregate measures of the social movement environment are included as independent variables. The unit of analysis in this case is the year of observation (for a more formal treatment, see Minkoff 1995: Appendix B). The longitudinal data I collected enabled me to count the number of women's and civil rights SMOs formed each year between 1955 and 1985 and to construct an annual time series that also included annually updated measures of the social movement environment collected from a variety of official sources (for variable description, see Minkoff 1995: Appendix C). I was also able to construct counts of population density, which organizational ecologists argue is a critical feature of the environment (Hannan and Carroll 1992).

To illustrate the logic of my approach, column I in Table 10.1 reproduces results from a Poisson regression analysis of organizational founding reported in Minkoff (1995: ch. 4). The dependent variable is a combined measure of the number of women's and racial and ethnic minority SMOs founded yearly from 1955 to 1985. The independent variables include movement-specific features relevant for women's and civil rights activism, more general "structural facilitators" (McCarthy and Zald 1973), and a quadratic measure of the density of the organizational population. Briefly, the results suggest that, as expected by political opportunity theory, SMO founding rates are significantly higher during periods of Democratic control of the White House and, as predicted by resource mobilization theory, the founding rate increases with improvements in educational attainments and external funding. I interpret the negative effect of increases in societal affluence (measured by per capita disposable income) and federal social welfare funding in terms of a "demand effect"; that is, organizational formation is less likely if organizers and supporters observe that economic conditions are consistently improving over time. Finally, the analysis confirms the density-dependence hypothesis that in the early stages of population growth, founding rates increase, but as the field becomes more dense, interorganizational competition takes over and limits the ability of new groups to enter the population (in this case, after 1970).

McCarthy and colleagues (1988) illustrate an alternative approach to modeling processes of organizational founding. Their interest is in the *timing*

Table 10.1 Women's and racial and ethnic SMO founding and survival rates (1955–85)[1]

Independent Variables	I: Founding	II: Disbanding
1966–73	-0.240	0.506
	(0.262)	(0.704)
1974–78	-0.379	0.989
	(0.354)	(0.934)
1979–85	-0.601	-0.164
	(0.532)	(1.212)
Federal social welfare support	-0.025[a]	-0.017[c]
	(0.009)	(0.009)
Democratic president	0.414[a]	-0.052
	(0.113)	(0.202)
Black congressional representation	0.108	-0.032
	(0.068)	(0.065)
Women's and black educational attainment	0.239[a]	0.343[b]
	(0.117)	(0.137)
External funding	0.360[a]	0.275[c]
	(0.092)	(0.148)
Per capita disposable income	$-0.211e-2^{a}$	$-0.132e-2^{b}$
	$(0.055e-2)$	$(0.034e-2)$
Organizational density	0.014[a]	$-0.842e-2$
	(0.003)	$(0.544e-2)$
Density^2 (/1,000)	$-0.160e-4^{a}$	$0.114e-4^{c}$
	$(0.067e-4)$	$(0.068e-4)$
Age	n/a	0.066[a]
		(0.020)
Age^2	n/a	$-0.112e-2^{a}$
		$(0.034e-2)$
Est. pre-1955	n/a	-0.733[c]
		(0.410)
Racial-ethnic SMO	n/a	-0.009
		(0.145)
Constant	-0.670[b]	-5.044[a]
	(0.342)	(0.885)
Log-Likelihood	-99.43	-1040.2
No. observations	31	11441
No. events	n/a	218

[1] Column I reports Poisson regression estimates of organizational founding: column II reports logistic regression estimates of organizational disbanding. Standard errors in parentheses. Results reproduced form Minkoff 1995:87, 93.

[a] $p < 0.01$

[b] $p < 0.05$

[c] $p < 0.10$

of the founding of the first local anti–drunken driving SMO in a given county, using the founding dates derived from their census of local groups described earlier. The dependent variable in their analysis is the instantaneous rate of founding of the first organization in each county based on historical time. They use Cox's partial likelihood method, which takes into account the time elapsed before an event takes place; in this manner they are able to control for the dependence of organizational founding on time. One way to think about this is that McCarthy and colleagues examine how "conducive" (or susceptible) a community is to a (first) SMO founding. They find that population size and rapid population growth are positively related to the founding rate, as is the resource mobilization base of the county (indexed by median household income of the county, percent college graduates, and percent middle class). Alternatively, neither the level of local government resources nor grievances (variously measured by the number of fatal accidents and fatalities associated with drunken driving) are significant predictors of the rate at which communities create local anti–drunken driving groups.

Event History Analysis of Organizational Failure and Change

The longitudinal database that I compiled on the population of women's and racial and ethnic minority organizations has two features that make it ideal for systematically analyzing the correlates of organizational failure. The first is that I was able to create an observation, or spell, for each year of the organization's existence, updating information on a yearly basis.[5] A second advantage of this research design is that I could append the time-varying measures of the social movement environment discussed above to each spell and therefore estimate the effects of both organizational attributes (e.g., age, size, targets, strategies, goals) and yearly change in external conditions on the rate of failure using the maximum likelihood discrete-time event history method elaborated by Allison (1984). This is a logistic regression strategy that estimates the probability of event occurrence (in this case, organizational failure), given that an organization had survived until that point (i.e., taking each organization's prior history into account).

Column II in Table 10.1 reproduces results from the event history analysis of organizational disbanding between 1955 and 1985, also reported in Minkoff (1995: ch. 4). The dependent variable is a dichotomous measure coded 1 if the SMO became defunct since the prior year (coded 0 if it was still active). In addition to the independent variables included in the founding rate analysis, I also control for three core organizational attributes: age (quadratic specification), whether the SMO was established prior to 1955, and whether the organization represents women or one of the racial-ethnic groups included in the study (focus on women is the baseline category).[6]

The first point to note is that the political and resource environment appears to play less of an overall role in determining the survival chances of women's and civil rights SMOs than is the case for SMO formation. In addition, factors that promote the SMO founding rate do not necessarily promote SMO survival or vice versa. For example, improvements in the social welfare environment and per capita disposable income lower the chances of failure, at the same time that they diminish the rate of SMO founding. Increases in foundation funding and educational attainments, which provide a favorable context for group formation, tend to significantly increase the SMO failure rate. And increases in organizational density tend to place competitive pressures on the survival of active SMOs, with little significant benefit gained from the early phase of population growth that promoted SMO formation. These divergent results point to the importance of conceptualizing SMO formation and survival as distinct processes that respond differently to environmental change.

More recently, I have used the same event history data to examine transitions between protest, advocacy, and service forms of organization and the relationship between change and organizational disbanding (Minkoff 1999). Again, the results demonstrate that the social movement environment provides distinct, and at times contradictory, opportunities for SMO development. Integrating those findings with the results of the founding rate analysis described above, for example, demonstrates that Democratic control of the presidency, which does not significantly influence survival, improves the prospects for SMO formation and the transition rate from advocacy to protest forms of organization. Increases in feminist and civil rights protest, in contrast, tend to diminish the rate of change, at the same time that they provide a more general buffer against organizational failure. Finally, improvements in external funding present positive opportunities for organizational formation and change but also increase the SMO failure rate. Regardless of external conditions, however, *any* experience with change increases the organizational failure rate. To some extent, organizational attributes offset this liability: age and formalization are correlated with both flexibility and survival. In addition, larger SMOs, although they are not significantly more likely to change their strategies, are more generally less likely to disband.

One implication that I draw from these results is that an integrated analysis of SMO founding, failure, and change demonstrates that whereas new group formation and adaptation are critically dependent on improvements in political and resource opportunities, the prospects for organizational survival hinge more on the positive political opportunities provided by cycles of protest and the adoption of administrative structures and strategies that signal stability and conformity to dominant models of social and political organization. Through processes of adaptation and selection older, more professional, and reform-oriented movement organizations begin to dominate the sector, making it increasingly difficult for younger, smaller, and more decentralized organizations to establish a viable national presence. Although these results are limited to the population of national women's and civil rights organizations, they illustrate the importance of analyzing central organizational processes separately and considering how, taken together, they provide a more complete picture of developmental dynamics of SMO populations.

Panel Analysis of Organizational Failure and Change

Panel studies provide an alternative approach to analyzing SMO mortality and changes in movement populations. Such research uses organizational characteristics measured in the first wave of the survey to predict whether groups remained active or disbanded by the time of the second wave of the study. The appropriate method of analysis in this case is logistic regression, which estimates how the odds of disbanding are affected by organizational attributes. This is the approach taken in Edwards and Marullo's (1995) study of the demise of movement organizations during the declining phase of the peace movement (between 1988 and 1992), which emphasized the differential survival rates of small, large, and national PMOs. Weed (1991) likewise uses logistic regression analysis to study organizational mortality between 1985 and 1987 in the sample of local anti–drunken driving groups described earlier. His focus is on the relationship between chapter failure and self-reported organizational attributes (e.g., chapter age, evaluation of goal performance, influence of the central office and officers, cooperative efforts, and external community relations). Weed also includes two control variables to index community-level effects on mortality: 1980 population size and percentage of the population over twenty-five with sixteen or more years of education. Edwards and McCarthy (n.d.) adopt a similar approach to analyzing mortality of local MADD chapters between 1985 and 1988, controlling for both organizational and community-level characteristics.

In an interesting example of the use of panel data to document frame changes in the U.S. peace movement between 1988 and 1992, Marullo, Pagnucco, and Smith (1996) use the PMO survey described above to document shifts in movement rhetorics and differences between surviving and defunct PMOs. This illustrates a promising method of using such data to map aggregate changes in movement characteristics, while also taking into account the interpretative dimension that is central to the framing perspective.

The central limitation of this set of studies is that they cannot take prior organizational histories, or time, into account, although measuring age tends to be the proxy used to ascertain the typical form of age-dependence on failure. The ability to control for the macro-political and social context is likewise limited to measurement at a single, earlier point in time. Finally, the time period covered by these studies tends to be quite short, examining change over a period of three to five years. Nonetheless, these kinds of analysis can shed important light on what factors promote organizational survival, and from there, it is possible to begin developing a profile of which organizational forms are most likely to endure over time.

Movement Organization and Protest Mobilization

A final issue that I will briefly address is the relationship between social movement organization and protest. The evolution of movement organizational structures may be an interesting topic in its own right, but the argument of this chapter is that the dynamics of protest behavior and collective "claims-making" (Koopmans and Statham 1999) are in large part shaped by organizational processes. An emphasis on organizational ecologies may be misplaced, then, unless the relationship between protest mobilization and the characteristics of the SMO system can be established empirically.

I have used the data collected on national women's and civil rights organizations in conjunction with civil rights and feminist protest event data to model the structure of protest cycles in the United States, which provides some insight into the relationship between macro-organizational developments and protest dynamics (Minkoff 1997). As with the founding rate analysis described earlier, I use Poisson regression to analyze the effect of civil rights protest and the density of civil rights SMOs on the rate of feminist protest and SMO formation. In contrast to the prevailing view that the diffusion of protest hinges on a demonstration effect that signals the feasibility of protest to a broad spectrum of activists (Tarrow 1994; McAdam 1995), I show that increases in the density of civil rights *organizations,* not the number of civil rights protest events, promoted feminist collective action between 1955 and 1985. In fact, it appears that civil rights protest increases feminist activism only when political allies are in positions of power; otherwise increases in protest by African Americans decrease the number of feminist protests. These findings suggest that the expansion of the SMO structure of "initiator movements" (McAdam 1995) is critical in creating protest opportunities for other challengers. And more to the point of this chapter, this kind of analysis, which counterposes independently derived measures of the organizational system and protest events, provides a means of systematically and empirically documenting the importance of organizational infrastructures for maintaining the potential for protest over time.

Other researchers are also beginning to analyze the relationship between protest and SMO systems, although this research remains fairly descriptive and is limited to detailing the kinds of organizations that sponsor protest events and how this changes over time (Koopmans 1993; Kriesi et al. 1995; Rucht 1998, 1999). Rucht (1998), for example, documents a notable shift in organizational sponsorship of protest events in Germany since 1950 (including East German protests since 1989): whereas most demonstrations were organized by large formal pressure groups in the 1950s and 1960s, after 1970 informal groups and networks, along with political parties, also became key sponsors. Formal pressure groups are still the dominant sponsors (they organized 46 percent of protests in 1990–92) but not exclusively so. Importantly, the volume of mass protest also increased over this period, despite occasional declines. This is particularly the case with demonstrative events (demonstrations, marches, rallies, and strikes), but there is also some indication of a recent rise in violent protests (consisting of property damage, physical aggression, and personal injuries). Rucht draws the conclusion that although many protest groups have become more professionalized and institutionalized, the result has not been a "deradicalization of protest" (1998: 52).

Rucht's analysis makes use of the Prodat data described in the chapter in this volume by Koopmans and Rucht. Organizational information is derived from newspaper coverage of protest events in Germany between 1950 and 1992, which means that trend data are limited to those organizations that the media report as involved in organizing or participating in the event. The available information on the groups involved is also limited, and organizations are mainly identified by issue domain and whether they are formal associations, informal groups, or political parties. Although this research design adequately captures trends in organizational sponsorship or support for social protest across a number of domains, it can provide only limited information on the full population of SMOs that are "at risk" of engaging in protest.[7] These data are also inadequate for analyzing organizational processes of the sort discussed in this chapter. In a more recent article, however, Rucht (1999) makes use of a panel survey of alternative organizations in Berlin conducted in 1991 and 1993, the first of which included a number of retrospective questions about organizational characteristics in 1989, 1984, and 1978. This approach represents a promising direction for future research since it provides an independent source of information on SMO structures and activities across a number of protest domains.

Macro-Organizational Analysis: Strengths and Limits

My purpose in this chapter has been to advocate for a social movement research program that builds on recent theoretical and methodological advances in macro-organizational analysis. In my own work, I have found that organizational ecology provides a set of powerful tools for systematically enumerating and analyzing the development of national SMO populations, but this framework is more broadly applicable, whether the boundaries are drawn at the transnational, national, or local level and whether the object of inquiry is a single movement industry, family, or sector. In particular, macro-organizational analysis reorients researchers to the premise that social movement organizations, unlike occasional outbursts of dissent, are burdened with the requirements of organizational survival. They need resources—members, leaders, money—to establish and maintain themselves, embedding them in competitive and institutional environments that delimit the activities of single organizations at the same time that they shape the diversity and development of organizational populations over time.

This chapter has emphasized the tasks of compiling the kind of longitudinal data on SMOs necessary for documenting processes of population-level change and demonstrating available strategies for data collection and analysis. The use of published directories or other documentary sources for enumerating organizational censuses is most obviously limited by the relatively schematic information available and the difficulties of locating resources that span a meaningful period of movement activity. In addition, documentary sources that are not generated by movements themselves are likely to underestimate the number of groups engaged in the very forms of protest behavior that are considered to be the sine qua non of social movement activity. The payoff, however, is a comprehensive view of the models and actors that serve as the carriers of broad-based collective challenges over time.

Censuses of SMO populations also provide the necessary data for systematic model testing with the use of quantitative methods. By utilizing the kinds of multivariate techniques described in this chapter, it becomes possible to model and compare processes of SMO formation, disbanding, and transformation and to understand how the evolution of organizational forms is linked to broader social and political changes and to developmental pressures arising from internal population dynamics such as density-dependence. As I have demonstrated, such factors influence social movement development in ways that may not only contradict theoretical expectations but also clarify the kinds of environmental and organizational contingencies that activists must negotiate in practice. Further, such models and methods provide the opportunity to analyze how the dominant features of movement populations influence the timing and direction of protest cycles, although a great deal of work remains to be done on this topic. Finally, analyses of the relationship between organizational and protest dynamics provide a promising template for the systematic analysis of movement outcomes (see, e.g., Meyer and Minkoff 1997). By treating measurable policy attainments as the dependent variable, for example, it should be possible to analyze the differential effects of protest activity and organizational expansion in order to better understand governmental responsiveness to different forms of movement activity in the context of independent changes in the political context.

Without the analytic leverage provided by macro-organizational theories, it would not be possible to draw conclusions regarding the more general environmental and organizational dynamics that set the context within which individual social movement organizations operate. There are, of course, trade-offs that researchers make when shifting to organizational populations as the unit of analysis. In-depth information on organizational histories—the circumstances that lead to their formation, internal conflicts that influence their development, and general decision-making processes within the group—are considered of secondary importance. In addressing such questions, case study research is better suited to provide in-depth narratives of organizational life histories. By the same token, historical studies of particular movements, for example, McAdam's (1982) study of the American civil rights movement and Staggenborg's (1991) analysis of the pro-choice movement, may provide a more nuanced account of the changing interaction dynamics between movements, authorities, and opponents (although in principle such relationships are amenable to the modeling techniques described earlier if appropriate data can be collected). Nonetheless, as I have tried to illustrate, the rise and fall of movement organizations and movements themselves are only fully discernable at a population level. And it is the aggregate processes of organizational formation, survival, and change that shape the social movement sector that provides the essential infrastructure for mobilizing the wide variety of institutional and extra-institutional challenges that comprise the subject area of social movement analysis.

Notes

1. I worked with McCarthy and Zald's (1977: 1218) definition of a social movements as "a set of opinions and beliefs in a population representing preferences

for changing some elements of the social structure or reward distribution, or both, of a society" and focused on delineating the relevant social movement industries (defined as "all SMOs that have as their goal the attainment of the broadest preferences of a social movement"). In retrospect, I implicitly employed della Porta and Rucht's (1995) concept of social movement family in electing to study women's and racial and ethnic minority organizations within a common analytic framework.

2. Some examples in the protest category (defined as using outsider tactics or disruptive means, such as sit-ins, boycotts, and demonstrations, to influence policies, public officials, or public opinion) are the Student Non-Violent Coordinating Committee (SNCC), the Black Panthers, and Radical Women. The advocacy category (using routine means, like lobbying and litigation, to influence policies and public opinion in a variety of institutional settings) includes political organizations such as the National Organization for Women, the NAACP, and the National Congress for Puerto Rican Rights, as well as such groups as Black Citizens for a Fair Media and the Association of Asian American Pacific Artists. Examples of service or resource providers (which target private resources and services to the constituency, such as job training, community development programs, or shelters for battered women) include traditional service groups such as the United Negro College Fund, the National Federation of Women's Exchanges, and the Japanese American Citizen's League. The database also includes politically oriented resource groups, such as Women's Direct Response Group, the Mexican-American Legal Defense Fund, and the Scholarship, Education and Defense Fund for Racial Equality (SCORE). Finally, some examples of organizations that emphasize cultural activities (such as sponsoring arts festivals, maintaining libraries or museums, or media production efforts) are Free Southern Theatre, the Women's History Network, and the Institute for the Study of the Hispanic American in U.S. Life and History.

3. Smith also conducted checks for intercoder reliability on two dimensions: the selection of transnational SMOs for inclusion and codebook reliability. Using the 1993 volume, a list of transnational SMOs was drawn a second time and compared to the original list, yielding a 0.89 reliability estimate. A 10 percent random sample of organizations was also coded by a second coder, resulting in a 0.97 reliability estimate. These reliability estimates are quite high and demonstrate procedures for ensuring both the reliability of the data and the population parameters measured (Smith 1997).

4. Annual budget information reported in the directory was used to stratify the PMO sample: 491 organizations that reported a 1986 budget greater than $30,000 represented the first strata, and a 5 percent random sample was drawn from the remaining 7,160 groups listed to yield a sample of 346 small-budget PMOs. The final sample comprised 411 peace movement groups (with a response rate of 56 percent for large-budget groups, and 43 percent for small-budget groups). In 1992, a

follow-up survey of these groups was conducted. In all, 91 (22 percent) of the 411 organizations surveyed in 1988 had disbanded by the time the 1992 survey was administered.

5. The first entry for an organization corresponds to its founding year (or the first year of the study if the association was formed prior to 1955, which was the case for 98 groups), and the last record corresponds either to the year the group became defunct or inactive (as reported in the *Encyclopedia*) or to the last year of the study (1985). Each organization could therefore have as few as one or as many as thirty-one observations (which would be the case for organizations established before 1955 and still active in 1985, such as the NAACP). The final database included 11,441 entries (organization-years) for 878 national organizations for which information on central variables was available (see Minkoff 1995: Appendix B).

6. The controls for age and movement affiliation reported in Table 10.1 indicate that racial or ethnic SMOs do not have significantly different survival chances than feminist groups, that organizations formed earlier than 1955 are marginally less likely to fail, and that this set of SMOs face a liability of newness that lasts well into their first decade of activity. See Minkoff (1993) for a more in-depth analysis of how organizational attributes influence survival chances independent of environmental conditions.

7. Jenkins and Ekert's (1986) study of the consequences of foundation funding for the development of the civil rights movement represents an early example of using media sources to document the carriers of protest events, distinguishing between unaffiliated individuals, crowds, local community organizations, classical SMOs, and professional SMOs. Everett (1992) similarly uses newspaper data to map changes in the U.S. social movement sector between 1961 and 1983, focusing on the differentiation of group interests (issues) over four two-year periods.

References

Aldrich, Howard. 1999. *Organizations Evolving.* Thousand Oaks, Calif.: Sage.

Allison, Paul D. 1984. *Event History Analysis: Regression for Longitudinal Event Data.* Beverly Hills, Calif.: Sage.

Brulle, Robert J. 2000. *Agency, Democracy, and Nature.* Cambridge: MIT Press.

Burstein, Paul. 1999. "Social Movements and Public Policy." In *How Social Movements Matter,* edited by M. Giugni, D. McAdam, and C. Tilly, 3–21. Minneapolis: University of Minnesota Press.

Cameron, A. Colin, and Pravin K. Trivedi. 1986. "Econometric Models Based on Count Data: Comparisons and Applications of Some Estimators and Tests." *Journal of Applied Econometrics* 1: 29–53.

Clemens, Elisabeth. 1993. "Women's Groups and the Transformation of U.S. Politics, 1892–1920." *American Journal of Sociology* 98: 755–98.

Curtis, Richard, and Louis Zurcher. 1973. "Stable Resources of Protest Movements: The Multi-Organizational Field." *Social Forces* 52: 53–60.

Dalton, Russell J. 1994. *The Green Rainbow.* New Haven, Conn.: Yale University Press.

della Porta, Donatella, and Dieter Rucht. 1995. "Left-Libertarian Movements in Context: A Comparison of Italy and West Germany, 1965–1990." In *The Politics of Social Protest,* edited by J. C. Jenkins and B. Klandermans, 229–72. Minneapolis: University of Minnesota Press.

Diani, Mario. 1995. *Green Networks.* Edinburgh: University of Edinburgh Press.

Edwards, Bob, and Sam Marullo. 1995. "Organizational Mortality in a Declining Movement: The Demise of Peace Movement Organizations in the End of the Cold War Era." *American Sociological Review* 60: 908–27.

Edwards, Bob, and John McCarthy. n.d. "Social Capital, Strategic Choice and the Contingent Value of Strong Social Ties for the Short-term Persistence of Social Movement Organizations." Unpublished manuscript.

Everett, Kevin Djo. 1992. "Professionalization and Protest: Changes in the Social Movement Sector, 1961–1983." *Social Forces* 70: 957–75.

Garner, Roberta Ash, and Mayer N. Zald. 1987. "The Political Economy of Social Movement Sectors." In *Social Movements in an Organizational Society,* edited by M. N. Zald and J. D. McCarthy, 293–317. New Brunswick, N.J.: Transaction Publishers.

Haines, Herbert H. 1984. "Black Radicalization and the Funding of Civil Rights: 1957-1970." *Social Problems* 32: 31-43.

Hannan, Michael, and Glenn R. Carroll. 1995. "The Population Ecology of Organizations." In *Organizations in Industry: Strategy, Structure, and Selection,* 17–31. New York: Oxford University Press.

Hannan, Michael, and John Freeman. 1989. *Organizational Ecology.* Cambridge: Harvard University Press.

Jenkins, J. Craig, and Craig M. Ekert. 1986. "Channeling Black Insurgency." *American Sociological Review* 51: 812–29.

Jenkins, J. Craig, and Bert Klandermans, eds. 1995. *The Politics of Social Protest.* Minneapolis: University of Minnesota Press.

Klandermans, Bert. 1992. "The Social Construction of Protest and Multiorganizational Fields." In *Frontiers in Social Movement Theory,* 77–103. New Haven, Conn.: Yale University Press.

Knoke, David. 1989. "Resource Acquisition and Allocation in U.S. National Associations." *International Social Movement Research* 2: 129–54.

Koopmans, Ruud. 1993. "The Dynamics of Protest Waves: West Germany, 1965 to 1989." *American Sociological Review* 58: 637–58.

Koopmans, Ruud, and Paul Statham. 1999. "Challenging the Liberal Nation State?

Postnationalism, Multiculturalism, and the Collective Claims-Making of Migrants and Ethnic Minorities in Britain and Germany." *American Journal of Sociology* 3: 652–96.

Kriesi, Hanspeter. 1996. "The Organizational Structure of New Social Movements in a Political Context." In *Comparative Perspectives on Social Movements,* edited by D. McAdam, J. D. McCarthy, and M. N. Zald, 152–184. New York: Cambridge University Press.

Kriesi, Hanspeter, Ruud Koopmans, Jan Willem Duyvendak, and Marco G. Giugni. 1995. *New Social Movements in Western Europe: A Comparative Analysis.* Minneapolis: University of Minnesota Press.

Marullo, Sam, R. Pagnucco, and J. Smith. 1996. "Frame Changes and Social Movement Contraction: U.S. Peace Movement Framing after the Cold War." *Sociological Inquiry* 66: 1–28.

McAdam, Doug. 1982. *Political Process and the Development of Black Insurgency.* Chicago: University of Chicago Press.

———. 1995. "'Initiator' and 'Spin-Off' Movements: Diffusion Processes in Protest Cycles." In *Repertoires and Cycles of Collective Action,* edited by M. Traugott, 217–39. Durham, N.C.: Duke University Press.

McCarthy, John D. 1996. "Constraints and Opportunities in Adopting, Adapting, and Inventing." In *Comparative Perspectives on Social Movements,* edited by D. McAdam, J. D. McCarthy, and M. N. Zald, 141–51. New York: Cambridge University Press.

McCarthy, John D., Mark Wolfson, David P. Baker, and Elaine Mosakawski. 1988. "The Founding of Social Movement Organizations: Local Citizens' Groups Opposing Drunken Driving." In *Ecological Models of Organization,* edited by G. Carroll, 71–84. Cambridge, Mass.: Ballinger.

McCarthy, John D., David W. Britt, and Mark Wolfson. 1991. "The Institutional Channelling of Social Movements by the State in the United States." *Research in Social Movements, Conflict, and Change* 13: 45–76.

McCarthy, John D., and Mark Wolfson. 1996. "Resource Mobilization by Local Social Movement Organizations: Agency, Strategy, and Organization in the Movement against Drinking and Driving." *American Sociological Review* 61: 1070–88.

McCarthy, John D., and Mayer N. Zald. 1973. *The Trend of Social Movements in America: Professionalization and Resource Mobilization.* New Brunswick, N.J.: Transaction Publishers.

———. 1977. "Resource Mobilization and Social Movements." *American Journal of Sociology* 82: 1212–41.

Meyer, David S., and Debra C. Minkoff. 1997. "Operationalizing Political Opportunity." Paper presented at the 1997 annual meeting of the American Sociological Association, Toronto, Canada.

Minkoff, Debra C. 1993. "The Organization of Survival." *Social Forces* 71: 887–908.

———. 1994. "From Service Provision to Institutional Advocacy: The Shifting Legitimacy of Organizational Forms." *Social Forces* 72: 943–69.

———. 1995. *Organizing for Equality: The Evolution of Women's and Racial Ethnic Organizations in America, 1955–1985.* New Brunswick, N.J.: Rutgers University Press.

———. 1997. "The Sequencing of Social Movements." *American Sociological Review* 62: 779–99.

———. 1999. "Bending with the Wind: Strategic Change and Adaptation by Women's and Racial Minority Organizations." *American Journal of Sociology* 6: 1666–1703.

Olzak, Susan, and Johan L. Olivier. 1998. "Comparative Event Analysis: Black Civil Rights Protest in South Africa and the United States." In *Acts of Dissent: New Developments in the Study of Protest,* edited by D. Rucht, R. Koopmans, and F. Neidhardt, 253–83. Berlin: Edition Sigma.

Rucht, Dieter. 1996. "The Impact of National Contexts on Social Movement Structures: A Cross-Movement and Cross-National Comparison." In *Comparative Perspectives on Social Movements,* edited by D. McAdam, J. D. McCarthy, and M. N. Zald, 185–204. New York: Cambridge University Press.

———. 1998. "The Structure and Culture of Collective Protest in Germany." In *The Social Movement Society: Contentious Politics for a New Century,* edited by D. Meyer and S. Tarrow, 29–58. New York: Rowman and Littlefield.

———. 1999. "Linking Organization and Mobilization: Michels's Iron Law of Oligarchy Reconsidered." *Mobilization* 4: 151–69.

Smith, Jackie. 1997. "Characteristics of the Modern Transnational Social Movement Sector." In *Transnational Social Movements and Global Politics: Solidarity beyond the State,* edited by J. Smith, C. Chatfield, and R. Pagnucco, 32–58. Syracuse, N.Y.: Syracuse University Press.

Staggenborg, Suzanne. 1991. *The Pro-Choice Movement.* New York: Oxford University Press.

Stinchcombe, Arthur. 1965. "Social Structure and Organizations." In *Handbook of Organizations,* edited by James March, 142–93. New York: Rand McNally.

Tarrow, Sidney. 1994. *Power in Movement: Social Movements, Collective Action and Politics.* New York: Cambridge University Press.

Tilly, Charles. 1978. *From Mobilization to Revolution.* New York: Random House.

Weed, Frank. 1991. "Organizational Mortality in the Anti-Drunk Driving Movement: Failure among Local MADD Chapters." *Social Forces* 69: 851–68.

Zald, Mayer N., and John D. McCarthy. 1980. "Social Movement Industries: Competition and Cooperation among Movement Organizations." *Research in Social Movements, Conflict and Change* 3: 1–20.

11

Comparative Politics and Social Movements

Donatella della Porta

The aim of this chapter is to discuss the problems and peculiarities of comparative politics as a method for the analysis of social movements. After a discussion of what comparative politics is, I present the principal methodological strategies and describe the underlying logic of the comparative method. Important issues include the formation of concepts, the number of cases, the use of time, and the choice of similar or different contexts. I conclude with a discussion of different perspectives in the field. Throughout, research on social movements will be the center of attention, providing illustrations of the main problems (and solutions) in the field.

What Is Comparative Politics?

Although considered to be the method most typically used by political scientists, comparative politics is not easy to define: many scholars agree that it is easier to state what the comparative method is *not* than what it is.[1] In a very wide perspective, comparison is viewed as the basis of any knowledge (Lasswell 1968: 3; Almond 1970: 254). That is to say, conceptualization necessitates comparing the reality we are interested in with something else. In this sense, any definition of social movements is comparative insofar as it builds boundaries between the phenomena we consider as social movements, and other phenomena such as interest groups, coalitions, or crowds (della Porta and Diani 1999: ch. 1). Any description of specific social movements as being radical or moderate, aggressive or tame, strong or weak requires comparison with other social movements in other times and places. For a definition of comparative politics, however, this all-encompassing understanding

286

of the concept is of little help. Many political scientists have in fact convincingly rejected the view that all research is comparative (Sartori 1990: 400) and have looked for more specific definitions of comparative politics.

Comparative politics is often defined as referring to a particular *field of study*: "the branch of political science concerned with comparing nations" (Verba 1991: 33).[2] In this sense, the comparative method responds to the need for "broadening the territorial scope and depth" of political information (Lasswell 1968: 3). It is "an attempt to develop concepts and generalizations at a level between what is true of all societies and what is true of one society in one point in time and space" (Bendix 1963: 532). We can see this broadening at work in social movement studies, where cross-national research has received more and more attention.

The Theory of Development and the First Wave of Cross-National Comparison

The field of comparative politics developed in the 1960s, together with the acknowledgment of "the accelerated interdependence of the world arena" (Lasswell 1968: 3). Increasing attention paid to comparative politics pushed political scientists to extend their range of interest from Western democracies to second- and third-world countries, shifting their concern from formal institutions to the real political processes. Theories of development dominated the field, with strong emphasis being placed on global comparison as a means of furthering the normative aim of bringing "Western-style" economic and political modernization to the underdeveloped countries.

Research on political violence in the 1960s reflected the search for invariant causes that can facilitate or thwart modernization. For instance, in his analysis of political violence in 114 polities between 1961 and 1965, Gurr (1968) explained the magnitude of civil strife in very different countries with the high level of discontent and frustration that, at the individual level, produces aggressive reactions. In a society, violence is likely to develop when there is widespread relative deprivation, defined as a perceived discrepancy between a person's value expectations (i.e., the goods and conditions of life to which people believe themselves to be rightfully entitled) and his or her value capabilities (i.e., the goods and conditions they think they are capable of attaining or maintaining). Relative deprivation spreads with all the structural conditions that increase levels of expectation without increasing capabilities: for instance, gains for other groups or a sudden disillusion. The political expression of such frustration is influenced by other societal conditions such as the cultural acceptance of aggression as a political means, the past success of political violence, and the degree of legitimation of the state as well as its capacity for repression. Economic dependence, discrimination, a low legitimation of the regime, and low levels of institutionalization—all elements that are typical of non-Western societies facilitated the explosion of frustration into political violence.

Decline and Reemergence of Cross-National Comparisons

It was the Vietnam War that first highlighted the dramatic consequences of intervention justified by the goal of "helping developing countries." The practical and political effects of such intervention were soon reflected in the work of scholars. In fact, as the 1970s progressed, scholars began to strongly criticize assumptions about a unique pattern of development in political and economic life based on the Western experience, and to attack the developmental approach for its "Cold War origins and overtones" (Wiarda 1991: 21). The effect was a decline in comparative studies in general that also affected the (then growing) field of social movements. With the reappraisal and gradual reappearance of cross-national comparison in the 1980s, global theories were abandoned along with the developmental approach, leaving space for various middle-range theories in different subfields of the discipline.

In the 1980s and 1990s social movement researchers also conducted many cross-national comparative studies, focusing predominately, however, on Europe and the United States. Among the first systematic comparisons of various countries were Nelkin and Pollack's (1981) work on the antinuclear movements in France and Germany; the study by Rochon (1988) on the peace movements in France, Great Britain, Germany, and the Netherlands; Joppke's (1993) analysis of the antinuclear movements in Germany and the United States; the research project directed by Flam (1994) on the antinuclear movements in Austria, Great Britain, the Netherlands, France, Sweden, Norway, and Italy; the analysis carried out by Rucht (1994) on the ecological and the environmental movements in France, Germany, and the United States; the study of new social movements in Germany, France, Switzerland, and the Netherlands developed by Kriesi and his collaborators (Kriesi et al. 1995); and my work on political violence in Italy and Germany (della Porta 1995). All these used the comparison of a limited number of national cases to describe the political opportunities for protest in the Western world. Moreover, they all focused on a certain type of movement: the so-called left-libertarian movements.

The Comparative Method

Recently, the awareness of the methodological peculiarity of comparative politics has increased, although comparativists still disagree on the logics behind the comparative method and, therefore, the type of knowledge comparative research should aim at.

One and the Same Logic

The comparative *method* has been defined as one of the scientific methods available to test hypotheses on the relations between two or more variables, keeping all potentially disturbing elements constant. As Smelser has authoritatively summarized,

> The process of gaining empirical control over sources of variation is clarified by referring to the distinction between causal conditions treated as parameters and causal conditions treated as operative variables. Parameters are conditions that are known or suspected to influence a dependent variable but, in the investigation at hand, are assumed or made not to vary. Operative variables are conditions that are known or suspected to influence the dependent variable and, in the investigation, are allowed or made to vary in order to assess this influence. By converting variables into parameters, most of the potentially operative conditions are made not to vary, so that the influence of one or a few conditions may be isolated and analyzed. (Smelser 1976: 154)

There are in fact three methods that perform, to various extents, the task of "converting variables into parameters": the experimental method, the statistical method, and the comparative method. In the *experimental* method, the conversion of variables into parameters is reached during the creation of data. Via experiments, we are able to test the effect of any changes in the values of an operative variable on the values of the other variables: in an experimental situation it is in fact possible to allow changes only in the variable on which we focus our attention. In this sense, as Lijphart (1971) stated, the method is very strong, offering robust criteria to choose between rival theories. Unfortunately, only a limited number of social phenomena can be investigated via experiments: while we can boil water as often as we want, we cannot produce riots to order.

The *statistical* method, based on the mathematical elaboration of empirically significant data (Lijphart 1971), approximates the experimental method by intervening after the data are created. Parameterization is here obtained via the mathematical manipulation of empirical evidence. We build subsamples in which potentially disturbing variables are kept constant, and calculate partial correlations between the two or more variables included in our hypotheses. Although the statistical method is weaker than the experimental method, it still provides good tests for eliminating rival theories. Its main problem is its need for large sample sizes: the higher the number of variables that potentially "disturb" the measuring of a correlation coefficient, the larger the number of cases we need in order to build subsamples large enough to be statistically significant. In social movement studies, the statistical method has been used to analyze individual political participation or protest events, but it has proved more difficult to apply to macro-units of analysis, such as nations.

Comparative politics provides an alternative to the statistical method in those research designs in which the number of cases is too small to allow for statistical manipulation. It supplements with *logical reasoning* the lack of a sufficient number of cases required for systematic tests via partial correlations. Dealing with a *small number of cases,* usually between two and twenty, the comparative method is a preferred strategy for political scientists when they investigate institutions or other macropolitical phenomena. Comparative politics is regarded as the only choice for testing hypotheses that apply to large units, such as countries, that by their very nature present too few cases for statistical analysis. Although the quality of control of the relationship between variables is low, it is often the *only* scientific method that is available for the study of the macrodimensional and institutional processes (Eisenstadt 1968).

In social movement studies, comparative analyses were used mainly to investigate the impact of national political characteristics or important historical changes on social movements (Tilly 1986; Tarrow 1989; Kriesi et al. 1995; della Porta 1995). Traditionally, social movement studies have been the domain of sociologists, and, not surprisingly, they hold a very central position in this field. But research on the kind of unconventional political participation associated with social movements also developed in political science, albeit more slowly. It was in the 1980s that the political preconditions of social movements, together with the political role they played, began to interest political scientists. Attention began to move toward the politics of social movements, and the comparative perspective also began to develop. While case studies and local research had been sufficient instruments for understanding the microdynamics of collective action, and opinion polls had allowed for statistical analysis on political participation, the use of the comparative method spread as attention begun to focus on the macroconditions for the development of protest and the effects of social movements on the political system.

For scholars such as Smelser and Lijphart, the logic of the comparative method is identical to that of the other two methods, "in that it attempts to develop explanations by the systematic manipulation of parameters and operative variables" (Smelser 1976: 158). The comparative method, like the other methods, aims at establishing general, empirical relations between two variables and testing them by keeping all the other variables constant (Lijphart 1971).[3] In this sense, comparative politics adopts the logic of the statistical method, adapting it to those situations in which complex phenomena are dealt with, but we lack the large number of cases necessary for a statistical analysis—the famous state of "many variables, small N" (Lijphart 1971: 686). The comparative method is used when the number of cases available is so small that cross-tabulation cannot be used to test hypotheses: "the comparative method resembles the statistical method in all respects except one. The crucial difference is that the number of cases it deals with is too small to permit systematic control by means of partial correlation" (Lijphart 1971: 684). Conversely, "as soon as the number of units becomes large enough to permit the use of statistical techniques, the line between the two is crossed" (Smelser 1976: 161).

According to this perspective, statistical methods are preferable when there are enough units to work with. For instance, the comparative method may be the only option if we want to test the effects of national institutions on protest strategies, but we might be able to use statistical techniques to assess their effects on local political opportunities. Statistical techniques were used, in fact, in one of the first pieces of research on the political opportunities of protest: Eisinger's (1973) study of the effects of local governments on the mobilization and success of urban social movements.

Durkheim versus Weber: Two Logics of Scientific Knowledge

The assimilation of statistical and comparative methods has not gone unchallenged. According to Ragin and Zaret (1983), there are two different logics in science, and these are reflected in the preference for either statistical or historical data. In statistical analyses, we look for concomitant variations in a variable-based design oriented toward building lawlike statements.[4] Collecting data on hundreds of riots in dozens of countries, for example, we may end up discovering that a sudden increase in unemployment increases the chances of people rioting. In line with Durkheim's approach, generalizations prevail over details. We are not interested in discovering to what extent the correlation holds in individual countries, or to which specific historical conditions it is related. Concomitant variation is used to single out permanent causes,[5] with no space given to plural causation: an effect cannot have different causes in different contexts. We measure, for instance, how strong the correlation is between growth in unemployment and frequency of rioting—not what are the historical characteristics of those countries in which that correlation does not hold. Adequate explanations have thus the form of "transhistorical propositions based on patterns observed in the widest possible populations of units" (Ragin and Zaret 1983: 739). In this perspective, scientific research should aim at discovering the causes that are present, always and everywhere, where there is political violence. The main aim is to construct the building of lawlike statements that hold true, no matter what the context.

Critics of this logic have stressed, however, the inadequacy of a method based on concomitant variations for research on macro-phenomena. Correlations are, in fact, only statistically probable. This brings about significant results when we are interested not in the specificity of single units of analysis but in the general pattern of correlation between two or more variables. In comparative politics, however, we often want to explain a certain phenomenon in its historical specificity: the knowledge of single units is considered as an important goal in itself (Ragin 1994). In this case, statistical correlation may be of little help. If we have a statistical analysis of the causes of, say, terrorism, and we try to explain terrorism in Italy on this basis, we may well end up with very little understanding of this specific case. We will have lost many intervening variables, and perhaps focused on factors that are not really relevant in that specific historical case, which may well be an exception to a statistically tested hypothesis.

If the units belonging to a statistical sample are "anonymous"—that is, we are not interested in Mr. X or Ms. Y—the comparison of macro-units requires us instead to take into account the historical specificity of the units under analysis. In a Weberian approach, the comparative method is inherently historical insofar as it tests empirical relationships between variables in different *systems*; the aim is an in-depth understanding of the context rather than establishing relationships between variables. A qualitative, historical comparison based on a case strategy "produces explanation and generalization, but unlike Durkheim's variable-based strategy, explanation is genetic, not functional, and generalizations are historically concrete, not abstractly ahistorical" (Ragin and Zaret 1983: 740).[6] This approach privileges, therefore, the understanding of specific contexts over the building of general lawlike statements.

The choice of the comparative method in the field of social movements is not a residual one: it was instead often justified by its capacity to go beyond descriptive statistic measures toward an in-depth understanding of historical processes. As Rucht (1994: 20) writes, explaining his choice for a cross-national comparison, "theory building in social science is historical. It remains linked to the spatial and temporal boundaries of its object of study.

Insofar as my research is concerned, it means that the interaction between modernization and social movements cannot be understood ahistorically." Most comparative studies in social movements do stress the historic peculiarity of each country, referring to the significance of path-dependency in the evolution of national political systems. The frequently mentioned effects of national prevailing strategies (Kriesi et al. 1995; Rucht 1994) or past experiences with authoritarian regimes (della Porta 1995; Flam 1994) on repertoires of collective actions point at the resilient effects of a national history dealing with contemporaneous movements.

Concepts in Comparative Politics

As a method, comparative politics is very sensitive to concept building; while statistical analyses can be inductive (at least to a certain extent), comparative analysis desperately needs theory. Dealing with complex, macrohistorical units, comparativists must reduce the number of variables to be kept under control as much as possible. Each variable that is introduced in the explanation forces us to multiply our number of cases in order to have at least one case for each value of that variable. For instance, if we want to check if violent repertoires are more common in countries with repressive traditions or in countries with liberal traditions, we may compare Italy as a country meeting the first characteristic and France as a case meeting the second one. If we think, however, that the type of governmental coalition also has an effect, we may start to think about including at least one country led solely by a socialist party, one country led by a socialist party in a coalition with the Greens, a country led by a nonsocialist left-wing party, a country with a coalition of socialist and Christian-democratic parties, a country led by a conservative party, one led by a Christian-democratic party, one led by a neoliberal party, and one led by a coalition including a radical-right party. Increasing the number of countries in order to account for all these possible differences is of course much more difficult than increasing the number of interviewees in a survey.

In cross-national comparison, the much needed simplification of the explanatory model can be done in two ways. One way is to aggregate cases by reducing the number of values on a single variable. For example, we might decide to differentiate only left-wing and right-wing governments. A second way is by theorizing, that is, by building the research design on previous theories so that only a few variables have to be checked each time. We may, for instance, focus our attention only on countries with a repressive tradition, and check what facilitated political violence in their historical evolution. A good research design is thus the first requirement "in order to be able to decide what, how and when to compare" (Pennings, Keman, and Kleinn 1999: 9).

Concepts That Travel

Theory, of course, needs concepts—that is, abstract ideas about objects belonging to the same class—and the problems involved in concept building are accentuated in comparative studies. In comparative politics, concept building is necessary primarily to single out the units of analysis. A main problem for a comparativist is in fact to define *what* is comparable, or, to put it better, *in what regard* two or more objects are comparable. As Sartori (1990: 402) warned us, to compare we need objects that are not identical but not too dissimilar either. If we want to investigate the effect of class on the political behavior of voters, we are usually fairly sure about who the voters are, but if we want to compare countries with an open opportunity structure and countries with a closed opportunity structure, we first need to clarify the concept of "political opportunity structure."

Good concepts are necessary to build hypotheses. In general, concepts are not true or false but rather more or less useful for understanding reality. In comparative politics, good concepts must be, as Sartori (1970: 18) put it, "able to travel," in particular, to travel beyond Western civilization. In fact, "social scientists who analyze only one country may proceed step by step, without structured hypotheses, building analytical categories as they go. Comparativists have no such freedom. They cannot advance without tools. Confronted with a variety of contexts, they are obliged to rely on abstractions, to master concepts general enough to cope with the diversity of the cases under consideration" (Dogan and Pelassy 1990: 3).

Comparativists aim to overcome ethnocentrism, improving the knowledge of one country by contrasting it with other cases. By helping to detect what is typical and what is not, comparison allows for the shift from description to explanation. However, the search for nonethnocentric concepts is not easy. Many of our concepts are developed within a single culture; they are useful in describing a specific situation but are less adaptable to other countries and cultures. One of the effects of this is that we may eventually place phenomena that do not belong together in the same class. We may arbitrarily extend the meaning of "locally-based" concepts, using them for phenomena that are "not-comparable"—we may, that is, *"stretch"* our concepts (Sartori 1970: 1034; 1971: 20), exporting concepts that have been created for domestic use. In this way, we end up with amorphous concepts that do not define empirical universals and cannot therefore be of use in the empirical verification of hypotheses. Alternatively, to avoid this stretching process, we may be tempted to build new concepts that are *all-encompassing* but empty of meaning. As Smelser pointed out, "The comparative investigator can thus be regarded as fighting a continuous struggle between the 'culture-boundness' of system-specific categories and the 'contentlessness' of system-inclusive categories" (1976: 178).

Concepts and Classification

To avoid these risks, Sartori has recommended using the following form of *classification*: proceeding *per genus et differentiam* (identity and difference, or inclusion and exclusion), concepts must be organized ("unpacked") into homogeneous groups and ranked at different levels of abstraction. Comparative knowledge requires the organization of concepts along so-called *scales of abstraction*, on which each gain in *extension* (or denotation)—that is, the range of phenomena covered—is paid for in terms of loss in *intention* (or connotation)—that is, the characteristics peculiar to a term. At the highest level of the scale, there are *universal concepts*, which may be used in any point in time and space; at the middle level, there are *general concepts*, with some capacity for generalization in middle-range theories and area studies; at the lowest level, there are *configurative concepts* proper to an ideographic knowledge.[7] Going up and down on the scale of abstraction, we can select the concepts at the right level of abstraction for our scientific purposes.

Concepts and Comparative Analysis of Social Movements

In the field of social movements, the development of cross-national comparison brought about a much-needed reflection on concepts. To be useful for scientific purposes, a concept has to be neutral and univocal, communicable and discriminating. This is rarely the case for the concepts used in social movement studies, which are often taken from current political debates. Cross-national research projects stimulated a conceptual dialogue that facilitated the meeting and merging of American and European traditions, which had initially proceeded along diverging paths in their conceptualization of social movements.

In Europe, research on social movements had developed within the tradition of research on the labor movement, which highlighted the role of an antagonistic class actor, carrying the vision and praxis of an alternative society. In the United States, social movement research grew out of a dominant pluralistic approach, which was interested in the way in which multiple interests and groups mobilized. Only with cross-national comparative studies on social movements did the need for a common understanding of the core concepts of the field of study emerge. A common definition developed of social movements as actors formed by networks of informal relationships, based on shared beliefs and solidarity, which are mobilized around conflictual issues through the frequent use of various forms of protest (della Porta and Diani 1999: ch. 1). In other words, comparative politics helped to shift concepts from the configurative to the general. Since, however, with few exceptions, the focus of social movement research remained on Western democracies, there was little development of any universal concepts. In fact, often the attempt to extend research on social movements to the "Second" and "Third" Worlds meets with serious definitional problems about what should and should not be included in the concept of social movements.

The Number of Cases

Unlike statistical analysis, where samples are usually random, in comparative politics the selection of cases requires the appreciation of their relevance for a specific set of hypotheses. Smelser lists five criteria that can guide our choice: units of analysis "must be [1] appropriate to the kind of theoretical problem posed by the investigator . . . [2] causally relevant to the phenomenon being studied . . . [3] empirically invariant with respect to their classificatory criterion . . . [4] reflect the degree of availability of data referring to this unit . . . [and 5] decisions to select and classify units of analysis should be based on standardized and repeatable procedures" (Smelser 1976: 174).

However, even with these specifications, comparative politics remains a very wide field, and many different strategies of comparison are available. First, we have different types of comparison as far as the *number of cases* is concerned, with obvious consequences for the degree of generalizability of the hypotheses.

Case Studies

The most intensive type of strategy is the *case study,* in which a single case is researched in depth. Although some scholars consider case studies noncomparative, others include them in the comparative approach if they are theoretically oriented; that is, case studies are in a sense comparative if they analyze in a single national case the validity of hypotheses developed for other national cases. In this way, case studies are useful in building knowledge of particular phenomena. When the research begins on a specific topic, case studies of instances where the phenomenon under investigation was particularly relevant may help to build up hypotheses on its causes, dynamics, and effects. Additional case studies may then increase our understanding by allowing hypotheses to be tested in various contexts. One particularly fruitful strategy is the investigation of so-called deviant cases, in which a hypothesis, confirmed in other cases, does not work. While the logic of statistical analysis is probabilistic, an important question for the comparative method is the number of exceptions necessary to falsify the hypothesis. Cases that do not fit a theory may be extremely useful for specifying under which conditions a hypothesis holds true and under which conditions it does not, that is, singling out the correct level of abstraction (or generalizability) for each hypothesis (Sartori 1984) and developing new hypotheses.

Paired Comparisons

To test the hypotheses developed through case studies, we usually want to compare more cases together. To do this, we can choose between paired and multilevel comparison. *Paired comparisons*—which usually involve two cases (binary comparison), but the same logic applies to comparisons of up to four cases—extend the range of applicability of the case study results. At the same time, they privilege a historical approach, providing "contrasted illustrations for a broad, encompassing theoretical reflection" (Dogan and Pelassy 1990: 127). A paired comparison allows us to test hypotheses that have arisen from single case studies, without losing the "thick description" of the units of analysis.

For instance, my research on terrorism in Italy led me to develop some hypotheses on the interaction between state strategies and movement strategies (della Porta 1990). However, many other hypotheses present in the literature related these phenomena with other characteristics of the Italian situation, such as its political culture and economic dualism. As a result, I decided to test my hypotheses by developing a research project on terrorism in another country, Germany, which had a different political culture and no strong economic differences across its territory (della Porta 1995). By comparing the two countries, I was able to provide an in-depth understanding of political developments during the past few decades. In work with other colleagues, I was then able to further test my hypotheses on clandestine groups by adding two additional cases, Japan and the United States (Zwerman, Stenhoff, and della Porta 2000). Dealing with four cases, we were still able to provide explanations that took the historical context into account but at the cost of a limited capacity for generalization. In other words, our explanations of left-wing terrorism in Italy, Germany, Japan, and the United States do not necessarily apply beyond capitalist democracies in a specific historical period.

Multicase Comparisons

Multicase comparisons—involving upwards of twenty to twenty-five cases—are stronger in generalization capacity. In the 1960s, such large-scale comparisons were prevalent. Increasing the number of cases was considered to be the best strategy for a more solid and rigorous control of causal relations.

However, multicase strategies have many shortcomings in cross-national comparison. First, by increasing the number of cases, we also increase the number of "third variables," that is, variables external to the hypothesis we want to control that can either reduce the reliability of the inference or impose a new increase in N (Morlino 1990: 387–88).[8] Moreover, the problem of measurement is particularly complex for cross-country and cross-time analyses. Working with many countries in a field in which few "hard data" are available enormously increases the risk of building on an insufficient knowledge of each country.[9] The choice of indicators is also complicated by the different criteria for collecting data in different countries as well as the different meanings of similar data in different cultures (Smelser 1976: 189).

Research in social movements indicates that even carefully designed cross-national surveys might, for example, end up with shaky evidence due to the difficulty of "translating" the same phrase in different languages. In the Eurobarometer's data on support for various types of movements, apparently basic concepts presented serious translation problems, since the same wording refers to different phenomena in different countries. For instance, the German word *Friedensbewegun* refers to a heterogeneous net of religious and political groups; its French translation, *mouvement pour la paix,* refers to an organization close to the communist party (Fuchs and Rucht 1992).

Number of Cases and Comparative Research on Social Movements

Because of the difficulties related to multicase comparisons, the most commonly used model in current comparative politics research is based on a small number of countries, often analyzed over long time periods. Correspondingly, there has been no increase in research based on large-scale comparison with statistical data (Collier 1990: 478, 487).[10] A growing interest in the interpretative social sciences pushed analysis toward "thick descriptions" of a few cases (Geertz 1973), aiming at "conjunctural causality," that is, causality linked to specific contexts (Ragin 1987). Today, most comparative research is designed so as to apply to a limited set of cases: "The more recent school of comparativists have contented themselves with a relatively middle-range or even low level of abstraction, in which the specificity of context become crucial determinants" (Mair 1996: 316).

A similar development can be found in the field of social movements. As mentioned, the search for global theories underpinned research on political violence in the 1960s, with multicase comparisons of countries from different regions in the world. This strategy produced poor results, however, since most of the available indicators of political violence are unreliable and not comparable. Later on, case studies produced an ideographic, noncumulative body of knowledge that was difficult to integrate into more general analyses because of the lack of a common theoretical framework. An intermediate approach did develop, however, between the (often unreliable) large-scale comparisons and idiosyncratic case studies. This occurred in the 1980s, when cross-national comparisons of two to four cases allowed more general hypotheses to be made, in particular on the role of political opportunities for movement choices. Thick descriptions of a few cases improved the understanding of the development of a limited type of social movement: the left-libertarian movements of the Western democracies in the 1970s and the 1980s. Together with theory building, much attention was given to the interpretation of specific historical phenomena.

Time and History in Comparative Politics

Another strategic choice also involved in the definition of the units of analysis is the use of time and temporal duration.

Cross-Time Comparison

Cross-national comparison can be either synchronic or diachronic: it may address either a single point in time or several such points in the history of a country. For example, case studies often analyze the development of some characteristics in a single unit over a certain time span (Bartolini 1993); comparison is then developed between single periods. Allowing for the parameterization of many variables, and an in-depth historical knowledge, *cross-time comparison within a single unit* offers many advantages for hypotheses building. The historical analyses of a single country are in fact usually "strong" in their development of hypotheses in new fields, insofar as they are able to keep under control—or at least offer knowledge about— a vast range of the independent variables that might intervene to "disturb" the testing of hypotheses. As well as taking into account the timing of some events, historical case studies may help to develop new hypotheses on the bases of an in-depth analysis of a single country.

What is true in a certain country (with a particular culture, social structure, model of economic development, and especially the configuration of many different variables) is not, however, necessarily true in others. *Cross-national diachronic studies* allow for a higher level of generalization to be reached, and specify the hypotheses developed in historical case studies. Additionally, in cross-national comparisons time can be used to increase the number of cases: by building periodizations, we can compare the case of country A in times Y and X with that of country B in times Y and Z. While increasing the number of countries has the disadvantage of increasing the number of variables to be kept under control, expanding the time span reduces that risk, allowing an in-depth historical knowledge of a few countries to be maintained.

For both diachronic case studies and diachronic cross-national comparisons, *periodization* allows cases to be singled out as temporal units. While spatial units are generally easy to detect, temporal units are not (Bartolini 1993). To understand how a variable changed in time, significant points in time need to be chosen and defined. Various periodizations might seem to be legitimate, but what is needed is a periodization that is significant according to our theoretical model. It should take into account the main changes in the dependent variable but cannot overlook the evolution of the other operative variables. Even in a single-country design, the need to take into account variables that have divergent timings may imply difficult choices between different periodizations. For instance, if I want to test the hypothesis that political violence increases when governments adopt exclusive strategies and no political allies are available for protestors, I can distinguish periods on the basis of (a) the degree of violence, (b) law-and-order policies adopted, and (c) the position of potential allies. The three periodizations do not necessarily overlap.

In cross-national designs, we have to deal with the additional problem of finding comparable periodizations in various countries; similar phases may well develop in different historical periods. For example, if we want to compare social movements during phases of transition and build a periodization based on the different steps in a transition to a new regime, we may have to choose different historical periods for different countries and thereby introduce a great deal of national variation.

Time as a Variable

An additional way to use time in comparative politics is to treat it as a *variable*: in this case we analyze processes and try to control for how timing influences the relationships between variables. These types of historical comparisons form the base of "grand theories of development," where the perspective is the illustration of large systemic changes (Bartolini 1993). In Rokkan's research, for instance, the timing of the different processes of nation building and industrialization influenced the evolution of the main social cleavages that have survived until today (Rokkan 1970). Sequences here acquire a central role: the timing of the various phases, steps, and thresholds involved in the pattern of political modernization is particularly illuminating for understanding democratization in various countries. The analyses of cycles, trends, processes, and dynamics all imply the use of time as a variable.

Time and Social Movements

In social movement studies, as in other fields, historical case studies provided path-breaking suggestions on movement dynamics that were then enriched by cross-country diachronic comparisons. This is the case, for instance, in Tarrow's research on the Italian protest cycle in the 1960s and the 1970s. Studying the Italian case between 1965 and 1975, Tarrow looked at the "forms of political actions and how these have evolved over time" (1989: 7). The focus on evolution over a long time span implied the need for highly desegregated data on the time variable; he therefore collected systematic information on protest events, as reported in one main daily newspaper. Using time as a variable, and looking at the daily number and form of protests, he developed the concept of the protest cycle. Though varying in dimension and duration, protest cycles have a number of common characteristics. They coincide with "a phase of heightened conflict and contention across the social system that includes: a rapid diffusion of collective action from more mobilized to less mobilized sectors; a quickened pace of innovation in the forms of contention; new or transformed collective action frames; a combination of organized and unorganized participation; and sequences of intensified interactions between challengers and authorities which can end in reform, repression and sometimes revolution" (Tarrow 1994: 153).

As in culture and the economy, there is a recurrent internal dynamic of ebb and flow in collective mobilization. By demonstrating the vulnerability of the authorities, the first movements to emerge lower the cost of collective action for other actors. In addition, the victories they obtain undermine the previous order of things, provoking countermobilization. The systematic collection of data on a daily basis allowed the changes of protest repertoires over time to be measured. Tarrow was able to observe that in the initial stages of protest the most disruptive tactics are often most prominent. The collective identities that are in the process of forming require radical action: new actors invent new tactics. As the cycle of protest is extended, the reaction of the authorities produces simultaneous processes of radicalization and institutionalization. The analysis of protest cycles is particularly useful for an understanding of the development of political violence—frequently one (though not the only nor the most important) of a protest's outcomes. The forms of violence used tend to vary according to the stage of the cycle.

The extent and characteristics of political violence in Italy in the 1960s and the 1970s were not, however, influenced only by cyclical dynamics: political violence was conditioned by various features of the national polity. Cross-national diachronic analysis was effective in singling out these characteristics.

I used this method in my comparative research on five periods of protest in Italy and Germany between the 1960s and the 1990s. By comparing the evolution of political violence in the two countries, I was able to identify some common processes, as well as the differences introduced by different external circumstances on internal dynamics. In particular, I described how small radical organizations espousing violence evolved within and then broke away from the larger, nonviolent social movement organizations. Exploiting environmental conditions conducive to militancy, these groups underwent further radicalization and eventually created new resources and occasions for violence. These radical groups, in other words, became agents, or entrepreneurs, for the propagation of violence. Like Tarrow's one-nation diachronic study of the Italian protest cycle, my cross-national diachronic comparison of escalation also aimed at describing a process. Comparing two countries over time, I was able to single out how internal dynamics interacted with external conditions. One example of this was that the timing of the trend of encapsulation was dependent on the environmental conditions that influenced the degree of isolation of the underground groups.

Most-Similar or Most-Different Design?

The degree of generalizability depends not only on the number of cases but also on the similarities and differences between them. Two different strategies are available: the "most-similar" system, and the "most-different" system designs.

Most-Similar Systems

Working with *similar countries* facilitates the so-called *ceteris paribus* rule; that is, it reduces the number of "disturbing" variables needing to be kept under control. In Lijphart's definition, the comparative method is "the method of testing hypothesized empirical relationships among variables on the basis of the same logic that guides the statistical method, but in which the cases are selected in such a way as to *maximize the variance of the independent variables and to minimize the variance of the control variables*" (1975: 164; emphasis added). Within a most-similar system design, we assume that the factors common to the countries sampled are irrelevant in explaining some observed differences, and focus, instead, on the sets of variables that are different.

Area studies, for example, deal with countries belonging to a common geographical area and sharing general historical traditions, geopolitical location, stage of economic development, and so on. One advantage of this grouping is that many variables are transformed into "parameters"; if we have more or less the same historical traditions, geopolitical location, stage of economic development, and so on, we can consider these characteristics as constant, and check the influence of other factors. Thus, general similarities allow the remaining differences to be better perceived (Dogan and Pelassy 1990: 134). Moreover, area studies have another advantage in that they reflect different bodies of knowledge, given that comparativists tend to specialize in particular geographical areas, such as western Europe, eastern Europe, or Latin America.

One disadvantage here, however, is that we cannot go beyond so-called middle-range theories, that is, theories that apply only to a restricted range of phenomena. Moreover, the comparison of similar cases leaves a risk of *overdetermination* (i.e., of including too many independent variables): "Although the number of differences among similar countries is limited, it will almost invariably be sufficiently large to 'overdetermine' the dependent phenomenon" (Przeworski and Teune 1970: 34). In fact, many variables may intervene, and we cannot control for their influence. As Dogan and Passy synthesized, "Never will the context of the compared situations be sufficiently similar to permit considering as null the influence of the environment; never will the researcher be in a position to validly exclude from his conclusions those contextual variables that he cannot keep constant" (1990: 16).

Most-Different Systems

By *maximizing the differences* between the cases, we may instead generalize beyond a restricted area, but at the cost of an increase in the number of independent variables that need to be kept under control. Przeworski and Teune (1970) noticed that a most-different system design allows for the checking of invariant correlations across countries. Confident that "human and social behavior can be explained in terms of general laws established by observation," Przeworski and Teune suggested looking for general statements that could be universally true (4).[11] The research strategy that can produce such statements is based "on random samples of the world population, regardless of the social systems to which individuals, groups, or subsystems belong" (7). In the most-different system design, the choice is in fact to sample *different* countries in order to "identify those independent variables, observed within systems, that do not violate the assumption of the homogeneity of the total population" (35).

The most-different system design usually privileges variables referring to the individual over those referring to the system. The assumption is that we have to look for correlations that apply "whenever and wherever" (Przeworski and Teune 1970: 17); consequently research on individual participation sampled individuals from different countries with the aim of finding common patterns. In line with the most-different system design is the classic research by Verba, Nie, and Kim (1978) on the impact of social inequalities on political participation in seven countries from the "First," "Second," and "Third" Worlds. The main focus of this study was to find an invariant relationship between political participation and social status, notwithstanding the type of political regime. Although focusing on Western democracies, some more recent survey-based cross-national studies on new forms of participation (such as Barnes et al. 1979; Inglehart 1977) also privilege the search for a common explanation of individual behavior over the analysis of historical or national specificity. The emphasis of this research is placed more on common patterns of post-materialist values and unconventional political participation than on cross-country differences.

Useful for investigating some of the microdynamics of participation, the most-different system design presents various shortcomings, however, when used to test causal correlations between variables. The most ambitious projects, aiming at explaining phenomena worldwide, risk ending with hypotheses that explain very little. As past attempts have shown, the hope for successful global theories is likely to be frustrated. For instance, the search to explain development once and for all led to explanations that "were too big to allow for accurate and satisfactory empirical work" (Verba 1991: 39). Similarly, the relative deprivation theory, based on the macrocomparison of a large number of different countries (most-different system design), was criticized when in-depth case studies indicated that grievances are always present in a society, but they are mobilized only when resources are available for the aggrieved groups. Currently, a widely shared assumption is that scientific theories of social change cannot go beyond processes that are situated in time and place (Boudon 1984).

Cycles of Research on Social Movements

In sum, the most-different design is used to obtain highly generalizable results, that is, to look for historically invariant correlations. The most-similar design instead looks for the specification of a hypothesis in other countries beyond that in which it has been developed.[12] Empirical research usually involves, however, different types of comparisons simultaneously, mixing the ideal types, although there is often an implicit or explicit preference for one design or the other.

Besides the individual preferences of the researcher, the various research designs tend to follow a certain order in the accumulation of knowledge about a certain phenomenon (Skocpol and Somers 1980). We can observe the presence of "research cycles" in which the comparative method is used, first, to generate hypotheses on the basis of systematic covariations in case studies; second, to specify these hypotheses in similar contexts; and, third, to test which hypotheses hold true in different contexts.

In the analysis of social movements, similar cycles—or, even better, spirals—of accumulation of knowledge can be seen in the development of the main hypotheses about political opportunities and cycles of protest. Turning first to the macrovariables that influence the evolution of protest repertoires, various studies have suggested that—besides the internal resources of the movement and the dynamics of the protest cycle—the most relevant variables to explain movement repertoires are to be found in the political process. In particular, the impact of political opportunities on single movements was observed in McAdam's research (1982) on Black insurgency, and Jenkins's work (1985) on the farmers' movement in the United States.

More fully developed in the research on the temporal evolution of protest actions, the concept of political opportunities referred mainly to the opening or closing of the political system, depending, in particular, on available alliances and the strength of opponents (McAdam 1982). Within a diachronic case study, Tarrow (1989) was able to specify the dynamics of the interaction between challengers and elites during the evolution of a protest cycle.

Applied to cross-national paired comparisons of social movements in a small number of countries, the concept of political opportunities started to take into account the role of specific institutions by looking at such variables as the degree of geographic centralization and functional differentiation of power. A comparison of movements' strategies in Germany, France, Switzerland, and Holland—and, in particular, the analysis of France as a deviant case—allowed Kriesi and his collaborators (Kriesi et al. 1995) to add on to the institutional aspects of the political opportunity structure some *informal* aspects. Comparing the women's and ecological movements in France, Germany, and the United States, Rucht (1994) specified the effects of political opportunities on different types of movements. Combining a diachronic design with a paired cross-national comparison of Italy and Germany, my research aimed at singling out the common dynamics of violent escalations, but also the way in which different opportunities are reflected in different repertoires of protest (della Porta 1995).

This research formed part of the tradition of area studies dealing with cases that were *similar* under many (social, economic, geographic) characteristics, and contrasting the cases in order to reflect on the differences in the national values of all the operative variables. This choice was conscious and explicit in many of the cross-national research projects on social movements.

To quote a few examples, Kriesi and his collaborators openly stated that "looking for differences between the mobilization patterns of Western European countries, [they] have adopted a 'most similar system design' which tries to control as large a number of explanatory variables as possible" (1995: xxii). Rucht (1994: 25) justifies his choice to compare Germany, France, and the United States with regard to the similarities in their economic, political, and sociocultural systems within the frame of a most-similar system design. I explained my selection of Italy and Germany as case studies with the fact that "the choice of similar countries—what comparative scholars define as the 'most-similar' context, as opposed to the 'most-different' context—allowed me to reduce the range of variables, although at the cost of a reduced range of applicability of the research results" (della Porta 1995: 15).

Focusing on Western democracies, these studies developed a number of hypotheses on the effects of the party system, interest representation, governmental institutions, and cultural traditions on forms of protest movements. In particular, they indicated that the more radical the movement strategy, the less assimilative the state strategy, and, conversely, the more moderate the movement strategy, the more assimilative the state strategy. These observations refer only to Western democracies; we do not know if the same explanatory model also applies in different contexts. In my research, the choice of two similar cases allowed me to reduce the range of variables but at the cost of a reduced range of applicability of the research results. My cross-national and historical approach lends itself to a middle-range level of generalization. It could not, for example, reach conclusions as to the causes and dynamics of all the different forms of political violence, or even of some forms of political violence. The research design did, however, avoid the complications inherent in any attempt to compare very diverse forms of violence and very different external contexts. It thus allowed some conclusions to be reached on at least one particular, historically defined form of political violence: the ideologically based violence connected with the development of new types of social movements in the late 1960s and 1970s.[13]

A more recent research project is based on another strategy. In their *Dynamics of Contention,* McAdam, Tarrow, and Tilly (2001) apply a most-*different* design to paired comparisons in order to look not for correlations between variables but for common mechanisms. The analysis of "most-different" countries and historical periods aims to avoid mistaking historically specific features of Western polities for general features of contention and checks the possibility of extending concepts and explanations across distinctively different political settings without distorting those settings (ch. 1).

This kind of strategy allows us to check if processes observed in contemporary Western democracies are also at work in other geographic areas and historical periods.

Comparing Social Movements: Some Perspectives

I have, up to this point, discussed the advantages and difficulties of the comparative method and its various strategies. Regarding the advantages of comparison for the building of scientific knowledge, we can state, with Dogan and Pelassy, that "by enlarging the field of observation, the comparativist searches for rules and tries to bring to light the general causes of social phenomena" (1990: 3). We can add that not only is the comparative method often the only one available for the analysis of macro, political phenomena, but also that comparative analysis allows us to shift from merely singling out a statistical correlation toward understanding more clearly the causality and meaning of a certain situation for the actors involved.

As for the difficulties, the comparative method is—as already mentioned—weak in the test of rival theories. It has been stated that "comparison is strongest as a choosing and provoking, not a proving, device: a system for questioning, not for answering" (Stretton 1969: 247). Many methodological problems that are proper to empirical research—such as concept building, choosing indicators, finding reliable sources—are exponentially multiplied when we work with various countries and cultures. This said, we can conclude with Tilly that due to the difficulties inherent in cross-national or cross-time comparison (in the comparison of "big structures" and "large processes"), we should learn to live with solutions that are far from perfect:

> No one would take the rules to require a search for the perfect pair of structures or processes: exquisitely matched on every variable except the purported cause and the supposed effect. Nor should anyone take them to require the pursuit of final causes; we should be delighted to discover the proximate causes of social phenomena. Nor do the rules forbid us to seek principles of covariation beginning "in so far as . . .". Nor, finally, do they demand complete explanations—explanations leaving no ounce of variance unaccounted for. The rules enjoin us to examine apparent covariation with high seriousness and to eliminate spurious causes with great ruthlessness. (Tilly 1984: 80)

As for the future, social movement studies seem to reflect some general tendencies noticed in the general field of comparative studies. First, in social movements as in other areas, a renewed attention is given to institutions, and, in particular, to their effects. While the global developmental approach had shifted attention away from these, the revival of small-N comparison and of middle-range theorization has helped to bring the historical context back:

> For once comparisons become more limited in scope, whether by restricting the focus to one region, or to a small number of cases, it becomes possible to bring into play a degree of conceptual specificity and intensiveness which is simply not feasible at the level of global, all-embracing comparisons. In other words, institutions and the state come back in not only because they are seen to be more important per se, but also because the lower levels of abstraction involved have allowed them to come back in, and have created the room for this type of grounded analysis. (Mair 1996: 315)

Since the 1980s, analysts have increasingly employed comparative methods to address questions dealing with the economic aspects of politics, the international context, interest groups, state structures and performances, and nationalism and ethnic cleavages (Rogowski 1993: 320). In general, attention has shifted from the causes of political phenomena to their consequences: "Comparative political inquiries are now much more likely than before to ask about the differences which politics makes, rather than to ask what makes politics different" (Mair 1996: 322). In social movement research, these trends are reflected in the growing attention to the effects of social movements on policy making and policy implementation (Giugni, McAdam, and Tilly 1999), the role of social movements in a globalizing world (della Porta, Kriesi, and Rucht 1999), the action of movement organizations as interest groups (via lobbying or concertation), and the development of movement politics beyond the "left-libertarian family."

Together with trends of attention, challenges also migrate from the general field of comparative politics to comparative social movements. In recent years there has been an increasing compartmentalization of comparativists into autonomous groups: "For not only has the growth of the discipline acted to cut regional specialists off from one another, but, even within the different regions, it has also tended to foster the self-sufficiency of specialist fields, each with its own narrow network and its own set of journals . . . " (Mair 1996: 318). The risk that social movement comparisons are developing in isolation from the other fields of comparative politics, "talking" only to social movement specialists, must be overcome if we want to introduce new ideas in the field.

Another challenge comparativists face refers to the choice of geographical units. While the nation-state still plays an important role in defining the political opportunities available for social movements, the levels of cross-national diffusion have increased enormously along with the role of transnational networks (della Porta and Kriesi 1999). Thus, although cross-national comparison becomes more important then ever in these circumstances, what is open to discussion is the extent to which nations are still meaningful units of analysis.[14]

Notes

I wish to thank Sidney Tarrow and the editors of this volume for their useful comments on an earlier version of this chapter.

1. Comparative politics "is not merely a vague perspective on a certain subject matter or a special set of substantive concerns; nor is it synonymous with the scientific method in general; nor is it merely a method of measurement" (Lijphart 1975: 159).

2. In the United States "comparative politics has traditionally been thought of as one of the major fields in political science. The other fields are American politics, political theory, public administration, international relations, public law and state and local government" (Wiarda 1991: 3).

3. According to Sartori (1971: 8), "comparison is a control method of generalizations, previsions or laws in the form of 'if . . . then'"; it can be used in cases in which stronger methods are not available.

4. A lawlike statement is "a generalization, with explicative power, that captures a regularity" (Sartori 1990: 399).

5. In Durkheim's approach (1964), inductive reasoning on empirical data aims at reconstructing the different species of social phenomena, and the systemic needs of each species explain the concomitant variations.

6. The interest in historical differences is implicit in the construction of ideal types oriented at generalization about historical divergence (Weber 1949). As Ragin and Zaret noticed, "Ideal types thus occupy a middle ground between the uniqueness of historical events and the generality of laws. . . . Central to this methodological strategy is Weber's conviction that social reality is sufficiently complex as to be unknowable in the absence of theoretical interests that guide construction of one-sided type concepts" (Ragin and Zaret 1983: 731–32).

7. In a similar vein, Tilly distinguished a world-historical level, referring to the property of an era; a world-systemic level, dealing with the largest sets of strongly interdependent social structures; a macrohistorical level, at which "we seek to account for particular big structures and large processes and to chart their alternate forms" (1984: 61); and a microhistorical level, looking at the way in which individuals experience these big structures and large processes.

8. The inclusion of historical trends and the extension of the analysis to subnational regions are strategies used to increase the number of cases without overly expanding the number of variables.

9. In fact, there is a clear problem concerning "the reliability of the various measures and indicators which are used in order to translate national experiences into comparable operational categories, a problem which has become even more pronounced as scholars have attempted to build into their analyses measures of variation in political institutions and political structures" (Mair 1996: 325).

10. This trend was also stimulated by new statistical techniques that are better suited to the analysis of comparative politics (with small Ns), because they reduce the impact of deviant cases and allow for simulations that increase the number of cases artificially (Collier 1990: 495).

11. As Przeworski and Teune state, "If all relevant factors were known, then the same multivariate statement would yell a deterministic explanation regardless of time and place" (1970: 7).

12. Tilly (1984: 81) noticed, however, that we may have other choices. Macro-historical analysis has been, and continues to be, pursued in different ways: by looking for single or multiple forms of a phenomenon, and by trying to explain one, a few, many, or all cases. Among the studies that privilege the search for a single form, *individualizing* comparisons single out the uniqueness of each case, while *universalizing* comparisons look for properties shared by all instances of a phenomenon (Tilly 1984: 81). Other studies identify multiple forms of a phenomenon, either to explain, in an *encompassing* way, a single instance, or by *finding variations* between all instances.

13. Recently, McAdam and Sewell (2001) have reflected on the events that mediate long-term processes of change and cycles of contention.

14. In fact, an increasingly used alternative is to dissolve countries into particular systems according to specific variables (Mair 1996).

References

Almond, Gabriel. 1970. *Political Development: Essays in Heuristic Theory.* Boston: Little, Brown and Co.

Barnes, Samuel, et al. 1979. *Political Action: Mass Participations in Five Democracies.* London: Sage.

Bartolini, Stefano. 1993. "On Time and Comparative Research." *Journal of Theoretical Politics* 5: 131–67.

Bendix, Reinhard. 1963. "Concepts and Generalizations in Comparative Sociological Studies." *American Sociological Review* 28: 532–38.

Boudon, Raymond. 1984. *La place du désordre.* Paris: PUF.

Collier, David. 1990. "Il metodo comparato: Due decenni di mutamento." *Rivista Italiana di Scienza Politica* 20: 477–504.

Daalder, Hans. 1993. "The Development of Study of Comparative Politics." In

Comparative Politics, edited by Hans Keman, 11–30. Amsterdam: Free University Press.

della Porta, Donatella. 1990. *Il terrorismo di sinistra.* Bologna: Il Mulino.

———. 1995. *Social Movements, Political Violence and the State.* New York: Cambridge University Press.

della Porta, Donatella, and Mario Diani. 1999. *Social Movements.* Oxford: Blackwell.

della Porta, Donatella, and Hanspeter Kriesi. 1999. "Social Movements in a Globalizing World: An Introduction." In *Social Movements in a Globalizing World,* edited by Donatella della Porta, Hanspeter Kriesi, and Dieter Rucht, 3–22. London: Macmillan.

della Porta, Donatella, Hanspeter Kriesi, and Dieter Rucht, eds. 1999. *Social Movements in a Globalizing World.* London: Macmillan.

Dogan, Mattei, and Dominique Pelassy. 1990. *How to Compare Nations.* 2d ed. Chatham, N.J.: Chatham House.

Durkheim, Emil. 1964. *The Rules of the Sociological Method.* New York: Free Press.

Eisenstadt, Samuel N. 1968. "Comparative Study." In *International Encyclopedia of the Social Sciences,* edited by David L. Sills. New York: Macmillan.

Eisinger, Peter. 1973. "The Conditions of Protest Behavior in American Cities." *American Political Science Review* 67: 11–28.

Flam, Helena, ed. 1994. *States and Antinuclear Movements.* Edinburgh: Edinburgh University Press.

Fuchs, Dieter, and Dieter Rucht. 1992. *Support for New Social Movements in Five Western European Countries.* Discussion Paper FS III 92-102. Wissenschaftszentrum Berlin.

Geertz, Clifford. 1973. *The Interpretation of Cultures.* New York: Basic Books.

Giugni, Marco, Doug McAdam, and Charles Tilly, eds. 1999. *How Movements Matter.* New York: Rowman and Littlefield.

Gurr, Ted. 1968, "A Causal Model of Civil Strife: A Comparative Analysis Using New Indices." *American Political Science Review* 62: 1104–24.

Inglehart, Ronald. 1977. *The Silent Revolution: Changing Values and Political Styles among Western Publics.* Princeton: Princeton University Press.

Jenkins, Craig J. 1985. *The Politics of Insurgency: The Farm Worker Movement in the 1960s.* New York: Columbia University Press.

Joppke, Christian. 1993. *Mobilizing against Nuclear Energy: A Comparison of Germany and the United States.* Berkeley: University of California Press.

King, Gary, Robert O. Keohane, and Sidney Verba. 1994. *Designing Social Inquiry: Scientific Inference in Qualitative Research.* Princeton: Princeton University Press.

Kriesi, Hanspeter, Ruud Koopmans, Jan-Willem Duyvendak, Marco Giugni, and Hein-Anton van der Heijden. 1995. *New Social Movements in Western Europe.* Minneapolis: University of Minnesota Press.

Lasswell, Harold D. 1968. "The Future of the Comparative Method." *Comparative Politics* 1: 3–18.

Lijphart, Arendt. 1971. "Comparative Politics and the Comparative Method." *American Political Science Review* 65: 682–93.

———. 1975. "The Comparable-Case Strategy in Comparative Research." *Comparative Political Studies* 8: 158–77.

Mair, Peter. 1996. "Comparative Politics: An Overview." In *A New Handbook of Political Science,* edited by Robert E. Goodin and Hans-Dieter Klingemann, 309–35. Oxford: Oxford University Press.

McAdam, Doug. 1982. *Political Process and the Development of Black Insurgency: 1930–1970.* Chicago: University of Chicago Press.

McAdam, Doug, and William H. Sewell Jr. 2001. "Temporality in the Study of Social Movements and Revolutions." In *Silence and Voice in the Study of Contentious Politics.* New York: Cambridge University Press.

McAdam, Doug, Sidney Tarrow, and Charles Tilly. 2001. *Dynamics of Contention.* New York: Cambridge University Press.

Morlino, Leonardo. 1990. "Problemi e scelte nella comparazione." *Rivista Italiana di Scienza Politica* 20: 381–96.

Nelkin, Dorothy, and Michael Pollak. 1981. *The Atom Besieged. Extraparliamentary Dissent in France and Germany.* Cambridge, Mass.: MIT Press.

Pennings, Paul, Hans Keman, and Jan Kleinn. 1999. *Doing Research in Political Science: An Introduction to Comparative Methods and Statistics.* London: Sage.

Przeworski, A., and H. Teune. 1970. *The Logic of Comparative Social Inquiry.* New York: John Wiley.

Ragin, Charles. 1987. *The Comparative Method.* Berkeley: University of California Press.

———. 1994. *Constructing Social Research.* Thousand Oaks, Calif.: Pine Forge Press.

Ragin, Charles, and David Zaret. 1983. "Theory and Method in Comparative Research: Two Strategies." *Social Forces* 63: 731–54.

Rochon, Thomas R. 1988. *Mobilizing for Peace: The Antinuclear Movements in Western Europe.* Princeton: Princeton University Press.

Rogowski, R. 1993. "Comparative Politics." In *Political Science: The State of the Discipline,* edited by A. W. Finer, 431–40. Washington D.C.: American Political Science Association.

Rokkan, Stein. 1970. *Citizens, Elections, Parties.* Oslo: Universitetsforlaget.

Rucht, Dieter. 1994. *Modernizierung und Soziale Bewegungen.* Frankfurt am Main: Campus.

Sartori, Giovanni. 1970. "Concept Misformation in Comparative Politics." *American Political Science Review* 64: 1033–53.

———. 1971. "La politica comparata: premesse e problemi." *Rivista Italiana di Scienza Politica* 1: 7–66.

———. 1984. "Guidelines for Concept Analysis." In *Social Science Concepts: A Systematic Analysis,* edited by Giovanni Sartori, 15–85. Beverly Hills, Calif.: Sage.

———. 1990. "Comparazione e metodo comparato." *Rivista Italiana di Scienza Politica* 20: 397–416.

Skocpol, Theda, and Margaret Somers. 1980. "The Uses of Comparative History in Macrosocial Inquiry." *Comparative Studies in Society and History* 12: 174–97.

Smelser, Neil J. 1973, "The Methodology of Comparative Analysis." In *Comparative Research Methods,* edited by D. Warwick and S. Osherson. Englewood Cliffs, N.J.: Prentice Hall.

———. 1976. *Comparative Methods in the Social Sciences.* Englewood Cliffs, N.J.: Prentice-Hall.

Stretton, H. 1969. *The Political Sciences: General Principles of Selection in Social Sciences and History.* London: Routledge and Kegan Paul.

Tarrow, Sidney. 1989. *Democracy and Disorder: Protest and Politics in Italy, 1965–1975.* Oxford: Clarendon Press.

———. 1994. *Power in Movements.* New York: Cambridge University Press.

Tilly, Charles. 1984. *Big Structures, Large Processes, Huge Comparisons.* New York: Russell Sage Foundation.

———. 1986. *The Contentious French.* Cambridge: Harvard University Press.

Verba, Sidney. 1991. "Comparative Politics: Where Have We Been, Where Are We Going." In *New Directions in Comparative Politics,* edited by Howard J. Wiarda, 31–42. Rev. ed. Boulder, Colo.: Westview Press.

Verba, Sidney, Norman H. Nie, and Jae-on Kim. 1978. *Participation and Political Equality.* New York: Cambridge University Press.

Weber, Max. 1949. *The Methodology of the Social Sciences.* New York: Free Press.

Wiarda, Howard J. 1991. "Comparative Politics: Past and Present." In *New Directions in Comparative Politics,* edited by Howard J. Wiarda, 3–30. Rev. ed. Boulder, Colo.: Westview Press.

Zwerman, Gilda, Patricia G. Steinhoff, and Donatella della Porta. 2000. "Disappearing Social Movements: Clandestinity in the Cycle of New Left Protest in the U.S., Japan, Germany and Italy." *Mobilization* 5: 85–104.

Conclusion: Blending Methods and Building Theories in Social Movement Research

Bert Klandermans, Suzanne Staggenborg, and Sidney Tarrow

Social movement researchers have built an impressive body of work by using a battery of methods to conduct theoretically informed research. In this concluding chapter, we examine the processes through which social movement theory has advanced, discuss some issues of controversy, assess the field's strengths and challenges, and explore some areas of potential expansion. In what follows, although we draw on the chapters in this volume, our focus is on the process of blending methods and building theories rather than on specific methods or findings.

The successes of social movement research during the past two decades are not easy to summarize; they emerge from mutually reinforcing theory and substantive research. Social movement scholars have continued to produce theoretical essays containing new ways of conceptualizing movement phenomena and new testable propositions (e.g., Zald and Ash 1966; McCarthy and Zald 1973, 1977; Meyer and Staggenborg 1996; Amenta and Young 1999). They have consistently conducted empirical research informed by theory, using a range of methods, and employed their findings to test and develop new theoretical ideas. They have meaningfully synthesized the theoretical and empirical work in the area (e.g., Buechler 2000; Klandermans 1997; McAdam, McCarthy, and Zald, 1988, 1996; Melucci 1996; Tarrow 1998; Tilly 1978). And they have begun to extend the insights of social movement research into broader areas of contentious politics (Aminzade et al. 2001; Goldstone 1998; McAdam, Tarrow, and Tilly 2001). We turn to these extensions of social movement research in a later section.

Where social movement theory falls short, it is not for lack of adequate

methods but because theoretical ideas have yet to develop in ways that encourage innovative empirical research. For example, many scholars have
called for cultural approaches to social movements, but these remain more at
the level of rousing calls to action than empirical achievements. And, although there are a few valiant efforts in this direction, systematic work on
social movements outside Western democracies is still relatively rare.[1] Moreover, theoretical syntheses capable of stimulating exciting new research are
lacking for many topics, although promising efforts are under way (Aminzade
et al. 2001; McAdam, Tarrow, and Tilly 2001; Snow, Soule, and Kriesi forthcoming). Such syntheses are critical in underdeveloped areas of research, but
they are also important to further advances in areas on which considerable
progress has already been made. We begin our survey with the sources of the
robustness of social movement research, illustrate them in three areas of research, move from there to some current challenges and lacunae, and close
by outlining some opportunities for expanding social movement research.

The Art of Social Movement Research

We use the term *art* of social movement research, not because we think such
research is unsystematic, unscientific, or literary, but because we think systematic, social-scientific work is, in fact, creative. The enterprise's successes
during the past few decades are the result of an artful convergence of numerous factors rather than a single method or approach: the intersection of multiple methods, an emphasis on middle-range theory, the infusion of new
ideas from the "real world" of social movements and from cognate fields, a
growing reliance on comparative methods, and an avoidance of the epistemological wars that have wounded other areas of research. Instead, the field
has proceeded through a dialectical process of what we call *contained contention,* which has encouraged scholars to use a variety of methods, build on
one another's research findings, and constructively criticize each other's theoretical perspectives.

Arraying Multiple Methods

As the contributions to this volume make eloquently clear, a major advantage of social movement research has been the use of multiple methods.
Some scholars have not hesitated to employ several methods within single
studies, though this is demanding and expensive in time and resources.
Others employ new methods to study the same phenomena previously studied with different methods. Overall, movement scholars have built on one
another's work regardless of the methods employed, which sometimes im-
pairs the certainty of research results but increases their range considerably.

Whether in a single study or in different studies of the same phenomenon, triangulation of methods ultimately produces stronger theories than multiple replications and permutations of the same method. Indeed, the essays in this book show how widely varying methods can converge on a range of research problems.

All methods have advantages and disadvantages, and a careful combining of methods intended to offset the disadvantages of one another is highly desirable (Brewer and Hunter 1989). For example, a survey can provide generalizable information, while in-depth interviews or focus groups can supplement such data by showing the processes or mechanisms behind respondents' beliefs and actions. Combinations of qualitative methods, such as documentary analysis, participant observation, and in-depth interviews, are probably most common, although some researchers have also combined quantitative and qualitative methods, such as surveys and in-depth interviews, or quantitative records and archival information on contentious politics.

Studies that employ multiple methods, including qualitative and quantitative ones, suggest that there are considerable benefits of doing so. Banaszak's (1996) multi-method study used quantitative measures to show "objective" political opportunities and resources, and qualitative methods to demonstrate "subjective" perceptions and rationales for strategies. Lichterman's (1996) survey of activists from the antitoxics movement and the Greens established differences in class background, education, and lifestyle between the two groups, while his extensive participant observation and in-depth interviews showed how these differences translate into distinct styles of political activism. In her study of the Coalition of Labor Union Women, Roth (1997, 2000) used a variety of qualitative and quantitative methods, including life-history interviews, participant observation, and a survey of members. Based on the interviews, she developed a membership typology, which she used in analyzing the survey results.

Should qualitative researchers strive to replicate the analytical logic of their quantitative colleagues, as one influential study argues (Keohane, King, and Verba 1995)? Although few would argue against analytical rigor, replicability, and the search for robust processes, it seems reductive to hold all forms of research to the standards of the most cutting-edge quantitative methods. (Indeed, as the past few decades have shown, what one generation of quantitative researchers considers "cutting-edge" tends to dull its edge as more sophisticated methods develop!)

Consider the interactive influence of two studies in the 1970s: Gamson's *Strategy of Social Protest* (1990 [1975]) and Piven and Cloward's *Poor People's Movements* (1977), the first largely quantitative, and the second qualitative.

How much would we know today about the impact of social movement activity had we held Piven and Cloward's case-study methodology to quantitative standards of evidence or read Gamson's book as a series of case studies? Different forms of evidence triangulating on a similar set of theoretical problems have taken us further than even a large number of replications of either one methodology or the other.

Emphasizing Middle-Range Theory

The process of theory building in the social movement area is, of course, similar to that in other areas of social science. Although a comparison of social movement research with other areas of social scientific research is beyond the scope of this chapter, our discussion of the theoretical and methodological reasons for the successes and shortcomings of social movement theory is relevant to a general understanding of the art of doing scholarly work (see Alford 1998). We see the best theories built by synthesizing arguments from different perspectives, making connections between different levels of analysis, and using a variety of methods and data.

Good social theory in any substantive area needs to avoid the pitfalls of grand theory on the one hand, and abstracted empiricism on the other (Mills 1959). A strategy of middle-range theorizing (Merton 1968; Pawson 2000) allows researchers to engage in theory-driven empirical research that identifies causal mechanisms operating within particular social contexts to explain processes such as movement mobilization. While such theory is limited in scope, research at different levels of analysis and in different historical contexts can be compared and connected to develop a more integrated theory of phenomena, such as contentious action (see McAdam, Tarrow, and Tilly 2001).

In the social movement domain, we are hard pressed to come up with examples of either grand theory or abstracted empiricism. Some European scholars who started with a tendency toward abstract theorizing made their theories more concrete as they "were forced to focus on political institutions" (see McAdam, Tarrow, and Tilly 1997: 145). At the other extreme, there are largely descriptive case studies and atheoretical survey analyses of movement support, but these are the exception rather than the rule. In our section "Advances in Social Movement Research," we present what we see as successful examples of middle-range theorizing from research on the impacts of organizational structures in social movements, movement recruitment and participation, and movement trajectories.

If social movement scholarship has largely avoided both grand theory and abstracted empiricism, why is this the case? Social movement theory had the advantage of expanding at a time—post-1968—when middle-range theorizing had gained popularity in the social sciences as a result of the work of theorists like Mills and Merton. Seminal works in the 1970s focused on social movements as a fairly delimited phenomenon that lent itself more to middle-range theorizing than to the grand theories aimed at political and social systems. The result was that most scholars who entered this area were both animated by theory and in touch with concrete manifestations of social movement activity.

Infusions from Social Movements and Cognate Research Areas

Many scholars entered the field of social movement studies from careers of activism, armed with concrete knowledge of movement tactics and organizations and looking for ways of making sense of their experiences. The largest such infusion, of course, came in the wake of the civil rights, student, women's, environmental, and peace movements in the 1960s in both Western Europe and North America. The ongoing presence of the last three movements, notably the women's movement, nourished social movement research on both continents through the 1970s and 1980s. To a much greater degree than in related areas, like voting and interest group behavior, social movement scholars knew and shared the concerns of those they studied. This experience helped scholars gain access to movement activists and aided them in asking penetrating questions regarding movement organizations.

Important infusions also came from the cognate area of organizational analysis in the form of resource mobilization theory, notably the work of McCarthy and Zald, which specified units of analysis (e.g., social movement organizations) that were amenable to middle-range empirical research. Although McCarthy and Zald have recently joined others in stressing the need to broaden our conceptualization of social movements (e.g., McCarthy 1996; Zald 2000), a focus on organizations has encouraged a great deal of theoretically informed empirical work, including case studies of social movement organizations and studies of organizational and interorganizational dynamics (e.g., Gamson 1990; Jenkins 1985; Kleidman 1993; Minkoff 1995; Morris 1984; Rupp and Taylor 1987; Staggenborg 1991; Walsh 1988; Zald and McCarthy 1987).

Social movement theory has been enriched from other directions too, in some cases bringing together theories from different disciplines and in other cases bringing together theories from distinct areas within the same discipline (Tarrow 2001). This infusion of "other voices" from different areas and disciplines has been critical to the growth of social movement research, laying the groundwork for theoretical linkages among micro, meso, and macro levels of analysis. For example, the new "history from below" from British social historians like Hobsbawm (1959), Rudé (1964), and Thompson (1966) was an inspiration in the work of many social movement scholars. Tilly (1978) and his collaborators (Shorter and Tilly 1974; Snyder and Tilly 1972; Tilly, Tilly, and Tilly 1975) then connected the study of collective action to the larger study of political processes in a way that avoided abstract generalizations by focusing on the concrete actions of collective actors and their interactions with authorities. Later theorists (e.g., Gamson 1992a; Klandermans 1997) transported insights from social psychology to social movement theory in ways that made theoretical connections to larger organizational, cultural, and political processes. Granovetter (1973), Gould (1995), and Diani (1995) brought insights from network theory to the social movement domain, allowing for connections between individual and organizational levels of analysis. More recently, scholars have connected social movement theory to areas such as space and social geography (Miller 2000; Sewell 2001), emotions (Aminzade and McAdam 2001), temporality (McAdam and Sewell 2001), and institutional theory (Raeburn, forthcoming).

Comparing Movements

When two of the authors of this chapter collaborated in a collective volume on comparing social movements in the mid-1980s (Klandermans, Kriesi, and Tarrow 1988), there were precious few studies of social movements that crossed borders. This omission was in part the result of distinct research traditions (e.g., the American "collective behavior" approach left little trace among Western European scholars of the 1950s and 1960s, many of whom came out of a Marxian tradition). It was also a perverse result of the fact that many movement scholars experienced in the particular movements of their countries were indifferent to or ignorant of movements elsewhere. And it was in part a result of the absence of international connections within social movements—with the partial exception of organized labor, whose members were brought together internationally in a variety of venues, but which had essentially ceased to act as a social movement.

The two decades between the late 1960s and the late 1980s reversed each of these conditions:

- Research traditions were converging, as American scholars developed new organizational and political approaches to social movements, and Europeans moved beyond a sterile Marxism that had its feet so solidly planted in macrostructural conditions that little attention remained for movement dynamics.

- Movements themselves were converging, from the informal interactions among student militants from different countries to the organized collaboration of the peace, environmental, and women's movements.
- Scholars from these countries also began to interact and spend periods of time researching and teaching in one another's countries.
- As we have seen in previous chapters of this volume, methodological advances in protest event analysis (see Koopmans and Rucht's chapter), survey methodology (see Klandermans and Smith's chapter), and structured comparative case studies (see della Porta's chapter) lent substance to calls for increased comparative analysis.

Though much work remains to be done, Klandermans and Tarrow's call in 1988 for increased comparative work seems to have been answered. The one remaining lacuna is the comparison of social movements, using similar methods and theoretical concepts, outside the range of North America and Western Europe.

Making Progress through Contained Contention

Finally, social movement theory has been enhanced by the area's ability to grow through debates between different perspectives. Fundamental differences have not been lacking, but research has progressed more through sequences of empirical research and theoretical synthesis than through the continued pitting of cardboard theories against one another. This is not to say that the debates have not been acrimonious at times, nor that they have all been resolved. But most of these debates have been beneficial in exposing weaknesses in the field and directing scholars to clarify ideas, develop new evidence, and adjust concepts and propositions. Here are two examples, one from the 1980s and the other from the 1990s:

- *Resource Mobilization and Collective Behavior*: For a time, American practitioners were absorbed in debates between collective behavior and resource mobilization theorists that pitted theories of "breakdown" or "strain" against "solidarity" models and contrasted a focus on "spontaneity" and expressive action with an emphasis on "organization" and rational choice. Early resource mobilization theorists appeared indifferent to grievances and to the role of collective action in constructing claims; in turn, some collective behavior theorists balked at charges of "irrationality" in what they considered resource mobilization theorists' caricatures of their arguments (see Killian 1984; Turner 1981). However, theorists on both sides prevented an impasse by offering clarifications of terms and assumptions, more empirical evidence, and sharper theoretical elaborations that provided bases for synthesis (see Useem 1980; Klandermans 1989a; and Rosenthal and Schwartz 1989).

• *Political Opportunity Structure*: In a more recent debate, social movement theorists have been disputing the definition and merit of the concept of "political opportunities" currently used in much movement scholarship. Theorists employ different measures of political opportunity and disagree on how broadly to define the concept (cf. Gamson and Meyer 1996; McAdam 1996). In a lively exchange in *Sociological Forum,* Goodwin and Jasper (1999) sharply criticized political process theory, arguing that the key concept of political opportunities creates a structural bias that omits cultural processes and leads to a focus on state-oriented social movements. Goodwin and Jasper's critics acknowledged the value of many of Goodwin and Jasper's points, but also disputed their characterizations of political process theory and challenged them to build a better mousetrap. Recent respecifications of the concept have linked opportunities to threats (Goldstone and Tilly 2001) and focused more on the attribution of opportunity by potential actors than on objective structures of opportunity (McAdam 1999; McAdam, Tarrow, and Tilly 2001). The debate also raised other useful issues, including how to deal with cultural opportunities, how to distinguish between "stable" and "volatile" elements of opportunity (Gamson and Meyer 1996), and how to take into account the ways in which movement strategies affect political structures and opportunities.

In summary, the combination of multiple methods, middle-range theory, infusions from real social movements and other areas of research, comparative perspectives, and contained contention has enriched the field of social movements with theoretical insights and empirical applications. We now turn to three areas of research in which sociologists and political scientists, European and North American scholars, have converged, to emphasize how the factors outlined have helped to advance the field of social movement studies.

Advances in Social Movement Research

Although many methodological problems remain unsolved in social movement research as in other areas, the field has advanced considerably. In the following subsections, we present examples of research questions on which we think a great deal of theoretical progress has been made: (1) the effects of various types of movement organization structures; (2) recruitment and participation; and (3) the dynamics of movement careers, cycles, and trajectories of contention. For these examples, we do not attempt a complete review of the literature but try to show how theoretical advances have been made through the use of multiple methods, middle-range theory, infusions from real social movements, the uses of the comparative method, and sequential interactions among theory and research, criticism and response. We might have used many other areas of research to illustrate advances in social movement research, but we chose these areas because one or the other of us has been associated with their development.

Organizational Characteristics and Impacts

The study of organizational features of "social movement organizations" (SMOs) or "challenging groups" and the effects of these characteristics on strategies and outcomes has advanced greatly because scholars have developed concepts and propositions that have been tested and expanded with empirical research using a variety of methods. Some empirical studies have taken a multi-method approach, and numerous case studies have specified the characteristics of movement organizations that produce various outcomes.

Theoretical ideas were important in launching this area of inquiry. Zald and Ash's (1966) seminal essay identified "movement organizations" as units of analysis and distinguished features of the movement environment from internal organizational characteristics. Specifying different types of organizational changes, such as factionalism and leadership transformation, Zald and Ash laid out a series of propositions about the ways in which environmental factors and internal processes affect these outcomes, which numerous researchers have since tested and elaborated. In another key work, Gamson (1990 [1975]) developed hypotheses regarding the effects of different types of organizational characteristics and goals on outcomes. Using a representative sample of American challenging groups active between 1800 and 1945, Gamson provided both empirical evidence and stimulating theoretical arguments about how factors such as bureaucratic structure and single-issue goals influence the outcomes of challenges.[2] These works and others, including influential papers by McCarthy and Zald (see Zald and McCarthy 1987), encouraged social movement theorists to view movement organizations as complex organizations operating in changing political contexts.

Movement scholars have used a variety of methods to investigate interactions between SMOs and their environments and the ways in which organizational structures affect tactics, mobilization, and outcomes (see Klandermans 1989b). They have also continued to develop theoretical ideas about the range of mobilizing structures important to movements and the organizational and environmental contexts, both political and cultural, in which SMOs operate (cf. Kriesi 1996; McCarthy 1996; Tarrow 1998).

To take one example of how theoretical development has occurred, Zurcher and his colleagues used multiple methods to build on the ideas of Zald and Ash and others in their study of two antipornography organizations located in different communities (see Zurcher and Kirkpatrick 1976; Curtis and Zurcher 1973, 1974; Zurcher and Curtis 1973). Individual-level data from questionnaires allowed the researchers to show the affiliations of SMO members with a variety of community organizations. Organizational documents and observations provided lists of community organizations aligned with the SMOs in their antipornography crusades, and observations of the campaigns and interviews with participants made it possible to assess how well integrated the antipornography groups were with aligned organizations and what impact this had on recruitment, goals and strategies, and outcomes.

Using both individual-level and organizational-level network data, Curtis and Zurcher (1973) conceptualized the antipornography organizations as operating within a "multi-organizational field." By comparing their cases, the researchers were able to observe how greater integration into the multi-organizational field allowed for recruitment through organizations, affected organizational characteristics, and created greater goal specificity and clarity, which influenced organizational success and longevity. Thus, an important theoretical concept, together with new propositions and tests of previous arguments, came out of a multi-method study that carefully specified the characteristics of two cases. Other scholars have since refined the concept (see Klandermans 1992) and analyzed processes such as recruitment in multi-organizational fields (e.g., Fernandez and McAdam 1989).

A number of researchers have used qualitative case studies to build theory about organizational dynamics in a way that allows other researchers to make comparisons with their own cases. Taylor (1989) used historical documents and in-depth interviews with members of the National Women's Party (NWP) to show how organizational characteristics such as centralization and exclusiveness, together with the elaborate culture of the NWP, kept the women's movement in "abeyance" during the period of "doldrums" between passage of suffrage in 1920 and the 1960s (Rupp and Taylor 1987). Staggenborg (1989) used similar methods to provide a detailed comparison of two local movement organizations, which shows how organizational formalization reduces internal disputes, and how an inclusive organizational structure can leave a group open to domination by outsiders. Thus, detailed knowledge of an organizational case allows a researcher to build on existing theory and to specify further how organizational characteristics produce particular outcomes. This can be accomplished with various methods. As Lichterman argues in this volume, a close-up understanding of organizational processes can be achieved through participant observation as well as in-depth interviews, with each providing different types of understandings of participant motivations and organizational arrangements (see Lichterman 1996).

It would be impossible to survey here all of the various ways in which theoretical contributions have been made. Indeed, this is one of the topics for which synthetic review essays are badly needed to bring together what we already know about organizational characteristics and their impacts in social movements. But suffice it to say that researchers exploring internal organizational dynamics will benefit from a rich empirical literature that includes detailed organizational case studies. To be sure, there is room for a great deal more research, but that research will benefit from a firm theoretical and methodological foundation.

Movement Recruitment and Participation

Participation in protest has always fascinated social scientists, perhaps because they were amazed that people would make sacrifices for a cause, sometimes even risking their lives. Amazement may also have led to the view of movement participation as an irrational act carried out by isolated and marginal members of society (Le Bon 1960 [1895]; Hoffer 1951; Kornhauser 1959). We have since moved far beyond theories that framed movement participation as irrational. The theories and models of today are complex and sophisticated frameworks that take into account a multifaceted set of factors in explaining movement participation. Indeed, it is a long way from the early studies of relative deprivation and movement participation to the mathematical modeling, the sophisticated survey designs, and the network analyses of recruitment and participation described in this volume.

Since the study of movement participation took an empirical turn, virtually every suitable research method has been used to investigate recruitment and participation. To mention only a few examples: White (1989) employed interviews in his study of micromobilization of the IRA; Andrews (1991) and Roth (1997) conducted life-history interviews with movement participants; Keniston (1968), Klandermans (1984), Opp (1989), Walsh and Warland (1983), and Stürmer (2000) employed survey techniques to study movement participants; Fernandez and McAdam (1989) used network analysis to explore recruitment; Martin (1986), Kelly and Breinlinger (1996), and Simon et al. (1998) applied experimental designs to investigate recruitment and participation.

Initially, cross-sectional comparisons of participants and nonpartici-pants dominated the field, but increasingly scholars began to employ longi-tudinal research designs and to build time into their research strategies and models. In his study of a mobilization campaign of a Dutch labor union, Klandermans (1984) argued that mobilization and participation are pro-cesses that evolve over time and therefore require longitudinal research de-signs to be adequately understood. He distinguished between consensus and action mobilization and hypothesized that action mobilization builds on successful consensus mobilization. He was able to demonstrate that in the course of a union's mobilization campaign, the preparedness of the union members to take part in industrial action fluctuated depending on the values of the parameters specified in his model.

In his study of applicants for the Mississippi Freedom Summer cam-paign, McAdam (1988) argued that the comparison made in most studies of movement participants between participants and nonparticipants is inap-propriate because most nonparticipants would never participate in a move-ment, either because they do not sympathize with its goals or because they would never participate in political protest of any sort. While conducting archival research, McAdam happened across a gold mine in an Atlanta li-brary: the application forms of both actual participants and "no shows" (those who applied to participate but ended up withdrawing) for Freedom Summer. The knowledge of who showed up and who dropped out allowed McAdam to construct an ideal data set with which he could test predictions about who would participate and who would not.

Marwell and Oliver (1993) demonstrated that mathematical modeling is an extremely useful means of testing hypotheses about the effectiveness of various recruitment strategies for different forms of participation. Their simu-lations suggest that free riding is likely only when participation has a decel-erating production function. That is, free riding is a problem when a few participants at the start suffice to produce the collective good, for instance, in a neighborhood committee negotiating with a municipality. But as Oliver (1984) showed elsewhere, people who are prepared to take such positions upon themselves do not typically worry about free riders, and under those circumstances, free riders do not jeopardize the achievement of the collective goal. In other words, the free riders who have so occupied the social move-ment literature may not be a major concern (see also Klandermans 1988).

Several decades of empirical work have broken recruitment and partici-pation down into three separate processes, each of which has been researched with a variety of methods:

- *The generation of mobilization potential.* This became the domain of research on consensus mobilization and framing processes. Case studies, participant observation, and textual analyses have generated insights into how organizers attempt to influence people to support a movement (see Benford 1997; and Benford and Snow 2000 for overviews).
- *The transformation of mobilization potential into actual participation.* This involves two different processes, which have each been the subject of numerous studies, namely targeting and motivating people. The first process became the domain of network analyses, which quickly refuted early conceptions of movement participants as isolated and marginalized (see Kitts 2000 for a recent review). Studies of motivations for participation and of how effective organizers are in motivating potential participants have been at the roots of social movement research for years. Although numerous methods have been applied to this area of study, it is here that sophisticated survey research has proved to be of great value.
- *Sustained participation and withdrawal from participation.* Interestingly, sustained participation and withdrawals from participation have been among the most neglected areas of research on recruitment and participation. A variety of research methods are applicable in this domain as well. Downton and Wehr (1997) applied survey techniques, case studies, and participant observation, and Klandermans (1994) used survey techniques in a panel design. Kitts (2000) argues for the use of network analysis to study sustained participation and withdrawal.

Careers, Cycles, and Trajectories of Contention

In understanding the dynamics of protest, three phases of theory building can be located, identified with three different historical phases of research:[3]

- *The movement career model* emerged from the core tradition of Weberian-Michelsian sociology (Alberoni 1968). It posited spontaneous noninstitutional origins for movement organizations, a linear trend toward deradicalization and bureaucracy, and a shift from charismatic leaders calling for radical change to organizational specialists more intent on defending their positions (Michels 1962). As a result, contention was seen as a rough parabola from movement to interest group, from a mood of *statu nascenti* to one of rational decision-making, and from principled opposition to institutions to participation in pragmatic politics (Lowi 1971; Piven and Cloward 1977).

That model summarized aptly what could happen to single classical movement organizations in the course of their maturation. But by the 1960s, the modal movement organization was decentralized and informal, and activism was more likely to take the form of "transitory teams" than bureaucratic monoliths, recruiting supporters on a campaign basis rather than depending on the ongoing participation of loyal members (McCarthy and Zald 1977; Rosenthal and Schwartz 1989). Many of these SMOs also belied the inexorable trend to deradicalization that Michels predicted. Most importantly, the movement career model privileged the internal dynamics of single movement organizations, detaching them from the interactions that influence their goals, organization, and tactics (Oliver 1989). This takes us to a second and more ambitious approach to contentious trajectories.

- *The protest cycle model* abandoned the idea of tracing episodes of contention through the careers of single movement organizations and observed broader trajectories involving a variety of groups and actors (Tarrow 1989a, 1989b). It posited a phase of heightened conflict and intensity of interaction across the social system, a rapid diffusion of collective action from more mobilized to less mobilized sectors of society, a heightened pace of innovation in the forms of contention, the creation of new or transformed collective action frames, and a combination of organized and unorganized contention. It also identified mechanisms of change like competition, polarization, and repression (Brockett 1995) as factors in moving the cycle along but produced no solid predictions about their interactions at different phases of the cycle.

The cyclical model combined the idea of expanding political opportunities, new and old organizational resources, the organization of collective action around "master frames" such as rights or autonomy, and an explosion of innovative collective action. In some versions it emphasized the alteration in identities over the course of a cycle (Klandermans 1994), in others it emphasized changes in organizational ecology (Minkoff 1995), and in still others it emphasized the structure of alignment and conflict (Koopmans 1993; Kriesi et al. 1995). In contrast to the movement career model, it could accommodate both radicalization and institutionalization (Tarrow 1989a: ch. 11).

The strength of the theory was that it was far more interactive than that of the movement career. The theory's weakness was that—like the movement career—it remained a *stage theory* based on a deductively posited phase of mobilization followed by a separate phase of demobilization, failing to account for mobilizations that emerge at various stages of the cycle and leaving untheorized the relations between actors, their actions, and identities. And by positing an invariant parabolic shape to episodes of contention, cyclical theory begged the question of whether there are episodes that take a different form altogether.

- These criticisms are leading some social movement scholars to a looser concept of *trajectories of contention* that focuses not on phases of mobilization and demobilization but on how different mechanisms and processes concatenate in different episodes of contention (McAdam, Tarrow, and Tilly 2001). For example, Mueller (1998) found a different pattern of radicalization and polarization in East Germany in 1989 than Tarrow found in Italy in the 1960s and 1970s. This is all to the good: once we realize that single movements are embedded in different contexts of contention and interact with other actors in an iterative dance of mobilization and demobilization, of identity formation and innovative collective action, and understand that trajectories of contention need not take a parabolic form, we are free to focus on how different mechanisms produce different overall shapes and intensities of contention, and different outcomes.

Challenges of Social Movement Research

Despite the advances in many areas, not all is golden in the broad trajectory of social movement research. Some scholars, in the name of rational choice theory, are uncomfortable with the field's preference for middle-range theory and synthesis among different theoretical traditions. Writers like Lichbach (1997) call instead for a search for general laws and for confrontation between broad research paradigms. Other scholars, coming from phenomenological or culturalist backgrounds, make exactly the opposite critique, calling for a greater emphasis on narrative, agency, and interpretation (Selbin 1997). Our answer, which we imagine would satisfy neither school of thought, is "a *praise* on both your houses!" We doubt that epistemological and ontological issues can ever be resolved through empirical research—certainly not in the field of social movement studies alone. We prefer to learn from other perspectives rather than engage them in paradigm warfare (Tarrow 1999).

The social movement field has already followed this strategy of selective absorption. Two examples will suffice to illustrate this:

- Though rational choice theorists search for general laws of "collective action," social movement scholars, both through resource mobilization and political process theory, absorbed essential rationalist insights and applied them selectively to specific situations and conditions.

- While culturalists and phenomenologists were insisting that there was too much "normal science" in the way social movement scholars worked, the field was quietly absorbing key concepts like framing, collective identity, and narrativity.

Our own worries about the social movement field are more frankly practical: we worry about conceptualizing new problems, especially the assimilation of macro concepts like "culture"; we are anxious about a tendency we see here and there for what we call "method-driven" research; we see a need to incorporate time more centrally in our models; we are concerned about the problems of planning ahead and the costs of employing multiple methods; and we would like to see more standardization. We summarize each of these concerns briefly before turning to a broader issue in social movement research: the expansion of the boundaries of the field.

Conceptualizing New Problems: The Example of Culture

Some issues are difficult to conceptualize in ways that make them amenable to empirical study. For example, social movement theorists have recently shown a great deal of interest in "culture," but have produced more theoretical "think pieces" than empirical studies (see Johnston and Klandermans 1995; Laraña, Johnston, and Gusfield 1994). Consider the outcomes of social movements: whereas Gamson (1990) provided a straightforward way of measuring political and policy outcomes, later expanded by others (see Burstein, Einwohner, and Hollander 1995), it is much more difficult to figure out how to assess cultural changes (Guigni 1998). As Gamson (1998: 57) remarks, "the referents for cultural change are all around us, diffused through the civil society in a thousand ways, but this does not tell us where to look to assess impact. If the changes are everywhere, then one can look anywhere."

We should not despair: social movement scholars are just beginning to find empirical referents for culture and relating it in interesting ways to the core issues of how social movements emerge, grow, decline, and effect change. For example, Gamson (1998) suggests focusing on mass media discourse as a way of evaluating cultural changes produced by social movements. He adapts the criteria of success developed in *The Strategy of Social Protest* to measure outcomes in terms of "media standing" (acceptance) and changes in media discourse or "framing" (new advantages), which he and his collaborators elaborate in a study of media discourse on abortion (Ferree et al.

2002). Rochon (1998) has also made progress in figuring out how to study cultural impacts of movements empirically. In examining how new cultural values spread, Rochon's work is particularly helpful in linking questions of culture and mobilization, identifying "critical communities" as groups that create new ideas, and showing how some cultural innovations, but not all, become linked to movements. Others, like Johnston (this volume), Polletta (1997), and Steinberg (1999), are adding to the array of tools used to ferret out difficult-to-identify cultural variables from social movements.

Avoiding Method-Driven Research

A second concern is that we tend to investigate problems for which we have methods. For example, the availability of protest event data and methods makes it more likely that we will focus on visible protests than on behind-the-scenes cultural or organizational activities. Not only can this procedure miss critical junctures or accumulations of small events, but it can also lend an exaggeratedly conflictual aura to periods in which most people may be minding their own business and tending their own gardens. Careful sampling and multiple sources can help to overcome this problem, but without complementary methods, we often lack qualitative information on what goes on in a protest, what was aimed at by its organizers, or its outcomes.

Use of a variety of methods, particularly qualitative ones, is especially important in exploring new phenomena and developing innovative theoretical ideas. In this volume, Snow and Trom highlight the open-ended character of case studies and how they often lead to the discovery of new data sources and unexpected findings, and stress the ways in which case studies can be designed to enhance theoretical development. Lichterman argues that a theory-driven version of participant observation allows researchers to understand how social structures shape social movement activities and to extend theory with their discoveries. Blee and Taylor show how open-ended semi-structured interviews advance our theoretical understandings in a variety of ways, and they emphasize that interviews are one way to provide a longitudinal view of social movements.

Incorporating Time

Incorporating time into social movement research is a key issue, as movements are affected by social changes and create changes that influence future collective action; by definition, movements are *sustained interactions* with authorities, countermovements, and other targets (cf. Tilly 1984; Tarrow 1998). Much movement research has failed, however, to examine movements over time owing to both data limitations and to the theoretical complexities introduced by longitudinal models. This is particularly true for new theoretical models and pioneering empirical research. For example, Tilly (1978: 142) acknowledged that his mobilization model "has no time in it" and is only a first step that simplifies initial analysis. Gamson's (1990) study of movement outcomes was limited by a "single-outcome-as-goal" model that did not take into account the effects of previous outcomes on later ones (Snyder and Kelly 1979).

Once theoretical ideas are better developed, and new data sources are found, scholars should be able to incorporate time into their research designs and theoretical models (McAdam and Sewell 2001). Protest event analysis is particularly helpful in allowing us to link a large number of protest events to large-scale changes. However, as Koopmans and Rucht (this volume) acknowledge, the method is limited in what it can tell us about social movements; protest event analysis cannot provide insight on issues such as public reactions, mobilizing structures, or participants' perceptions of events. Surveys can provide measures of actors' perceptions, but they are often cross-sectional; however, as Oegema and Klandermans (1994) demonstrate, surveys done at different points in a campaign offer an important means of incorporating time into studies (see Klandermans and Smith, this volume). Research that combines qualitative sources such as interviews and historical documents with quantitative data such as protest event data and survey data is particularly important in allowing researchers to connect levels of analysis over time, showing how changes in large-scale political and cultural contexts, organizational forms, and micro-level perceptions are linked.

Planning Ahead

Another difficulty in our current practice of social movement research is that we often lack the opportunity for advanced planning in our studies of social movements. In addition to studying past movements, we can learn a great deal about the dynamics of social movements by watching events as they happen in current movements and new instances of collective action. Because collective action often occurs unexpectedly, we need to think through theory and methods in advance. Although some events are unpredictable, an understanding of social movements should allow us to predict the occurrence and trajectory of some instances of collective action and plan for their study. As Klandermans and Smith discuss in this volume, attention to cycles of mobilization allows for a great deal of advance planning in research designs that involve time comparisons.

Even when we know that an event is going to occur, movement activists are not always ready to stop what they are doing as they engage in collective action to provide information to even the most sympathetic of social movement scholars. Two new approaches offer alternatives. First, some intrepid French researchers have made efforts to interview activists in the act of collective action (Favre et al. 1990). Second, the increasing diffusion of information on the World Wide Web by movement organizations provides a rich source of data. Both of these data sources must be used with caution, the first because of problems of sampling and what we may call the "excitement bias" brought by interviewing people in the act of protest; the second because of the danger that deliberate strategies of movement activists to influence public opinion in the guise of electronic news will be taken as fact. For example, Hellman (1999) has shown how deceptive much of the information was that was diffused through more-or-less biased sources during the Chiapas rebellion of 1994.

Sharing Data

Beyond these problems, an obvious obstacle to greater triangulation of methods is cost, together with the extreme difficulty of collecting multiple types of data without assembling a large research team. One way in which we can reduce the costs of studying collective action through multiple methods is by finding more ways to share data. With access to data archives, researchers could supplement one type of data with another at a low cost, and they could also conduct more comparative studies based on a single method. Most developed countries today have archives and procedures for storing and sharing quantitative data. Although such resources are less common for qualitative data, some projects are under way to encourage archiving of qualitative data for secondary analysis and to solve some of the problems, such as confidentiality concerns, associated with secondary use of qualitative data. Some oral histories, including interviews with American suffrage and civil rights activists, are now available on the Internet, which has great potential as a means of low-cost archiving and distribution of available data. A number of libraries have already begun to make data in their archives available on-line, and researchers in areas like social movements might initiate projects to make secondary data available, perhaps through professional associations.

Researchers interested in sharing qualitative research can draw on the resources of the Qualitative Data Archival Resource Centre (Qualidata) at the University of Essex (see www.essex.ac.uk/qualidata), which operates a service that evaluates qualitative data for suitability, catalogs it, organizes its transfer to suitable archives, lists repositories of qualitative data, and provides other resources, such as advice to researchers on how to make data available. Qualidata has worked out guidelines for addressing concerns typically raised about secondary use of qualitative data such as confidentiality, informed consent, and control over access to the data. Although many qualitative researchers are likely to be skeptical about the feasibility of sharing data such as field notes and interviews—and not all qualitative data are suitable for secondary analysis—the work of Qualidata shows that many concerns can be addressed. If more qualitative data are made available for secondary analysis in the social movement domain, as well as in other areas of social science, multi-method studies will become more feasible.

Standardization

Along with the need for more sharing of data, greater standardization in data collection and reporting is necessary to allow for comparative research. In the case of protest event data, some progress has been made on this problem as a result of the collaborations of international research teams. But researchers also need to find ways of standardizing other methods, including qualitative ones. Standardization of qualitative methods, we want to emphasize, does not imply a mechanical handling of qualitative data. It does mean greater clarity in reporting of procedures used, such as questions asked in interviews and methods of coding and analysis. Although the analysis of qualitative data—like quantitative analysis—requires creativity, it should also be systematic. With their increased use, computer programs for qualitative analysis can potentially make the process of systematic coding and comparison of data more transparent. Although they do not substantially alter methods of analysis developed previously by qualitative researchers, qualitative analysis programs make it much easier to list codes and concepts used and to map connections among concepts grounded in different pieces of data, such as interviews and field notes.

Standardization of case studies also means clearer specification of the conditions that hold in particular cases, so that they can be compared to other cases on various dimensions. Vaughan (1992: 175) describes "a method for developing general theories of particular phenomena through qualitative case analysis" that involves careful selection of cases based on organizational form and function and units and levels of analysis. By making clear the characteristics of our cases, we can compare them for similarities and differences and then make theoretical arguments based on the comparisons (178). If the features of cases were clearly specified in published works, other researchers could compare their own case findings to published cases, and further specify the conditions under which various outcomes can be expected. For example, Banaszak (1996) details differences in the Swiss and American suffrage movements, such as the extent to which they were connected with other movements. Other researchers might select one or more cases based on this feature and compare the effects of connections to other movements to Banaszak's findings regarding strategies and outcomes in her cases. Such comparison would permit further elaboration of the ways in which connections among movements influence strategy and outcomes in different situations.

Extending Social Movement Research

Assimilating and operationalizing difficult concepts, avoiding methods biases, incorporating time, planning ahead, sharing data, and standardizing research findings: these are challenges that social movement scholars have been confronting and to some extent surmounting, as our collaborators' chapters indicate. Broader challenges involve, first, extending existing methods to new sources of data; second, assessing the relationship between contentious and institutional politics; and third, expanding the scope conditions for social movement research, including the particular problem of studying transnational social movements.

Extending Existing Methods

Social movement research has grown over the past three decades largely by absorbing and modifying methods inherited from other areas of research. Even protest event analysis—the field's most characteristic invention—was adapted from the study of strike waves (Shorter and Tilly 1974) and from "official" studies of the 1960s race riots. Surveys and case studies were certainly not invented by social movement scholars, but they take on characteristic turns when used by skilled social movement practitioners. Even the original approach to framing and discourse analysis elaborated by Johnston in this volume is an expansion of methods developed elsewhere.

The syncretic impulse of social movement research remains one of the field's great strengths. Here are some examples of current areas of methodological expansion:

- Adapting a method first employed by Merton, Fiske, and Kendall (1990 [1956]) to examine wartime propaganda films, and then by Lazarsfeld in advertising and marketing, focus group methodologies moved from electoral campaigning to studying social movement constituencies. First Gamson (1992b), and more recently Taylor and Gamson (cited in Blee and Taylor, this volume), have experimented with this technique. Its use in studying social movement constituencies poses rather different problems than those found in market or electoral research—for example, the generally greater political sophistication of the subjects—but it is extremely promising as a way of studying activists' interaction and "negotiation" of collective identity (Melucci et al. 1985).

- Expanding the study of repertoires of contention from classifying them by their nominal forms to the dramatic, ludic, and threatening presentation of collective self in contentious politics. Once we get below gross classification (e.g., the strike, the demonstration, the sit-in), we often find that what are nominally the same forms differ widely in their mood, internal logics, and symbolism, yet few studies of the repertoire have zeroed in on their presentation of collective self (but see Steinberg 1999). Parallels with the study of political theater are proving helpful here, as are historical studies of monuments, dress, and festivals (Mosse 1975; Hunt 1984, 1992). But we still lack the instruments to allow concerted attention to the presentation of self in contentious politics.

- Expanding the method of the systematic study of protest events to noncontentious and less contentious forms, as Koopmans and Statham (1999) have attempted in their recent work. Much progress also remains to be made in linking time-series protest event history to covariates in the environments of social movements (for example, increases in inequality) and in organizational type and density. We have also made little progress in relating the intensity or durability of protest waves to the type and extent of public policy response.

Relating Contentious and Institutional Politics

The social movement field is based on the recognition of the boundary between institutionalized and noninstitutionalized politics.[4] We agree with that distinction, but as an unfortunate consequence, analysts have neglected or misunderstood both the parallels and the interactions between the two. Reification reached its peak in American social science during the 1950s and 1960s, as political science claimed "normal" prescribed politics as its bailiwick, leaving social movements (in Gamson's ironic phrase) to "the social psychologist whose intellectual tools prepare him to better understand the irrational" (Gamson 1990: 133). Sociologists claimed movements as their chosen terrain, frequently ignoring their complex relations to institutional politics.

During the past thirty years, this neat disciplinary division of labor has largely dissolved; we ourselves (a social psychologist, sociologist, and political scientist) have contributed to its destruction. Yet we are left with a language and a set of categories (revolution, social movement, interest groups, electoral politics, and so on) that reproduce the original duality. Boundaries between institutionalized and noninstitutionalized politics are hard to draw with precision. More important, the two sorts of politics interact incessantly and involve similar causal processes. Coalitions, strategic interaction, and identity struggles occur widely in the politics of established institutions as well as in social movements. Virtually all broad social movements, revolutions, and similar phenomena grow from roots in less visible episodes of institutional contention. Understanding the relations and interactions among conventional and noninstitutional politics is a major current challenge of social movement research.

These issues have become particularly acute because of the expansion and institutionalization of classically social movement–like forms of behavior over the past few decades (Dalton 1996; Meyer and Tarrow 1998). When provincial English matrons protesting against the export of calves to the continent join irate Parisian students and American schoolteachers in the use of blockades and demonstrations, we must reexamine many of the assumptions that have separated the field of social movement studies from that of conventional political participation.

It is not just the expansion of contentious forms of action that concerns us but the more routinized relations that develop around them between protesters and authorities. The studies of della Porta and Reiter (1998), McCarthy and his collaborators (McCarthy, McPhail, and Smith 1996; McCarthy and McPhail 1998), and Fillieule (1997) all demonstrate a shift in police behavior toward protesters from repression to containment and selective facilitation. Favre (1990) regards the demonstration as a form of ritualized political participation, with its characteristic roles, behaviors, and audiences. When behaviors that were recently regarded as forbidden, or behaviors of minorities that were barely tolerated, come to be employed by vast sectors of the public and are facilitated by police and authorities, social movement scholars must ask indeed, as Zald (2000) urges, whether there is still something particular about their subject.

Expanding Scope Conditions

We do not go as far as Zald in his belief that the significant differences between social movements and other forms of collective action pale in comparison to their similarities.[5] We do, however, wish to suggest that much can be gained from comparing social movements to other forms of contentious politics. For although this book focuses on movements, it is undeniable that a wide range of comparable pathways and trajectories connect movements to other types of contentious politics, including revolutions, strike waves, ethnic mobilizations, democratization, and nationalism.

In recent decades, specialized scholars have made substantial advances in describing and explaining each of these important contentious forms, but for the most part, they have paid little attention to each other's discoveries. Students of strikes, for example, rarely draw on the burgeoning literature on ethnic mobilization. Students of ethnic mobilization return the compliment by ignoring analyses of strikes. Yet there are strong family resemblances between movements and other forms of contention, such as revolutions. Strong, if partial, parallels exist between strikes and ethnic mobilization, and between these two forms and social movements, for example, in the ways that actions of third parties affect their success or failure and in the impact of previously existing interpersonal networks on their patterns of recruitment. Even nationalism and democratization, which have spawned their own distinct literatures, are frequently studied as if they had nothing to do with the study of social movements.

But how can we respond to these analogies? Surely not by melting down all forms of contentious politics in one great pot—variously called "conflict," "struggle," or "collective action"! For, in addition to abandoning the benefits of middle-range theory, such a practice would lead the analyst to neglect the very cultural and political specificities to which we have learned to attend. We suggest instead that applying the findings of social movement research comparatively may be the best strategy for understanding what is specific to movements and what is characteristic of other varieties of contention.

One group of scholars proposes a daring methodological strategy: expanding scope conditions by comparing social movements with other forms of behavior; not through either large-N studies of "most-different systems" or through small-N paired comparisons of similar movements (see della Porta, this volume), but through small-N paired comparisons of different forms of contention (McAdam, Tarrow, and Tilly 2001: ch. 3). They do so by focusing on the causal mechanisms that drive different episodes of contention, searching for robust mechanisms and combinations of mechanisms across wide varieties of contention.

For example, consider the formation of actor identities: many social movement scholars have noted the formation of new actors and new identities in the course of a contentious episode (Klandermans 1994), but little work has been done to specify how this process occurs. Focusing on a process they call "actor constitution," McAdam, Tarrow, and Tilly (2001: ch. 10) hypothesize that new actors are constructed in contentious episodes through the mechanisms of social appropriation of existing institutions; innovative collective action; certification of actors, their actions, and their claims by external parties; and category formation—creation of a set of sites sharing a boundary distinguishing all of them and relating all of them to at least one set of sites visibly excluded by the boundary.

These authors use a foundational social movement case to illustrate how the process of actor constitution can work: the American civil rights movement. They show that following the Montgomery bus boycott determined efforts were made by the organizers to constitute a new identity, "the new Negro." Appropriating existing organizations, calling on certification by federal authorities and the national press, participants in the boycott were engaged in "signifying work," or what Jenson (1998) has termed "group naming." As Martin Luther King wrote, "In Montgomery we walk in a new way. We hold our heads in a new way. Even the Negro reporters who converged on Montgomery have a new attitude. One tired reporter, asked at a luncheon in Birmingham to say a few words about Montgomery, stood up, thought for a moment, and uttered one sentence: 'Montgomery has made me proud to be a Negro'" (quoted in Burns 1997: 244).

How robust is this process of actor constitution? McAdam, Tarrow, and Tilly claim to see elements of the same process in a very different case, the formation of a "Red Guard" identity in the Chinese Cultural Revolution. Drawing heavily on the work of Walder, they argue that shifts in identity did not so much motivate action in Beijing as develop as a logical consequence of contentious interaction in a highly risky and uncertain political context. As Walder (2000: 1) writes:

> Factions did not form until after participants took initial actions under ambiguous political circumstances that varied widely across schools. These individual choices split pre-existing status groups and local political networks, and in turn imposed new political identities that had potentially severe consequences for the movement activists who would lead opposed factions. These identities constrained choice, sharply defined interests for the first time, and subsequently served as a basis for group formation and conflict.

China in 1966 was nothing like Montgomery a decade earlier, which is exactly the point of the comparison. It suggests that scholars of social movements would do well to compare their subjects with other forms of contentious politics—not to dissolve them all into a great soup but to better understand what is specific to social movements and what unites them with other forms of contention. Such an exercise of expanding scope conditions has become more urgent in recent years with the realization that the traditional boundaries of social movements—the national state—have become permeable to corporations, governments, and social movements. With the advent of the transnational social movement, a new set of challenges are on the horizon for students of social movements.

This brings us to a final set of challenges, which are perhaps even greater: until quite recently most social movement research was lodged securely within domestic politics and society. Indeed, for some theorists, the *national* social movement was the key subject of the study of contentious politics, at least in the West (Tilly 1984; Tarrow 1998). But with the recent expansion of the authority of international institutions, the growth of international nongovernmental organizations, and the ease with which citizens of the new century can travel and engage in contention, social movement scholars are challenged to adapt their theories and methods to contention beyond borders (Keck and Sikkink 1998; Guidry, Kennedy, and Zald 2000; Risse, Ropp, and Sikkink 1999; Smith, Chatfield, and Pagnucco 1997). Whether these new global phenomena will fit within the canon of social movement research or require a qualitatively new theoretical effort is the most exciting issue in the field of contentious politics today.

Coda

We have chosen as a title "Blending Methods and Building Theories" for this closing chapter, and in a way, this can be read as a programmatic statement: we think scientists ought to blend methods to build theories. Social movement research, like all science, is nothing more or less than an attempt to understand reality, be it individuals' willingness to sacrifice, a sudden wave of protest, or a process of transition. Theories, no matter how masterfully built, are of course only hypothetical models of reality, and research methods are our tools for testing and expanding them. With this book we have tried to provide a tool kit, a user's guide, and a handbook for innovators who want to take part in the exciting art of social movement research. The authors have offered their collective expertise to those who want to do empirical research to develop their theories. Researchers will find some guidance in how to use a method, and we hope they will feel challenged to try new approaches and directions with their own blend of methods.

Notes

1. This is, of course, *not* true of the extensive body of work on revolutions, or of that inchoate but nevertheless important borderland of contentious politics called "resistance."

2. Gamson also published his coding scheme and data, enabling other researchers

to reanalyze the data using multivariate statistical techniques (see the papers reprinted in Gamson 1990, and Frey, Dietz, and Kalof 1992).

3. This section draws on McAdam, Tarrow, and Tilly 2001.

4. This section draws on McAdam, Tarrow, and Tilly 2001: ch. 1; and Meyer and Tarrow 1998.

5. This section draws on McAdam, Tarrow, and Tilly 2001: ch. 3.

References

Alberoni, Francesco. 1968. *Statu nascenti*. Bologna: Il Mulino.

Alford, Robert R. 1998. *The Craft of Inquiry: Theories, Methods, Evidence*. New York: Oxford University Press.

Amenta, Edwin, and Michael P. Young. 1999. "Democratic States and Social Movements: Theoretical Arguments and Hypotheses." *Social Problems* 46 (2): 153–68.

Aminzade, Ronald R., Jack A. Goldstone, Doug McAdam, Elizabeth Perry, William H. Sewell Jr., Sidney Tarrow, and Charles Tilly, eds. 2001. *Silence and Voice in the Study of Contentious Politics*. Cambridge: Cambridge University Press.

Aminzade, Ronald R., and Doug McAdam. 2001. "Emotions and Contentious Politics." In *Silence and Voice in the Study of Contentious Politics,* edited by Ronald R. Aminzade, Jack A. Goldstone, Doug McAdam, Elizabeth Perry, William H. Sewell Jr., Sidney Tarrow, and Charles Tilly, 14–50. Cambridge: Cambridge University Press.

Andrews, Molly. 1991. *Lifetimes of Commitment: Aging, Politics, Psychology*. Cambridge: Cambridge University Press.

Banaszak, Lee Ann. 1996. *Why Movements Succeed or Fail: Opportunity, Culture, and the Struggle for Woman Suffrage*. Princeton, N.J.: Princeton University Press.

Benford, Robert D. 1997. "An Insider's Critique of the Social Movement Framing Perspective." *Sociological Inquiry* 67 (4): 409–30.

Benford, Robert D., and Scott A. Hunt. 1992. "Dramaturgy and Social Movements: The Social Construction and Communication of Power." *Sociological Inquiry* 62 (1): 36–55.

Benford, Robert D., and David A. Snow. 2000. "Framing Processes and Social Movements: An Overview and Assessment." *Annual Review of Sociology* 26: 611–39.

Brewer, John, and Albert Hunter. 1989. *Multimethod Research: A Synthesis of Styles*. Newbury Park, Calif.: Sage.

Brockett, Charles D. 1995. "A Protest-Cycle Resolution of the Repression/Popular Protest Paradox." In *Repertoires and Cycles of Collective Action*, edited by Mark Traugott, 117–44. Durham, N.C.: Duke University Press.

Buechler, Steven M. 2000. *Social Movements in Advanced Capitalism*. New York: Oxford University Press.

Burns, Stewart. 1997. *Daybreak of Freedom*. Durham, N.C.: Duke University Press.

Burstein, Paul, Rachel L. Einwohner, and Jocelyn A. Hollander. 1995. "The Success of Social Movements: A Bargaining Perspective." In *The Politics of Social Protest: Comparative Perspectives on States and Social Movements,* edited by J. Craig Jenkins and Bert Klandermans, 275–95. Minneapolis: University of Minnesota Press.

Curtis, Russell L., Jr., and Louis Zurcher Jr. 1973. "Stable Resources of Protest Movements: The Multi-Organizational Field." *Social Forces* 52: 53–61.

———. 1974. "Social Movements: An Analytical Exploration of Organizational Forms." *Social Problems* 21 (3): 356–70.

Dalton, Russell. 1996. *Citizen Politics: Public Opinion and Political Parties in Advanced Industrial Democracies*. 2d. ed. Chatham, N.J.: Chatham House.

della Porta, Donatella, and Herbert Reiter, eds. 1998. *Policing Protest: The Control of Mass Demonstrations in Western Democracies*. Minneapolis: University of Minnesota Press.

Diani, Mario. 1995. *Green Networks: A Structural Analysis of the Italian Environmental Movement*. Edinburgh: Edinburgh University Press.

Downton, James, Jr., and Paul Wehr. 1997. *The Persistent Activist: How Peace Commitment Develops and Survives*. Boulder, Colo.: Westview Press.

Favre, Pierre, et al. 1990. *La Manifestation*. Paris: Presses de la Fondation Nationale des Sciences Politics.

Fernandez, Roberto M., and Doug McAdam. 1989. "Multiorganizational Fields and Recruitment to Social Movements." *International Social Movement Research* 2: 315–43.

Ferree, Myra Marx, William A. Gamson, Jürgen Gerhards, and Dieter Rucht. 2002. *Shaping Abortion Discourse: Democracy and the Public Sphere in Germany and the United States*. Cambridge: Cambridge University Press.

Fillieule, Olivier. 1997. *Stratégies de la rue. Les manifestations en France*. Paris: Presses de la Fondation Nationale des Sciences Politiques.

Frey, Scott R., Thomas Dietz, and Linda Kalof. 1992. "Characteristics of Successful American Protest Groups: Another Look at Gamson's 'Strategy of Social Protest.'" *American Journal of Sociology* 98 (2): 368–87.

Gamson, William A. 1990. *The Strategy of Social Protest*. 2d ed. Belmont, Calif.: Wadsworth Publishing Co.

———. 1992a. "The Social Psychology of Collective Action." In *Frontiers in Social Movement Theory,* edited by Aldon D. Morris and Carol McClurg Mueller, 53–76. New Haven, Conn.: Yale University Press.

———. 1992b. *Talking Politics*. Cambridge: Cambridge University Press.

———. 1998. "Social Movements and Cultural Change." In *From Contention to Democracy,* edited by Marco G. Giugni, Doug McAdam, and Charles Tilly, 57–77. Lanham, Md.: Rowman and Littlefield.

Gamson, William A., and David S. Meyer. 1996. "Framing Political Opportunity." In *Comparative Perspectives on Social Movements: Political Opportunities, Mobilizing Structures, and Cultural Framings,* edited by Doug McAdam, John D. McCarthy, and Mayer N. Zald, 275–90. Cambridge: Cambridge University Press.

Goldstone, Jack. 1998, "Social Movements or Revolutions? On the Evolution and Outcomes of Collective Action." In *From Contention to Democracy,* edited by Marco G. Giugni, Doug McAdam, and Charles Tilly, 125–48. Lanham, Md.: Rowman and Littlefield.

Goldstone, Jack, and Charles Tilly. 2001. "Threat and Opportunity." In *Silence and Voice in the Study of Contentious Politics,* edited by Ronald R. Aminzade, Jack A. Goldstone, Doug McAdam, Elizabeth Perry, William H. Sewell Jr., Sidney Tarrow, and Charles Tilly, 179–94. Cambridge: Cambridge University Press.

Goodwin, Jeff, and James M. Jasper. 1999. "Caught in a Winding, Snarling Vine: The Structural Bias of Political Process Theory." *Sociological Forum* 14 (1): 27–54.

Gould, Roger V. 1995. *Insurgent Identities: Class, Community, and Protest in Paris from 1848 to the Commune.* Chicago: University of Chicago Press.

Granovetter, Mark. 1973. "The Strength of Weak Ties." *American Journal of Sociology* 78: 1360–80.

Guidry, John A., Michael D. Kennedy, and Mayer N. Zald, eds. 2000. *Globalizations and Social Movements.* Ann Arbor: University of Michigan Press.

Guigni, Marco G. 1998. "Was It Worth the Effort? The Outcomes and Consequences of Social Movements." *Annual Review of Sociology* 98: 371–93.

Hellman, Judith. 1999. "Real and Virtual Chiapas: Magic Realism and the Left." In *Socialist Register 2000: Necessary and Unnecessary Utopias,* edited by Leo Panitch and Colin Leys, 161–86. London: Merlin.

Hobsbawm, E. J. 1959. *Primitive Rebels.* New York: W. W. Norton and Co.

Hoffer, Eric. 1951. *The True Believer.* New York: Harper and Row.

Hunt, Lynn. 1984. *Politics, Culture and Class in the French Revolution.* Berkeley: University of California Press.

———. 1992. *The Family Romance of the French Revolution.* Berkeley: University of California Press.

Jenkins, J. Craig. 1985. *The Politics of Insurgency: The Farm Worker Movement in the 1960s.* New York: Columbia University Press.

Jenson, Jane. 1998. "Social Movement Naming Practices and the Political Opportunity Structure." Working Paper 1998/114, Instituto Juan March De Estudios e Investigaciones, Madrid.

Johnston, Hank, and Bert Klandermans, eds. 1995. *Social Movements and Culture.* Minneapolis: University of Minnesota Press.

Keck, Margaret, and Kathryn Sikkink. 1998. *Activists beyond Borders.* Ithaca, N.Y.: Cornell University Press.

Kelly, Caroline, and Sarah Breinlinger. 1996. *The Social Psychology of Collective Action.* Basingstoke: Taylor and Francis.

Keniston, Kenneth. 1968. *Young Radicals.* New York: Harcourt Brace Jovanovich.

Keohane, Robert, Gary King, and Sidney Verba. 1995. *Designing Social Inquiry: Scientific Inference in Qualitative Research.* Princeton: Princeton University Press.

Killian, Lewis M. 1984. "Organization, Rationality, and Spontaneity in the Civil Rights Movement." *American Sociological Review* 49: 770–83.

Kitts, James A. 2000. "Mobilizing in Black Boxes: Social Networks and Participation in Social Movement Organizations." *Mobilization* 5: 241–57.

Klandermans, Bert. 1984. "Mobilization and Participation: Social-Psychological Expansions of Resource Mobilization Theory." *American Sociological Review* 49 (5): 583–600.

———. 1988. "The Formation and Mobilization of Consensus." *International Social Movement Research* 1: 173–96.

———. 1989a. "Grievance Interpretation and Success Expectations: The Social Construction of Protest." *Social Behavior* 4 (2): 113–25.

———. 1989b. "Introduction: Social Movement Organizations and the Study of Social Movements." *International Social Movement Research* 2: 1–17.

———. 1992. "The Social Construction of Protest and Multiorganizational Fields." In *Frontiers in Social Movement Theory,* edited by Aldon D. Morris and Carol McClurg Mueller, 77–103. New Haven, Conn.: Yale University Press.

———. 1994. "Transient Identities? Membership Patterns in the Dutch Peace Movement." In *New Social Movements: From Ideology to Identity,* edited by Enrique Laraña, Hank Johnston, and Joseph Gusfield, 168–84. Philadelphia: Temple University Press.

——— 1997. *The Social Psychology of Protest.* Oxford: Blackwell Publishers.

———, ed. 1989. *Organizing for Change: Social Movement Organizations in Europe and the United States.* Greenwich, Conn.: JAI Press.

Klandermans, Bert, Hans-Peter Kriesi, and Sidney Tarrow, eds. 1988. *From Structure to Action: Comparing Social Movement Participation across Cultures.* Greenwich, Conn.: JAI Press.

Kleidman, Robert. 1993. *Organizing for Peace: Neutrality, the Test Ban, and the Freeze.* Syracuse, N.Y.: Syracuse University Press.

Koopmans, Ruud. 1993. "The Dynamics of Protest Waves: West Germany, 1965–1989." *American Sociological Review* 58: 637–58.

Koopmans, Rudd, and Paul Statham. 1999. "Ethnic and Civic Conceptions of Nationhood and the Differential Success of the Extreme Right in Germany and Italy." In *How Social Movements Matter,* edited by Marco Giugni, Doug McAdam, and Charles Tilly, 225–51. Minneapolis: University of Minnesota Press.

Kornhauser, William. 1959. *The Politics of a Mass Society.* New York: Free Press.

Kriesi, Hans-Peter. 1996. "The Organizational Structure of New Social Movements in a Political Context." In *Comparative Perspectives on Social Movements,* edited by Doug McAdam, John D. McCarthy, and Mayer N. Zald, 152–184. Cambridge: Cambridge University Press.

Kriesi, Hans-Peter, Ruud Koopmans, Jan Willem Duyvendak, and Marco G. Giugni. 1995. *New Social Movements in Western Europe: A Comparative Analysis.* Minneapolis: University of Minnesota Press.

Laraña, Enrique, Hank Johnston, and Joseph R. Gusfield, eds. 1994. *New Social Movements: From Ideology to Identity.* Philadelphia: Temple University Press.

Le Bon, Gustave. 1960 [1895]. *The Crowd.* New York: Viking.

Lichbach, Mark I. 1997. "Contentious Maps of Contentious Politics." *Mobilization* 2: 87–98.

Lichterman, Paul. 1996. *The Search for Political Community.* New York: Cambridge University Press.

Lowi, Theodore. 1971. *The Politics of Disorder.* New York: Free Press.

Martin, Joanne. 1986. "The Tolerance of Injustice." In *Relative Deprivation and Social Comparison: The Ontario Symposium, Volume 4,* edited by James M. Olson, C. Peter Herman, and Mark P. Zanna, 217–42. Hillsdale, N.J.: Lawrence Erlbaum.

Marwell, Gerald, and Pamela Oliver. 1993. *The Critical Mass in Collective Action: A Micro-Social Theory.* Cambridge: Cambridge University Press.

McAdam, Doug. 1986. "Recruitment to High-Risk Activism: The Case of Freedom Summer." *American Journal of Sociology* 92 (1): 64–90.

———. 1988. *Freedom Summer.* New York: Oxford University Press.

———. 1996. "Conceptual Origins, Current Problems, Future Directions." In *Comparative Perspectives on Social Movements: Political Opportunities, Mobilizing Structures, and Cultural Framings,* edited by Doug McAdam, John D. McCarthy, and Mayer N. Zald, 23–40. Cambridge: Cambridge University Press.

———. 1999. *Political Process and the Development of Black Insurgency.* 2d ed. Chicago: University of Chicago Press.

McAdam, Doug, John D. McCarthy, and Mayer N. Zald. 1988. "Social Movements." In *Handbook of Sociology,* edited by Neil J. Smelser, 695–737. Newbury Park, Calif.: Sage.

———, eds. 1996. *Comparative Perspectives on Social Movements: Political Opportunities, Mobilizing Structures, and Cultural Framings.* Cambridge: Cambridge University Press.

McAdam, Doug, and William H. Sewell Jr. 2001. "Temporality in the Study of Contentious Politics." In *Silence and Voice in the Study of Contentious Politics,* edited by Ronald R. Aminzade, Jack A. Goldstone, Doug McAdam, Elizabeth Perry, William H. Sewell Jr., Sidney Tarrow, and Charles Tilly, 89–125. Cambridge: Cambridge University Press.

McAdam, Doug, Sidney Tarrow, and Charles Tilly. 1996. "To Map Contentious Politics." *Mobilization* 1: 17–34.

———. 1997. "Toward an Integrated Perspective on Social Movements and Revolution." In *Comparative Politics: Rationality, Culture, and Structure,* edited by Mark I. Lichbach and Alan S. Zuckerman, 142–73. New York: Cambridge University Press.

———. 2001. *Dynamics of Contention.* Cambridge: Cambridge University Press.

McCarthy, John D. 1996. "Constraints and Opportunities in Adopting, Adapting, and Inventing." In *Comparative Perspectives on Social Movements,* edited by Doug McAdam, John D. McCarthy, and Mayer N. Zald, 141–51. Cambridge: Cambridge University Press.

McCarthy, John D., and Clark McPhail. 1998. "The Institutionalization of Protest in the United States." In *The Social Movement Society: Contentious Politics for a New Century,* edited by David S. Meyer and Sidney Tarrow, 83–110. Lanham, Md.: Rowman and Littlefield.

McCarthy, John D., Clark McPhail, and Jackie Smith. 1996. "Images of Protest: Estimating Selection Bias in Media Coverage of Washington Demonstrations." *American Sociological Review* 61: 478–99.

McCarthy, John D., and Mayer N. Zald. 1973. *The Trend of Social Movements in America: Professionalization and Resource Mobilization.* Morristown, N.J.: General Learning Press.

———. 1977. "Resource Mobilization and Social Movements: A Partial Theory." *American Journal of Sociology* 82 (6): 1212–41.

Melucci, Alberto. 1996. *Challenging Codes: Collective Action in the Information Age.* Cambridge: Cambridge University Press.

Melucci, Alberto, et al. 1985. *Altri codici.* Bologna: Mulino.

Merton, Robert K. 1968. *Social Theory and Social Structure.* Enlarged ed. New York: Free Press.

Merton, Robert K., Marjorie Fiske, and Patricia L. Kendall. 1990 [1st ed., 1956]. *The Focused Interview.* 2d. ed. New York: Free Press.

Meyer, David S., and Suzanne Staggenborg. 1996. "Movements, Countermovements, and the Structure of Political Opportunity." *American Journal of Sociology* 101 (6): 1628–60.

Meyer, David S., and Sidney Tarrow, eds. 1998. *The Social Movement Society.* Lanham, Md.: Rowman and Littlefield.

Michels, Robert. 1962. *Political Parties*. New York: Collier Books.

Miller, Byron A. 2000. *Geography and Social Movements: Comparing Antinuclear Activism in the Boston Area*. Minneapolis: University of Minnesota Press.

Mills, C. Wright. 1959. *The Sociological Imagination*. New York: Oxford University Press.

Minkoff, Debra. 1995. *Organizing for Equality: The Evolution of Women's and Racial-Ethnic Organizations in America, 1955–1985*. New Brunswick, N.J.: Rutgers University Press.

Morris, Aldon D. 1984. *The Origins of the Civil Rights Movement: Black Communities Organizing for Change*. New York: Free Press.

Mosse, George. 1975. *The Nationalization of the Masses*. New York: H. Ferrig.

Mueller, Carole McClurg. 1998. "Claim 'Radicalization'? The 1989 Protest Cycle in the GDR." Paper presented to the Second Conference on Protest Event Analysis, WZB Berlin. July.

Oegema, Kirk, and Bert Klandermans. 1994. "Why Social Movement Sympathizers Don't Participate: Erosion and Nonconversion of Support." *American Sociological Review* 59: 703–22.

Oliver, Pamela. 1984. "'If You Don't Do It, Nobody Else Will': Active and Token Contributors to Local Collective Action." *American Sociological Review* 49 (5): 601–10.

———. 1989. "Bringing the Crowd Back In: The Nonorganizational Elements of Social Movements." *Research in Social Movements, Conflict and Change* 11: 1–30.

Opp, Karl-Dieter. 1989. *The Rationality of Political Protest*. Boulder, Colo.: Westview.

Pawson, Ray. 2000. "Middle-Range Realism." *European Journal of Sociology* 41 (2): 283–325.

Piven, Frances Fox, and Richard A. Cloward. 1977. *Poor People's Movements: Why They Succeed, How They Fail*. New York: Vintage Books.

Polletta, Francesca. 1997. "Culture and Its Discontents: Recent Theorizing on the Cultural Dimensions of Protest." *Sociological Inquiry* 67 (4): 431–50.

Raeburn, Nicole C. Forthcoming. *Inside Out: The Struggle for Lesbian, Gay, and Bisexual Rights in the Workplace*. Minneapolis: University of Minnesota Press.

Risse, Thomas, Stephen C. Ropp, and Kathryn Sikkink, eds. 1999. *The Power of Human Rights*. Cambridge: Cambridge University Press.

Rochon, Thomas R. 1998. *Culture Moves*. Princeton, N.J.: Princeton University Press.

Rosenthal, Naomi, and Michael Schwartz. 1989. "Spontaneity and Democracy in Social Movements." *International Social Movement Research* 2: 33–59.

Roth, Silke. 1997. *Political Socialization, Bridging Organization, Social Movement Interaction: The Coalition of Labor Union Women, 1974–1996*. Ph.D. diss., University of Connecticut, Storrs.

———. 2000. "Developing Working-Class Feminism: A Biographical Approach to Social Movement Participation." In *Self, Identity, and Social Movements,* edited by Sheldon Stryker, Timothy J. Owens, and Robert W. White, 300–303. Minneapolis: University of Minnesota Press.

Rudé, George. 1964. *The Crowd in History, 1730–1848.* London: Lawrence and Wishart.

Rupp, Leila, and Verta Taylor. 1987. *Survival in the Doldrums: The American Women's Rights Movement, 1945 to the 1960s.* New York: Oxford University Press.

Selbin, Eric. 1997. "Contentious Cartography." *Mobilization* 2: 99–106.

Sewell, William, Jr. 2001. "Space in Contentious Politics." In *Silence and Voice in the Study of Contentious Politics,* edited by Ronald R. Aminzade, Jack A. Goldstone, Doug McAdam, Elizabeth Perry, William H. Sewell Jr., Sidney Tarrow, and Charles Tilly, 51–88. Cambridge: Cambridge University Press.

Shorter, Edward, and Charles Tilly. 1974. *Strikes in France, 1830–1968.* Cambridge: Cambridge University Press.

Simon, Bernd, Michael Loewy, Stefan Stürmer, Ulrike Weber, Claudia Kampmeier, Peter Freytag, Corinna Habig, and Peter Spahlinger. 1998. "Collective Identity and Social Movement Participation." *Journal of Personality and Social Psychology* 74: 646–58.

Smith, Jackie, Charles Chatfield, and Ron Pagnucco, eds. 1997. *Transnational Social Movements and Global Politics.* Syracuse, N.Y.: Syracuse University Press.

Snow, David, E. Burke Rochford Jr., Steven K. Worden, and Robert D. Benford. 1986. "Frame Alignment Processes, Micromobilization, and Movement Participation." *American Sociological Review* 51: 464–81.

Snow, David, Sarah Soule, and Hans-Peter Kriesi, eds. Forthcoming. *The Blackwell Companion to Social Movements.* Oxford: Blackwell.

Snyder, David, and William R. Kelley. 1979. "Strategies for Investigating Violence and Social Change: Illustrations from Analyses of Racial Disorders and Implications for Mobilization Research." In *The Dynamics of Social Movements: Resource Mobilization, Social Control, and Tactics,* edited by M. N. Zald and J. D. McCarthy, 212–37. Cambridge, Mass.: Winthrop.

Snyder, David, and Charles Tilly. 1972. "Hardship and Collective Violence in France, 1830–1960." *American Journal of Sociology* 37: 520–32.

Staggenborg, Suzanne. 1989. "Stability and Innovation in the Women's Movement: A Comparison of Two Movement Organizations." *Social Problems* 36 (1): 75–92.

———. 1991. *The Pro-Choice Movement: Organization and Activism in the Abortion Conflict.* New York: Oxford University Press.

Steinberg, Marc W. 1999. *Fighting Words.* Ithaca, N.Y.: Cornell University Press.

Stryker, Sheldon, Timothy J. Owens, and Robert W. White, eds. 2000. *Self, Identity, and Social Movements.* Minneapolis: University of Minnesota Press.

Stürmer, Stefan. 2000. "Soziale Bewegungsbeteiligung: Ein psychologisches Zwei-Wege Modell." Unpublished Ph.D. diss., University of Kiel.

Tarrow, Sidney. 1989a. *Democracy and Disorder: Protest and Politics in Italy 1965–1975*. Oxford: Oxford University Press.

———. 1989b. *Struggle, Politics and Reform: Collective Action, Social Movements, and Cycles of Protest*. Center for International Studies, Cornell University.

———. 1998. *Power in Movement: Social Movements and Contentious Politics*. 2d ed. New York: Cambridge University Press.

——— 1999. "Paradigm Warriors: Regress and Progress in the Study of Contentious Politics." *Sociological Forum* 14: 71–78.

——— 2001. Introduction to *Silence and Voice in the Study of Contentious Politics*, edited by Ronald R. Aminzade, Jack A. Goldstone, Doug McAdam, Elizabeth Perry, William H. Sewell Jr., Sidney Tarrow, and Charles Tilly, 1–13. Cambridge: Cambridge University Press.

Taylor, Verta. 1989. "Social Movement Continuity: The Women's Movement in Abeyance." *American Sociological Review* 54: 761–75.

Thompson, E. P. 1966. *The Making of the English Working Class*. New York: Vintage.

Tilly, Charles. 1978. *From Mobilization to Revolution*. Reading, Mass.: Addison/Wesley Publishing Co.

———. 1984. "Social Movements and National Politics." In *Statemaking and Social Movements*, edited by Charles Bright and Susan Harding, 297–317. Ann Arbor: University of Michigan Press.

Tilly, Charles, Louise Tilly, and Richard Tilly. 1975. *The Rebellious Century: 1830–1930*. Cambridge: Harvard University Press.

Turner, Ralph. 1981. "Collective Behavior and Resource Mobilization as Approaches to Social Movements: Issues and Continuities." *Social Movements, Conflicts and Change* 4: 1–24.

Useem, Bert. 1980. "Solidarity Model, Breakdown Model, and the Boston Anti-Busing Movement." *American Sociological Review* 45: 357–69.

Vaughan, Diane. 1992. "Theory Elaboration: The Heuristics of Case Analysis." In *What Is a Case?* edited by Charles C. Ragin and Howard S. Becker, 173–202. Cambridge: Cambridge University Press.

Walder, Andrew. 2000. "Identities and Interests in the Chinese Red Guard Movement." Unpublished paper, Stanford University Department of Sociology.

Walsh, Edward J. 1988. *Democracy in the Shadows: Citizen Mobilization in the Wake of the Accident at Three Mile Island*. Westport, Conn.: Greenwood Press.

Walsh, Edward J., and Rex H. Warland. 1983. "Social Movement Involvement in the Wake of a Nuclear Accident: Activists and Free Riders in the TMI Area." *American Sociological Review* 48 (6): 764–80.

White, Robert W. 1989. "From Peaceful Protest to Guerrilla War: Micromobilization of the Provisional Irish Republican Army." *American Journal of Sociology* 94 (6): 1277–1302.

Zald, Mayer N. 2000. "Ideologically Structured Action: An Enlarged Agenda for Social Movement Research." *Mobilization* 5 (1): 1–16.

Zald, Mayer N., and Roberta Ash. 1966. "Social Movement Organizations: Growth, Decay, and Change." *Social Forces* 44 (3): 327–41.

Zald, Mayer N., and John D. McCarthy, eds. 1987. *Social Movements in an Organizational Society: Collected Essays.* New Brunswick, N.J.: Transaction Books.

Zurcher, Louis A., and Russell L. Curtis. 1973. "A Comparative Analysis of Propositions Describing Social Movement Organizations." *Sociological Quarterly* 14 (2): 175–88.

Zurcher, Louis A., and R. George Kirkpatrick. 1976. *Citizens for Decency: Anti-Pornography Crusades as Status Defense.* Austin: University of Texas Press.

Contributors

KATHLEEN M. BLEE is professor of sociology and director of women's studies at the University of Pittsburgh. Her books include *Women of the Klan: Racism and Gender in the 1920s*; *No Middle Ground: Women and Radical Protest*; *Inside Organized Racism: Women in the Hate Movement*; and, with Dwight Billings, *The Road to Poverty: The Making of Wealth and Hardship in Appalachia*.

ELISABETH S. CLEMENS is associate professor of sociology at the University of Arizona. Building on organizational theory and political sociology, her research has addressed the role of social movements and voluntary organizations in processes of institutional change. Her book *The People's Lobby: Organizational Innovation and the Rise of Interest Group Politics in the United States, 1890–1925* received the 1998 Max Weber Award and the award for the best book in political sociology in 1997–98.

DONATELLA DELLA PORTA is professor of political science at the University of Florence. She is the author of numerous publications on social movements and political violence, including *Social Movements, Political Violence, and the State* and *Social Movements: An Introduction* (with Mario Diani). She is coeditor, with Herbert Reiter, of *Policing Protest: The Control of Mass Demonstrations in Western Democracies* (Minnesota, 1998).

MARIO DIANI is professor of sociology at the University of Trento and the European editor of *Mobilization: An International Journal*. His publications include *Social Movements,* with Donatella della Porta; *Green Networks*; *Studying Collective Action,* coedited with Ron Eyerman; and *Social Movements and Networks,* coedited with Doug McAdam.

MARTIN D. HUGHES is a Ph.D. candidate in sociology at the University of Arizona. He specializes in comparative and historical methods.

HANK JOHNSTON is the editor of *Mobilization: An International Journal* and professor of social psychology at San Diego State University. He is author of *Tales of Nationalism: Catalonia, 1939–1979,* as well as numerous articles on social movement theory and movements against repressive states. He is editor of *Social Movements and Culture* (with Bert Klandermans; Minnesota, 1995), *New Social Movements* (with Enrique Laraña and Joseph Gusfield), and *Globalization and Resistance* (with Jackie Smith).

BERT KLANDERMANS is professor of applied social psychology at Free University, Amsterdam. He has published widely on social movement participation and has conducted several large-scale studies of participation in the peace movement, labor unions, the women's movement, farmers' protests, and protest in South Africa during the years of transition. He is author of *The Social Psychology of Protest* and coeditor of *Social Movements and Culture* (with Hank Johnston; Minnesota, 1995) and *The Politics of Social Protest: Comparative Perspectives on States and Social Movements* (with J. Craig Jenkins; Minnesota, 1995).

RUUD KOOPMANS is a senior researcher at the Science Center Berlin (WZB). His current research includes political mobilization on immigration and ethnic relations in five European countries; civic engagement and political trust among immigrant communities in Berlin and Amsterdam; and the transformation of political communication and mobilization through the process of European integration.

PAUL LICHTERMAN is assistant professor of sociology at the University of Wisconsin–Madison. He studies political culture, social movements, and moral commitment, and he is author of *The Search for Political Community: American Activists Reinventing Commitment.* He recently completed a participant-observation study of faith-based volunteer groups for his forthcoming book on religion and civic engagement.

DEBRA C. MINKOFF is associate professor of sociology at the University of Washington, Seattle. Her work explores the organizational dynamics of contemporary American social movements, particularly the civil rights and women's movements. Her current research focuses on the structure and determinants of the national U.S. social movement sector, comparing a diverse range of domestic movements and countermovements with respect to organizational forms, strategies, and network relationships.

DANIEL J. MYERS is associate professor of sociology at the University of Notre Dame. His current research focuses on diffusion models for collective behavior, media coverage of collective violence, racial rioting, and game theory.

PAMELA E. OLIVER is professor of sociology at the University of Wisconsin–Madison. She developed formal "critical mass" models of collective action and is now working on diffusion models of the interplay of repression and protest in protest cycles. Her recent empirical research, published in the *American Journal of Sociology*, centered on the selection structures of news coverage of protest events.

DIETER RUCHT is professor of sociology at the Social Science Research Center Berlin. His research interests include modernization processes in comparative perspective, social movements, and political protest. Currently he is engaged in a study of the patterns of protest in Germany since 1950 and a study of the transformation of environmental activism in seven European countries.

JACKIE SMITH is assistant professor of sociology at the State University of New York at Stony Brook. She is coeditor of *Transnational Social Movements and Global Politics: Solidarity beyond the State* and has written a number of articles on transnational organizations and social movements.

DAVID A. SNOW is professor of sociology at the University of California, Irvine. He has published widely on various aspects of social movements, framing processes in the context of movements, conversion processes, self and identity, ethnographic field methods, and homelessness. He is coauthor (with Leon Anderson) of *Down on Their Luck: A Study of Homeless Street People*, coeditor (with Doug McAdam) of *Social Movements: Readings on*

Their Emergence, Mobilization, and Dynamics, and coeditor (with Sarah Soule and Hanspeter Kriesi) of *The Blackwell Companion to Social Movements.*

SUZANNE STAGGENBORG is professor of sociology at McGill University. Her work includes *The Pro-Choice Movement: Organization and Activism in the Abortion Conflict; Gender, Family, and Social Movements;* and a number of articles about abortion politics and social movements in the United States and Canada.

SIDNEY TARROW is Maxwell M. Upson Professor of Government and Sociology at Cornell University. He is the author of *Power in Movement: Collective Action, Social Movements, and Politics.* With Charles Tilly and Doug McAdam, he has completed a broad study of contentious politics, social movements, and revolutions, *Dynamics of Contention;* with Doug Imig, he recently published *Contentious Europeans.*

VERTA TAYLOR is professor of sociology at the University of California, Santa Barbara. She is coauthor, with Leila J. Rupp, of *Survival in the Doldrums: The American Women's Rights Movement, 1945 to the 1960s* and *What Makes a Man a Man: Drag Queens at the 801 Cabaret;* coeditor, with Laurel Richardson and Nancy Whittier, of *Feminist Frontiers;* and author of *Rock-a-by Baby: Feminism, Self-Help, and Postpartum Depression,* along with numerous articles on social movement theory, the women's movement, and the gay and lesbian movements.

DANNY TROM is a researcher at the Groupe de Sociologie Politique et Morale at the Ecole des Hautes Etudes en Sciences Sociales in Paris. He studies social movements, ethnographic and historical approaches to mobilization, and environmental activism.

Series page continued from page ii.

Index